Get Updates and More on Nolo.com

Go to this book's companion page at:

www.nolo.com/back-of-book/FEMP.html

When there's an important change to the law affecting this book, we'll
post updates. You'll also find articles and other related materials.

Legal Forms, Books, & Software
Hundreds of do-it-yourself products—all written in plain English,
approved, and updated by our in-house legal editors.

Legal Articles
Get informed with thousands of free articles on everyday legal
topics. Our articles are accurate, up to date, and reader friendly.

Find a Lawyer
Want to talk to a lawyer? Use Nolo to find a lawyer who can
help you with your case.

NOLO
LAW for ALL

⚖ NOLO The Trusted Name
(but don't take our word for it)

6th Edition

The Essential Guide to Federal Employment Laws

Lisa Guerin, J.D. & Attorney Sachi Barreiro

SIXTH EDITION   APRIL 2019

Cover Design   SUSAN PUTNEY

Book Design   TERRI HEARSH

Proofreading   IRENE BARNARD

Index   THÉRÈSE SHERE

Names: Guerin, Lisa, 1964- author. | Barreiro, Sachi, author.
Title: The essential guide to federal employment laws / Lisa Guerin, J.D. and
   Attorney Sachi Barreiro.
Description: Sixth edition. | Berkeley, CA : Nolo, 2019. | Includes
   bibliographical references and index.
Identifiers: LCCN 2018049381 (print) | LCCN 2018056255 (ebook) | ISBN
   9781413326161 (ebook) | ISBN 9781413326154 (pbk.)
Subjects: LCSH: Labor laws and legislation--United States--Popular works.
Classification: LCC KF3455 (ebook) | LCC KF3455 .G835 2019 (print) | DDC
   344.7301--dc23
LC record available at https://lccn.loc.gov/2018049381

This book covers only United States law, unless it specifically states otherwise.

Please note

We believe accurate, plain-English legal information should help you solve
many of your own legal problems. But this text is not a substitute for
personalized advice from a knowledgeable lawyer. If you want the help of a
trained professional—and we'll always point out situations in which we think
that's a good idea—consult an attorney licensed to practice in your state.

Acknowledgments

The authors would like to thank:

Jake Warner, who came up with the idea that turned into this book. His encouragement and advice were invaluable.

Janet Portman, for helping us trim the fat, explain the technicalities, and bring this material down to earth.

Albin Renauer, for his amazing database and his help in organizing the book.

Laura Lawson and **Margaret Clark**, for their thoughtful comments and assistance on the first edition.

Christopher Anzalone, manager of book publishing, and **Allen Smith**, manager for workplace law content, and our other reviewers from the **Society for Human Resource Management**, for their assistance and insightful comments.

Attorney Dan Feinberg of Sigmund, Lewis and Feinberg in Oakland, California, and **Attorney Lee Trucker** of Trucker Huss in San Francisco, California, for their generous assistance.

Ella Hirst, for her unsurpassed research skills and for creating most of the 50-state charts that appear in this book.

Alayna Schroeder, Drew Wheaton, and **Stephen Stine** for updating and streamlining the state material.

Stan Jacobsen, for his research assistance and general good cheer.

Susan Putney, for making the book look good.

About the Authors

Lisa Guerin, J.D.

Lisa Guerin is the author or coauthor of several Nolo books, including *The Manager's Legal Handbook, Dealing With Problem Employees, The Essential Guide to Workplace Investigations,* and *Create Your Own Employee Handbook.* Ms. Guerin has practiced employment law in government, public interest, and private practice where she represented clients at all levels of state and federal courts and in agency proceedings. She is a graduate of Boalt Hall School of Law at the University of California at Berkeley.

Sachi Barreiro, Attorney

Sachi Barreiro is an attorney, the coauthor of *The Manager's Legal Handbook,* and the author of *Your Rights in the Workplace.* Prior to working in legal publishing, Ms. Barreiro practiced as an employment lawyer, advising businesses on their legal obligations to employees and litigating a variety of employment matters. Sachi received her law degree with high honors from the University of San Francisco School of Law.

Table of Contents

Overview

Most managers and human resources professionals—particularly those who work for larger companies—have to deal with federal employment laws every day. These laws apply in nearly every stage of the employment relationship, from hiring and first-day paperwork, to providing benefits and time off, to terminations and layoffs. Whether you are developing workplace policies, creating forms and notices for your company to use with employees, or handling employee performance and discipline issues, you need to understand your company's legal obligations—and make sure that you don't inadvertently violate the law.

It can be tough to find out exactly what these federal laws require. That's where this book comes in. It explains all of the major federal employment laws: whom they protect, who has to follow them, what they require, and what they prohibit. Each chapter in this book covers a single federal employment law and describes the obligations employers have under each law, including deadlines, posting requirements, and record-keeping rules. If you need more information, each chapter includes a list of additional resources. And many chapters include charts that provide information on state laws.

What This Book Doesn't Cover

Some employment situations are *not* covered in this book. If you fall into one of the following categories, the information you need is likely beyond the scope of this book:

- **Government employers.** Although we explain which (if any) federal, state, and local government workers are covered by each law, we don't detail the special rules that may apply to government employees. For example, although federal government workers are protected from certain types of discrimination by Title VII (see Chapter 18), they must follow a special complaint process that doesn't apply to private companies. We don't cover that process here.

- **Federal contractors.** Private employers that contract to do work for the federal government are subject to additional employment laws. We don't cover those laws here.

This overview chapter provides the information you need to get the most out of this book. First, we explain how to figure out which federal laws your company has to follow and when and how state and local laws might come into play. Next, we cover a handful of practical strategies that will help your company comply with these laws, such as consulting with a lawyer, documentation, and training. Finally, we explain what to do if you need more help.

Which Laws Your Company Must Follow

Employment law comes from many sources. Each of the federal laws (also called "statutes") covered in this book has been interpreted and refined by court decisions and sometimes by regulations issued by the federal agency responsible for enforcing and administering the law. Many of the topics covered by these laws are also addressed by state, and sometimes even local, laws. If more than one law applies, employers generally must follow whichever law is more beneficial to employees.

You can use this book to figure out which federal laws apply to your company, which employees are protected by those laws, and whether those laws apply to the situation you are facing. "Which Federal Laws Apply," below, will help you get to this information quickly.

This book also provides charts that summarize the laws of the 50 states and the District of Columbia, at the end of some chapters. However, you may have to do some research on your own—or talk to a lawyer—to find out whether a state or local law applies to your situation. This topic is covered in "Which State and Local Laws Apply," below.

Which Federal Laws Apply

Federal employment law consists of three components: the statutes themselves, any regulations issued by the federal agency responsible for administering the law, and court decisions interpreting the law and regulations. Together, these sources define what the terms in the law mean, what employers have to do to comply with the law, and how violations of the law will be handled. Each chapter of this book covers a federal employment statute, any regulations interpreting it, and the major court cases decided under the law.

Because the employment laws explained here are federal statutes, they apply throughout the country, regardless of what state the company or worker is in. This means that every federal law in this book has the potential to apply to your company if it operates in the United States. We say "potential" because none of these laws apply to every employer and employee, in every situation. Instead, most laws specify which employers need to follow them, which employees are protected by them, and what actions they prohibit and require.

Different Rules for Unions

If your company is unionized, the first place to look for answers to your employment questions is not the law, but the collective bargaining agreement (CBA) between the union and the company. A CBA is a binding contract, so if it gives workers more rights in certain areas (most commonly, wage and hour issues, time off, discipline, and termination procedures), it supersedes the law.

For example, let's say you want to know how much time an employee can take off for childbirth and parental leave. You look up the Family and Medical Leave Act in this book and see that it requires covered employers to provide up to 12 weeks of unpaid leave. Your company's CBA, however, gives employees up to 16 weeks of paid leave. Because the CBA is more generous than the law, you must follow its provisions.

Generally, unions are not allowed to bargain away their members' federal rights in a collective bargaining agreement. Therefore, a CBA typically cannot provide workers with less than what the federal law requires. However, there are some exceptions to this rule. For example, most courts have upheld a common CBA provision that requires workers to make certain workplace claims only through the union grievance procedure, rather than bringing them to court (which they would otherwise have the right to do). And some laws allow unions and management to bend the rules in a CBA; for example, although some state laws require employers to give workers specified meal and rest breaks, these laws may not apply to a workplace governed by a CBA.

Sources of Federal Employment Law

Statutes start out as bills passed by the U.S. Congress, which are then signed into law by the president. Statutes are collected in a set of books called the U.S. Code. The first page of each chapter of this book includes the location of the statute in the U.S. Code. For example, the Age Discrimination in Employment Act (ADEA) is found at 29 U.S.C. §§ 621–634; this means that it's located in Title 29 of the U.S. Code, at Sections 621 through 634. Each chapter also provides a link to a website where you can view the statute online.

Regulations are administrative rules issued by federal agencies. When Congress passes a law, it usually designates a federal agency to interpret and enforce that law. In employment law, these agencies are often responsible for receiving employee complaints, creating paperwork (such as posters or notice forms) that employers must use to comply with the law, and imposing penalties on employers that don't meet their obligations. Sometimes agencies also issue regulations— rules that fill in some of the gaps not addressed by the statute. Regulations are collected in the Code of Federal Regulations (C.F.R.). If regulations have been issued interpreting one of the laws we cover, you'll find a citation for those regulations—and a website where you can access them online—at the beginning of the chapter. Regulations are updated frequently; our citation is to the most recent version, but you should always check to see whether the regulations have been revised.

Court decisions are opinions written by judges deciding the outcome of a lawsuit. Often, judges must interpret what a law means in order to decide who should win in court. For example, a court might have to decide what constitutes a reasonable accommodation for an employee with a disability or whether an employer's decision to transfer an employee who complained of harassment constitutes illegal retaliation. Decisions by the U.S. Supreme Court are the most influential, because they dictate how federal employment laws will be interpreted throughout the country. Decisions by lower courts, such as the U.S. Courts of Appeal and the U.S. District Courts, are binding only in the states or regions those courts cover.

To figure out whether a particular federal employment law applies to your company and your situation, you'll need to answer these five questions:

- Does your company have enough employees?
- Is your company otherwise covered by the law?
- Is the employee covered by the law?
- Do all of the law's provisions apply?
- Is this situation covered by the law?

Does Your Company Have Enough Employees?

Many employment laws apply only to employers that have a minimum number of employees. You'll find these rules under the heading "Covered Employers" in each chapter. For example, an employer with only 20 employees is not covered by the Family and Medical Leave Act (FMLA); only employers with at least 50 employees must comply with that law.

Is Your Company Otherwise Covered?

Some employment laws don't impose a minimum size requirement, but instead apply only to companies that engage in "interstate commerce" (and, in a few cases, meet a minimum of business volume requirement). These rules are included in the chart, "Laws That Apply by Size or Operations of Employer," below.

All but the smallest local companies are engaged in interstate commerce within the meaning of these laws. For example, if your company buys, sells, or handles materials or products that have come from or will go to another state, or if your company's employees communicate across state lines as part of their job duties, your company is most likely engaged in interstate commerce.

For decades, the U.S. Supreme Court has defined "interstate commerce" very broadly, to encompass virtually any activity that crosses—or could cross—a state's borders. This expansive definition allows the Court to uphold Congressional legislation: The Constitution gives Congress the right to regulate interstate commerce, so Congress has the widest possible reach when interstate commerce is defined in broad strokes.

In recent years, however, the Court has been scaling back this definition to occasionally find that Congress has overstepped its bounds. For example, although the Court ultimately upheld the Affordable Care Act (the health care reform law) on other grounds, a majority of the Court found that Congress exceeded its authority to regulate interstate commerce. This holding signals

Laws That Apply by Size or Operations of Employer

Law	Acronym	Involved in interstate commerce	Involved in interstate commerce or have $500,000 or more in annual gross sales	All public companies (publicly traded or required to register with the SEC)	All private employers (1 or more employees)	15 or more employees	20 or more employees	50 or more employees	100 or more employees
Age Discrimination in Employment Act	ADEA						■	■	■
Americans with Disabilities Act of 1990	ADA					■	■	■	■
Consolidated Omnibus Budget Reconciliation Act	COBRA						■	■	■
Employee Polygraph Protection Act	EPPA		■						
Equal Pay Act	EPA		■						
Fair Credit Reporting Act	FCRA				■	■	■	■	■
Fair Labor Standards Act	FLSA		■						
Family and Medical Leave Act	FMLA							■	■
Genetic Information Nondiscrimination Act	GINA					■	■	■	■
Immigration Reform and Control Act of 1986	IRCA				■	■	■	■	■
National Labor Relations Act	NLRA	■							

Laws That Apply by Size or Operations of Employer (continued)

Law	Acronym	Involved in interstate commerce	Involved in interstate commerce or have $500,000 or more in annual gross sales	All public companies (publicly traded or required to register with the SEC)	All private employers (1 or more employees)	15 or more employees	20 or more employees	50 or more employees	100 or more employees
Occupational Safety and Health Act	OSH Act				■	■	■	■	■
Older Workers Benefit Protection Act	OWBPA						■	■	■
Personal Responsibility and Work Opportunity Reconciliation Act	PRWORA				■	■	■	■	■
Pregnancy Discrimination Act	PDA					■	■	■	■
Sarbanes-Oxley Act of 2002	SOX			■					
Section 1981 of the Civil Rights Act of 1866	Section 1981				■	■	■	■	■
Title VII of the Civil Rights Act of 1964	Title VII					■	■	■	■
Uniformed Services Employment and Reemployment Rights Act	USERRA				■	■	■	■	■
Worker Adjustment and Retraining Notification Act	WARN								■

that the definition of interstate commerce remains in flux. If, after reading the relevant chapter in this book, you believe that your company is not covered, you should probably check your conclusion with a lawyer.

Even laws that impose a minimum size requirement don't apply to every employer that is large enough to be covered. Some laws include exceptions for particular types of employers and some apply only to certain types of companies. For example, the Sarbanes-Oxley Act of 2002 applies only to companies that are publicly traded or required to register with the Securities and Exchange Commission. You'll find this information under the heading "Covered Employers" in each chapter.

Is the Employee Covered?

Some employment laws apply only to employees who have worked for the employer for a certain period of time. Some exclude independent contractors, apply only to employees in certain occupations, or apply to people who don't even work for the employer. For example, the Consolidated Omnibus Budget Reconciliation Act (COBRA) applies not only to employees and former employees, but also to their spouses and dependents, if they are covered by the employer's group health insurance plan. Each chapter explains whom the law protects under the heading "Covered Workers."

Do All of the Provisions Apply?

Some laws have provisions that apply only to certain workers and/or certain employers. For example, the provisions of the Fair Labor Standards Act that require employers to pay overtime and minimum wages don't apply to certain types of employees, including certain computer specialists, seamen, and criminal investigators. Similarly, only employers with at least four employees are subject to the antidiscrimination provision of the Immigration Reform and Control Act (IRCA), but all employers—regardless of size—must comply with IRCA's verification provision, which requires employers to verify that their employees are legally authorized to work in the United States.

You can find this additional coverage information within the discussion of each provision of the law, under the headings "Covered Employers" and/or "Covered Workers."

Is Your Situation Covered?

Each law covers a limited spectrum of employment issues and may not extend to the problem or question you're facing. We've included two charts below to help you figure out which chapters to review. The first, "What Each Law Covers," gives a very brief summary of the law. The second, "Laws That Apply to Common Employment Situations," lets you know which aspects of the employment relationship are covered by each law. Once you decide which laws might apply, you'll need to read the sections called "What's Prohibited" and "What's Required" in the chapters covering those laws to find out whether your particular situation is addressed.

For example, if you have a question about discrimination, you'll see that several laws prohibit discrimination in employment. You'll also see that these laws prohibit different types of discrimination—for instance, the Civil Rights Act of 1866 prohibits race discrimination, while the Equal Pay Act prohibits gender-based wage discrimination. To find out precisely what each law requires and prohibits, turn to the appropriate chapters.

In addition, some laws make exceptions for certain situations in which employers are not required to comply with the law. You can find this information in the "Exceptions" section of each chapter. For example, although the Worker Adjustment and Retraining Notification Act (WARN) generally requires large employers to give employees advance notice of a layoff, employers don't have to give notice if the layoff results from the closing of a temporary facility.

Which State and Local Laws Apply

Even if you follow every applicable federal employment law to the letter, your company could still be violating other legal obligations to its employees. The federal government isn't alone in regulating the employment relationship—state and local governments have been increasingly active in passing their own employment laws as well. If your company and situation are covered by more than one law, you must follow the law that is the most beneficial to the employee in a particular situation.

This book will help you get started in figuring out which state laws might apply. At the end of many chapters, you'll find charts summarizing the laws of the 50 states and the District of Columbia on the same topic. For example,

What Each Law Covers

Law	Summary
ADEA	**Age Discrimination in Employment Act:** prohibits employers from discriminating against employees who are 40 and older
ADA	**Americans with Disabilities Act:** prohibits discrimination against qualified employees with disabilities; requires employers to make reasonable accommodations for employees and applicants with disabilities
COBRA	**Consolidated Omnibus Budget Reconciliation Act:** requires employers to provide continued group health insurance coverage for up to 36 months to employees (and possibly their spouses and dependents) who would otherwise lose coverage
EPPA	**Employee Polygraph Protection Act:** prohibits employers from requiring or asking employees or applicants to take a polygraph test in most circumstances
EPA	**Equal Pay Act:** requires employers to give male and female employees equal pay for doing equal work
FCRA	**Fair Credit Reporting Act:** requires employers to provide notice and get consent before ordering a credit report or other types of background or investigative reports on employees or applicants; requires employers to give certain information to employees or applicants before taking negative action based on a report; establishes standards employers must follow to destroy consumer records
FLSA	**Fair Labor Standards Act:** establishes the minimum wage; determines what constitutes work time for purposes of calculating pay; requires overtime pay for certain employees; restricts child labor
FMLA	**Family and Medical Leave Act:** entitles eligible employees to take up to 12 weeks of unpaid leave per year, with continued health benefits, for their own serious health conditions, to bond with a new child, to care for a family member with a serious health condition, or for a qualified exigency due to a family member's call to active military duty; family members of servicemembers who suffer a serious injury or illness may take up to 26 weeks of leave in a single 12-month period (military caregiver leave)
GINA	**Genetic Information Nondiscrimination Act:** prohibits employers from making employment decisions based on genetic information or requiring employees to provide genetic information; requires employers to keep employees' genetic information confidential
IRCA	**Immigration Reform and Control Act:** prohibits discrimination on the basis of citizenship and national origin in every aspect of employment; requires employers to verify that employees are authorized to work in the United States and keep records to that effect

What Each Law Covers (continued)

Law	Summary
NLRA	**National Labor Relations Act:** regulates the relationship of employers and unions; prohibits employers and unions from engaging in unfair labor practices; protects employees who engage in concerted activities to improve working terms and conditions, whether the workplace is unionized or not
OSH Act	**Occupational Safety and Health Act:** requires employers to comply with workplace safety and health standards
OWBPA	**Older Workers Benefit Protection Act:** prohibits age discrimination in the provision of benefits for employees 40 and older; explains the criteria to be used in determining whether equal benefits have been provided; requires employers to include particular language in a waiver of an employee's right to sue for age discrimination
PRWORA	**Personal Responsibility and Work Opportunity Reconciliation Act:** requires employers to report new hires to a state registry, which uses the information to enforce child support obligations
PDA	**Pregnancy Discrimination Act:** prohibits discrimination on the basis of pregnancy or childbirth in every aspect of employment; requires employers to treat pregnant women who are temporarily unable to work the same way they treat workers who are temporarily disabled for other reasons
SOX	**Sarbanes-Oxley Act of 2002:** prohibits employers from retaliating against employees who complain of shareholder fraud; requires companies to establish procedures allowing employees to submit anonymous complaints about accounting and auditing practices; requires companies to establish procedures for taking, handling, and retaining such complaints
Section 1981	**Section 1981 of the Civil Rights Act of 1866:** prohibits race discrimination in the making or enforcement of contracts, which includes every aspect of the employment relationship
Title VII	**Title VII of the Civil Rights Act of 1964:** prohibits discrimination on the basis of race, color, national origin, religion, and sex in every aspect of employment
USERRA	**Uniformed Services Employment and Reemployment Rights Act:** prohibits discrimination against applicants and employees who serve in the armed services; requires employers to reinstate employees who take up to five years off to serve in the armed services and to restore their benefits; prohibits employers from firing reinstated employees, except for cause, for up to one year after they return
WARN	**Worker Adjustment and Retraining Notification Act:** requires employers to give 60 days' notice to employees who will lose their jobs through large layoffs or plant closings, with limited exceptions

Laws That Apply to Common Employment Situations*

Law	Hiring	Background Checks	Testing	First-Day Paperwork	Benefits	Compensation	Hours	Health and Safety	Investigations	Discrimination/Harassment	Leave/Time Off	Unions/Organizing	Whistleblowing	Layoffs	Terminations
ADEA	■	■	■		■	■	■		■	■	■			■	■
ADA	■	■	■		■	■	■	■	■	■	■			■	■
COBRA					■									■	■
EPPA	■		■						■						■
EPA					■	■				■					
FCRA	■	■							■						■
FLSA						■	■	■			■				
FMLA					■						■			■	■
GINA	■	■	■		■	■	■		■	■	■			■	■
IRCA	■	■	■	■					■	■				■	■
NLRA					■					■		■		■	
OSHA								■	■				■		
OWBPA					■	■				■					■
PRWORA				■											
PDA	■		■		■	■	■	■		■	■			■	■
SOX									■	■			■		■
Sec. 1981	■	■	■		■	■	■		■	■				■	■
Title VII	■	■	■		■	■	■		■	■				■	■
USERRA	■	■	■		■	■	■		■	■				■	■
WARN														■	

* You'll see that most of the antidiscrimination laws appear with nearly every issue. Because these laws prohibit discrimination in every aspect of employment, employers could violate them by undertaking any common employment practice with the intent to discriminate. For example, let's say an employer required only applicants who have served in the military to take a psychological test, based on the hiring manager's belief that such applicants are more likely to be mentally unstable. This would violate USERRA's ban on discrimination against those who have served in the military, even though USERRA doesn't explicitly address the issue of testing.

at the end of the chapter on the FLSA, you'll find charts on state minimum wage, overtime, and meal and rest break laws. However, these charts may not provide the details you need. In that case, you should contact your state's labor or fair employment practices department (you can find contact information in Appendix A), consult a resource on the employment laws of your state, or talk to a local employment lawyer.

To find out whether local laws might come into play, you'll have to find out what your city or county requires. Some local governments post their laws (often called "ordinances") or information for local employers on their websites; you can find links to many city and county websites at www. statelocalgov.net. You can also find out what local laws require by talking to a local employment attorney.

State and local laws can be quite similar to federal employment laws: They cover similar topics, apply to only certain employers (often those with a minimum number of employees), and protect only certain types of employees. However, state and local laws often provide workers with more benefits and apply to a wider set of employers. If you live in a large metropolitan area, chances are good that local ordinances will apply to your company.

Putting It All Together

Here are a couple of examples to illustrate how to figure out which laws your company has to follow.

EXAMPLE 1: The only manager of a four-employee graphic design company in Berkeley, California, wants to know what the company's obligations are to applicants with disabilities. The federal Americans with Disabilities Act governs this issue, but it applies only to private employers with at least 15 employees. California also has an antidiscrimination law that prohibits disability discrimination, but it applies only to employers with at least five employees. However, the city of Berkeley prohibits all companies that contract with the city from discriminating on the basis of disability. Therefore, if the company wins a bid to redesign the city's website, it will have to comply with this municipal law.

EXAMPLE 2: A national restaurant chain is considering expanding to New Mexico. Its HR director does some research and learns that New Mexico's minimum wage is $7.50 an hour. Because this is higher than the current federal minimum wage ($7.25 an hour), the chain will have to pay its workers at least the higher state amount. But if the chain decides to open in Santa Fe County, it will have to pay workers at least $11.40 an hour, because the county has adopted a living wage law that applies to all employers that are required to have a business license from the county. Both federal and New Mexico law require employers to pay tipped workers a wage of at least $2.13 an hour, as long as they make enough in tips to earn the applicable minimum wage. However, Santa Fe County requires employers to pay tipped employees a base wage of at least $3.41 per hour. So, the restaurant will have to pay its tipped workers in Santa Fe County at least $3.41 per hour, and the employee's total pay—including tips— must add up to at least the county's minimum wage of $11.40.

As you can see, things can get confusing if your company is covered by two or more laws that impose different requirements or seem to contradict each other. If you find yourself in this position, you may need some help figuring out what to do. This is a good time to consult with an employment lawyer.

Basic Compliance Tools

This book will help you understand which federal employment laws your company must follow and what those laws mean. However, to stay out of legal trouble, your company must do more than simply follow the letter of the law. It will also have to adopt some practical strategies to make sure that it meets its legal obligations. These compliance tools are not strictly "required" by the laws covered in this book, but a company that wants to avoid legal problems should consider them standard operating procedures.

This section briefly explains a handful of basic strategies every company should follow, but it is only an introduction to these important topics. The ins and outs of creating an effective compliance program are well beyond the scope of this book. However, Nolo has plenty of detailed resources that will help you design and implement procedures for compliance; see "If You Need More Information," below.

Lawyers

Even the most conscientious HR professional occasionally needs help from a lawyer. Although you can handle many employment issues on your own, some are particularly tricky and require some legal expertise. As you read this book, you'll see that we sometimes advise you to consult with a lawyer if you need more information on a difficult topic. And with good reason: Although lawyers don't come cheap, your company can save money by paying a lawyer for advice and information that would be very time-consuming and difficult to research on your own.

There are no hard and fast rules that determine when you should consult with a lawyer. You'll have to decide when it's time to get some expert help based on a number of factors, including your own comfort level, how important the issue is, how many employees are affected, whether your company is facing significant legal exposure, and your company's budget. However, as a general rule, it's better to consult with a lawyer sooner rather than later in any potentially difficult situation.

You can use a lawyer for a variety of tasks, including:

- **Document drafting or review.** A lawyer can create or edit documents you use over and over again, such as employment contracts, employee notice forms, waivers, your employee handbook, and other written policies.
- **Advice on employment decisions.** Of course, your company would quickly go out of business if it consulted a lawyer every time an employee was hired or disciplined, but there are times when a lawyer's advice will be very valuable. If, for example, you are considering firing a worker who is on FMLA leave or has recently complained of sexual harassment, a lawyer can help you make sure that you have adequate legal support for your decision.
- **Help understanding your legal obligations.** As noted above, companies must follow whichever law—federal, state, or local—provides the most benefits for workers. A lawyer can help you untangle these obligations and assist you in figuring out your responsibilities when several laws overlap.
- **Representation in legal or administrative proceedings.** If an employee files a complaint with an administrative agency or a lawsuit, your company should consult with a lawyer right away. Good legal advice at the outset can mean the difference between winning and losing the case.

Training

Training is a great way to reduce your company's legal exposure and give your company an opportunity to deal with potential problems early on, before they have a chance to escalate. Training is a vital component of a company's efforts to combat harassment and discrimination, for example. In this type of training, employees learn about harassment and discrimination and how to report possible misconduct to the appropriate people. Managers should also be trained to recognize harassment and discrimination and take appropriate action in response. You can learn more about discrimination and harassment training from the Training Institute of the Equal Employment Opportunity Commission, www.eeotraining.eeoc.gov.

As a legal matter, training can help limit your company's liability if it faces a harassment lawsuit. Companies that take reasonable care to prevent and correct harassment—by adopting an antiharassment policy, training managers in their responsibilities, investigating complaints effectively, and taking swift action if harassment occurs—have a potential legal defense to certain harassment claims.

You can also use training to help your company maintain a safe and healthy workplace (a requirement of the OSH Act). In fact, the OSH Act requires companies in certain industries to provide specific types of training to their employees. Safety training might include information on how to use particular tools or equipment, ergonomics, working with hazardous materials, and reporting possible unsafe conditions. You can learn more about safety training from OSHA's Directorate of Training and Education Training Resources, www.osha.gov/dte.

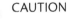

CAUTION

With sexual harassment making headlines in numerous industries recently, more states are passing laws to protect employees. Some states, such as California, require larger employers to provide sexual harassment training to managers and supervisors only; other states, such as New York, require all employers to provide harassment training to all employees. Contact your state fair employment practices agency to learn more (see Appendix A for contact information).

Policies

Your company's written policies or employee handbook can make or break your efforts to comply with the law and can help limit your company's legal exposure. By clearly communicating what it expects from its employees and managers, a company can nip certain legal problems in the bud—or at least give itself an opportunity to resolve problems when they first arise. If everyone at your company understands, for example, what retaliation is and that the company will not tolerate it, managers will be less likely to retaliate against employees who raise concerns or complaints, and employees will be more likely to report retaliation right away, before their relationship with the company has been damaged beyond repair.

When writing or updating your company's policies, you must choose your words with care: At the most basic level, your company's policies must not contradict what the law requires or allows. For example, if your company's employee handbook says that employees may take only four weeks off per calendar year, strict enforcement of that policy could well violate several federal employment laws, including the Family and Medical Leave Act, the Uniformed Services Employment and Reemployment Rights Act, the Pregnancy Discrimination Act, and the Americans with Disabilities Act. If your company's policies lead employees to believe that they aren't entitled to the rights provided by these laws, the company could face major legal problems.

As you'll learn in later chapters, a company's policies sometimes also determine its legal responsibilities to employees. In some situations, a company may take certain actions only if its policies provide for it, even though the actions are otherwise legally allowed. For example, a company is legally allowed to pay less than the minimum wage to employees who earn tips (known as taking a "tip credit") under the Fair Labor Standards Act, but only if the company clearly informs employees that it will do so. To take full advantage of its legal rights, your company must make sure that its policies meet these standards.

Some policies can also be used as a legal defense to claims of harassment and discrimination. As noted above under "Training," companies that have antiharassment and antidiscrimination policies and take quick action to investigate and resolve complaints may be able to avoid liability for certain harassment and discrimination claims. Every company should have written policies prohibiting harassment and discrimination and outlining the steps the company will take if an employee comes forward with a complaint.

Companies that don't have written policies, or don't review their policies periodically to make sure that they are legally valid and up to date, are placing themselves at legal risk.

Responding to Legal Violations

If you learn of a possible legal violation—for example, hazardous working conditions, discriminatory statements by a supervisor, or a manager's refusal to allow an eligible employee to take FMLA leave—you must take action right away. You may need to investigate the situation first, to find out what happened and who is responsible. Once you know that your company has a problem, however, you should step in quickly to resolve it.

There are several good reasons for taking action to correct legal violations. Perhaps most important, taking action will show employees that the company cares about their well-being and wants to do the right thing. This will help build the type of loyalty and positive feelings that can provide a strong deterrent to lawsuits. Putting a stop to illegal behavior will also limit the amount of money an employee can recover (called "damages"), if he or she decides to take legal action against the company. And dealing quickly with troublemakers will send the strong message that your company doesn't tolerate misconduct, which will help prevent similar problems in the future.

Outsourcing

A few of the laws in this book—particularly those that deal with benefit plans, such as COBRA—can be difficult to understand and administer. That's why many companies hire outside service providers to handle their obligations under these laws. Outsourcing these responsibilities is a great way to maximize efficiency: Rather than spending weeks of your time trying to understand what these laws require, you can hire a company that specializes in compliance to take care of everything for you.

But use caution when hiring a third party to discharge your company's obligations. Generally, your company will remain legally liable for any actions taken by an outside provider. This means that an employee can still sue your company and collect damages (although, your company may be able to sue the provider to recoup your costs). This is why you must choose service providers very carefully; create a clear, written agreement about what you expect the provider to do for your company; monitor the provider's performance; and periodically review your outside contracts to make sure that your company is getting what it pays for.

Among the factors your company should consider when hiring an outside service provider are:

- **The services to be provided.** Is your company looking to outsource its entire HR function or only the administration of its pension plan or benefits programs?

- **Performance benchmarks.** How will you measure whether the provider is meeting its obligations to your company?

- **Pricing.** What will your company pay, and how will the price be calculated (for example, per employee, per task, or a set monthly or annual rate)?

- **Control.** Does your company want to have some input on the tasks you are outsourcing, or will the provider be solely responsible for those issues?

- **Liability.** Does using an outside provider create additional obligations or legal exposure? (For example, an employer's obligations under the Fair Credit Reporting Act are triggered when it hires another party to perform credit or background checks on applicants and employees.) If an employee or applicant sues, will the provider indemnify (repay) your company?

- **Handling problems.** How will you deal with disagreements or other problems in your company's relationship with the provider, and under what circumstances can either of you end the arrangement?

By carefully considering these issues up front, and getting some legal assistance in drafting and reviewing provider contracts, you can ensure that your company gets the most out of outsourcing administrative functions.

Documentation and Record-Keeping

As you'll see, many of the laws we cover require companies to keep certain documents—for example, payroll records, job applications, or forms signed by employees. In addition to complying with these legal requirements, your company should carefully document in writing all important decisions and required actions relating to its employees. Even if this type of documentation is not specifically required by the law, it's the best way to prove that you complied with the law, if necessary.

For example, the Fair Credit Reporting Act requires covered employers to provide written notice and obtain an applicant's or employee's consent before ordering a consumer report on that person. Because the law doesn't specifically require employers to keep copies of these records, an employer is technically free to shred these documents. But what if the employee claims never to have consented to the report? If the employer saves these records, it will have a written consent signed by the employee. If not, it will have no written proof that it complied with the law.

Companies should also carefully document employment decisions. For example, when a manager fires, promotes, disciplines, gives a pay raise to, or transfers an employee, or otherwise changes an employee's status or situation, he or she should fully document the reasons for the action. This will help the company if the employee later complains that the action was taken for illegal reasons (for example, discrimination or retaliation). The manager will have an easier time remembering the details and explaining the basis for the decision. The company will have a contemporaneous record (that is, one made at the time of the decision) of what it did and why. And, ultimately, documents will help the company persuade a government agency, jury, or judge that it acted properly.

As you will see, some federal laws require employers to keep records only for a certain period of time (for example, one or two years). However, you may want to retain these documents for longer than required by the federal law. For example, a state law may allow an employee to bring a lawsuit three years after a violation of state antidiscrimination laws. If you have thrown out relevant documents after only one or two years, you will have a difficult time defending against the claim. To find out how long you should keep specific employment records, consult with an employment lawyer in your area.

If You Need More Information

You may need more information than this book provides. You may have to figure out exactly how your company can comply with apparently conflicting federal, state, and local laws on the same topic. You may need help with the practical aspects of compliance, such as how to conduct an investigation of sexual harassment or develop an appropriate procedure for taking anonymous complaints of shareholder fraud under Sarbanes-Oxley. Or, you may need help developing employment contracts or an employee handbook. This section will direct you to some other resources that might help.

Government Agencies

Your first stop should be the federal or state agency that administers and enforces the law you're interested in. At the end of our discussion of each law, we give you a list of resources available from the relevant federal agency. But these lists aren't exhaustive—some of these agencies have dozens of fact sheets, guidance memoranda, and special bulletins for employers and small businesses that can help you figure out the law's requirements. These agencies also have staff members available to answer your questions or point you toward the information you need.

If your question involves state law, you can start your research by contacting the state agency that enforces the law. For questions about employment discrimination, contact your state fair employment practices agency. For other employment-related questions, contact your state labor department. Appendix A includes contact information for the federal agencies that enforce and interpret the laws covered in this book, as well as the fair employment practices agency and labor department of each of the 50 states and the District of Columbia.

Nolo Resources

Nolo provides a number of resources on employment law, policies and procedures, and other issues of special interest to the HR profession. The Nolo.com website has numerous articles on employment law and HR topics, as well as books and legal forms. See Appendix B for a list of resources you might find helpful.

Get Updates and More Online

When the information in this book changes, we'll post updates at this book's online companion page:

www.nolo.com/back-of-book/FEMP.html

You'll find information there on evolving issues in employment law, such as important Supreme Court cases or new regulations.

Age Discrimination in Employment Act (ADEA)

Statute: 29 U.S.C. §§ 621 and following
To view the statutes, visit https://uscode.house.gov and select "Title 29" and "Chapter 14."

Regulations: 29 C.F.R. §§ 1625–1627
To view the regulations, visit www.govinfo.gov and search "29 CFR 1625," "29 CFR 1626," and "29 CFR 1627."

Overview of the ADEA

The Age Discrimination in Employment Act (ADEA) prohibits age discrimination against employees and applicants age 40 or older. Congress passed the ADEA in 1967 to address the difficulties older employees face in the workplace, including mandatory retirement cutoffs and discrimination in the hiring process. Although the ADEA outlaws age discrimination, it does create a few limited exceptions, recognizing that advanced age may, in some circumstances, affect a worker's ability to perform certain jobs effectively.

Covered Employers

The ADEA covers:

- private employers with 20 or more employees (defined as an employer that has 20 or more employees on each working day during each of 20 or more calendar weeks in the current or previous calendar year)
- state and local governments (but state employees may not sue their employer for ADEA violations; see "Covered Workers," below)
- the federal government
- employment agencies, and
- labor organizations.

The ADEA covers multinational employers with operations in the United States or its territories, unless the employer is covered by a treaty or other binding international agreement—for example, a treaty permitting the company to give its own citizens preference for specific jobs.

The ADEA covers employers with operations in other countries if the employer is incorporated in the United States, based in the United States, or controlled by a U.S. company. However, an employer is exempt from the ADEA's requirements if complying with the ADEA would violate a law of the country in which it operates.

One section of the ADEA (29 U.S.C. § 633a) prohibits most federal agencies from discriminating on the basis of age against employees or applicants who are at least 40 years old.

Definitions

Terms that appear in italics throughout this chapter are defined below.

Bona fide employee benefit plan: A benefit plan that has been accurately described, in writing, to all employees and that actually provides the benefits promised.

Bona fide executive: A top-level employee who exercises substantial executive authority over a significant number of employees and a large volume of business. Examples include the head of a large regional operation of a national employer or the head of a major corporate division.

Bona fide occupational qualification (BFOQ): A limited exception to the ADEA that allows employers to discriminate on the basis of age if the nature of the job requires them to do so.

Bona fide seniority system: A seniority system that uses length of service with the employer as the primary criterion for deciding who will receive available employment opportunities and privileges. For the system to qualify as "bona fide," its essential terms and conditions must be communicated to employees and applied uniformly to all workers, regardless of age.

Firefighter: An employee whose primary duties are to perform work directly connected with controlling and extinguishing fires or maintaining and using firefighting apparatus and equipment, including an employee engaged in any of these activities who is transferred to a supervisory or administrative position.

High policy-making position: A top-level position that carries significant responsibility, held by someone who plays a substantial role in the development and effective implementation of corporate policy. This definition may include employees who do not supervise other workers, such as a company's chief research scientist or head economist.

Law enforcement officer: An employee whose primary duties are the investigation, apprehension, or detention of those suspected or convicted of violating criminal laws, including an employee engaged in any of these activities who is transferred to a supervisory or administrative position. Prison guards and other employees assigned to guard incarcerated prisoners are law enforcement officers.

Covered Workers

The ADEA protects employees and applicants who are at least 40 years old and who work for a covered employer. Unlike other antidiscrimination laws, the ADEA does not prohibit "reverse discrimination." Those who are younger than 40 have no rights under the law.

Although state government workers are protected by the ADEA, they do not have the right to sue their employers (the states for which they work) in court to enforce those rights; only the EEOC may sue a state to protect state employees from age discrimination.

The ADEA protects foreign nationals working for a covered employer, even if the employees are not authorized to work in the United States. Such employees still have rights under the ADEA, however, their available remedies may be limited. For example, although reinstatement is a common remedy for an unlawfully fired employee, a foreign national will not be reinstated to a job in the United States if he or she is not authorized to work in the United States.

The ADEA also protects U.S. citizens working outside the United States for employers that are incorporated in the United States, based in the United States, or controlled by a U.S. employer.

Did You Know ...

- According to the Bureau of Labor Statistics (BLS), workers age 40 and older made up over one-third of the workforce in 2017. By 2024, the BLS projects that around 41 million U.S. workers will be 55 and older.
- In 2017, nearly 22% of all discrimination charges filed with the EEOC included a claim of age discrimination.
- An AARP survey, conducted in May 2018, found that more than 60% of older respondents had experienced or witnessed age discrimination in the workplace. More than half of respondents believed that age discrimination starts in a worker's 50s.

What's Prohibited

The ADEA prohibits age discrimination against applicants and employees who are at least 40 years old. The ADEA applies to all aspects of employment, including:

- hiring
- firing
- compensation
- benefits
- job assignments and transfers
- employee classifications
- promotions
- layoffs and recalls
- training and apprenticeship programs
- retirement plans, and
- time off.

The ADEA also prohibits employers from retaliating against employees who complain of age discrimination or otherwise assert their rights under the law. (For more information, see "Retaliation," below.)

Key Facts

- The ADEA protects workers who are at least 40 years old from age discrimination. It does not apply or provide any rights to workers who are younger than 40, and it does not prohibit an employer from favoring older workers over younger workers.
- There are several explicit exceptions for firefighters, law enforcement officers, and certain types of executives and policy makers. In addition, an employer may discriminate based on age if it can prove that age is a bona fide occupational qualification for the job.
- Like Title VII of the Civil Rights Act of 1964, the ADEA prohibits neutral policies and practices that have a disproportionately negative impact on older workers. However, different rules apply to these so-called "disparate impact" lawsuits under the ADEA and Title VII. (See Chapter 18 for more on Title VII.)

Discrimination

Among the practices that might constitute age discrimination under the ADEA are:

- requiring workers to retire once they reach a certain age
- treating older workers worse than younger workers by, for example, targeting them for layoffs or discipline
- giving younger workers higher pay, more favorable assignments, or more responsibilities than older workers because of age, and
- making decisions based on stereotypes about older people (for example, refusing to include older workers in training programs because of a belief that they are unwilling or unable to learn new things).

The ADEA's prohibitions apply even if the "younger" workers who receive better treatment are 40 or older. For instance, an employer who treats a 50-year-old worker more favorably than a 70-year-old worker because of age has violated the ADEA, even though both workers are protected from age discrimination under the law. However, the opposite is not true: Employers may favor a 70-year-old employee over a 50-year-old employee without violating the ADEA.

The ADEA also prohibits employers from adopting facially neutral policies or practices that have a disproportionately negative effect on older workers. These "disparate impact" claims often come up in layoff cases, when a significant number of the employees who lose their jobs are 40 or older.

The ADEA gives employers a defense to disparate impact claims: An employer can escape liability if it can prove that the policy or practice that created the disparate impact was based on a reasonable factor other than age (RFOA). In 2008, the Supreme Court decided that the RFOA is an affirmative defense, which means the employer must prove it at trial. (*Meacham v. Knolls Atomic Power Laboratory,* 554 U.S. 84 (2008).) But this left open the question of exactly what qualifies as an RFOA, including which factors are "reasonable" for an employer to consider when making job decisions and how much responsibility an employer has to try to reduce the negative impact on older workers.

In 2012, the EEOC issued final regulations that attempt to answer these questions. Among other things, the regulations define an RFOA as a "non-age" factor that is objectively reasonable when viewed from the position of a prudent employer mindful of its obligations under the ADEA. The employer must show both of the following:

- that the employment practice it used was reasonably designed to achieve a legitimate business purpose, and
- that the employer applied the factor in a way that reasonably achieves that purpose.

The regulations make clear that a court must consider all of the relevant facts and circumstances in deciding whether an employer has adequately proven an RFOA. Specific items to consider include:

- the factor's relationship to the employer's stated business purpose
- the extent to which the employer defined the factor accurately and applied it fairly and accurately, including whether managers and supervisors received training as to how to apply the factor in making decisions and avoid discrimination
- whether (and how much) the employer limited supervisors' discretion to evaluate employees subjectively, particularly if the factor is known to be subject to negative stereotypes based on age
- whether the employer assessed the adverse impact of its practice on older employees, and
- how much the practice harmed older workers (in severity and number) and whether the employer took steps to reduce that harm, given the burden involved in taking such steps.

Mixed Motive Cases Under the ADEA

A mixed motive case is one in which the employer potentially had both a discriminatory and a nondiscriminatory motive for an adverse employment action. Under Title VII, an employee can succeed in this type of claim by showing that the protected characteristic, such as race or gender, was a motivating factor in the employment decision. The burden then shifts to the employer to prove that it would have made the same decision regardless of the protected characteristic, based on a nondiscriminatory motive.

However, in *Gross v. FBL Financial Services, Inc.*, 557 U.S. 167 (2009), the United States Supreme Court held that this burden-shifting scheme does not apply to discrimination claims under the ADEA. Rather, the plaintiff must prove that the discriminatory motive was the "but for" cause of the employment decision—that is, the decision would not have been made if not for the employee's age. In *Gross*, the plaintiff claimed that he was reassigned to a different position due to his age. The employer argued that the reassignment was part of a larger corporate restructuring and that the position was a better fit for his skills. Based on the Court's decision, the plaintiff needed to show that, had it not been for his age, he would not have been reassigned.

Harassment

Harassment occurs when an employee is forced to put up with offensive, age-related conduct as a condition of employment or when such conduct is severe or pervasive enough to create a hostile work environment. Harassment might include:

- age-related slurs or offensive remarks
- offensive jokes about a worker's age
- cartoons or pictures that depict older people unfavorably
- threats, intimidation, or hostility, or
- physical violence.

Although there was originally some doubt as to whether the ADEA prohibited harassment in addition to discrimination, courts have generally recognized an employee's right to sue for age-related workplace harassment.

These claims are generally treated in the same manner as harassment claims under Title VII.

Advertising Prohibitions

The ADEA specifically prohibits employers from printing or publishing any job advertisement or notice that expresses a preference or limitation based on age. Terms such as "college student," "youthful," or "recent college graduate" all run afoul of this rule. Terms such as "energetic," "flexible," and "willingness to learn new things" may also indicate a discriminatory motive. Job notices seeking applicants of a particular age are also illegal.

Retaliation

The ADEA prohibits employers from retaliating against employees who complain about age discrimination, file a charge of age discrimination with the EEOC, participate in an investigation of age discrimination, file or testify in a lawsuit alleging age discrimination, or otherwise exercise their rights under the ADEA.

An employer retaliates when it takes an adverse job action against an employee for exercising his or her legal rights. This might include firing, demotion, discipline, pay cuts, or less-favorable job assignments.

In a 2008 case, the U.S. Supreme Court found that federal employees are also protected from retaliation for complaining of age discrimination. (*Gomez-Perez v. Potter*, 553 U.S. 474 (2008).)

Exceptions

Employers may use age as a basis for employment decisions in a few limited circumstances. If an employer that relies on one of these exceptions is sued for age discrimination, the employer will bear the burden of proving that its actions fell within the exception.

Bona Fide Seniority System

An employer may use a *bona fide seniority system* as a basis for employment decisions, even if that results in more favorable treatment of younger workers. For example, an employer can adopt a policy of laying off workers who have the least seniority with the company, even if older workers disproportionately lose their jobs as a result.

This exception is rarely used. Because older workers tend to have greater seniority than younger workers, they are unlikely to be disadvantaged by an employer's decision to lay off workers who have little or no seniority. A "reverse" seniority system that benefits workers with less seniority or penalizes workers with more seniority does not qualify as a bona fide seniority system under the ADEA.

Bona Fide Occupational Qualification

An employer may discriminate on the basis of age in filling a particular job if age is a *bona fide occupational qualification (BFOQ)* for the position—that is, if the job, by its very nature, must be filled by an employee of a particular age. In age discrimination cases, the BFOQ defense comes up most often in the context of age limits, when an employer refuses to hire anyone older than a certain age for certain positions.

An employer may use the BFOQ defense only if the age limit or other age-related policy is reasonably necessary to the essence of the employer's business and either of the following is true:

- All or substantially all people who are older than the age limit would be unable to perform the job.
- Some people who are older than the age limit would be unable to perform the job and testing each person individually would be impossible or highly impractical for the employer.

If the employer's goal in using the BFOQ is public safety, the employer must show not only that the challenged age limit achieves that goal, but also that there is no acceptable alternative that is less discriminatory.

Bona Fide Employee Benefit Plan

In some cases, an employer may reduce benefits paid to older workers if the employer acts in accordance with a *bona fide employee benefit plan.* This exception is discussed in detail in Chapter 13, which covers the Older Workers Benefit Protection Act.

Firefighters and Law Enforcement Officers

State and local governments may institute a mandatory retirement age of 55 or older for firefighters and law enforcement officers.

Bona Fide Executives and High Policy Makers

Employers may require a high-ranking employee to retire or step down to a lesser position if all of the following conditions are met:

- The employee is at least 65 years old.
- The employee has worked for at least the previous two years as a *bona fide executive* or in a *high policy-making position* (see "Definitions," at the beginning of this chapter).
- The employee is entitled to an immediate, nonforfeitable annual retirement benefit of at least $44,000 from the employer. A benefit is immediate if payments start (or could have started, at the employee's election) within 60 days of the effective date of the employee's retirement. A benefit is nonforfeitable if no plan provisions could cause payments to cease. For example, if the plan requires payments to be suspended if the employee files a lawsuit, that benefit would be forfeitable. In calculating whether a benefit pays at least $44,000 annually, employers may not count Social Security contributions, employee contributions, contributions of former employers, or rollover contributions.

How the ADEA Is Enforced

Individual Complaints

Employees may file a complaint (also called a charge) of age discrimination with the EEOC. The deadlines for filing a charge depend on whether the state where the discrimination charge will be filed also has an antidiscrimination law. In states without antidiscrimination laws, an employee has 180 days from the date of the discriminatory act to file a complaint. In states that have their own laws prohibiting age discrimination, this deadline is extended to 300 days. (You can find a list of states with antidiscrimination laws, and information on what those laws prohibit, at the end of Chapter 18.)

An employee may also file a lawsuit for age discrimination. However, the employee first must file a charge of discrimination with the EEOC and get a "right to sue" letter (see "Agency Enforcement," below). The employee must then file the lawsuit within 90 days.

Agency Enforcement

The federal agency responsible for investigating ADEA complaints is the EEOC. (See Appendix A for contact information for the EEOC.) An employee usually initiates the process by filing a charge of age discrimination with the EEOC, although the agency can also act on its own initiative. The EEOC has the power to investigate, negotiate with employers, and bring lawsuits against employers to stop discriminatory practices.

Complying With the ADEA

Reporting Requirements

The ADEA imposes no reporting requirements.

Posting Requirements

All covered employers must post a notice regarding the ADEA. Employers must post this notice in a prominent location, where it can be easily seen and read by employees and job applicants. The EEOC has created a poster, *Equal Employment Opportunity Is the Law*, which fulfills this requirement. You can download the poster in English, Spanish, Arabic, or Chinese from the EEOC's website. (See "Agency Resources," below.)

Record-Keeping Requirements

Employers must make and keep records for three years that contain the following information for each employee:
- name
- address
- date of birth
- occupation
- pay rate, and
- weekly compensation.

Employers must keep any records relating to the following employment matters for one year:

- job applications, résumés, responses to job advertisements, inquiries about jobs, and any other records relating to the failure to hire any applicant
- promotion, demotion, transfer, selection for training, layoff, recall, or termination
- job orders submitted by the employer to an employment agency or labor organization to recruit applicants for job openings
- test papers completed by applicants for any position
- results of any physical examination considered by the employer in connection with any personnel action, and
- job notices or advertisements relating to job openings, promotions, training programs, or opportunities to work overtime.

Employers must also keep copies of any employment benefit plan and any written seniority system and merit system for one year beyond the date when the plan expires. If such a plan or system is not in writing, the employer must keep a memorandum fully outlining its terms and the manner in which it has been communicated to employees for the same time period.

Remedies

If a court finds that an employer has violated the ADEA, the employer may be ordered to do any or all of the following:

- Pay the employee all wages, benefits, and other forms of compensation lost as a result of the discrimination.
- Take action to remedy the results of the discrimination by, for example, reinstating or promoting the worker. If the court finds that such action is warranted but impractical (for example, if the employee's position has been eliminated or the work relationship is irrevocably poisoned), the court may award the employee "front pay"—compensation for future earnings lost—instead.
- Pay a penalty (called "liquidated damages"), equal to all of the wages, benefits, and other compensation owed the employee at the time of trial, if the employer knew that its conduct was illegal or showed reckless disregard as to whether its conduct violated the ADEA.
- Pay the employee's court costs and attorneys' fees.

Agency Resources

- The downloadable notice employers must post regarding the ADEA:

  Equal Employment Opportunity Is the Law
  www1.eeoc.gov/employers/poster.cfm

- Information about the EEOC's charge-processing procedures:

  What You Can Expect After a Charge is Filed
  www1.eeoc.gov/employers/process.cfm

- Basic facts about the ADEA:

  Facts About Age Discrimination
  www1.eeoc.gov/eeoc/publications/age.cfm

State Laws Relating to Age Discrimination

Most states have antidiscrimination laws, many of which prohibit age discrimination. Some states follow the ADEA's lead by prohibiting discrimination only against workers 40 and older. Other states prohibit discrimination against workers of all ages. To find out whether your state has an age discrimination law, consult the chart at the end of Chapter 18.

Americans with Disabilities Act of 1990 (ADA)

Statute: 42 U.S.C. §§ 12101 and following
To view the statutes, visit http://uscode.house.gov and select "Title 42" and "Chapter 126."

Regulations: 29 C.F.R. §§ 1630 and following
To view the regulations, visit www.govinfo.gov and search "29 CFR 1630."

Overview of the ADA

The Americans with Disabilities Act of 1990 (ADA) is a sweeping civil rights law that protects people with *disabilities* in many contexts, including employment, government services, public accommodations, and telecommunications. This book covers only the ADA's employment provisions, which can be found in Title I of the Act.

The ADA's main employment provisions prohibit covered employers from discriminating against *qualified individuals with a disability*. This prohibition applies to all terms, conditions, and privileges of employment, and it protects both applicants and current employees. In addition, the ADA requires employers to provide *reasonable accommodations* to qualified individuals with a disability, to enable them to perform the job.

In 2008, President Bush signed the Americans with Disabilities Act Amendments Act (ADAAA), which makes a number of changes to the ADA. The stated purpose of the ADAAA was to make clear that Congress intended for the term "disability" to be interpreted broadly, in order to provide a national mandate to end discrimination against people with disabilities. The ADAAA explicitly overturned several Supreme Court decisions that had limited the scope of the ADA. This discussion includes the provisions of the ADAAA, which went into effect in 2009.

Covered Employers

The following employers must comply with the ADA's employment provisions:
- private employers with 15 or more employees
- employment agencies
- labor organizations
- joint labor/management committees, and
- local governments.

State employers are also required to follow the ADA, but their employees may not sue them for money damages for violating the law. However, state employees may sue their employers for injunctive relief—that is, to ask the court to require the state to take some action or refrain from taking some action (for example, to prohibit the state from requiring all applicants to submit to a physical or to require the state to provide reasonable test-taking accommodations to applicants

Definitions

Terms that appear in italics throughout this chapter are defined below.

Direct threat: A significant and immediate risk of substantial harm to the health or safety of an employee with a disability or others that cannot be reduced or eliminated by a *reasonable accommodation*.

Disability: A long-term physical or mental impairment that substantially limits a *major life activity*; a history of such an impairment; or being regarded as having such an impairment.

Essential functions: The fundamental duties of a job, as opposed to the marginal ones.

Major bodily functions: The proper working of bodily processes, functions, or systems, such as the immune system, normal cell growth, and the digestive, bowel, bladder, neurological, brain, respiratory, circulatory, endocrine, and reproductive functions.

Major life activities: Activities that are of central importance to daily life, including *major bodily functions*.

Mitigating measures: Equipment, supplies, technology, aids, appliances, and other devices or items used to ameliorate the effects of a physical or mental condition, such as medication, medical supplies, prosthetics, hearing aids, mobility devices, assistive technology, oxygen therapy equipment, and learned behavioral or adaptive neurological modifications.

Qualified individual with a disability: A person who has a *disability* and who, with or without a *reasonable accommodation*, can perform the *essential functions* of a job that the person holds or would like to hold. The ADA protects only qualified individuals with a disability.

Reasonable accommodation: Providing assistance or making changes in the job or workplace that will enable a worker with a disability to do the job.

Retaliation: A negative employment action taken by an employer (or someone who works for the employer) against an employee for complaining about harassment or discrimination.

with disabilities for civil service exams). State employees may also be able to sue their employers under state antidiscrimination laws. And, the EEOC can sue state employers on behalf of state employees whose ADA rights have been violated.

The ADA does not cover the federal government, but a similar law—the Rehabilitation Act of 1973 (29 U.S.C. § 701 and following)—does.

The ADA covers multinational employers with operations in the United States or its territories, unless the employer is covered by a treaty or another binding international agreement—for example, a treaty permitting the company to prefer its own citizens for specific jobs.

The ADA covers an employer with operations in other countries if the employer is incorporated in the United States, based in the United States, or controlled by a U.S. company. However, an employer is exempt from the ADA's requirements if complying with the ADA would violate a law of the country in which it operates.

Covered Workers

To get the benefits of the ADA's employment provisions, a person must:
- be a current or prospective employee of a covered employer (including part-time or probationary employees)
- be qualified for the position, and
- have a disability within the meaning of the ADA.

The sections below explain these requirements.

Current or Prospective Employee

The ADA's employment provisions protect only current employees or applicants for jobs with a covered employer. The ADA's employment provisions do not cover independent contractors, vendors, or customers (though they may be covered by some of the ADA's other provisions, such as those mandating access to public accommodations).

The ADA covers foreign nationals working for a covered employer, even if the employee is not authorized to work in the United States. Such an employee still has rights under the ADA, although his or her available remedies may be limited. For example, although reinstatement is a common remedy for an unlawfully fired employee, a foreign national may not be reinstated if he or she is not authorized to work in the United States.

The ADA also protects U.S. citizens working outside the United States for employers that are:

- incorporated in the United States
- based in the United States, or
- controlled by a U.S. employer.

Qualified for the Position

A person is qualified for a position if both of the following are true:

- The person satisfies the prerequisites for the position (for example, has the right level of education, employment experience, skills, and licenses).
- The person is able to perform the *essential functions* of the position, with or without a reasonable accommodation from the employer.

The term essential functions refers to the fundamental duties of a job, as opposed to the marginal ones. A job duty is an essential function if any of the following are true:

- The reason the job exists is to perform that function (for example, an essential function of a pilot is to fly the plane).
- A limited number of employees are available to perform the function.
- The function is so highly specialized that the employer hires people into the position specifically because of their expertise in performing that function.

The following types of information are relevant to determining whether a job duty is an essential function:

- written job descriptions prepared before advertising or interviewing for a position
- the employer's opinion, as to the importance of the job duty
- the amount of time that people who hold that job have to spend performing that duty
- the consequences of giving the job to someone who could not perform that duty
- the terms of a collective bargaining agreement
- the work experience of people who have held the job in the past, and
- the work experience of people who are currently holding the job.

With a Disability

Not all physical or mental impairments qualify as disabilities under the ADA. The ADA establishes three ways for a worker to qualify as having a disability:

- The worker has a physical or mental impairment that substantially limits a *major life activity*, without taking *mitigating measures* into account.
- The worker has a record or history of such an impairment.
- The employer incorrectly regards the worker as having a disability.

Temporary or minor impairments, such as pregnancy, the flu, or broken bones, are not covered by the ADA (but they may be covered by other laws).

The EEOC's regulations specifically say that the following are not disabilities: transvestism, transsexualism, pedophilia, gender identity disorders (other than those that result from a physical impairment), other sexual behavior disorders, compulsive gambling, kleptomania, pyromania, psychoactive substance use disorders resulting from current illegal drug use, homosexuality, and bisexuality.

Physical or Mental Impairment

A physical impairment means a disorder, condition, cosmetic disfigurement, or an anatomical loss that negatively affects the body's functioning. A mental impairment is any mental or psychological disorder—for example, mental retardation, organic brain syndrome, emotional or mental illness, or a learning disability.

An impairment is different from a condition or trait. Only impairments can be disabilities; conditions and traits cannot. For example, height and weight, when they are in the normal range, are traits, not impairments. Personality traits, such as poor judgment or a quick temper, are also not impairments (unless they are symptoms of a mental or psychological disorder).

The regulations interpreting the ADA provide a list of impairments that will "as a factual matter, virtually always" be disabilities, because of their effect on major life activities. These impairments include deafness, blindness, intellectual disabilities, missing limbs or mobility impairments requiring the use of a wheelchair, autism, cancer, cerebral palsy, diabetes, epilepsy, HIV infection, muscular dystrophy, major depressive disorder, bipolar disorder, posttraumatic stress disorder, obsessive-compulsive disorder, and schizophrenia.

Substantial Limitation

An impairment that substantially limits a major life activity is a disability. Prior to the passage of the ADAAA, the EEOC and the courts used to interpret this standard to mean that a person had to be either:

- unable to perform a major life activity, or
- significantly restricted in the condition, manner, or duration of performing that activity to qualify as having a disability.

In enacting the ADAAA, however, Congress stated that this definition was too narrow and excluded too many people from the ADA's reach. Congress instructed the EEOC to revise its regulations to redefine "substantially limits" more broadly.

In keeping with this directive, the final regulations interpreting the ADAAA state that the term is "not meant to be a demanding standard." They also clarify that a person can be substantially limited in performing a major life activity even if that person is not prevented, or significantly restricted, from performing that activity. The final regulations indicate that the condition, manner, and duration of the person's performance of the activity should be examined. For example, can the person perform the activity only for a brief period? Must the person expend significant effort to perform the activity? Is it painful or otherwise difficult for the person to perform the activity? Do the side effects of medication or other treatment make it harder for the person to perform the activity?

Conditions that are in remission or are episodic in nature are now covered by the ADA, as long as they would substantially limit a major life activity when they are active. For example, an employee whose cancer is in remission or who suffers from chronic asthma would likely be covered.

Major Life Activities

Major life activities are activities that are of essential importance to daily life, including:

- caring for oneself
- performing manual tasks
- walking
- seeing
- hearing
- speaking
- breathing
- learning, and
- working.

The ADAAA added *major bodily functions* to the list of major life activities. This means that serious conditions that have not yet appeared as outwardly debilitating will be covered as disabilities. For example, many types of cancer wreak havoc on the body's internal functioning (such as proper cell growth or the normal functioning of the immune or other bodily systems) before they substantially limit a person's ability to breathe, walk, or work. These conditions are now covered by the ADA without question.

Did You Know ...

- According to the *2016 Disability Status Report* by Cornell University, more than 10% of the working age population (ages 21 through 64) has a disability. The most common disabilities were ambulatory disabilities, independent living disabilities, and cognitive disabilities, hearing disabilities, self-care disabilities, and visual disabilities. More than one-third of working age adults with disabilities were employed, as compared to more than three-quarters of the working age population without a disability.

- The same report states that the median annual income of Americans with disabilities who were employed full time for a full year was $43,300, which was $2,000 less than those without disabilities earned. Those with hearing disabilities earned the most, while those with cognitive disabilities earned the least.

- When the EEOC drafted its proposed regulations on the ADAAA in 2009, it pulled together various statistics and studies on the cost of reasonable accommodations. Those studies show significant variations in the reported mean cost of an accommodation, ranging from $462 up to more than $1,400. Where the studies agree, however, is that many reasonable accommodations are free. In fact, in an ongoing study by the Job Accommodation Network— a service of the U.S. Department of Labor's Office of Disability Employment Policy—participating employers reported that 59% of the accommodations they made cost them nothing. Employers that incurred a one-time cost to make an accommodation spent an average of $500.

Mitigating Measures

The ADAAA also changed the rules on mitigating measures. Previously, courts (including the Supreme Court) held that mitigating measures had to be considered when determining whether someone had a disability. For example, an employee who takes medication to control seizures would be found to have a disability only if his or her impairment, as medicated, substantially limited a major life activity. This meant that employees whose disabilities were largely controlled or ameliorated by equipment, medication, or other assistive devices were often found not to have disabilities.

The ADAAA overturned this rule so that more employees would be found to have disabilities under the ADA. Now, an employee's condition must be considered without mitigating measures in determining whether an employee has a disability. The only exception to this rule is for ordinary prescription eyeglasses and contact lenses, which may be considered in evaluating an employee's condition. In other words, someone who has 20/20 vision while wearing glasses does not have a disability.

Alcoholism

Alcoholism is a recognized disability under the ADA. Employers may not discriminate against employees because they are alcoholics or have a history of alcoholism. Employers must also provide reasonable accommodations to alcoholic employees. This might include, for example, changing work hours so an employee can attend Alcoholics Anonymous meetings or providing time off work to attend rehab. However, employers still have the right to enforce an alcohol-free workplace and prohibit employees from showing up to work under the influence of alcohol. They can also hold alcoholics to the same workplace standards as other employees, provided they don't single out alcoholics for harsher treatment. For example, an employer may discipline an alcoholic employee who continually misses work on Mondays after a weekend bender.

Illegal Drug Use

An applicant or employee who currently engages in illegal drug use (including abuse of prescription drugs) is not a qualified individual with a disability and is, therefore, not entitled to the ADA's protections.

This exception applies only to employees and job applicants who are currently using drugs illegally. The ADA still protects employees and applicants who:

- have successfully completed a drug rehabilitation program and are no longer using drugs illegally
- are currently participating in a drug rehabilitation program and are no longer using drugs illegally, or
- are erroneously believed to use drugs illegally when, in fact, they do not.

Because marijuana is still illegal under federal law, employers are not required to make reasonable accommodations for medical marijuana use under the Americans with Disabilities Act. In states where medical marijuana is legal, some states require employers to accommodate medical marijuana use while others do not. In fact, in several states with medical marijuana laws, employees can be fired for using marijuana with a valid prescription during nonwork hours.

What's Prohibited

Discrimination

Covered employers may not discriminate against qualified individuals with a disability in any aspect of employment, including:

- recruitment
- job application procedures
- hiring
- promotion and training
- time off
- job assignments
- benefits
- wages, and
- layoff and termination.

Covered employers also may not discriminate against employees or applicants for associating with a person with a disability. For example, a covered employer cannot refuse to hire someone because his or her spouse has AIDS. Nor may an employer refuse to hire someone with a developmentally disabled child because the employer fears the person will miss work too often.

Key Facts

- The ADA prohibits discrimination in all aspects of employment against qualified individuals with disabilities and requires employers to make reasonable accommodations to allow those with disabilities to apply for a position or to perform a job.
- Employers may not inquire about a job applicant's disabilities. However, an employer may ask an applicant to describe how he or she would perform the essential functions of a job.
- An employer may refuse to hire a qualified individual with a disability if doing so would pose a *direct threat* to the employee's own health or safety or to the health or safety of others.

Tests and Qualification Standards

An employer may not base tests or qualification standards for a job on an employee's uncorrected vision unless such a requirement is job related and consistent with business necessity.

Harassment

The ADA prohibits harassment of employees with disabilities. Harassment consists of unwelcome comments or offensive conduct that the employee must put up with as a condition of employment or that is severe or pervasive enough to alter the conditions of employment. This test is the same as that used under Title VII. (See Chapter 18 for more about harassment.)

Segregation

Employers may not segregate employees with disabilities. For example, if coworkers feel uncomfortable working with a person who has a disability, the employer may not transfer that person or require him or her to work at home.

Medical Examinations

Covered employers may not require job applicants to take a medical examination until a conditional offer of employment is made. After extending a conditional offer of employment, the employer may require a medical exam, but only if all of the following are true:

- All entering employees are required to take the exam regardless of whether they have a disability.
- The medical exam is the last stage in the applicant-screening process (for example, after the background check).
- The employer keeps the medical exam results in a separate and confidential medical file.

A test for illegal drug use is not a medical exam and is, therefore, not prohibited or governed by the ADA. (It may be governed by other laws, though. For example, some states have laws limiting when and how employers may test applicants and employees for drugs and alcohol.)

An employer may require current employees to take a medical examination only if the employer reasonably believes either of the following:

- The employee is unable to perform the essential functions of the job due to a medical condition.
- The employee poses a *direct threat* to himself or herself or other employees because of a medical condition.

Inquiries About Disabilities

During the pre-offer period, employers may not ask job applicants questions about whether they have a disability or about the nature or severity of a disability. However, employers can explain what the hiring process involves and ask applicants whether they will need a reasonable accommodation. They can also explain what the job entails and ask applicants whether they are capable of performing job-related functions.

After making a conditional offer of employment, an employer may ask an applicant about his or her health or disability, but only if such questions are asked of all applicants who are extended a job offer (in other words, not just applicants with obvious disabilities).

Retaliation

Covered employers may not take a negative employment action against an individual for asserting his or her rights under the ADA. Negative employment actions might include demotion, discipline, firing, salary reduction, or change in job assignment. To do so constitutes illegal *retaliation*. (See Chapter 18 for more information on retaliation.)

What's Required

Employers must provide reasonable accommodations for qualified individuals with disabilities who need them to apply for a job, perform a job, or access work facilities and benefits. Employers are excused from providing an accommodation only if it would cause the employer undue hardship. (See "Undue Hardship," below.)

Accommodating a worker means providing assistance or making changes in the job or workplace that will enable the worker to do the job. For example, an employer might lower the height of a desktop to accommodate a worker in a wheelchair, provide TDD telephone equipment for a worker whose hearing is impaired, or provide a quiet, distraction-free workspace for a worker with Attention Deficit Disorder.

Reasonable accommodations fall into three broad categories:
- changes to the job application process that enable a qualified individual with a disability to apply and be considered for the position
- changes to the work environment, the circumstances in which the job is performed, or the manner in which the job is performed that enable a qualified individual with a disability to perform the job's essential functions, and
- changes that enable an employee with a disability to enjoy the same benefits and privileges that other employees enjoy.

It is generally the applicant's or employee's responsibility to request the accommodation initially. The employer does not have to guess or anticipate the need for accommodation. (However, if the disability is obvious or the employer is otherwise on notice of the need for an accommodation, the employer might need to inquire further.) Employees or job applicants do not have to make the request in writing, nor do they have to use any particular words—for example, they don't have to mention the ADA or use the words "reasonable accommodation." They simply need to request that some change be made because of a medical condition or impairment. Someone other than the applicant or employee (such as a spouse, friend, or coworker) can request the accommodation on the worker's behalf.

Once the request is made, the employer and the worker must talk and work together to see if a reasonable accommodation is possible. The employer does not have to grant the specific accommodation that the employee or applicant requests, as long as the employer provides an effective alternative accommodation.

If the disability or need for accommodation is not obvious, the employer may ask the employee to submit medical verification of the disability and the employee's limitations.

Employers are not required to make accommodations that are unreasonable, including the following:

- eliminating an essential function of the job
- lowering production or performance standards, or
- providing personal use items, such as a wheelchair, eyeglasses, hearing aids, or a prosthetic limb.

An employee who is protected from discrimination under the ADA because the employer incorrectly "regards" the employee as disabled is not entitled to a reasonable accommodation.

Exceptions

There are four major exceptions to employers' responsibilities under the ADA:

- *Undue hardship.* Employers are not required to make a reasonable accommodation if it would cause the employer an undue hardship.
- *Direct threat.* Employers may refuse to hire a qualified applicant with a disability if it would pose a direct threat to the applicant's own health or safety or to the health or safety of others.
- *Religious institutions.* Churches and other religious institutions may prefer applicants who conform to the tenets of their religion over otherwise qualified applicants with a disability for ministerial positions.

- *Food handling.* If a job requires food handling, an employer can refuse to hire someone with an infectious or communicable disease if a reasonable accommodation cannot eliminate the risk of transmitting the disease.

Undue Hardship

An accommodation creates an undue hardship if it would involve significant difficulty or expense for the employer or if it would fundamentally alter the nature or operation of the business. Whether an accommodation creates an undue hardship depends on a number of factors, including:

- the accommodation's cost
- the size and financial resources of the business
- the structure of the business, and
- the effect the accommodation would have on the business.

An undue hardship can be financial, but it doesn't have to be. For example, suppose a library clerk with a hearing disability requested that a loud bell and speaker be added to the telephone, which would enable him to hear and answer calls. Although the accommodation is probably inexpensive, it would disturb library patrons and destroy the quiet atmosphere of the library. Because of this, the accommodation would probably create an undue hardship for the library.

Direct Threat

A covered employer may refuse to hire qualified individuals with disabilities— or may transfer or terminate them without violating the ADA—if hiring them for the job would pose a direct threat to their own health or safety or to the health or safety of others. To determine whether a direct threat exists, the employer must make an individualized assessment of a person's ability to safely perform the essential functions of the job, taking into account the judgment of a medical professional. The following factors should be considered:

- the duration of the risk
- the nature and severity of the potential harm to the person with the disability, his or her coworkers, and the public
- the likelihood of harm occurring, and
- whether the harm is imminent.

Religious Institutions

Religious institutions may give preference to job applicants of a particular religion. For example, a Jewish temple may hire a qualified Jewish applicant instead of a qualified applicant with a disability who is not Jewish. Religious institutions may also require that the applicant conform to the tenets of the religion. For example, a Catholic college may fire a professor with a disability who renounces his faith, even though he is otherwise able to perform his job.

The Supreme Court has clarified that applicants for, and employees in, ministerial positions may not sue religious employers for discrimination or retaliation under the ADA. The First Amendment's guarantee of religious freedom requires courts to steer clear of religious employers' decisions about who will preach their message and mission. This exception applies only to employees who act as "ministers" of the religious employer's faith.

The Supreme Court declined to adopt a bright-line rule as to who qualifies as a minister. Instead, the determination should be made on a case-by-case basis by looking at all of the facts. In one case in particular, the Court held that a teacher for a Lutheran school was a minister because she had significant religious training, was formally commissioned as a minister, taught a religion class, led students in prayer, took students to a weekly church service, and occasionally led the church service. The fact that the teacher spent most of her time performing secular duties (such as teaching non-religious school subjects) did not alter her status as a minister, nor did the fact that non-commissioned teachers performed the same religious duties that she did. (*Hosanna-Tabor Evangelical Lutheran Church & School v. EEOC*, 132 S. Ct. 694 (2012).).

Infectious Diseases

If a job requires food handling, an employer can refuse to hire someone with an infectious or communicable disease that is transmittable through food handling only if a reasonable accommodation cannot eliminate the risk of transmitting the disease.

How the ADA Is Enforced

Individual Complaints

The ADA is enforced under the same procedures as Title VII, including through applicant and employee complaints to the Equal Employment Opportunity Commission (EEOC). (See Chapter 18.)

Agency Enforcement

The ADA is enforced under the same procedures as Title VII, including through investigations and lawsuits brought by the EEOC. (See Chapter 18.)

Complying With the ADA

Reporting Requirements

The reporting requirements for the ADA are the same as those for Title VII. Larger employers must file annual reports with the EEOC. (See Chapter 18.)

Posting Requirements

Covered employers must post notices informing current and prospective employees about the ADA. This notice is included in the poster, *Equal Employment Opportunity Is the Law*, available from the EEOC. (See Chapter 18 for more information.)

Record-Keeping Requirements

The record-keeping requirements for the ADA are the same as those for Title VII. Covered employers must keep employment records for one year. When an employee is involuntarily terminated, personnel records must be kept for one year after the termination. (See Chapter 18.)

Remedies

For the most part, failure to comply with the ADA carries the same penalties as failure to comply with Title VII. (See Chapter 18.) However, courts disagree on whether plaintiffs who bring a lawsuit for retaliation under the ADA may recover compensatory damages (for out-of-pocket expenses and the emotional harm caused by the employer's actions), or punitive damages (intended to punish the employer for egregious violations of the law). This conflict has not yet been resolved by the U.S. Supreme Court.

In addition to the penalties available under Title VII, a court might order an employer to make a reasonable accommodation for an employee's disability.

Agency Resources

- Basic information on the ADA

    Facts About the Americans with Disabilities Act
    www.eeoc.gov/facts/fs-ada.html

    The ADA: Questions and Answers
    www.eeoc.gov/facts/adaqa1.html

- Information for employers about their obligations under the ADA

    The ADA: Your Responsibilities as an Employer
    www.eeoc.gov/facts/ada17.html

- A detailed handbook on how to comply with the ADA

    The Americans with Disabilities Act: A Primer for Small Business
    www.eeoc.gov/eeoc/publications/adahandbook.cfm

- A guide to reasonable accommodations under the ADA for small businesses

    Small Employers and Reasonable Accommodation
    www.eeoc.gov/facts/accommodation.html

- A guide to the ADA during the job application process

    Job Applicants and the Americans with Disabilities Act
    www.eeoc.gov/facts/jobapplicant.html

- Facts on telecommuting as a reasonable accommodation
  Work At Home/Telework as a Reasonable Accommodation
  www.eeoc.gov/facts/telework.html

- A detailed guide to the ADA for the food service industry
  How to Comply with the Americans with Disabilities Act:
  A Guide for Restaurants and Other Food Service Employers
  www.eeoc.gov/facts/restaurant_guide.html

- Question and answer series on the ADA and specific issues or disabilities
  Questions & Answers About Blindness and Vision Impairments in the
  Workplace and the Americans with Disabilities Act (ADA)
  www.eeoc.gov/eeoc/publications/qa_vision.cfm

  Questions & Answers About the Association Provision of the Americans
  with Disabilities Act (ADA)
  www.eeoc.gov/facts/association_ada.html

  Questions & Answers About Cancer in the Workplace and the Americans with
  Disabilities Act (ADA)
  www.eeoc.gov/laws/types/cancer.cfm

  Questions & Answers About Diabetes in the Workplace and the Americans
  with Disabilities Act (ADA)
  www.eeoc.gov/laws/types/diabetes.cfm

  Questions & Answers About Epilepsy in the Workplace and the Americans
  with Disabilities Act (ADA)
  www.eeoc.gov/laws/types/epilepsy.cfm

  Questions & Answers About Persons with Intellectual Disabilities in the
  Workplace and the Americans with Disabilities Act
  www.eeoc.gov/laws/types/intellectual_disabilities.cfm

State Laws Relating to Disability Discrimination

At the end of Chapter 18, you'll find a chart of state laws that prohibit
employment discrimination, including disability discrimination.

Consolidated Omnibus Budget Reconciliation Act (COBRA)

Statute: 29 U.S.C. §§ 1161–1169
To view the statutes, visit http://uscode.house.gov and select "Title 29," "Chapter 18," and "Subchapter I."

Regulations: 26 C.F.R. § 54.4980B-0 and following
To view the regulations, visit www.govinfo.gov and search "26 CFR 54.4980B."

Overview of COBRA

The Consolidated Omnibus Budget Reconciliation Act of 1985 (COBRA) enables employees and their families to continue health care coverage under an employer's *group health plan* after they experience an event—such as a layoff or termination—that would end their coverage under ordinary circumstances.

Employees and their families must pay the entire cost of COBRA coverage: the full premium at the employer-negotiated group rate, which is often less expensive than an individual policy.

This continued coverage lasts for 18 to 36 months, depending on the *qualifying event* that entitled the *qualified beneficiary* to coverage.

COBRA requires both the employer and qualified beneficiaries to meet certain notice requirements. Many employers choose to outsource their administrative obligations under COBRA; others take on those responsibilities themselves.

Covered Employers

COBRA covers private employers with 20 or more employees. (See "Counting Employees," below, for information on how to figure out which workers to count.)

Separate provisions of COBRA apply to state and local governments. (42 U.S.C. § 300bb-1.) These provisions are administered and enforced by the Department of Health and Human Services. Although COBRA does not cover the federal government, federal employees and their families are covered by similar, but not identical, provisions in the Federal Employees Health Benefits Amendments Act. (5 U.S.C. § 8905a.)

COBRA does not cover *church plans*.

Counting Employees

Figuring out whether your company has 20 or more employees for purposes of COBRA is not always a simple matter of counting heads. To determine whether COBRA applies, follow these rules:

- Count both full-time and part-time employees. Each part-time employee counts as a fraction of an employee, equal to the fraction of a full-time

Definitions

Terms that appear in italics throughout this chapter are defined below.

Church plan: A *group health plan* that is established and maintained by a church or an association or convention of churches that is tax exempt under Internal Revenue Code § 501(a).

Election notice: A document the plan administrator must send to *qualified beneficiaries* after a *qualifying event* has occurred, letting them know how to elect continued health care coverage under COBRA.

ERISA: The Employee Retirement Income Security Act, a federal law that sets minimum standards for establishing, administering, and maintaining certain employee benefit plans, including most group health plans sponsored by employers.

Gross misconduct: Employee wrongdoing that is willful, intentional, reckless, or deliberately indifferent to the employer's interests. COBRA coverage is not available when an employee is terminated for gross misconduct. Neither the statute nor the regulations define this term, but court decisions consistently hold that *gross misconduct* must be something more than mere carelessness or incompetence. Examples of gross misconduct include:

- theft
- embezzlement
- intentional violation of company policy
- lying
- driving a vehicle under the influence of alcohol, or
- physical violence.

Group health plan: An employee benefit plan that provides medical care to participants (typically employees, their spouses, and their dependents). Medical care includes inpatient and outpatient hospital care, physician care, surgery and other major medical benefits, prescription drugs, dental care, and vision care. It does not include life insurance, disability benefits, or amounts employers contribute to a *medical savings account*.

Initial/general notice: A document the plan administrator must give to employees and their spouses when they become eligible to participate in an employer's *group health plan*. The notice must provide specific information about continuation coverage under the plan.

Definitions (continued)

Medical savings account: A tax-exempt account employees can use to pay for certain medical expenses. A medical savings account may be funded by employer or employee contributions.

Multiemployer plan: A plan to which more than one employer is required to contribute and which is maintained pursuant to at least one collective bargaining agreement between at least one employee organization and more than one employer. Multiemployer plans are allowed to follow slightly different rules for COBRA notices.

Noncompliance period: A period of time used to calculate the excise tax an employer must pay for failing to comply with COBRA. The noncompliance period begins on the first day the employer fails to continue coverage for a *qualified beneficiary* and ends on the earlier of (1) the date the employer corrects the violation, or (2) six months after the last day of the *qualified beneficiary's* coverage period.

Qualified beneficiary: An individual who is covered by an employer's *group health plan* on the day before a *qualifying event*. Individuals who are qualified beneficiaries are eligible to receive COBRA benefits.

Qualifying event: An event that makes a *qualified beneficiary* eligible for COBRA coverage. For a current employee, a qualifying event is one that would otherwise disqualify the employee from the employer's *group health plan*, such as a resignation or layoff. If the employee's dependents are covered through the employer's *group health plan*, the employee's death or divorce are qualifying events as well.

Qualifying event notice: Notice provided by the employer or by a *qualified beneficiary* to the plan, stating that a *qualifying event* has occurred.

Second qualifying event: A qualifying event that occurs after a first *qualifying event* and would have caused the *qualified beneficiary* to lose coverage under the plan had the first *qualifying event* not already done so. A second qualifying event (sometimes referred to as a "subsequent qualifying event") may entitle the *qualified beneficiary* to an extension of COBRA coverage.

day that employee works. For example, if a part-time employee works four hours a day, but full-time employees work eight hours a day, then the part-time employee would count as half an employee.

- Don't count self-employed people, independent contractors, and corporate directors as employees. However, if you are a covered employer, some of these workers may still be entitled to COBRA coverage (see "Covered Workers," below).

Covered Workers

To be eligible for COBRA's benefits, a person must:
- be a qualified beneficiary, and
- have a relationship with the employer that will be affected by a qualifying event. Those who have such a relationship to the employer include employees, former employees, family members of current and former employees, and others associated, formerly associated, or in a business relationship with the employer (including members of a union who are not currently employees).

Unlike most other employment laws, COBRA provides benefits not only to current and former employees, but also to their spouses and children if they were covered by the employer's group health plan.

As a result of the Supreme Court's decision to legalize same-sex marriage in 2015, same-sex spouses must now be covered under COBRA in all 50 states. (See "Legal Developments" in Chapter 8 for more information.)

Qualified Beneficiary

A qualified beneficiary is a person (typically, an employee, the employee's spouse, or the employee's dependent child) covered by the employer's group health plan on the day before a qualifying event, such as a layoff. Employees and their family members who were not covered by their employer's group health plan prior to the qualifying event are not entitled to COBRA's coverage or notice rights.

Retired employees, their spouses, and their dependent children can also be qualified beneficiaries if the employer files for certain types of bankruptcy. We don't cover these rules here.

If a child is born to a covered employee or placed for adoption with a covered employee while the employee is on COBRA, the child is a qualified beneficiary.

Agents, independent contractors, and directors who are not employees, but who nonetheless participate in the group health plan, can also be qualified beneficiaries.

Qualifying Event

There are many events that affect an individual's relationship with an employer, but only a qualifying event makes the individual eligible for COBRA coverage. What constitutes a qualifying event differs for employees, their spouses, and their dependents.

Employees

The following are qualifying events for employees:
- The employee quits or otherwise voluntarily terminates the employment.
- The employee is involuntarily terminated for reasons other than *gross misconduct*. For example, the employee is laid off for economic reasons or fired because he or she lacks the necessary skills for the position.
- The employee's work hours are reduced to an amount that would otherwise make the employee ineligible for benefits. For example, if an employer provides health insurance benefits only to employees who work 40 hours a week, and a full-time employee chooses to switch to a 30-hour work week schedule, that employee becomes ineligible for health insurance benefits under the employer's rules.

Spouses

The following are qualifying events for spouses of employees:
- The employee experiences any of the events listed under "Employees," above.
- The employee becomes entitled to Medicare.
- The spouse and the employee divorce or legally separate.
- The employee dies.

Dependent Children

The qualifying events for dependent children are the same as those listed under "Spouses," above, with one addition: It is a qualifying event if the child loses dependent status under the plan. For example, if the plan states that children are covered as dependents only until they turn 18, a child's 18th birthday is a qualifying event that triggers the child's right to continuation coverage.

Did You Know ...

- According to the Bureau of Labor Statistics, 69% of all employees in private industry had access to medical care benefits through their employers, and 50% of all private employees actually participated in their employers' plans, as of March 2018.
- Most private industry employees who receive medical care benefits from their employers are required to contribute to the cost of coverage. In 2018, employees contributed an average of 21% of individual coverage and 33% of the cost of family coverage.
- Employees and their families who opt for COBRA coverage have to foot the whole bill themselves. How much does coverage run? In 2017, a survey by the Kaiser Family Foundation showed that the average total cost of employer-provided health insurance was $6,690 a year for individuals and $18,764 for families.

What's Prohibited

Employers may not refuse COBRA coverage to a qualified beneficiary because that person would not have been insurable on the day before the qualifying event. If the group health plan actually covered the employee, spouse, or dependent on the day before the qualifying event, then that person is entitled to COBRA coverage, regardless of whether the plan would choose to insure him or her at that time in ordinary circumstances. This rule prevents termination of benefits to those who arguably need them the most: people with serious health conditions that might make it difficult for them to find insurance coverage otherwise.

Key Facts

- COBRA enables employees and their families to continue health care coverage under an employer's group health plan after an event—such as a layoff or termination—that would otherwise end their coverage. Usually, employees and their families must pay the entire cost of the coverage, but they get to pay at the employer-negotiated group rate, which is usually less expensive than an individual rate.
- Employers must give employees several different notices relating to COBRA eligibility, as well as notices for unavailability or early termination of COBRA coverage. Specific rules govern the content and timing of each notice.
- If a qualified beneficiary elects continuation coverage under COBRA, the group health plan must continue to cover the beneficiary for 18 or 36 months, depending on the type of beneficiary and the qualifying event.

What's Required

Notice Requirements

A plan administrator—who may either be the employer (if it administers the health care plan itself) or a third party hired by the employer to administer the plan—has several notice obligations under COBRA. (Slightly different rules apply to *multiemployer plans*; these rules are not covered in this book.)

General Notice

A plan administrator must provide a *general notice* to employees when they become eligible to participate in the group health plan—for example, when they are hired, if their employer allows new hires to immediately be covered by health insurance. Plan administrators must provide this notice in writing to a covered employee and to his or her spouse within 90 days after coverage begins. If the employee and spouse enroll in the plan within the same 90-day period and reside at the same address, the plan administrator can send one notice to both; otherwise, it must send a separate notice to each. The employer need not send separate notices to any dependent children who reside with the employee and/or spouse.

Because employers typically have to provide a summary plan description to new participants during this same time period, a plan administrator may include the general COBRA notice along with the summary plan description. This is fine as long as it is given to the employee within the required 90-day period and the spouse is properly notified.

The notice must provide the plan's name; the name, address, and telephone number of a person to contact for information about the plan; a description of the continuation coverage available; and information on how to notify the plan of qualifying events, among other things. The Department of Labor publishes a *Model General Notice of COBRA Continuation Coverage Rights* that single-employer group health plans may use to satisfy the general notice requirement. (For information on how to download these publications, see "Agency Resources," below.)

Qualifying Event Notice

Either the employer or the qualified beneficiary is responsible for notifying the plan, depending on the type of qualifying event. This is done by sending a *qualifying event notice* to the plan administrator.

The employer has 30 days to notify the plan administrator of the following qualifying events:

- voluntary or involuntary termination of employment
- reduction of hours
- death of the covered employee, or
- the covered employee's entitlement to Medicare.

If the employer administers its own plan, it does not have to send itself a qualifying event notice.

The qualified beneficiary is responsible for notifying the plan administrator of the following qualifying events:

- divorce
- legal separation
- a child losing dependent status under the plan
- the employee's disability, or
- a *second qualifying event* that occurs after the qualified beneficiary is already eligible for continuation coverage under COBRA.

The plan must include reasonable procedures for qualified beneficiaries to provide notice of these qualifying events. These procedures should be included in the summary plan description and should allow enough time after the event for the beneficiary to give notice (at least 60 days), specify the time limits for giving notice, describe how and to whom notice must be given, and describe what information the notice must include. If a plan fails to establish reasonable procedures, a beneficiary can fulfill his or her obligation to notify the plan of a qualifying event by providing oral or written notice to the person or department that handles employee benefit issues for the employer.

The qualified beneficiary is required to notify the plan administrator if the Social Security Administration determines that the employee is no longer disabled. This notice must be provided within 30 days.

Election Notice

After a qualifying event, a plan administrator must provide an *election notice* to the qualified beneficiaries, informing them of their right to choose COBRA continuation coverage.

- If the employer has a separate plan administrator, the plan administrator has 14 days after learning of the qualifying event to provide an election notice to the qualified beneficiaries.
- If the employer is the plan administrator, and the qualifying event is one that the employee or another qualified beneficiary must report to the plan, then the employer has 14 days after learning of the qualifying event to provide an election notice to the qualified beneficiaries.
- If the employer is the plan administrator, and the qualifying event is one that the employer must report to the plan, then the employer must provide the election notice no later than 44 days after the qualifying event. Or, if the employer's plan states that COBRA coverage begins with the loss of regular coverage, the employer must provide the election notice no later than 44 days after the beneficiary loses coverage under the employer's plan due to a qualifying event.

The election notice must contain a significant amount of information as specified by the DOL. The DOL publishes a *Model COBRA Continuation Coverage Election Notice*, available for download at its website. (See "Agency Resources," below, for more information.)

Other Notices

If a plan denies a request for COBRA coverage or a request for an extension of COBRA coverage, the plan administrator must provide the beneficiary with a notice of unavailability of continuation coverage within 14 days after receiving the request. This notice must explain why the request was denied.

If a plan ends COBRA coverage before the maximum period allowed under the circumstances (18 or 36 months) has passed, the plan administrator must provide the beneficiary with a notice of early termination of continuation coverage as soon as possible and practicable after the decision to terminate the coverage is made. This notice must include the date coverage will end, the reason for terminating coverage, and any rights the beneficiary may have to elect other coverage.

Coverage Requirements

If a qualified beneficiary chooses to take advantage of COBRA benefits, the group health plan must continue to cover the beneficiary for either 18 or 36 months, depending on the type of beneficiary and the qualifying event, as shown in the chart below.

Coverage Periods

Qualifying Event	Qualified Beneficiary	Coverage Period
Voluntary termination Involuntary termination Reduction of hours	Employee Spouse Dependent child	18 months
Divorce Legal separation Employee's death Employee entitled to Medicare*	Spouse Dependent child	36 months
Loss of dependent child status	Dependent child	36 months

* But see "Medicare," below.

The law allows the employer to choose to extend COBRA benefits beyond the required statutory coverage period. In addition, the coverage periods described above may be lengthened if certain events occur, as described in "Exceptions," below.

COBRA beneficiaries are entitled to the same coverage they would have received if the qualifying event had not occurred. In other words, the employer or plan may not provide lesser or different benefits to those who receive coverage under COBRA.

The qualified beneficiary is responsible for paying the full premium. The employer may charge a 2% administrative fee, making the total cost to the employee 102% of the coverage costs. (Employers may choose to pay for the coverage, but the law does not require them to do so.)

Each qualified beneficiary has individual election rights. This means that even within the same family, some qualified beneficiaries could choose to elect coverage, while others could choose not to. For example, if an employee goes to work for a new employer that provides coverage for employees only, the employee might choose to enroll in the new plan while his or her spouse and child continue coverage under the former employer's plan, using COBRA.

Exceptions

The coverage periods described in "Coverage Requirements," above, may be lengthened in certain circumstances. Longer coverage may be required in case of either of the following:

- The qualified beneficiary has or develops a disability.
- A second qualifying event occurs.

Disability

If the qualifying event is voluntary or involuntary termination of employment or reduction in hours, COBRA coverage lasts for 18 months. However, if a qualified beneficiary is disabled at the time of the qualifying event or becomes disabled during the first 60 days of COBRA coverage, COBRA coverage can be extended for up to an additional 11 months (for a total of 29 months).

In order to qualify for this exception, the beneficiary must be determined by the Social Security Administration (SSA) to be disabled as defined by Titles II or XVI of the Social Security Act (42 U.S.C. § 401 and following or § 1381 and following, respectively). The SSA uses strict criteria to determine whether a person is disabled and, therefore, eligible for disability benefits. To be eligible, a person must be unable to do the work he or she did before or unable to adjust to other work because of his or her condition, and the disability must be expected to last at least a year or to result in the person's death. For detailed information on these criteria, go to the SSA's website, www.ssa.gov/benefits/disability.

If coverage is extended due to a disability, coverage is extended for all qualified beneficiaries who became entitled to COBRA because of the initial qualifying event. For example, if an employee is laid off, and that employee along with his or her spouse and dependent children all choose to continue coverage under COBRA, the entire family would be entitled to a disability extension if the employee became disabled.

The employer may increase the charge for the last 11 months of coverage from 102% of the premium to 150% of the premium.

Second Qualifying Event

If a beneficiary is using the 18-month coverage period and a second qualifying event occurs during that time, the beneficiary can extend the coverage period to 36 months from the date of the first qualifying event. To receive an extension, the second qualifying event must be one that would have resulted in loss of coverage had the first qualifying event never occurred. Death of the employee, divorce or legal separation, or a child losing dependent status are all second qualifying events that would result in extension of coverage. The employee's entitlement to Medicare may be a second qualifying event, but only in limited circumstances. (See "Medicare," below, for more information.)

Medicare

Under the Medicare Secondary Payer (MSP) rules, most group health plans are not permitted to terminate coverage for current employees or their families simply because the employee becomes entitled to Medicare. However, an employee's entitlement to Medicare can affect the length of continuation coverage for a spouse and dependent children. Where the employee became entitled to Medicare less than 18 months before the qualifying event, the employee's spouse and dependent children can receive continuation coverage for 36 months from the date the employee became entitled to Medicare. For example, suppose an employee became eligible for Medicare three months before she was fired (the qualifying event). Her spouse and dependent children would receive COBRA coverage for 33 months after the date of termination instead of 18. In this situation, the employee's own COBRA coverage would not be affected.

If a former employee becomes entitled to Medicare benefits while he or she is receiving COBRA coverage, coverage may be terminated for the employee. However, because Medicare does not cover the employee's family, spouses and dependents will not lose coverage.

How COBRA Is Enforced

Individual Complaints

Individuals may bring a civil action in court to enforce COBRA rights. These lawsuits fall under the civil enforcement provisions of the Employee Retirement Income Security Act of 1974 (ERISA).

Agency Enforcement

The Employee Benefits Security Administration of the DOL enforces COBRA's disclosure and notice provisions.

The Internal Revenue Service and the DOL share jurisdiction for enforcement of COBRA's eligibility, coverage, and premium provisions.

The Social Security Administration (SSA) determines whether someone is disabled under the Social Security Act.

Complying With COBRA

Deadlines

• The plan administrator must send the general notice within *90 days* after the employee and other qualified beneficiaries begin coverage under the plan.

- The employer must send a qualifying event notice to the plan administrator within *30 days* after the following qualifying events: the employee quits, the employee is laid off or fired for reasons other than gross misconduct, the employee becomes entitled to Medicare, or the employee's hours are reduced to a level that would make him or her ineligible for benefits under the employer's group health plan.
- The employee or another qualified beneficiary has at least *60 days* to send a qualifying event notice to the plan administrator after the following qualifying events: divorce, legal separation, a child losing dependent status under the plan, the employee being found to be disabled by the Social Security Administration, or a second qualifying event that occurs after the employee or another qualified beneficiary is already eligible for COBRA coverage.
- The employee has *30 days* to notify the plan administrator if the Social Security Administration determines that the employee is no longer disabled.
- The plan administrator has *14 days* after receiving the qualifying event notice to send the employee and other qualified beneficiaries an election notice. If the employer is also the plan administrator, the employer also has *14 days* to send the election notice, if the qualifying event is one that the employee or another qualified beneficiary must report to the plan administrator.
- The employer has *44 days* after a qualifying event to send the employee and other qualified beneficiaries an election notice, if the employer is also the plan administrator and the qualifying event is not one that the employee or another qualified beneficiary must report to the plan administrator.
- If a plan denies a request for COBRA coverage or a request for an extension of COBRA coverage, the plan administrator must provide the beneficiary with a notice of unavailability of continuation coverage within *14 days* after receiving the request.

Reporting Requirements

COBRA has no specific reporting requirements.

Posting Requirements

COBRA imposes no posting requirements.

Record-Keeping Requirements

COBRA has no specific record-keeping requirements.

Remedies

A private sector employer that fails to comply with COBRA may face any or all of the following sanctions:

- excise taxes (see "Excise Taxes," below, for more information)
- fines imposed by the Department of Labor for failing to satisfy COBRA's notice and disclosure rules
- civil liability to individuals who suffered losses because they did not receive the health insurance coverage to which they were entitled, and
- attorneys' fees.

Excise Taxes

The IRS may impose a $100 excise tax (also called a penalty tax) for every day that an employer fails to meet the health coverage continuation rules during the *noncompliance period*. This excise tax applies separately for each qualified beneficiary for whom the employer fails to provide the required coverage. However, if the affected qualified beneficiaries are in the same family, then the tax is capped at $200 per day for the family.

The noncompliance period begins on the first day of the violation and ends on the earlier of: (1) the date the employer corrects the violation, or (2) six months after the last day of the qualified beneficiary's coverage period.

The employer will not have to pay the excise tax if either of the following applies:

- The failure is not intentional, and the employer has a reasonable explanation.
- The employer corrects the violation within 30 days of finding out about the violation.

Agency Resources

- A detailed booklet describing employer rights and obligations under COBRA

    To view the guide, visit www.dol.gov/agencies/ebsa and select "Publications," followed by "Publications for Workers and Families."

- General Notice Form

    Model General Notice of COBRA Continuation Coverage Rights
    www.dol.gov/sites/default/files/ebsa/laws-and-regulations/laws/cobra/
    model-general-notice.doc (English)
    www.dol.gov/sites/default/files/ebsa/laws-and-regulations/laws/cobra/
    model-general-notice-spanish.doc (Spanish)

- Election Notice Form

    Model COBRA Continuation Coverage Election Notice
    www.dol.gov/sites/default/files/ebsa/laws-and-regulations/laws/cobra/
    model-election-notice.doc (English)
    www.dol.gov/sites/default/files/ebsa/laws-and-regulations/laws/cobra/
    model-election-notice-spanish.doc (Spanish)

- Information answering common questions on COBRA

    Visit www.dol.gov/agencies/ebsa and select "About EBSA,"
    "Our Activities," "Resource Center," "FAQs," and "Health."

State Laws Relating to Health Coverage Continuation

Many states also have laws requiring employers to provide continued health insurance coverage. These laws sometimes go beyond what COBRA requires. For example, some states require employers with fewer than 20 employees to provide continuation coverage, or require employers to continue coverage for vision, dental, or prescription drug benefits.

The chart below provides some basic information on state health insurance continuation laws. To find out more about your state's requirements, contact your state insurance department.

State Health Insurance Continuation Laws

Alabama

Ala. Code § 27-55-3(a)(4)

Special Situations: 18 months for subjects of domestic abuse who have lost coverage they had under abuser's insurance and who do not qualify for COBRA.

Arizona

Ariz. Rev. Stat. §§ 20-1377, 20-1408, 20-2330

Employers affected: All employers that offer group disability insurance. Under § 20-2330, employers that offer group health insurance and have 1 to 20 employees.

Eligible employees: Employees covered under an employer's health benefits plan for at least three months before a qualifying event.

Length of coverage for employee: Under § 20-2330, 18 months (or less if the employee fails to make timely payments or becomes eligible for Medicare or Medicaid or obtains other health coverage, or if the employer terminates group coverage for all employees).

Length of coverage for dependents: Insurer must either continue coverage for dependents or convert to individual policy upon death or divorce of covered employee. Coverage must be the same unless the insured chooses a lesser plan.

Under § 20-2330, 18 months, or less if dependent becomes eligible for Medicare or Medicaid or obtains any other health coverage. Dependents with disabilities are eligible for an additional 11 months' coverage.

Qualifying event: Death of an employee; change in marital status; any other reason stated in policy (other than failure to pay premium).

Under § 20-2330, voluntary or involuntary termination of employment other than for gross misconduct; reduction of hours required to qualify for coverage under group plan; divorce or separation; employee's death or eligibility for Medicare; dependent child ceases to qualify as dependent under group plan; retired employees or their spouses or dependent children lose coverage within a year before or after employer files for bankruptcy.

Time employer has to notify employee: No provisions for employer. Insurance policy must include notice of conversion privilege. Clerk of court must provide notice to anyone filing for divorce that dependent spouse entitled to convert health insurance coverage.

Under § 20-2330, 30 days after the qualifying event.

Time employee has to apply: 31 days after termination of existing coverage.

Under § 20-2330, 60 days after date of employer's notice.

Arkansas

Ark. Code Ann. §§ 23-86-114 to 23-86-116

Employers affected: All employers that offer group health insurance.

Eligible employees: Employees continuously insured for previous 3 months.

Length of coverage for employee: 120 days.

Length of coverage for dependents: 120 days.

Qualifying event: Termination of employment; change in insured's marital status. Employer may—but is not required to—continue benefits on death of employee.

Time employee has to apply: 10 days.

State Health Insurance Continuation Laws (continued)

California

Cal. Health & Safety Code §§ 1373.6, 1373.621; Cal. Ins. Code §§ 10128.50 to 10128.59

Employers affected: Employers that offer group health insurance and have 2 to 19 employees.

Employers that offer group health insurance and have 2 to 19 employees.

Eligible employees: All covered employees are eligible.

Length of coverage for employee: 36 months.

Length of coverage for dependents: 36 months.

Qualifying event: Termination of employment; reduction in hours; death of employee; change in marital status; loss of dependent status; covered employee's eligibility for Medicare (for dependents only).

Time employer has to notify employee: 15 days.

Time employee has to apply: 60 days.

Special situations: Employee who is at least 60 years old and has worked for employer for previous 5 years may continue benefits for self and spouse beyond COBRA or Cal-COBRA limits (also applies to COBRA employers). Employee who began receiving COBRA coverage on or after 1/1/03 and whose COBRA coverage is for less than 36 months may use Cal-COBRA to bring total coverage up to 36 months.

Colorado

Colo. Rev. Stat. § 10-16-108

Employers affected: All employers that offer group health insurance.

Eligible employees: Employees continuously insured for previous 6 months.

Length of coverage for employee: 18 months.

Length of coverage for dependents: 18 months.

Qualifying event: Termination of employment; reduction in hours; death of employee; change in marital status.

Time employer has to notify employee: 60 days.

Time employee has to apply: 30 days after termination; 60 days if employer fails to give notice.

Connecticut

Conn. Gen. Stat. Ann. §§ 38a-512a, 31-51n, 31-51o

Employers affected: All employers that offer group health insurance.

Eligible employees: All covered employees are eligible.

Length of coverage for employee: 30 months, or until eligible for Medicare benefits.

Length of coverage for dependents: 30 months, or until eligible for Medicare benefits; 36 months in case of employee's death, divorce, or loss of dependent status.

Qualifying event: Layoff; reduction in hours; termination of employment; death of employee; change in marital status; loss of dependent status.

Special situations: When facility closes or relocates, employers with 100 or more employees must pay for insurance for employee and dependents for 120 days or until employee is eligible for other group

State Health Insurance Continuation Laws (continued)

coverage, whichever comes first. (Does not affect employee's right to conventional continuation coverage, which begins when 120-day period ends.)

Delaware

18 Del. Code Ann. § 3571F

Employers affected: Employers that offer group health insurance and have 1 to 19 employees.

Eligible employees: Employees continuously insured for previous 3 months.

Length of coverage for employee: 9 months.

Length of coverage for dependents: 9 months.

Qualifying event: Employee's death; termination of employment; divorce or legal separation; employee's eligibility for Medicare; loss of dependent status.

Time employer has to notify employee: Within 30 days of the qualifying event.

Time employee has to apply: 30 days.

District of Columbia

D.C. Code Ann. §§ 32-731 to 32-732

Employers affected: Employers with fewer than 20 employees.

Eligible employees: All covered employees are eligible.

Length of coverage for employee: 3 months.

Length of coverage for dependents: 3 months.

Qualifying event: Any reason employee or dependent becomes ineligible for coverage, except employee's termination for gross misconduct.

Time employer has to notify employee: Within 15 days of termination of coverage.

Time employee has to apply: 45 days after termination of coverage.

Florida

Fla. Stat. Ann. § 627.6692

Employers affected: Employers with fewer than 20 employees.

Eligible employees: Full-time (25 or more hours per week) employees covered by employer's health insurance plan.

Length of coverage for employee: 18 months.

Length of coverage for dependents: 18 months.

Qualifying event: Layoff; reduction in hours; termination of employment; death of employee; change in marital status.

Time employer has to notify employee: Carrier notifies within 14 days of learning of qualifying event (beneficiary has 63 days to notify carrier of qualifying event).

Time employee has to apply: 30 days from receipt of carrier's notice.

Georgia

Ga. Code Ann. §§ 33-24-21.1 to 33-24-21.2

Employers affected: All employers that offer group health insurance.

Eligible employees: Employees continuously insured for previous 6 months.

Length of coverage for employee: 3 months plus any part of the month remaining at termination.

Length of coverage for dependents: 3 months plus any part of the month remaining at termination.

State Health Insurance Continuation Laws (continued)

Qualifying event: Termination of employment (except for cause).

Special situations: Employee, spouse, or former spouse, who is 60 years old and who has been covered for previous 6 months may continue coverage until eligible for Medicare. (Applies to companies with more than 20 employees; does not apply when employee quits for reasons other than health.)

Hawaii

Haw. Rev. Stat. §§ 393-11, 393-15

Employers affected: All employers required to offer health insurance (those paying a regular employee a monthly wage at least 86.67 times state hourly minimum— about $542).

Length of coverage for employee: If employee is hospitalized or prevented from working by sickness, employer must pay insurance premiums for 3 months or for as long as employer continues to pay wages, whichever is longer.

Qualifying event: Employee is hospitalized or prevented by sickness from working.

Idaho

Idaho Code § 41-2213

Employers affected: All employers that offer group disability insurance.

Eligible employees: Employees or dependents who are totally disabled at the time the policy ends. (Applies to policies that provide benefits for loss of time during periods of hospitalization, benefits for hospital or medical expenses, or benefits for dismemberment.)

Length of coverage for employee: Must provide a reasonable extension of coverage

(in the case of medical and hospital expenses, a reasonable extension is at least 12 months).

Length of coverage for dependents: Must provide a reasonable extension of coverage (in the case of medical and hospital expenses, a reasonable extension is at least 12 months).

Illinois

215 Ill. Comp. Stat. §§ 5/367e, 5/367.2, 5/367.2-5

Employers affected: All employers that offer group health insurance.

Eligible employees: Employees continuously insured for previous 3 months.

Length of coverage for employee: 12 months.

Length of coverage for dependents: Upon death or divorce, 2 years' coverage for spouse under 55 and eligible dependents who were on employee's plan; until eligible for Medicare or other group coverage for spouse over 55 and eligible dependents who were on employee's plan. A dependent child who has reached plan age limit or who was not already covered by plan, is also entitled to 2 years' continuation coverage.

Qualifying event: Termination of employment; reduction in hours; death of employee; divorce.

Time employer has to notify employee: 10 days.

Time employee has to apply: 30 days after termination or reduction in hours or receiving notice from employer, whichever is later, but not more than 60 days from termination or reduction in hours.

Iowa

Iowa Code §§ 509B.3, 509B.5

Employers affected: All employers that offer group health insurance.

State Health Insurance Continuation Laws (continued)

Eligible employees: Employees continuously insured for previous 3 months.

Length of coverage for employee: 9 months.

Length of coverage for dependents: 9 months.

Qualifying event: Any reason employee or dependent becomes ineligible for coverage.

Time employer has to notify employee: 10 days after termination of coverage.

Time employee has to apply: 10 days after termination of coverage or receiving notice from employer, whichever is later, but not more than 31 days from termination of coverage.

Kansas

Kan. Stat. Ann. § 40-2209(i)

Employers affected: All employers that offer group health insurance.

Eligible employees: Employees continuously insured for previous 3 months.

Length of coverage for employee: 18 months.

Length of coverage for dependents: 18 months.

Qualifying event: Any reason employee or dependent becomes ineligible for coverage.

Time employer has to notify employee: Reasonable notice.

Kentucky

Ky. Rev. Stat. Ann. § 304.18-110

Employers affected: All employers that offer group health insurance.

Eligible employees: Employees continuously insured for previous 3 months.

Length of coverage for employee: 18 months.

Length of coverage for dependents: 18 months.

Qualifying event: Any reason employee or dependent becomes ineligible for coverage.

Time employer has to notify employee: Employer must notify insurer as soon as employee's coverage ends; insurer then notifies employee.

Time employee has to apply: 31 days from receipt of insurer's notice, but not more than 90 days after termination of group coverage.

Louisiana

La. Rev. Stat. Ann. §§ 22:1045, 22:1046

Employers affected: All employers that offer group health insurance and have fewer than 20 employees.

Eligible employees: Employees continuously insured for previous 3 months.

Length of coverage for employee: 12 months.

Length of coverage for dependents: 12 months.

Qualifying event: Termination of employment; death of insured; divorce.

Time employer has to apply: By the end of the month following the month in which the qualifying event occurred.

Special situations: Surviving spouse who is 50 or older may have coverage until remarriage or eligibility for Medicare or other insurance.

Maine

Me. Rev. Stat. Ann. tit. 24-A, § 2809-A

Employers affected: All employers that offer group health insurance and are not subject to COBRA.

State Health Insurance Continuation Laws (continued)

Eligible employees: Employees employed for at least 6 months.

Length of coverage for employee: 1 year.

Length of coverage for dependents: 1 year.

Qualifying event: Temporary layoff; permanent layoff if employee is eligible for federal premium assistance for laid-off employees who continue coverage; loss of employment because of a work-related injury or disease.

Time employer has to notify employee: 31 days from termination of coverage.

Maryland

Md. Code Ann., [Ins.] §§ 15-407 to 15-409

Employers affected: All employers that offer group health insurance.

Eligible employees: Employees continuously insured for previous 3 months.

Length of coverage for employee: 18 months.

Length of coverage for dependents: 18 months upon death of employee; upon change in marital status, 18 months or until spouse remarries or becomes eligible for other coverage.

Qualifying event: Termination of employment; death of employee; change in marital status.

Time employer has to notify employee: Must notify insurer within 14 days of receiving employee's continuation request.

Time employee has to apply: 45 days from termination of coverage. Employee begins application process by requesting an election of continuation notification form from employer.

Massachusetts

Mass. Gen. Laws ch. 175, §§ 110G, 110I; ch. 176J, § 9

Employers affected: All employers that offer group health insurance and have fewer than 20 employees.

Eligible employees: All covered employees are eligible.

Length of coverage for employee: 18 months; 29 months if disabled.

Length of coverage for dependents: 18 months upon termination or reduction in hours; 29 months if disabled; 36 months upon divorce, death of employee, employee's eligibility for Medicare, or employer's bankruptcy.

Qualifying event: Involuntary layoff; death of insured employee; change in marital status.

Time employer has to notify employee: Carrier must notify beneficiary within 14 days of learning of qualifying event.

Time employee has to apply: 60 days.

Special situations: Termination due to plant closing: 90 days' coverage for employee and dependents, at the same payment terms as before closing.

Minnesota

Minn. Stat. Ann. §§ 62A.17; 62A.20; 62A.21

Employers affected: All employers that offer group health insurance and have 2 or more employees.

Eligible employees: All covered employees are eligible.

State Health Insurance Continuation Laws (continued)

Length of coverage for employee:
18 months; indefinitely if employee becomes totally disabled while employed.

Length of coverage for dependents:
18 months for current spouse or child after termination of employment; divorced or widowed spouse can continue until eligible for Medicare or other group health insurance. Upon divorce or death of employee, dependent children can continue until they no longer qualify as dependents under plan.

Qualifying event: Termination of employment; reduction in hours.

Time employer has to notify employee: Within 14 days of termination of coverage.

Time employee has to apply: 60 days from termination of coverage or receipt of employer's notice, whichever is later.

Mississippi

Miss. Code Ann. § 83-9-51

Employers affected: All employers that offer group health insurance and have fewer than 20 employees.

Eligible employees: Employees continuously insured for previous 3 months.

Length of coverage for employee: 12 months.

Length of coverage for dependents: 12 months.

Qualifying event: Termination of employment; divorce; employee's death; employee's eligibility for Medicare; loss of dependent status.

Time employer has to notify employee: Insurer must notify former or deceased employee's dependent child or divorced spouse of option to continue insurance

within 14 days of their becoming ineligible for coverage on employee's policy.

Time employee has to apply: Employee must apply and submit payment before group coverage ends; dependents or former spouse must elect continuation coverage within 30 days of receiving insurer's notice.

Missouri

Mo. Rev. Stat. § 376.428

Employers affected: All employers that offer group health insurance and are not subject to COBRA.

Eligible employees: All employees.

Length of coverage for employee: 18 months.

Length of coverage for dependents:
18 months if eligible due to termination or reduction in hours; 36 months if eligible due to death or divorce.

Qualifying event: Termination of employment; death of employee; divorce; reduction in hours; employee's eligibility for Medicare; loss of dependent status.

Time employer has to notify employee: Same rules as COBRA.

Time employee has to apply: Same rules as COBRA.

Montana

Mont. Code Ann. §§ 33-22-506 to 33-22-507

Employers affected: All employers that offer group disability insurance.

Eligible employees: All employees.

Length of coverage for employee: 1 year (with employer's consent).

Qualifying event: Reduction in hours.

State Health Insurance Continuation Laws (continued)

Special situations: Insurer may not discontinue benefits to child with a disability after child exceeds age limit for dependent status.

Nebraska

Neb. Rev. Stat. §§ 44-1640 and following, 44-7406

Employers affected: Employers not subject to federal COBRA laws.

Eligible employees: All covered employees.

Length of coverage for employee: 6 months.

Length of coverage for dependents: 1 year upon death of insured employee. Subjects of domestic abuse who have lost coverage under abuser's plan and who do not qualify for COBRA may have 18 months' coverage (applies to all employers).

Qualifying event: Involuntary termination of employment (layoff due to labor dispute not considered involuntary).

Time employer has to notify employee: Within 10 days of termination of employment must send notice by certified mail.

Time employee has to apply: 10 days from receipt of employer's notice.

Nevada

Nev. Rev. Stat. Ann. § 689B.0345

Employers affected: All employers that offer group health insurance.

Eligible employees: Employees who are on unpaid leave due to total disability.

Length of coverage for employee: Coverage must continue for 12 months, unless one of the following events occurs sooner: the employee is terminated, the employee obtains another health insurance policy, or the group health insurance policy is terminated.

Length of coverage for dependents: Coverage must continue for 12 months, unless one of the following events occurs sooner: the employee is terminated, the employee obtains another health insurance policy, or the group health insurance policy is terminated.

New Hampshire

N.H. Rev. Stat. Ann. § 415:18

Employers affected: All employers that offer group health insurance.

Eligible employees: All insured employees are eligible.

Length of coverage for employee: 18 months; 29 months if disabled at termination or during first 60 days of continuation coverage.

Length of coverage for dependents: 18 months; 29 months if disabled at termination or during first 60 days of continuation coverage; 36 months upon death of employee, divorce or legal separation, loss of dependent status, or employee's eligibility for Medicare.

Qualifying event: Any reason employee or dependent becomes ineligible for coverage.

Time employer has to notify employee: Carrier must notify beneficiary within 30 days of receiving notice of loss of coverage.

Time employee has to apply: Within 45 days of receipt of notice.

Special situations: Layoff or termination due to strike: 6 months' coverage with option to extend for an additional 12 months. Surviving, divorced, or legally separated

State Health Insurance Continuation Laws (continued)

spouse who is 55 or older may continue benefits available until eligible for Medicare or another employer-based group insurance.

New Jersey

N.J. Stat. Ann. §§ 17B:27-51.12, 17B:27A-27

Employers affected: Employers with 2 to 50 employees.

Eligible employees: Employed full time (25 or more hours).

Length of coverage for employee: 18 months; 29 months if disabled at termination or during first 60 days of continuation coverage.

Length of coverage for dependents: 18 months; 36 months upon death of employee, divorce or legal separation, loss of dependent status, or employee's eligibility for Medicare.

Qualifying event: Termination of employment; reduction in hours; change in marital status; death.

Time employer has to notify employee: At the time of qualifying event.

Time employee has to apply: Within 30 days of qualifying event.

Special benefits: Coverage must be identical to that offered to current employees.

Special situations: Total disability: Employee who has been insured for previous 3 months and employee's dependents entitled to continuation coverage that includes all benefits offered by group policy (applies to all employers).

New Mexico

N.M. Stat. Ann. § 59A-18-16

Employers affected: All employers that offer group health insurance.

Eligible employees: All insured employees are eligible.

Length of coverage for employee: 6 months.

Length of coverage for dependents: 6 months for termination of employment. May continue group coverage or convert to individual policies upon death of covered employee or divorce or legal separation.

Qualifying event: Termination of employment.

Time employer has to notify employee: Insurer or employer must give written notice at time of termination.

Time employee has to apply: 30 days after receiving notice.

New York

N.Y. Ins. Law § 3221(m)

Employers affected: All employers that offer group health insurance.

Eligible employees: All covered employees are eligible.

Length of coverage for employee: 36 months.

Length of coverage for dependents: 36 months.

Qualifying event: Termination of employment; death of employee; divorce or legal separation; loss of dependent status; employee's eligibility for Medicare.

Time employee has to apply: 60 days after termination or receipt of notice, whichever is later.

North Carolina

N.C. Gen. Stat. §§ 58-53-5 to 58-53-40

Employers affected: All employers that offer group health insurance.

State Health Insurance Continuation Laws (continued)

Eligible employees: Employees continuously insured for previous 3 months.

Length of coverage for employee: 18 months.

Length of coverage for dependents: 18 months.

Qualifying event: Termination of employment.

Time employer has to notify employee: Employer has option of notifying employee as part of the exit process.

Time employee has to apply: 60 days.

North Dakota

N.D. Cent. Code §§ 26.1-36-23, 26.1-36-23.1

Employers affected: All employers that offer group health insurance.

Eligible employees: Employees continuously insured for previous 3 months.

Length of coverage for employee: 39 weeks.

Length of coverage for dependents: 39 weeks; 36 months if required by divorce or annulment decree.

Qualifying event: Termination of employment; change in marital status, if divorce or annulment decree requires employee to continue coverage.

Time employee has to apply: Within 10 days of termination or of receiving notice of continuation rights, whichever is later, but not more than 31 days from termination.

Ohio

Ohio Rev. Code Ann. §§ 1751.53, 3923.38

Employers affected: All employers that offer group health insurance.

Eligible employees: Employees continuously insured for previous 3 months who were involuntarily terminated for reasons other than gross misconduct on the part of the employee.

Length of coverage for employee: 12 months.

Length of coverage for dependents: 12 months.

Qualifying event: Involuntary termination of employment.

Time employer has to notify employee: At termination of employment.

Time employee has to apply: Whichever is earlier: 31 days after coverage terminates; 10 days after coverage terminates if employer notified employee of continuation rights prior to termination; 10 days after employer notified employee of continuation rights, if notice was given after coverage terminated.

Oklahoma

Okla. Stat. Ann. tit. 36, § 4509

Employers affected: All employers that offer group health insurance.

Eligible employees: Employees insured for at least 6 months (all other employees and their dependents entitled to 30 days' continuation coverage).

Length of coverage for employee: 63 days for basic coverage; 6 months for major medical at the same premium rate prior to termination of coverage (only for losses or conditions that began while group policy in effect).

Length of coverage for dependents: 63 days for basic coverage; 6 months for major medical at the same premium rate prior to termination of coverage (only for losses or conditions that began while group policy in effect).

State Health Insurance Continuation Laws (continued)

Qualifying event: Any reason coverage terminates (except employment termination for gross misconduct).

Time employer has to notify employee: Carrier must notify employee in writing within 30 days of receiving notice of termination of employee's coverage.

Time employee has to apply: 31 days after receipt of notice.

Special benefits: Includes maternity care for pregnancy begun while group policy was in effect.

Oregon

Or. Rev. Stat. §§ 743B.343 to 743B.347

Employers affected: Employers not subject to federal COBRA laws.

Eligible employees: Employees continuously insured for previous 3 months.

Length of coverage for employee: 9 months.

Length of coverage for dependents: 9 months.

Qualifying event: Termination of employment; reduction in hours; employee's eligibility for Medicare; loss of dependent status; termination of membership in group covered by policy; death of employee.

Time employer has to notify employee: 10 days after qualifying event.

Time employee has to apply: Within the time limit determined by the insurer, which must be at least 10 days after the qualifying event or employee's receipt of notice, whichever is later.

Special situations: Surviving, divorced, or legally separated spouse who is 55 or older and dependent children entitled to continuation coverage until spouse remarries or is eligible for other coverage; must include dental, vision, or prescription drug benefits, if they were offered in original plan (applies to employers with 20 or more employees).

Pennsylvania

Pa. Stat. 40 P.S. § 764j

Employers affected: Employers that offer group health insurance and have 2 to 19 employees.

Eligible employees: Employees continuously insured for at least 3 months.

Length of coverage for employee: 9 months.

Length of coverage for dependents: 9 months.

Qualifying event: Termination of employment; reduction in hours; death of employee; change in marital status; employer's bankruptcy.

Time employer has to notify employee: 30 days after qualifying event.

Time employee has to apply: 30 days after receiving notice.

Rhode Island

R.I. Gen. Laws §§ 27-19.1-1, 27-20.4-1 to 27-20-4-2

Employers affected: All employers that offer group health insurance.

Eligible employees: All insured employees are eligible.

Length of coverage for employee: 18 months (but not longer than continuous employment); cannot be required to pay more than one month's premium at a time.

Length of coverage for dependents: 18 months (but not longer than continuous

State Health Insurance Continuation Laws (continued)

employment); cannot be required to pay more than one months' premium at a time.

Qualifying event: Involuntary termination of employment; death of employee; change in marital status; permanent reduction in workforce; employer's going out of business.

Time employer has to notify employee: Employers must post a conspicuous notice of employee continuation rights.

Time employee has to apply: 30 days from termination of coverage.

Special situations: If right to receiving continuing health insurance is stated in the divorce judgment, divorced spouse has right to continue coverage as long as employee remains covered or until divorced spouse remarries or becomes eligible for other group insurance.

South Carolina

S.C. Code Ann. § 38-71-770

Employers affected: All employers that offer group health insurance.

Eligible employees: Employees continuously insured for previous 6 months.

Length of coverage for employee: 6 months (in addition to part of month remaining at termination).

Length of coverage for dependents: 6 months (in addition to part of month remaining at termination).

Qualifying event: Any reason employee or dependent becomes ineligible for coverage.

Time employer has to notify employee: At the time of termination, employer must clearly and meaningfully advise employee of continuation rights.

South Dakota

S.D. Codified Laws Ann. §§ 58-18-7.5, 58-18-7.12; 58-18C-1

Employers affected: All employers that offer group health insurance.

Eligible employees: All covered employees.

Length of coverage for employee: 18 months; 29 months if disabled at termination or during first 60 days of continuation coverage.

Length of coverage for dependents: 18 months; 29 months if disabled at termination or during first 60 days of continuation coverage; 36 months upon death of employee, divorce or legal separation, loss of dependent status, employee's eligibility for Medicare.

Qualifying event: Termination of employment; death of employee; divorce or legal separation; loss of dependent status; employee's eligibility for Medicare.

Special situations: When employer goes out of business: 12 months' continuation coverage available to all employees. Employer must notify employees within 10 days of termination of benefits; employees must apply within 60 days of receipt of employer's notice or within 90 days of termination of benefits if no notice given.

Tennessee

Tenn. Code Ann. § 56-7-2312

Employers affected: All employers that offer group health insurance.

Eligible employees: Employees continuously insured for previous 3 months.

Length of coverage for employee: 3 months (in addition to part of month remaining at termination).

State Health Insurance Continuation Laws (continued)

Length of coverage for dependents:
3 months (in addition to part of month remaining at termination); 15 months upon death of employee or divorce (in addition to part of month remaining at termination).

Qualifying event: Termination of employment; death of employee; change in marital status.

Special situations: Employee or dependent who is pregnant at time of termination entitled to continuation benefits for 6 months following the end of pregnancy.

Texas

Tex. Ins. Code Ann. §§ 1251.252 to 1251.255; 1251.301 to 1251.310

Employers affected: All employers that offer group health insurance.

Eligible employees: Employees continuously insured for previous 3 months.

Length of coverage for employee: 9 months; for employees eligible for COBRA, 6 months after COBRA coverage ends.

Length of coverage for dependents:
9 months; for employees eligible for COBRA, 6 months after COBRA coverage ends. Three years for dependents with coverage due to the death or retirement of employee or severance of the family relationship.

Qualifying event: Termination of employment (except for cause); employee leaves for health reasons; severance of family relationship; retirement or death of employee.

Time employee has to apply: 60 days from termination of coverage or receiving notice of continuation rights from employer or insurer, whichever is later. Must give notice within 15 days of severance of

family relationship. Within 60 days of death or retirement of family member or severance of family relationship, dependent must give notice of intent to continue coverage.

Utah

Utah Code Ann. § 31A-22-722

Employers affected: All employers that offer group health insurance.

Eligible employees: Employees continuously insured for previous 3 months.

Length of coverage for employee: 12 months.

Length of coverage for dependents:
12 months.

Qualifying event: Termination of employment; retirement; death; divorce; reduction in hours; sabbatical; disability; loss of dependent status.

Time employer has to notify employee:
In writing within 30 days of termination of coverage.

Time employee has to apply: Within 60 days of qualifying event.

Vermont

Vt. Stat. Ann. tit. 8, §§ 4090a to 4090c

Employers affected: All employers that offer group health insurance.

Eligible employees: All covered employees are eligible.

Length of coverage for employee: 18 months.

Length of coverage for dependents: 18 months.

Qualifying event: Termination of employment; reduction in hours; death of employee; change of marital status; loss of dependent status.

State Health Insurance Continuation Laws (continued)

Time employer has to notify employee: Within 30 days of qualifying event.

Time employee has to apply: Within 60 days of receiving notice following the occurrence of a qualifying event.

Virginia

Va. Code Ann. §§ 38.2-3541 to 38.2-3542

Employers affected: All employers that offer group health insurance.

Eligible employees: Employees continuously insured for previous 3 months.

Length of coverage for employee: 12 months.

Length of coverage for dependents: 12 months.

Qualifying event: Any reason employee or dependent becomes ineligible for coverage.

Time employer has to notify employee: 14 days from termination of coverage.

Time employee has to apply: Within 31 days of receiving notice of eligibility, but no more than 60 days following termination.

Special situations: Employee may convert to an individual policy instead of applying for continuation coverage (must apply within 31 days of termination of coverage).

Washington

Wash. Rev. Code Ann. § 48.21.075

Employers affected: All employers that offer disability insurance.

Eligible employees: Insured employees on strike.

Length of coverage for employee: 6 months if employee goes on strike.

Length of coverage for dependents: 6 months if employee goes on strike.

Qualifying event: If employee goes on strike.

Special situations: All employers have option of offering continued group health benefits.

West Virginia

W. Va. Code §§ 33-16-2, 33-16-3(e);
W. Va. Code St. R. § 114-93-3

Employers affected: Employers providing insurance for between 2 and 20 employees.

Eligible employees: All employees are eligible.

Length of coverage for employee: 18 months in case of involuntary layoff.

Qualifying event: Involuntary layoff.

Time employer has to notify employee: Carrier must notify beneficiaries within 15 days of receiving notice from beneficiary of intent to apply.

Time employee has to apply: 20 days to send notice of intention to apply; 30 days to apply after receiving election and premium notice.

Wisconsin

Wis. Stat. Ann. § 632.897

Employers affected: All employers that offer group health insurance.

Eligible employees: Employees continuously insured for previous 3 months.

Length of coverage for employee: 18 months (or longer at insurer's option).

Length of coverage for dependents: 18 months (or longer at insurer's option).

State Health Insurance Continuation Laws (continued)

Qualifying event: Any reason employee or dependent becomes ineligible for coverage (except employment termination due to misconduct).

Time employer has to notify employee: 5 days from termination of coverage.

Time employee has to apply: 30 days after receiving employer's notice.

Wyoming

Wyo. Stat. § 26-19-113

Employers affected: Employers not subject to federal COBRA laws.

Eligible employees: Employees continuously insured for previous 3 months.

Length of coverage for employee: 12 months.

Length of coverage for dependents: 12 months.

Time employee has to apply: 31 days from termination of coverage.

Employee Polygraph Protection Act (EPPA)

Statute: 29 U.S.C. §§ 2001–2009
To view the statutes, visit http://uscode.house.gov and select "Title 29" and "Chapter 22."

Regulations: 29 C.F.R. § 801
To view the regulations, visit www.govinfo.gov and search "29 CFR 801."

Overview of the EPPA

The Employee Polygraph Protection Act (EPPA) prohibits most private employers from requiring job applicants or current employees to take lie detector tests, except in very limited circumstances. In the few situations when an employer is legally allowed to use a *polygraph* test, the EPPA places strict limits on how the test must be administered and how the results can be used.

The EPPA contains provisions on:

- **Polygraph use.** Employers generally may not ask or require workers to take a polygraph test, with a few narrow exceptions.
- **Test results.** Employers may use the results of a polygraph test against an employee only if additional evidence supports the decision.
- **Employees' rights.** Employees are entitled to certain information and protections before, during, and after a polygraph test.
- **Polygraph examiners.** Those who administer the test must meet certain job qualifications and render their conclusions in a prescribed format.
- **Retaliation.** Employers may not take any *adverse employment action* against employees who exercise their rights under the law.

Covered Employers

Private employers are subject to the EPPA if they are covered by the Fair Labor Standards Act (FLSA). (The FLSA covers most private employers; for more information, see Chapter 7.) The EPPA does not apply to governmental employers, whether federal, state, or local.

Foreign employers are subject to the EPPA for any actions they take within the United States relating to the administration of lie detector tests. For example, if a foreign corporation has an office in the United States and prepares paperwork in that office relating to polygraph testing, the EPPA applies to that employer, even if the polygraph tests will be conducted in a foreign country.

The EPPA also applies to any person acting in an employer's interest in relation to an employee or applicant. For example, employment placement agencies, job recruiting firms, and vocational trade schools may be subject to the EPPA for job applicants whom they refer to prospective employers. However, these referring organizations will be liable for violations of the EPPA only if they had reason to know that the prospective employer would require applicants to take a polygraph test or otherwise violate the EPPA.

Definitions

Access: The opportunity to cause, or help cause, a specific *economic loss or injury* to the employer's business. An employee need not have regular contact with property to have access to it. If the employee is able to get at the property (by working in its vicinity or knowing the combination to a safe where it is kept, for example), the employee has access, even if the employee's job does not require contact with or use of the property.

Adverse employment action: Firing, disciplining, discriminating against, or refusing to hire or promote an applicant or current employee.

Counterintelligence: Information gathered and activities conducted to protect against espionage and other clandestine intelligence activities, sabotage, terrorism, or assassinations conducted by or on behalf of foreign governments, foreign or domestic organizations, or people.

Currency, negotiable securities, and precious commodities: Assets that are typically handled by, protected for, and transported between commercial and financial institutions. Also includes cash assets handled by casinos, racetracks, lotteries, and other businesses in which cash constitutes the inventory or stock in trade. Also includes gold, silver, or diamonds.

Direct access: Contact with or responsibility for a controlled substance, as part of an employee's job responsibilities. An employee whose job requires dispensing, obtaining, manufacturing, storing, testing, distributing, packaging, transporting, taking inventory of, providing security for, or prescribing controlled substances has direct access, as long as the employee's job duties include either physical contact with the substances or the opportunity to get possession of such substances.

Economic loss or injury: Financial harm to an employer's business, including loss due to theft, embezzlement, misappropriation of trade secrets, or sabotage of an employer's property; use of an employer's business to commit a crime, such as money laundering or check kiting; or theft or harm to property belonging to a third party, if the employer is responsible for protecting that property. Examples of losses that do not fall within this definition are theft of a client's property (unless the employer is responsible for that property), threatened or potential

Definitions (continued)

harm, losses caused by legal or unintentional conduct (for example, damages caused by a workplace accident), or theft of another employee's property.

Facilities, materials, or operations having a significant impact on the national security of the United States or the health or safety of any state or political subdivision thereof: Facilities, operations, or materials that are targets of acts of sabotage, espionage, terrorism, or other destructive or illegal acts, where the consequences of such destructive acts could significantly affect the general public's safety or health or national security. Examples include government office buildings, prisons, nuclear or electric power facilities, the public water supply, shipment or storage of toxic waste, public transportation, public schools, military posts or laboratories, factories or plants used to produce, store, or process products related to the national defense, factories that produce hazardous chemicals, public and private energy supplies and reserves, the Federal Reserve System, and hospitals.

Lie detector test: Any mechanical or electrical device that is used, or the results of which are used, for the purpose of rendering a diagnostic opinion about whether a person is telling the truth. Polygraphs, deceptographs, voice stress analyzers, and psychological stress evaluators all constitute lie detector tests under the EPPA. However, medical tests to determine whether an employee has taken drugs or alcohol, written or oral honesty tests, and handwriting tests are not considered lie detector tests and are not subject to the EPPA's restrictions. (These tests may be covered by other laws, however.)

Ongoing investigation: A current investigation into a specific incident of economic loss or injury the employer has suffered.

Polygraph: An instrument that (1) records continuously, visually, permanently, and simultaneously any changes in cardiovascular, respiratory, and electro-dermal patterns and (2) is used, or the results of which are used, for the purpose of rendering an opinion about whether a person is being honest or dishonest.

Primary business purpose: For purposes of the security services exception (see the "Exceptions" sections under "Polygraph Use," below), an employer's primary business purpose is providing security services if at least 50% of its annual dollar volume of business is derived from that activity.

Definitions (continued)

Proprietary information: Business assets such as trade secrets, manufacturing processes, research and development data, and cost or pricing data.

Reasonable suspicion: A demonstrable factual basis for believing that a particular employee was involved in, or responsible for, an economic loss or injury to the employer's business. In deciding whether an employer had a reasonable suspicion for testing a particular employee, courts will consider all of the circumstances, including reliable information from coworkers, an employee's demeanor or conduct, or inconsistencies between facts or statements that come up during the investigation. Generally, an employee's opportunity to cause the loss will not be enough, on its own, to create reasonable suspicion.

Did You Know ...

- Polygraphs work by using sensors to measure things like pulse, breathing rate, blood pressure, and perspiration while the examinee is asked questions. Significant changes (typically, increases) in any of these vital signs while the employee is responding to a particular question are thought to indicate that the examinee is lying.
- A large number of Fortune 500 and 1000 companies use some form of psychological or personality testing in the hiring process. Some experts believe that use of these types of tests increased after the EPPA essentially prohibited the use of polygraph tests in hiring.

Covered Workers

The EPPA covers all job applicants and employees who work for a covered employer. It does not cover federal, state, or local government employees.

The EPPA also protects former employees from retaliation. For example, if an employee decides to quit rather than take a polygraph test, an employer may not threaten or take negative action against that person (by attempting to prevent him or her from getting another job, for example).

What's Prohibited

Employers are prohibited from requiring applicants or employees to take *lie detector tests*, except in very limited circumstances. When employers are legally allowed to conduct polygraph tests, they may not rely on the results to take an *adverse employment action* against an employee unless they have additional evidence of the employee's guilt.

What's Required

When employers are legally allowed to administer *polygraph* tests, they must carefully observe the tested employee's rights throughout the process. Among other things, this includes providing a written statement of the nature of and reasons for the test. Employers must also use polygraph examiners who meet certain qualifications and requirements as spelled out in the law.

Employers are also required to post a notice in the workplace (prepared by the Department of Labor) describing the EPPA's provisions. (See "Agency Resources," below.)

Exceptions

There are several exceptions to the EPPA's prohibition on private employers' use of lie detector tests. These exceptions are discussed in "Major Provisions of the EPPA," below.

Major Provisions of the EPPA

Polygraph Use

In general, the EPPA prohibits private employers from requiring any applicant or current employee to take a lie detector test. The law also prohibits private employers from firing, disciplining, retaliating against, or refusing to hire or promote any applicant or current employee for refusing to take a lie detector test.

However, the law lists several circumstances in which certain private employers may require employees or applicants to take polygraph tests. (See "Exceptions: Private Employers," below.) In addition, the law allows certain public employers to administer lie detector tests to employees of private employers. (See "Exceptions: Public Employers Testing Private Employees," below.)

Key Facts: Polygraph Use

- Generally, employers cannot require or ask an employee or applicant to take a lie detector test, nor can they discipline, fire, or refuse to hire an employee or applicant for refusing to take one.
- Public officials may require the employees of certain private employers to submit to lie detector tests, in limited circumstances.
- Private companies that deal with controlled substances or provide security services are allowed to require certain applicants and employees to take a polygraph test, in specified circumstances.
- A private company may require an employee to take a polygraph test as part of an ongoing investigation into economic loss or injury, but only if a number of conditions are met.

Covered Employers

All covered employers are subject to these provisions unless they fall within one of the law's exceptions.

Covered Workers

All covered workers are subject to these provisions.

What's Prohibited

Unless they fall within one of the exceptions outlined below, employers may not, directly or indirectly, require, suggest, request, or cause any applicant or employee to take or submit to a lie detector test.

What's Required

An employer that falls within one of the law's exceptions (see "Exceptions: Public Employers Testing Private Employees" and "Exceptions: Private Employers," below) and wishes to request or administer a test still has to meet the law's other requirements, as explained below.

Exceptions: Public Employers Testing Private Employees

There are two circumstances in which federal, state, or local authorities can require private employees to take lie detector tests. In these circumstances, the private employers for whom these employees work cannot be held liable for the testing under the EPPA.

Law Enforcement Exception

If a private employer reports a theft or another economic loss to law enforcement authorities, and those authorities deem it necessary in the normal course of investigating the incident to administer a polygraph test to a suspected employee, that testing is not prohibited by the EPPA. The employer may cooperate with law enforcement officials in the investigation—for example, by allowing the police to test a suspect on the employer's premises or letting the employee leave work early to take a polygraph test at the police station. However, if an employer participates actively in the testing, by administering the test itself or by reimbursing police for the costs of testing, the employer will be subject to the EPPA—and the employer will have violated the law unless one of the private employer exceptions (see "Exceptions: Private Employers," below) applies.

Federal Government Counterintelligence Exception

If a private employer does work for the federal government, the government may, in the performance of its *counterintelligence* functions, require its employees to take lie detector tests. This exception allows the government to require lie detector tests of:

- any expert or consultant under contract to, or any employee of any contractor of, the Department of Defense
- any expert or consultant under contract to, or any employee of any contractor of, the Department of Energy in connection with its atomic energy defense activities
- anyone assigned or detailed to, any expert or consultant under contract to, any employee of a contractor of, or any person assigned to, a space where sensitive cryptologic information is produced, processed, or stored for the National Security Agency, Defense Intelligence Agency, National Imagery and Mapping Agency, or the Central Intelligence Agency
- any expert or consultant under contract to, or any employee of any contractor of, any department, agency, or program of the federal government, if that person's duties involve access to information that has been classified as top secret or designated as being within a special access program, and
- any employee of any contractor to the Federal Bureau of Investigation, if that employee actually performs any work under the contract.

Exceptions: Private Employers

There are three exceptions available to private employers. These exceptions apply only to polygraph tests. Private employers are always prohibited from administering lie detector tests other than polygraph tests, even if one of the exceptions applies.

Controlled Substances Exception

Employers that are authorized by the Drug Enforcement Administration (DEA) to manufacture, distribute, or dispense specified controlled substances (those listed in Schedule I, II, III, or IV of the Controlled Substances Act (21 U.S.C. § 812)) may require polygraph testing only of:

- job applicants who would, if hired, have *direct access* to the manufacture, storage, distribution, or sale of a controlled substance, and

- current employees in connection with an *ongoing investigation* of criminal or other misconduct involving actual or potential loss or injury to the manufacture, distribution, or dispensing of a controlled substance, but only if the employee had access to the person or property that is the subject of the investigation.

This exception applies only to employers who have DEA authorization to deal in these controlled substances. It does not apply to other employers, even if their employees may come in contact with controlled substances as a normal part of their jobs, as might be true of truck drivers or warehouse employees.

The term "job applicants," as used in this exception, might include current employees who apply for transfer or promotion to a different position. For example, if an employee who currently works in a position with no direct access to controlled substances applies for a position that provides such access, that employee can be required to take a polygraph test as a job applicant under the rule.

Security Services Exception

Certain private employers that provide security services may require job applicants to take a polygraph test. This exception applies only if:

- the employer's *primary business purpose* is providing armored car personnel; personnel who design, install, and maintain security alarm systems; or other uniformed or plainclothes security personnel
- the employer's function includes protecting (1) *facilities, materials, or operations having a significant impact on the national security of the United States or the health or safety of any state or political subdivision thereof*; or (2) *currency, negotiable securities, precious commodities, or proprietary information*, and
- the applicant tested would be employed to protect the facilities, materials, operations, or assets listed above. An applicant for a position that would allow the opportunity to cause or participate in a security breach is covered by this requirement.

The term "job applicants," as used in this exception, might include current employees who apply for transfer or promotion to a different position. For example, if an employee who currently provides security for an appliance store applies for a position guarding a nuclear facility, that employee can be required to take a polygraph test under the rule applicable to job applicants.

Ongoing Investigation Exception

A private employer may ask an employee to submit to a polygraph test if all of the following conditions are met:

- The test is administered in connection with an ongoing investigation of *economic loss or injury* to the employer's business.
- The employee had *access* to the property that is the subject of the investigation.
- The employer has a *reasonable suspicion* that the employee was involved in the incident or activity under investigation.
- The employer gives the employee a written statement, at least two working days before the test, that:
  - describes the specific incident or activity under investigation and the basis for testing the employee
  - identifies the specific economic loss or injury to the employer's business
  - states that the employee had access to the property that is the subject of the investigation
  - describes the basis for the employer's reasonable suspicion of the employee, and
  - is signed by someone authorized to legally bind the employer, such as an officer or director of the company.

This statement must be signed by the employee and must indicate the time and date when the employee received the statement.

An employer may not request polygraph testing to determine whether any economic losses have been incurred; testing is allowed only in response to a specific, identifiable incident of loss. Nor may employers request polygraph testing to investigate a continuing loss. For example, regular inventory shortages that occur all the time in a warehouse would not be a sufficiently specific incident to allow testing.

Test Results

Unless one of the exceptions listed under "Polygraph Use," above, applies, employers may not:

- use, accept, refer to, or inquire about the results of any lie detector test taken by an applicant or a current employee, or

- take any adverse employment action against an employee or applicant on the basis of the results of a lie detector test or the employee's or applicant's refusal to take a lie detector test.

If one of the exceptions applies, employers may use the results of a polygraph test—or an employee's refusal to take a polygraph test—as one basis for taking an adverse employment action against the employee. However, the employer must administer the test properly, by following the requirements described in "Employees' Rights" and "Polygraph Examiners," below.

And the employer may not rely solely on the results of the polygraph test or the employee's refusal to take it. An employer must have additional evidence or grounds for the decision; what's required depends on the exception that applies.

Ongoing Investigation Exception

For the ongoing investigation exception, additional supporting evidence might include:

- evidence showing that the employee had access to the property that is the subject of the investigation, and
- evidence supporting the employer's reasonable suspicion that the employee was involved in the incident or activity under investigation.

Admissions or statements made by the employee before, during, or after the polygraph test may also create sufficient additional supporting evidence to act on the results of the test.

Controlled Substances and Security Services Exceptions

For the controlled substances and security services exception, additional supporting evidence might include:

- traditional factors on which employers rely to make job decisions, such as job performance or prior employment experience, or
- admissions or statements made by the employee before, during, or after a polygraph test.

Employees' Rights

Employers may rely on the results of a polygraph test only if they meet a long list of requirements designed to protect an employee's rights before, during, and after a polygraph test. Some of these requirements (for example, those about the manner in which the test is conducted) rely on the cooperation of the polygraph examiner. In these cases, the employer is responsible for ensuring that the examiner does not violate the employee's rights.

Key Facts: Employees' Rights

- Before a polygraph test, the employee who will be tested is entitled to written information about the test and a written notice detailing the employee's rights. The employee is also entitled to see every question that will be asked.
- During a polygraph test, the employee has the right to end the test at any time. In addition, the employee cannot be asked any questions that were not revealed in advance, any questions that are unnecessarily intrusive or degrading, or questions about religious beliefs, sexual activities, or certain other matters.
- If an employer plans to take action based on the results of the polygraph test, it must first interview the employee further and provide certain written information about the test questions and results.
- An employer may disclose the results of the test only to the employee; a court, mediator, agency, or other fact finder pursuant to a court order; or a law enforcement agency, if the employee admitted committing a crime.

Pretest Rights

The pretest phase of a polygraph test refers to the period of questioning and other methods of preparing an employee to take the test. During this phase, the employee must receive:

- written notice, in a language the employee understands, of the date, time, and location of the test, and the employee's right to consult with an attorney or an employee representative before each phase of the test. The notice must be signed by the employee and must indicate the date and time the employee received it. The employee must receive this notice two working days before the test.

- written and oral notice of the nature and characteristics of the polygraph instrument and examination, including an explanation of how the polygraph instrument works and the procedure to be used during the examination
- the opportunity to review, in writing, all questions the examiner will ask during the test
- written notice, in a language the employee understands, indicating:
  - whether the testing area contains a two-way mirror, camera, or another device to observe the employee
  - whether any other device (such as a tape recorder or another monitoring instrument) will be used during the test
  - that the employee has a right to record the test, as long as the employer is told of the recording
  - that the employee may stop the test at any time
  - that the employee has the right, and will be given the opportunity, to review all questions to be asked during the test
  - that the employee may not be asked questions that are degrading or needlessly intrusive
  - that the employee may not be asked any questions about religious beliefs or opinions, beliefs regarding racial matters, political beliefs or affiliations, matters of sexual behavior, or beliefs, affiliations, opinions, or lawful activities relating to unions or labor organizations
  - that the test may not be conducted if a physician provides sufficient written evidence that the employee suffers from a medical or psychological condition or is undergoing treatment that might cause abnormal responses during the test
  - that the test cannot be required as a condition of employment
  - that the employer may not take an adverse employment action against the employee based on the results of the test, or the employee's refusal to take the test, without additional evidence to support the action
  - if the test is given under the ongoing investigation exception, that the additional evidence required to support the adverse employment action may include evidence that the employee had access to the property and evidence supporting the employer's reasonable suspicion that the employee was involved in the incident

- that any statements the employee makes before, during, or after the test may provide additional evidence to support an adverse employment action
- that any admission of criminal conduct may be transmitted to an appropriate government law enforcement agency
- that information gained from the test may be disclosed by the examiner or the employer only to: the employee; any person whom the employee specifically authorizes, in writing, to receive the results; the employer; a court, governmental agency, arbitrator, or mediator, pursuant to court order; an official of the U.S. Department of Labor, if the employee authorizes such disclosure in writing; or an appropriate governmental law enforcement agency, if the information is an admission of criminal conduct
- a description of the employee's legal rights if the employer violates the law
- that the employee has the right to consult with legal counsel or another representative during every phase of the test, although that person may be excluded from the room when the test is actually conducted, and
- that the employee may not give up his or her rights under the EPPA, voluntarily or involuntarily, by contract or otherwise, except as part of a written settlement agreement.

The employer must give the employee this notice and read the notice to the employee. The Department of Labor has prepared a standard form that the employer can use to fulfill this requirement. (See "Agency Resources," below, for more information.)

Rights During the Test

During the polygraph test, the employee has the right:

- to end the test at any time
- not to be asked questions in a manner designed to degrade or needlessly intrude on the employee
- not to be asked any question about (1) religious beliefs or affiliations, (2) beliefs or opinions regarding racial matters, (3) political beliefs or affiliations, (4) any matter relating to sexual behavior, or (5) beliefs, affiliations, opinions, or lawful activities regarding unions or labor organizations

- not to be tested if a physician provides sufficient written evidence that the employee is suffering from a medical or psychological condition or is undergoing treatment that might cause abnormal responses to the test
- to be asked only questions that were presented to the employee for review, in writing, before the test, and
- to a test of at least 90 minutes in length (unless the employee ends the test before it is complete).

Rights After the Test

Before taking any adverse employment action based on the results of a test, the employer must:
- interview the employee further, based on the results of the test, and
- give the employee (1) a written copy of any opinion or conclusion rendered as a result of the test, and (2) a copy of the questions asked during the test and the corresponding charted responses (copies of the charts of the entire examination, showing the employee's physiological responses to each question).

Disclosure of Test Results

Although the employee who takes the test can disclose the results as he or she sees fit, the EPPA strictly limits the circumstances in which an employer or polygraph examiner may reveal test results.

An examiner may disclose results only to:
- the employee or any other person whom the employee authorizes, in writing, to receive the results
- the employer that requested the test, or
- any court, governmental agency, arbitrator, or mediator, pursuant to a court order requiring such disclosure.

An employer may disclose polygraph results only to:
- the employee or any other person whom the employee authorizes, in writing, to receive the results
- any court, governmental agency, arbitrator, or mediator, pursuant to a court order requiring such disclosure, or
- a governmental law enforcement agency, if the disclosed information is an admission of criminal conduct.

Polygraph Examiners

Even if an employer is entitled to request or conduct a polygraph test pursuant to one of the exceptions listed under "Polygraph Use," above, that test will violate the EPPA unless the employer uses a polygraph examiner who meets certain qualifications and requirements. The examiner must:

- have a valid, current license, if required in the state where the polygraph will be conducted (over half of states require licenses)
- maintain a minimum $50,000 bond or an equivalent amount of professional liability coverage
- administer no more than five polygraph tests in any single day on which a test or tests subject to the EPPA is conducted (not including any tests terminated voluntarily by the employee), and
- administer no polygraph examination that is less than 90 minutes long (unless the test is terminated voluntarily by the employee).

In addition, if the examiner renders any opinion or conclusion regarding the employee's truthfulness or deception, the report must:

- be in writing
- be based solely on an analysis of polygraph test charts
- not contain information other than admissions, information, case facts, and interpretation of the charts relevant to the purpose and stated objectives of the test, and
- not include any recommendation about the employment of the employee.

The examiner must also retain all opinions, reports, charts, written questions, lists, and other records relating to the test (including written notices signed by the employee and electronic recordings of the test) for at least three years after the test is conducted.

Retaliation

An employer may not fire, discipline, refuse to hire, or take another adverse employment action against an employee or job applicant for exercising rights granted the by EPPA (by, for example, filing an administrative complaint or testifying in a lawsuit).

How the EPPA Is Enforced

Individual Complaints

An employee who wishes to file a complaint under the EPPA has two options. The employee may make a complaint to the Wage and Hour Division of the Department of Labor (DOL). (See Appendix A for contact information.) Or, the employee may bypass the DOL and file a lawsuit in state court or in federal district court. The employee must file this lawsuit within three years of the date the employer violated the EPPA.

Agency Enforcement

If an employee files a complaint with the DOL, the agency may choose to investigate the employer—particularly if the employer conducts a lot of polygraph tests, which raises the possibility that many employees' rights have been violated.

DOL investigations are similar to audits. An investigator may contact the employer ahead of time or may simply show up at the workplace. The investigator will examine the employer's records and interview employees who may have information about the complaint. Once the investigation is complete, the investigator will meet with the employer to try to resolve any problems the investigation uncovered. The investigator will tell the employer whether it violated the law and how it can correct those violations—for example, by reinstating an employee who was fired illegally for refusing to take a polygraph test or by immediately ceasing to require all applicants to take a polygraph test.

If the employer refuses to comply, the secretary of labor can file a lawsuit in federal district court on behalf of the employees whose rights were violated.

The secretary may also impose civil penalties against the employer (see "Remedies," below, for more information).

Complying With the EPPA

Deadlines

If one of the exceptions to the EPPA applies and the employer is entitled to administer a polygraph test, the employee must receive written notice of the test, including the detailed information listed under "Employees' Rights," above, at least *two working days* before the test. The employer or the polygraph examiner may provide this notice.

Reporting Requirements

The EPPA imposes no reporting requirements.

Posting Requirements

Employers are required to post a notice (prepared by the DOL) in the workplace describing the EPPA's provisions. Employers must post this notice in a prominent spot in each of its business locations, where it can be easily seen and read by employees and job applicants. (See "Agency Resources," below, for information on how to download this poster.)

Record-Keeping Requirements

Employers must keep the following records for at least three years from the date the polygraph test is conducted (or from the date the employer asks the employee to take the test, if no test is ever conducted):

- a copy of the employer's written notice to the polygraph examiner identifying the person(s) to be tested
- copies of all opinions, reports, or other records that the polygraph examiner gives to the employer
- if the test is administered under the ongoing investigation exception, a copy of the statement to the employee setting forth the specific incident under investigation and the basis for testing that particular employee, and

- if the test is administered to a current employee under the controlled substances exception, records specifically identifying the loss or injury under investigation and the nature of the employee's access to the person or property investigated.

The employer must make these records available to the secretary of labor or an investigator from the DOL within 72 hours after they are requested.

Remedies

Employers that violate the EPPA may be required to:

- take action to remedy the violation, such as hiring, promoting, or reinstating a worker who was wrongfully asked or required to take a polygraph test, or who suffered some other adverse employment action in violation of the law
- pay the worker for any benefits or wages lost because of the employer's violation, and
- pay the worker's attorneys' fees and court costs.

The language of the EPPA does not specifically allow for compensatory damages (money awarded to the plaintiff for out-of-pocket costs and the emotional harm caused by the employer's actions). However, a couple of courts have awarded compensatory damages to successful plaintiffs. These courts have also indicated that punitive damages (a money award intended to punish the employer for particularly egregious misconduct) might be available under the law. These issues are still undecided because there are so few reported lawsuits interpreting the EPPA.

As the result of an audit by the DOL, the secretary of labor may impose civil penalties of up to $20,521 against an employer that violates the EPPA. These penalties are assessed in an administrative hearing process, not a lawsuit. If the employer objects to the penalties, it has the right to appeal to federal district court.

Agency Resources

- The DOL's poster on the EPPA

    Notice: Employee Polygraph Protection Act
    www.dol.gov/whd/regs/compliance/posters/eppa.htm

- A fact sheet on the EPPA's provisions

    Fact Sheet #36: The Employee Polygraph Protection Act of 1988
    www.dol.gov/whd/regs/compliance/whdfs36.htm

- A fact sheet explaining DOL audits

    Fact Sheet #44: Visits to Employers
    www.dol.gov/whd/regs/compliance/whdfs44.htm

- A list of the addresses and telephone numbers of local offices
  of the Wage and Hour Division

    District Office Locations
    www.dol.gov/whd/local

State Laws Relating to Polygraph Tests

Many states also have laws that prohibit or restrict employers from using
lie detector tests in connection with hiring or employment. Some of these
laws go further than the EPPA and prohibit employers from even suggesting
such a test. The chart below summarizes state polygraph testing laws.
If you need more information, contact your state department of labor
(Appendix A provides contact information).

State Employee Polygraph Examination Laws

Alaska

Alaska Stat. § 23.10.037

Employers covered: All

What's prohibited: Employer may not suggest, request, or require that employee or applicant take a lie detector test.

California

Cal. Lab. Code § 432.2

Employers covered: All

What's prohibited: Employer may not demand or require that employee or applicant take a lie detector test.

What's allowed: Employer may request a test, if applicant is advised in writing of legal right to refuse to take it.

Connecticut

Conn. Gen. Stat. Ann. § 31-51g

Employers covered: All, including employment agencies

What's prohibited: Employer may not request or require that employee or applicant take a lie detector test.

Delaware

Del. Code Ann. tit. 19, § 704

Employers covered: All

What's prohibited: Employer may not suggest, request, or require that employee or applicant take a lie detector test in order to obtain or continue employment.

District of Columbia

D.C. Code Ann. §§ 32-901 to 32-903

Employers covered: All

What's prohibited: Employer may not administer, have administered, use, or accept the results of any polygraph examination.

Hawaii

Haw. Rev. Stat. § 378-26.5

Employers covered: All

What's prohibited: Employer may not require employee or applicant to take lie detector test.

What's allowed: Employer may request test if current or prospective employee is told, orally and in writing, that refusing to take test will not result in being fired or hurt chances of getting job.

Idaho

Idaho Code § 44-903

Employers covered: All

What's prohibited: Employer may not require an employee or applicant to take a lie detector test.

Illinois

225 Ill. Comp. Stat. § 430/14.1

Employers covered: All

What's prohibited: Unless directly related to employment, examination may not include questions about:
- political, religious, or labor-related beliefs, affiliations, or activities (that are lawful)
- beliefs or opinions on racial matters, or
- sexual preferences or activity.

State Employee Polygraph Examination Laws (continued)

Iowa

Iowa Code § 730.4

Employers covered: All

What's prohibited: Employer may not request, require, administer, or attempt or threaten to administer a lie detector test; may not request or require that employee or applicant sign waiver of any action prohibited by this law.

Maine

Me. Rev. Stat. Ann. tit. 32, § 7364

Employers covered: All

What's prohibited: Employer may not request, require, suggest, or administer a polygraph test.

What's allowed: Employee may voluntarily request a test if these conditions are met:
- results cannot be used against employee
- employer must give employee a copy of the law when employee requests test, and
- test must be recorded or employee's witness must be present during the test, or both (upon employee's request).

Maryland

Md. Code Ann. [Lab. & Empl.] § 3-702

Employers covered: All

What's prohibited: Employer may not require or demand that employee or applicant take a lie detector test.

What's required: All employment applications must include specified notice that no person can be required to take a lie detector test as a condition of obtaining or continuing employment and must include space for applicant to sign and acknowledge notice.

Massachusetts

Mass. Gen. Laws ch. 149, § 19B

Employers covered: All

What's prohibited: Employer may not request, require, or administer a lie detector test.

What's required: All employment applications must include specified notice that it is unlawful to require a lie detector test as a condition of obtaining or continuing employment.

Michigan

Mich. Comp. Laws §§ 37.203, 338.1719

Employers covered: All

What's prohibited: Employer may not request, require, administer, or attempt or threaten to administer a lie detector test; may not request or require that employee or applicant sign waiver of any action prohibited by this law.

What's allowed: Employee may voluntarily request a test if all of these conditions are met:
- The employee is given a copy of the law before taking the test.
- The employee is given copies of the test results and reports.
- No questions are asked about sexual practices; marital relationship; or political, religious, or labor or union affiliations, unless the questions are relevant to areas under examination.
- The examiner informs employee:
  - of all questions that will be asked

State Employee Polygraph Examination Laws (continued)

- of right to accept, refuse, or stop test at any time
- that employee is not required to answer questions or give information, and
- that information volunteered could be used against the employee or made available to the employer, unless otherwise agreed to in writing.

Minnesota

Minn. Stat. Ann. §§ 181.75, 181.76

Employers covered: All

What's prohibited: Employer may not directly or indirectly solicit or require an applicant or employee to take a lie detector test.

What's allowed: Employee may request a test, but only if employer informs employee that test is voluntary. Results of voluntary test may be given only to those authorized by employee.

Montana

Mont. Code Ann. § 39-2-304

What's prohibited: Employer may not require an employee or applicant to take a lie detector test.

Nebraska

Neb. Rev. Stat. § 81-1932

Employers covered: All

What's prohibited: Employer may not require an employee or applicant to take a lie detector test.

What's allowed: Employer may request that test be taken, but only if all of these conditions are met:

- No questions are asked about sexual practices; marital relationship; or political, religious, or labor or union affiliations.
- An examinee is given written and oral notice that the test is voluntary and may be discontinued at any time.
- An examinee signs a form stating that the test is being taken voluntarily.
- Prospective employees are asked only job-related questions and are not singled out for testing in a discriminatory manner.
- An employee is requested to take the test only in connection with a specific investigation.
- The results of a test are not the sole reason for terminating employment.
- All questions and responses are kept on file by the employer for at least one year.

Nevada

Nev. Rev. Stat. Ann. §§ 613.480 to 613.510

Employers covered: All

Exceptions: Manufacturers or distributors of controlled substances; providers or designers of security systems and other security personnel; ongoing investigation.

What's prohibited: Employer may not directly or indirectly require, request, suggest, or cause a lie detector test to be taken; may not use, accept, refer to, or ask about the results of any test. May not take adverse employment action solely on the basis of test results or a refusal to take test.

What's allowed: Nevada law allows testing in the same limited circumstances as the federal EPPA, with similar rules and restrictions on when and how the test is given.

State Employee Polygraph Examination Laws (continued)

New Jersey

N.J. Stat. Ann. § 2C:40A-1

Employers covered: All

Exceptions: Employers that deal with controlled, dangerous substances.

What's prohibited: Employer may not influence, request, or require applicant or employee to take a lie detector test.

What's allowed: Employers who are allowed to test must observe all of these rules:

- The job must require direct access to the controlled substance.
- The test is limited to the preceding 5 years.
- Questions must be work-related or pertain to improper handling, use, or illegal sale of legally distributed controlled dangerous substances.
- The test taker has the right to legal counsel.
- The written copy of test results must be given to the test taker upon request.
- Test information may not be released to any other employer or person.
- The employee or prospective employee must be informed of the right to present results of a second independently administered test prior to any personnel decision being made.

New York

N.Y. Lab. Law §§ 733 to 739

Employers covered: All

What's prohibited: Employer may not require, request, suggest, permit, or use results of a lie detector test.

Oregon

Or. Rev. Stat. Ann. §§ 659.840, 659A.300

Employers covered: All

What's prohibited: Employer may not require an employee or applicant to take a lie detector test.

Pennsylvania

18 Pa. Cons. Stat. Ann. § 7321

Employers covered: All

Exceptions: Employers with positions that have access to narcotics or dangerous drugs.

What's prohibited: Employer may not require an employee or applicant to take a lie detector test.

Rhode Island

R.I. Gen. Laws §§ 28-6.1-1 to 28-6.1-4

Employers covered: All

What's prohibited: Employer may not request, require, subject, or directly or indirectly cause an employee or applicant to take a lie detector test.

Tennessee

Tenn. Code Ann. §§ 62-27-123, 62-27-128

Employers covered: All

What's prohibited: Employer may not take any personnel action based solely upon the results of a polygraph examination. No questions may be asked about:

- religious, political, or labor-related beliefs, affiliations, or activities (that are lawful)
- beliefs or opinions about racial matters
- sexual preferences or activities
- disabilities covered by the Americans with Disabilities Act, or

State Employee Polygraph Examination Laws (continued)

- activities that occurred more than five years before the examination, except for felony convictions and violations of the state drug control act.

(There is an exception where the examination is part of an investigation of illegal activity in one of the above subject areas.)

What's required: Prospective examinee must be told if examiner is a law enforcement or court official and informed that any illegal activity disclosed may be used against examinee. Must receive and sign a written notice of rights including:

- right to refuse to take the test or to answer any question
- right to terminate examination at any time
- right to request an audio recording of examination and pretest interview, and
- right to request examination results within 30 days of taking it.

Vermont

Vt. Stat. Ann. tit. 21, §§ 494 to 494e

Employers covered: All

Exceptions: Employers whose primary business is sale of precious metals, gems, or jewelry; whose business includes manufacture or sale of regulated drugs and applicant's position requires contact with drugs; employers authorized by federal law to require a test.

What's prohibited: Employer may not request, require, administer, or attempt or threaten to administer a lie detector test. May not request or require that employee or applicant sign waiver of any action prohibited by state law. May not discriminate against employee who files a complaint of violation of laws. When testing is allowed, no questions may be asked about:

- political, religious, or labor union affiliations
- sexual practices, social habits, or marital relationship (unless clearly related to job performance), or
- any matters unrelated to job performance.

What's required: Prior to taking test examinee must receive a copy of state laws and a copy of all questions to be asked. Must be told that any information disclosed could be used against examinee or made available to employer, unless there is a signed written agreement to the contrary. Examinee must be informed of rights including:

- right to accept or refuse to take examination
- right to refuse to answer any questions or give any information
- right to stop examination at any time, and
- right to a copy of examination results and of any reports given to employer.

Virginia

Va. Code Ann. § 40.1-51.4:3

Employers covered: All

What's prohibited: Employer may not require an applicant to answer questions about sexual activities in a polygraph test, unless the sexual activity resulted in a conviction for violation of state law.

What's required: Any record of examination results must be destroyed or maintained on a confidential basis, open to inspection only upon agreement of the employee.

State Employee Polygraph Examination Laws (continued)

Washington

Wash. Rev. Code Ann. § 49.44.120

Employers covered: All

Exceptions: Applicant or employee who manufactures, distributes, or dispenses controlled substances, or who works in a sensitive position directly involving national security.

What's prohibited: Employer may not require, directly or indirectly, that an employee or applicant take a lie detector test.

West Virginia

W.Va. Code §§ 21-5-5a to 21-5-5d

Employers covered: All

Exceptions: Employees or applicants with direct access to controlled substances.

What's prohibited: Employer may not require or request, directly or indirectly, that an employee or applicant take a lie detector test; may not knowingly use the results of a lie detector test.

Wisconsin

Wis. Stat. Ann. § 111.37

Employers covered: All

Exceptions: Manufacturers or distributors of controlled substances; providers or designers of security systems and other security personnel; ongoing investigation.

What's prohibited: Employer may not directly or indirectly require, request, suggest, or cause an applicant or employee to take a lie detector test; may not use, accept, refer to, or inquire about the results of a test. May not take adverse employment action solely on the basis of test results or a refusal to take test. May not discriminate or retaliate against employee who files a complaint of violation of laws.

What's allowed: Wisconsin law allows testing in the same limited circumstances as the federal EPPA, with similar rules and restrictions on when and how the test is given.

Equal Pay Act (EPA)

Statute: 29 U.S.C. § 206(d)
To view the statutes, visit http://uscode.house.gov and select "Title 29" and "Chapter 8."

Regulations: 29 C.F.R. §§ 516, 1620, and 1621
To view the regulations, visit www.govinfo.gov and search "29 CFR 516," "29 CFR 1620," and "29 CFR 1621."

Overview of the EPA

The Equal Pay Act (EPA) requires employers to give men and women equal pay for equal work. Congress passed the EPA to combat "the ancient but outmoded belief that a man, because of his role in society, should be paid more than a woman." (*Corning Glass Works v. Brennan,* 417 U.S. 188, 195 (1974).) Despite its gender-specific origins, however, the EPA protects both men and women from wage discrimination based on sex.

Covered Employers

Most government and private employers must comply with the EPA. The EPA also applies to unions.

Government Employers

All state and local governments must comply with the EPA.

Most, but not all, federal government agencies and departments must comply, including:

- military departments that employ civilians (only the civilian employees are covered by the law; see "Covered Workers," below)
- all executive agencies
- the United States Postal Service and Postal Rate Commission
- the Library of Congress
- any unit of the judicial or legislative branch that has positions in the *competitive service* (only employees in these positions are covered by the law; see "Covered Workers," below), and
- *nonappropriated fund instrumentalities.*

Private Employers

Generally, a business is covered by the EPA if it has $500,000 or more in annual gross sales, or if it is involved in interstate commerce. Practically speaking, this means that nearly all businesses are covered: An employer engages in interstate commerce when workers produce or buy goods that have come from or will be sent to another state; transport goods or services interstate; sell products or services that have come from or will go to another state; and/or communicate across state lines as part of their job duties.

Definitions

Terms that appear in italics throughout this chapter are defined below.

Competitive service: Jobs in the executive branch of the federal government that are subject to the federal civil service laws. Jobs at certain agencies, including the Federal Bureau of Investigation and the Central Intelligence Agency, are not part of the competitive service.

Effort: The amount of physical or mental exertion a job generally requires. In determining how much effort a job requires, courts will take into account aspects of the job that are particularly stressful or tiring, as well as job factors that alleviate fatigue. Two jobs may require equal effort even if they require different types of effort.

Establishment: A distinct physical place of business (such as a factory or an office) rather than an employer's entire business or enterprise. Separate workplaces can constitute a single establishment if their operations are connected and personnel and pay decisions are made centrally.

Nonappropriated fund instrumentalities: Federal organizations that are under the jurisdiction of the armed forces and whose activities are conducted for the support, pleasure, recreation, or improvement of members of the armed forces. Employees of these organizations are paid with nonappropriated funds (funds that are not appropriated by Congress, but that are generated by military and civilian personnel of the Department of Defense).

Responsibility: The level of accountability a job carries. In assessing responsibility, courts consider how important a particular task is to the employer, as well as how much time a worker spends on that task. Examples of job tasks that require significant responsibility include supervising other workers, generating substantial revenues, or approving financial transactions.

Skill: The abilities or aptitudes required to perform a job. Skill includes experience, training, education, and ability. In determining whether two jobs require equal skill, courts look only at the skills actually required to do the job, not any additional skills the employees may happen to possess.

Willful violation: An employer commits a willful violation of the EPA if it violates the law knowingly or with reckless disregard as to whether its conduct was illegal.

Working conditions: The environment in which a job must be performed. Working conditions include physical surroundings, such as temperature, ventilation, and location, as well as hazards, like exposure to toxic chemicals or dangerous terrain.

Unions

The EPA prohibits unions from causing, or trying to cause, employers to violate the law's provisions. If, for example, a union seeks a collective bargaining agreement that sets higher pay scales for men than for women doing equal work, the union has violated the EPA.

Did You Know ...

- The Bureau of Labor Statistics (BLS) reports that women who worked full time in 2016 earned about 82 cents for every dollar earned by men who worked full time. This is an improvement of more than 20 cents since the Equal Pay Act was signed in 1963.
- When broken down by ethnicity, the pay gap is generally even wider for minority women.
- According to the BLS, women in these professions earned the highest pay in 2016, calculated as a weekly median: chief executives ($1,876), pharmacists ($1,839), nurse practitioners ($1,753), computer and information systems managers ($1,680), and lawyers ($1,619).
- When the EPA was passed, a number of states had labor laws that distinguished between men and women—for example, laws that prohibited women from working overtime, that required employers to give women (but not men) breaks during the workday, and that allowed employers to refuse to hire women for jobs that required heavy lifting. Some opponents of the EPA argued that these protective laws made it more expensive for employers to hire women, so employees felt justified in paying them a lower wage.

Covered Workers

The EPA protects all employees who work for a covered employer, as defined above, except:

- uniformed service members, even if they are employed by a federal agency that also has civilian employees, and
- federal employees of the judicial or legislative branch of government, unless they are in the competitive service.

What's Prohibited

Employers are prohibited from paying workers of one sex more than workers of the opposite sex to do equal work.

Key Facts

- Most employers are covered by the Equal Pay Act. Unlike most antidiscrimination statutes, the EPA's application depends on the type and volume of business your company does, not the number of employees it has.
- The EPA requires companies to compensate men and women who do equal work at the same pay rate.
- Jobs qualify as "equal work" if they require substantially equal skill, effort, and responsibility, and if they are performed under similar working conditions.

What's Required

Employers must give equal pay to men and women for doing equal work. However, the equal pay requirement applies only to those working in substantially similar jobs, as defined by the EPA. And the EPA requires only that workers performing equal work be paid at the same pay rate, not that workers receive the same total amount of pay.

Equal Work

Male and female employees are entitled to equal pay even if their jobs are not identical. The equal pay requirement applies when the jobs are substantially equal—that is, the jobs require substantially equal *skill*, *effort*, and *responsibility*, and are performed under similar *working conditions* within the same *establishment*.

Two jobs may constitute equal work even if they require different types of skill, effort, or responsibility. For example, if two employees work as salespeople in a retail establishment and each has some additional responsibilities—one to keep the financial books and the other to supervise temporary sales help—a court might find that their jobs require equal responsibility, even though each has a different type of responsibility.

Generally, however, courts will find that two jobs constitute equal work only where they are quite similar. Although operating a jackhammer might require as much effort and skill as drafting detailed architectural designs, no court would find that these two jobs are equal work requiring equal pay.

Job titles do not determine whether two jobs are substantially equal. Courts will look at the actual tasks a worker must perform rather than the job description or designation. For example, an employer may not pay a male "administrative assistant" more than a female "secretary" if both do essentially the same tasks.

Equal Pay and Benefits

The EPA requires more than equal wages. If employees do equal work, they are also entitled to equal fringe benefits, such as insurance coverage, pensions, and use of a company car. And the EPA applies to other forms of compensation, such as vacation time, profit sharing, and bonuses.

However, the EPA requires only that employers pay workers at the same rate, not that they pay workers the same amount of total wages. If an employer pays on commission or by the piece, for example, the employer must use the same formula—such as 10% of the company's gross profit per sale or $1 per unit produced—to calculate pay for men and women. If one worker earns more than another because of higher productivity (making more sales or turning out more units), that does not violate the EPA.

Financial incentives for good performance work the same way. An employer may not offer men the opportunity to earn a bonus for high sales volume or productivity while denying the same opportunity to women. However, if a bonus is offered on the same fair terms to all employees and the only workers who meet the criteria for the bonus are men, an employer may legally pay the bonus to those men only.

Exceptions

There are four exceptions to the EPA. An employer may pay workers of one sex at a higher rate than workers of the opposite sex for doing equal work only if the difference is based on one of these factors:

- **Seniority.** An employer may pay more to workers who have been with the company longer, even if this results in workers of one sex getting paid more to do the same job.
- **Merit.** An employer may pay higher rates (by giving larger bonuses or performance-based raises, for example) to workers whose performance is better, regardless of gender.
- **Quantity or quality of production.** An employer may pay a higher rate for better quality work or pay workers based on their productivity (by the piece or on commission, for example), as long as both men and women have the opportunity to earn this higher rate.
- **Any factor other than sex.** This catchall exception is intended to encompass any legitimate reason why an employer might pay one worker more than another to do the same job, as long as that discrepancy isn't based on the workers' genders. It would not violate the EPA for an employer to pay a shift premium to all workers on the night shift, for example.

How the EPA Is Enforced

Individual Complaints

An employee who wants to file a complaint against an employer for violating the EPA can file a charge (also called a complaint) of discrimination with the Equal Employment Opportunity Commission (EEOC). (See Appendix A for contact information.)

However, an employee is not required to file a charge with the EEOC. Instead, the employee may bypass the agency and go straight to state or federal court to file a lawsuit.

The employee must file a lawsuit within two years after the employer violated the EPA. This time limit is extended to three years if the employer committed a *willful violation* of the law. These time limits can be extended if the employee did not know about the violation because the employer lied about it or concealed it.

Agency Enforcement

The federal agency responsible for investigating EPA complaints is the EEOC. An employee usually initiates the investigation process by filing a charge of wage discrimination with the EEOC, although the agency can also act on its own initiative. The EEOC has the power to investigate, negotiate with employers, and bring lawsuits against employers to stop discriminatory practices.

Complying With the EPA

Reporting Requirements

There are no reporting requirements under the EPA.

Posting Requirements

All covered employers must post a notice regarding the EPA. Employers must post this notice in a prominent location, where it can be easily seen and read by employees and job applicants. The EEOC has created a poster, *Equal Employment Opportunity Is the Law*, which fulfills this requirement. You can download the poster in English, Spanish, Arabic, or Chinese from the EEOC's website. (See "Agency Resources," below.)

Record-Keeping Requirements

The EPA is part of the Fair Labor Standards Act (FLSA). Employers subject to the EPA must keep basic wage and hour records, as required by the FLSA. (For a detailed description of these requirements, see Chapter 7.)

In addition to general wage and hour records, employers subject to the EPA must also keep all records relating specifically to differences in pay between men and women. This includes documents that:

- describe or explain the basis for any difference in wages between men and women, and
- may help show whether that differential is based on a factor other than sex.

Examples of such records include:
- payment of wages
- wage rates
- job evaluations
- job descriptions
- merit systems
- seniority systems
- collective bargaining agreements, and
- pay practices.

Remedies

If a court finds that an employer has violated the EPA, the employer may be ordered to do any or all of the following:
- pay back wages, equal to the difference between what the employee actually earned and what employees of the opposite sex earned for doing equal work; an employee can collect up to two years' worth of back pay, or three years' worth if the employer committed a willful violation of the EPA
- pay an additional penalty (called "liquidated damages") equal to the entire back pay award, unless the employer can demonstrate that it acted in good faith and had reasonable grounds to believe that its conduct did not violate the EPA
- pay the employee's costs of suit and attorneys' fees, and
- change its pay policies to avoid further violations of the law. In making these changes, an employer may not reduce any employee's pay rate. Rather, the employer must raise the pay of employees who were underpaid.

Agency Resources

- A fact sheet and other EEOC resources on equal pay
  Facts About Equal Pay and Compensation Discrimination
  www.eeoc.gov/eeoc/publications/fs-epa.cfm

- The EEOC's compliance manual on wage discrimination
  Compensation Discrimination
  www.eeoc.gov/policy/docs/compensation.html

- A list of the addresses and phone numbers of EEOC offices throughout the United States
  EEOC Field Offices
  www.eeoc.gov/field/index.cfm

State Laws Relating to Equal Pay

Most states have their own equal pay laws, many of which mirror the EPA. However, in recent years, several states have amended their equal pay laws to strengthen protections for employees. Some state laws may consider a broader range of jobs to be equal or might shift the burden of proof to the employer to justify pay differentials. A handful of states and cities have also passed laws banning employers from asking job applicants about their salary history. These laws recognize that when employers make job offers based on an applicant's previous salary, pay inequality tends to follow women from job to job. To find out your state's equal pay laws, contact your state department of labor. (See Appendix A for contact information.)

Fair Credit Reporting Act (FCRA)

Statute: 15 U.S.C. §§ 1681 and following
To view the statutes, visit http://uscode.house.gov and select "Title 15,"
"Chapter 41," and "Subchapter III."

Regulations: 16 C.F.R. §§ 600.1 and following
To view the regulation, visit www.govinfo.gov and search "16 CFR 602."

16 C.F.R. § 660 (Furnisher Rule)
To view the regulation, visit www.govinfo.gov and search "16 CFR 660."

16 C.F.R. § 641 (Address Discrepancy Rule)
To view the regulation, visit www.govinfo.gov and search "16 CFR 641."

16 C.F.R. § 682 (Disposal Rule)
To view the regulation, visit www.govinfo.gov and search "16 CFR 682."

Overview of the FCRA

The Fair Credit Reporting Act (FCRA) has two goals:

- to protect the privacy of consumer credit and other information by restricting access to those who have a legitimate need for the information and requiring the consent of the person whose records are sought, and
- to ensure the accuracy of that information by giving people the right to see their *consumer reports* (and other records, in some circumstances); the right to know whether someone has decided not to give them credit, employment, housing, or other benefits based on that information; and the right to dispute information that is incorrect or incomplete.

To those ends, the FCRA imposes a number of legal obligations on *consumer reporting agencies,* such as credit bureaus and companies that provide background check services. For example, these agencies must allow individuals to dispute inaccurate information and must remove negative information, such as arrests or bankruptcies, from consumer reports after a certain period of time. The FCRA also imposes rules on other parties who order consumer reports to make important decisions. For example, a bank might consider someone's credit report in deciding whether to extend a loan; a landlord might hire an agency to call the former landlords of prospective tenants and ask whether the tenants have paid rent on time, damaged rental property, or been evicted; or an employer might hire a company to run detailed background checks on applicants for high-level positions. This chapter covers only the aspects of the FCRA that impose obligations on employers.

The FCRA places limits and obligations on employers that hire consumer reporting agencies to investigate prospective and current employees and independent contractors. The FCRA does not apply to investigations that the employer conducts in house (although other laws may apply; for example, some state laws restrict an employer's use of arrest or conviction records in making employment decisions).

In the context of employment, the FCRA has five main provisions:

- **Notice, authorization, and certification procedures.** Before seeking a consumer report or an *investigative consumer report* for employment purposes, employers must notify the employee, applicant, or contractor, in writing, that they want a report. In addition, they must obtain written authorization from that person before actually ordering the report. They must then verify to the consumer reporting agency that they have given notice and received authorization.

- **Address-checking procedures.** If an employer receives a notice of address discrepancy from a consumer reporting agency from which it has requested a report, the employer must take steps to make sure that the report it receives actually relates to the intended employee, applicant, or contractor.
- **Adverse action procedures.** Employers that take an adverse action based on a consumer report or an investigative consumer report must provide the subject of the report with specific types of information about both the report and the consumer reporting agency that provided it.
- **Disposal rules.** Employers that gather or use consumer reports or information must limit access to that information. They must also follow specified methods of destroying the information to prevent identity theft and other unauthorized uses of that information.
- **Furnisher rules.** Certain employers that provide information on current or former employees to credit reporting agencies must take steps to ensure the information is accurate and complete. If an employee disputes that information, the employer must investigate, inform the employee of its findings, and correct any inaccurate information.

Covered Employers

The FCRA covers all employers, including:
- the federal government
- state governments
- local and municipal governments, and
- private employers, regardless of size.

Covered Workers

The FCRA applies to anyone about whom the employer gathers information in a way covered by the FCRA. This means that any time an employer seeks a credit report or an investigative consumer report for employment purposes, the employer must comply with the FCRA.

Definitions

Terms that appear in italics throughout this chapter are defined below.

Accuracy: When information a *furnisher* provides to a *consumer reporting agency* about someone identifies the correct person and correctly reflects the terms of the relationship and the person's performance and other conduct with respect to the relationship.

Adverse action: Any decision made by an employer for *employment purposes* that negatively affects an employee or applicant. Examples include refusing to hire, refusing to promote, and firing.

Consumer report: In the context of employment, written or oral information that (1) will be used for *employment purposes*, (2) comes from a *consumer reporting agency*, and (3) relates to a person's:
- creditworthiness
- credit standing
- credit capacity
- general reputation
- personal characteristics, or
- lifestyle.

Examples of consumer reports include criminal background checks, educational history checks, and license checks.

Consumer reporting agency: A person or an entity that regularly provides *consumer reports* to third parties. Examples of consumer reporting agencies include credit bureaus, private investigators, records search firms, law firms, and background-checking services. Employers are not consumer reporting agencies. A state entity that is required to keep certain information as a matter of public record—for example, a court clerk—is not a consumer reporting agency, and any information it provides is not a *consumer report*.

Employment purposes: To use information to decide whether to hire, promote, reassign, or terminate someone. Although the term refers to employment, it extends to applicants and independent contractors as well as employees.

Definitions (continued)

Furnisher: An entity that provides information relating to consumers to a *consumer reporting agency* for inclusion in a *consumer report*. A furnisher does not include:

- an entity that provides information to a consumer reporting agency for the sole purpose of obtaining a consumer report (for example, an employer that provides an applicant's identifying information in order to pull the applicant's credit report)
- a consumer reporting agency
- the person who is the subject of the information, or
- a neighbor or friend, an associate, or another person who is acquainted with or has knowledge of the subject of the report, and who provides information about the person's character, general reputation, personal characteristics, or mode of living in response to a specific request from a consumer reporting agency.

Integrity: When information a *furnisher* provides to a *consumer reporting agency* about someone is substantiated by the furnisher's records when it is provided, and is provided in a form and manner designed to minimize the likelihood that the information may be incorrectly reflected in a consumer report.

Investigative consumer report: A *consumer report* based at least in part on personal interviews that go beyond simply verifying facts that the person has provided to the employer. To qualify as an investigative consumer report, the information must have been gathered by a *consumer reporting agency*. For example, if a consumer reporting agency calls a college to verify the degree an applicant earned, a written record of that phone call would not be an investigative consumer report. If, however, the agency called the applicant's professors to get their opinions about the applicant, a written record of those phone calls would be an investigative consumer report.

Notice of address discrepancy: A notice sent by a consumer reporting agency to someone who requested a consumer report, stating that there is a substantial difference between the address provided to request the report and the address in the agency's file for the consumer.

Legal Developments

- **Some states restrict employer use of credit reports.** In response to the economic downturn that began in 2008, some states (and cities) passed laws restricting an employer's right to use credit reports in making hiring decisions. To date, at least 11 states (California, Colorado, Connecticut, Delaware, Hawaii, Illinois, Maryland, Nevada, Oregon, Vermont, Washington, and the District of Columbia) have enacted legislation prohibiting employers from pulling credit reports on applicants or limiting how and when employers may use them in making hiring and other job decisions. Because these state laws are more restrictive, they trump the federal law.

- **Employers may be furnishers, too.** Most employer responsibilities under the FCRA are as users of consumer reports. But employers may also contribute to consumer reports if they furnish information to credit reporting agencies regarding current or former employees (for example, by providing payroll or other information about employees to an outside agency to which the employer has outsourced its unemployment processing or reference checking). Under rules that went into effect in 2010, employers that act as furnishers must take steps to ensure the accuracy and integrity of the information they provide. If a current or former employee disputes the information, the employer must investigate the dispute and correct any inaccurate information provided.

Did You Know ...

- When the FCRA was passed in 1970, there were no federal restrictions on access to consumer credit information, and there was no way for a person to challenge the information in his or her credit report.
- Before the FCRA was amended in 2003, the Federal Trade Commission (FTC), the agency then responsible for interpreting and enforcing the law, took the position that it applied to investigations of workplace misconduct. The FTC announced this interpretation in the "Vail letter," an opinion letter providing guidance on the law's application in response to a question from an attorney. After human resources professionals pointed out the problems this interpretation created for employers, the law was amended to create an exception for workplace investigations.
- A 2017 survey conducted by HR.com and commissioned by the National Association of Professional Background Screeners revealed that 96% of responding employers conduct at least one type of background screening on job applicants. Of those employers, 83% screen for all full-time positions.

Major Provisions of the FCRA

Notice, Authorization, and Certification Procedures

Employers must follow the procedures described in this section before obtaining a consumer report or an investigative consumer report on an applicant or employee.

Covered Employers

All covered employers are subject to these provisions.

Covered Workers

All covered workers are subject to these provisions.

Key Facts: Notice Procedures

- Employers may request a consumer report or an investigative consumer report on an applicant or employee only for employment purposes.
- Before requesting a consumer report on someone, an employer must notify that person properly, obtain his or her written authorization, and then verify to the consumer reporting agency that notice was given and authorization received.
- Before obtaining an investigative consumer report, an employer must make additional disclosures to the person about whom the report will be obtained.
- Certain exceptions to these requirements exist for employers in the trucking industry and employers hiring third parties to investigate alleged employee misconduct.

What's Prohibited

Employers may request a consumer report or an investigative consumer report only for employment purposes. For example, an employer that is fighting a union cannot request reports on pro-union employees if the purpose of getting the reports is to gain information to hamper the organizing effort.

Employers cannot request a consumer report or an investigative consumer report without notifying the subject of the report and receiving his or her written authorization. (For more on this, see "What's Required," below.)

What's Required

Before obtaining a consumer report or an investigative consumer report on a current or prospective employee or contractor, employers must:
- notify the subject of the report, in writing, that they want to obtain a report (the notice cannot include any other information)
- obtain the subject's written authorization before asking a consumer reporting agency for a report, and
- verify to the consumer reporting agency that they have notified the subject of the report and obtained written authorization.

Special Rules for Investigative Consumer Reports

In addition to following the rules described above, an employer that wants an investigative consumer report must give the following information to the subject of the report, in writing, within three days after requesting the report:

- a statement that the requested report is an investigative consumer report
- a statement briefly identifying the type(s) of information the report will contain—such as information about the individual's character, general reputation, personal characteristics, or way of life, and
- a statement that the individual has the right to submit a written request for complete and accurate information about the nature and scope of the investigation.

Special Rules for Medical Information

When an employer seeks medical information as part of a consumer report on an applicant, employee, or independent contractor, both of these additional rules apply:

- The information must be relevant to the employment.
- The employer must get specific written consent from the applicant, employee, or independent contractor that describes in "clear and conspicuous language" how the information will be used.

Exceptions

Investigations of Alleged Workplace Misconduct

When an employer uses an outside party (such as an investigative agency or a law firm) to investigate a suspected employee misconduct, violation of a law or regulation, or violation of a written employment policy, the investigation is excluded from the definition of "consumer report" under the FCRA. This means that the employer need not provide notice and obtain authorization before conducting such an investigation. To fall within this exception, the investigation must be employment related, and its results must not be disclosed to anyone except the employer and certain governmental entities.

This exclusion is significant because the FTC had previously interpreted the requirements of the FCRA to apply to third-party investigations into alleged workplace misconduct. Requiring employers to inform—and get the consent of—the employee under investigation before proceeding created a number of problems. For example, what if an employer was legally obligated to investigate a sexual harassment claim, but the employee accused of harassment refused to consent to the investigation? The FCRA was amended, in part, in response to these concerns.

The amendments do, however, require the employer to disclose a summary of the report if the investigation results in an adverse employment action. (For more on this, see "Adverse Action Procedures," below.)

The Trucking Industry

Unlike other employers, which must notify individuals in writing and receive written authorization, the trucking industry can meet the notice and authorization requirements by oral, written, or electronic means. This exception applies only to job applicants, not current employees or contractors, and only if none of the interactions between the applicant and employer prior to obtaining the report have been in person. If there is any in-person contact between the employer and the applicant, the exception doesn't apply. For example, if the applicant stops by the employer's office to pick up a job application, the employer must follow the standard written notice and authorization rules.

Address-Checking Procedures

An employer that receives a notice of address discrepancy from a consumer reporting agency after requesting a consumer report must take steps to verify the identity of the subject of the report.

Covered Employers

All covered employers are subject to these provisions.

Covered Workers

All covered workers are subject to these provisions.

Key Facts: Address-Checking Procedures

- Once an employer receives a notice of address discrepancy, it must follow reasonable procedures to determine that the report is actually about the person who was the subject of the requested report.
- An employer can do this by checking its own records, verifying the information with the employee or applicant, or verifying the information through third-party sources.
- The employer must report the employee or applicant's correct address back to the agency in certain circumstances.

What's Required

If an employer asks a consumer reporting agency for a consumer report on someone, it might receive a notice of address discrepancy from the agency. This notice means that the address the employer supplied for the subject of the requested report is substantially different from the address in the agency's file.

Once an employer receives a notice of address discrepancy, it must follow reasonable procedures sufficient to form a reasonable belief that the employee or applicant about whom it requested the report is the same person described in the report. There are no legally required procedures, but examples of reasonable procedures might include:

- comparing the information provided by the agency to information in its own records, such as change of address notifications or employment applications
- checking the information provided by the agency with a third party source, and
- verifying the information provided by the agency directly with the employee or applicant.

The employer might also have to provide the employee or applicant's correct address to the agency, but only if all of the following apply:

- The employer reasonably believes that the report it received from the agency related to the intended employee, contractor, or applicant.

- The employer establishes a continuing relationship with that person (for example, by hiring him or her).
- The employer regularly furnishes information to the agency in the ordinary course of business.

If all of these criteria are met, the employer must provide the address it has reasonably confirmed as accurate as part of the information it regularly furnishes to the agency, in the reporting period in which it establishes a continuing relationship with the employee, contractor, or applicant.

Adverse Action Procedures

If an employer takes adverse action against an individual as a result of information learned from a consumer report or investigative consumer report, the employer must take some additional steps.

Key Facts: Adverse Action

- Before taking adverse action against someone based on a consumer report, an employer must provide the person with a copy of the report and a copy of the CFPB's document summarizing a consumer's rights under the FCRA.
- After taking adverse employment action against someone based on a consumer report, an employer must provide the person with an "adverse action notice" that contains certain disclosures about the consumer reporting agency and the individual's rights.
- Certain exceptions to these requirements exist for employers in the trucking industry, national security investigations, and third-party investigations of alleged employee misconduct.

Covered Employers

All covered employers are subject to these provisions.

Covered Workers

All covered workers are subject to these provisions.

What's Required

If an employer takes adverse action against someone based on information in a consumer report or an investigative consumer report, the employer must make certain disclosures to that person both before and after the adverse action.

Pre-Adverse Action Disclosure

Prior to taking adverse action, the employer must give the subject of the report two documents:

- a copy of the report, and
- a copy of a document from the Consumer Financial Protection Bureau (CFPB) called *A Summary of Your Rights Under the Fair Credit Reporting Act.* (To learn how to download a copy of this document, see "Agency Resources," below.)

Adverse Action Disclosure

After taking adverse action against someone, the employer must give that person an adverse action notice. This notice can be oral, written, or electronic and must contain the following information:

- the name, address, and phone number of the consumer reporting agency that supplied the report
- a statement that the consumer reporting agency did not make the decision to take the adverse action and cannot give the individual the specific reasons for the adverse action
- a statement that the individual has a right to dispute the accuracy or completeness of the information in the report, and
- a statement that the individual has a right to request a free copy of the report from the consumer reporting agency.

Exceptions

Investigations of Alleged Workplace Misconduct

The FCRA imposes more limited obligations on employers when they hire an outside party to investigate an employee's alleged misconduct, violation of law or regulation, or violation of a workplace rule. When an employer takes adverse action against an employee based on the results of the investigation, the employer must only provide the employee with a summary of the investigation report. The summary should cover the "nature and substance" of the investigation that led to the adverse action, but need not disclose the sources of the information (for example, the names of witnesses who provided information).

National Security Investigations

If a federal agency or department requests a consumer report or an investigative consumer report for employment purposes, it does not have to comply with the adverse action procedures if the head of the department or agency states all of the following in writing:

- The report is part of a national security investigation.
- The agency or department has jurisdiction over the investigation.
- Negative consequences—including danger to life or physical safety, destruction of evidence, or flight from prosecution—will result if the agency or department complies with the standard adverse action procedures.

The Trucking Industry

Because it is difficult to correspond with applicants who are on the road, trucking companies are allowed to take adverse action without prior notice for applicants who applied by mail, phone, or electronic means. However, the employer must send the adverse action notice within three business days after taking the adverse action.

Proper Disposal of Consumer Information

The FCRA also requires any person or business that has consumer information to dispose of it properly. Regulations created by the FTC deal with the proper destruction of consumer information, including both paper and electronic reports and information identifiable as derived from those reports. These regulations are known as the "Disposal Rule."

Key Facts: The Disposal Rule

- Under the Disposal Rule, all businesses must properly destroy consumer reports and information derived from them in both paper and electronic formats.
- Businesses must use reasonable and appropriate methods to avoid unauthorized access to or use of such consumer information—for example, by shredding paper and erasing disks or computer files.
- Any business that fails to follow these rules can be held liable for resulting damages (for example, unauthorized credit card charges).

Covered Employers

All covered employers are subject to these provisions.

Covered Workers

All covered workers are subject to these provisions.

What's Required

The Disposal Rule requires all businesses to safeguard and eventually destroy consumer reports and any information derived from those reports—for example, a manager's handwritten notes based on a background check of a potential employee.

To comply with these rules, businesses should store consumer reports and other documents that include consumer information securely—for example, in a locked cabinet or under a closely guarded password if stored on computers or electronically. Businesses should also limit access to trusted people who have a legitimate need for the information.

When an employer no longer has a legitimate business reason to keep consumer reports and information, it must dispose of them properly, using a level of document destruction that is reasonable in the context of the business. For example, a small business with only a few employees might shred paper documents and erase or render unreadable computer files, discs, CDs, and the like, whereas a major corporation with a large human resources department might want to contract with a disposal service. If an employer does contract with a disposal service, however, it must exercise due diligence to make sure that the service's disposal methods comply with the Disposal Rule.

The Disposal Rule does not impose time limits for destroying consumer information. When determining when to destroy consumer information, employers must remember that they may need these reports long after they've rejected or accepted an applicant—for example, to refute an employment discrimination claim.

Rules for Employers That Provide Information

Employers don't just order consumer reports; they may contribute to these reports as well. When an employer provides information on its employees to outside agencies to which it has outsourced functions such as checking references or processing claims for unemployment, the employer may qualify as a furnisher. For example, an employer that outsources its background checks may also regularly provide information to the outside firm on its own current and former employees. The employer's information may then become part of the firm's consumer reports about those employees. In this situation, the employer is considered a "furnisher" of information, which means it must establish procedures to ensure the accuracy and integrity of the information it provides. If an employee disputes the information provided, the employer must investigate and take steps to correct inaccuracies.

Key Facts: Employers Who Furnish Information

- Employers that provide information on current or former employees to outside consumer reporting agencies (other than for the sole purpose of obtaining a consumer report) must take steps to ensure the accuracy and integrity of the information. Such steps include reasonable written policies and procedures appropriate to the nature, size, complexity, and scope of the employer's activities.
- An employer that furnishes information must conduct a reasonable investigation of disputes raised by the current or former employee who is the subject of the information. If the investigation reveals a problem with the information the employer provided, the employer must notify the employee and the consumer reporting agency to which it furnished the information.

Covered Employers

All covered employers are subject to these provisions.

Covered Workers

All covered workers are subject to these provisions.

What's Required

Employers that furnish information about current or former employees to consumer reporting agencies, other than for the purpose of obtaining a consumer report, have additional obligations under the FCRA. Among other things, furnishers must implement reasonable written policies and procedures to ensure the *accuracy* and *integrity* of that information. These policies and procedures must be appropriate to the nature, size, complexity, and scope of the employer's activities. The rules suggest that employers should identify potential problem areas, evaluate current procedures for supplying information, and modify procedures as necessary. Some of the topics an employer's policies might address are standard formats and procedures for compiling and providing information, record-keeping requirements, internal controls for making sure information is accurate, training, and oversight of outside service providers.

If a current or former employee disputes the information an employer has provided, the employer must conduct a reasonable investigation. The regulations deal primarily with creditors and the information they provide regarding debt, payments, credit accounts, and so on. However, the rules state that a furnisher must investigate disputes over the person's "performance or other conduct concerning an account or other relationship with the furnisher," as well as disputes regarding information provided that bears on the person's "creditworthiness, credit standing, credit capacity, character, general reputation, personal characteristics, or mode of living," both of which encompass the type of information an employer might supply to a third-party consumer reporting agency.

To raise a dispute, the employee must provide the employer with identifying information, the specific information the employee is disputing, why the employee disputes the information, and all supporting documentation or other information necessary to substantiate the dispute (such as a copy of the consumer report that includes the disputed information). The employer must conduct its investigation and report the findings to the employee within

30 days. If the employer determines that the information it furnished was inaccurate, it must promptly notify every agency to which the information was sent and provide the correct information.

Exceptions

The employer does not have to investigate a dispute if any of the following are true:
- The dispute relates only to identifying information, such as the employee's name, birth date, Social Security number, address, or phone number.
- The dispute relates only to the identity of past or present employers.
- The dispute relates to information provided by a different furnisher or information derived from public records.
- The dispute relates to inquiries or requests for a consumer report.
- The employee did not provide sufficient information for the employer to investigate.
- The dispute is substantially the same as one previously submitted by, or on behalf of, the employee.

How the FCRA Is Enforced

Individual Complaints

Individuals who believe an employer has violated the FCRA can sue the employer in federal district court within two years of the violation. If the employer gives false information to the individual about its obligations or actions under the FCRA, then the individual can bring the lawsuit within two years after discovering the information was false.

Individuals may also file a complaint with the Consumer Financial Protection Bureau (CFPB).

Agency Enforcement

The CFPB enforces the FCRA and can, on its own initiative, investigate and bring a civil action against anyone it suspects of violating the FCRA. (For information on how to contact the CFPB, see Appendix A.)

The states and several other federal agencies and departments also have the power to enforce this law. (See "Complying With the FCRA," below, for more information.)

Complying With the FCRA

Reporting Requirements

The FCRA imposes no reporting requirements, other than the obligation, in some instances, to report an employee or applicant's correct address to a consumer reporting agency, as explained in "Key Facts: Address-Checking Procedures," above.

Posting Requirements

The FCRA imposes no posting requirements.

Record-Keeping Requirements

The FCRA does not require any particular record keeping. The FCRA does, however, require proper safeguarding and destruction of consumer information. (See "Proper Disposal of Consumer Information," above.)

Remedies

The penalties for violating the FCRA depend on who is bringing the lawsuit—an individual, a consumer reporting agency, the CFPB, another federal agency, or a state.

Liability to Individuals

If an individual sues an employer over violations of the FCRA, the penalties the employer might face depend on whether the employer's actions were willful or negligent. A willful action occurs when the employer knowingly and intentionally violates the law. A negligent action occurs when the employer doesn't know that it is violating the law, but should know.

Willful Actions. If an employer is found guilty of willfully failing to comply with any of the FCRA's provisions, it must:

- pay either of the following: the actual damages that the person can prove he or she suffered, or statutory damages of at least $100 but not less than $1,000
- pay any punitive damages that the court might order, and
- pay the attorneys' fees and court costs of the person bringing the action.

Negligent Actions. If an employer is found guilty of negligently failing to comply with the FCRA, the employer will have to pay the individual actual damages, and attorneys' fees and court costs.

Liability to Consumer Reporting Agencies

An employer that misleads a consumer reporting agency must pay the agency either its actual damages or $1,000, whichever is greater.

Liability to the Consumer Financial Protection Bureau

If the CFPB investigates an employer and finds that it has repeatedly and knowingly violated the FCRA, the employer must pay a penalty of not more than $2,500 per violation.

Liability to Others

Other federal agencies (including the Federal Deposit Insurance Corporation and the National Credit Union Administration) and state governments may also investigate and penalize wrongdoers. Those penalties are beyond the scope of this book.

Agency Resources

- A guide for employers on how to follow the FCRA when doing background checks on employees

    Using Consumer Reports: What Employers Need to Know
    www.ftc.gov/tips-advice/business-center/guidance/using-consumer-reports-what-employers-need-know

- The document that employers must give to individuals as part of the disclosure before taking an adverse employment action based on a consumer report

  A Summary of Your Rights Under the Fair Credit Reporting Act
  www.consumer.ftc.gov/articles/pdf-0096-fair-credit-reporting-act.pdf
  (English)

  www.consumidor.ftc.gov/articles/spdf-0096-fair-credit-reporting-act.pdf
  (Spanish)

- Information about businesses' responsibilities under the FTC's Consumer Report Disposal Rule

  Disposing of Consumer Report Information? Rule Tells How
  www.ftc.gov/tips-advice/business-center/guidance/disposing-consumer-report-information-rule-tells-how

- The FTC's main webpage about the FCRA; includes links and recent highlights

  www.ftc.gov/enforcement/statutes/fair-credit-reporting-act

- Compliance information on the identity theft rule

  Fighting Identity Theft With the Red Flags Rule
  www.ftc.gov/tips-advice/business-center/privacy-and-security/red-flags-rule

State Laws Relating to Credit Reporting

Some states have their own fair credit reporting laws. To find out about the laws of your state, contact the state agency that handles consumer issues (often called the consumer protection agency or department of consumer affairs).

Fair Labor Standards Act (FLSA)

Statute: 29 U.S.C. §§ 201–219
To view the statutes, visit http://uscode.house.gov and select "Title 29,"
and "Chapter 8."

Regulations: 29 C.F.R. §§ 500 and following
To view the regulations, visit www.govinfo.gov and search "29 CFR 500."

Overview of the FLSA

The Fair Labor Standards Act (FLSA) regulates wages and hours, how much workers must be paid, how many hours they can be required to work, and the special rules that apply to younger workers.

The law includes provisions on:

- minimum wages
- hours worked
- overtime, and
- child labor.

Covered Employers

The FLSA applies to most employers, including:

- the federal government
- state and local governments
- companies with annual gross sales of at least $500,000
- businesses that engage in interstate commerce or the production of goods for interstate commerce—that is, businesses whose employees:
  - handle, sell, produce, or otherwise work on goods or materials that have come from, or will go to, another state; or
  - use the mail, telephone, or other equipment to communicate across state lines
- hospitals and businesses that are primarily engaged in institutional care of the sick, aged, or mentally ill, and
- preschools, elementary schools, secondary schools, and schools for mentally or physically disabled or gifted children.

Covered Workers

The FLSA applies to all employees of covered employers, set forth above. In addition, the FLSA applies to any employee who is engaged in interstate commerce or the production of goods for interstate commerce. Even if an employer is not covered by the FLSA, some of its employees may be protected under this test. And, many workers (see "Exempt Employees," below) are not entitled to minimum wage or overtime under the FLSA, even though they are covered by the law.

Definitions

Terms that appear in italics throughout this chapter are defined below.

Agriculture: All aspects of farming, including soil cultivation and tilling; dairy work; production, cultivation, growth, and harvest of agricultural or horticultural products; raising livestock, bees, poultry, or fur-bearing animals; and any incidental practices on a farm, including forestry, lumbering, preparation for market, and delivery to storage, market, or carrier.

Exempt employee: An employee who is not covered by the FLSA's minimum wage and/or overtime compensation provisions.

Independent contractor: Someone who performs services for another person or business under contract, not as an employee. In determining whether a worker is an independent contractor rather than an employee, courts consider whether the worker has the right to control how to do the job, whether the worker has an opportunity for profit or loss depending on the worker's skill, whether the worker has invested in equipment or material or hired helpers, whether the worker's job requires special skills, the permanence of the work relationship, and whether the worker's job constitutes an essential part of the employer's business.

Outside salespeople: Employees who customarily and regularly work away from the employer's business selling, or taking orders to sell, goods, services, or the use of facilities.

Primary duty: The major, main, principal, or most important duty an employee performs.

Willful violation: A violation of the FLSA committed by an employer that knew its conduct was illegal or showed reckless disregard as to whether its conduct violated the law.

Legal Developments

- **Tip pooling rules.** In 2018, the FLSA was amended to clarify the rules around tip pooling. For many years, a Department of Labor regulation prohibited employers from including "back of house" staff—such as dishwashers and cooks—in tips pools. However, the new law allows this practice as long as the employer does not take a tip credit (discussed below).
- **Salary threshold for "white collar" exemptions.** In 2015, the Department of Labor passed a new regulation that would significantly increase the minimum weekly salary that executive, administrative, and professional employees would need to make in order to qualify as exempt from the FLSA's minimum wage and overtime requirements. This rule would have made a substantial number of employees eligible for overtime pay. However, the rule was blocked by a federal court in 2016, and the Department of Labor announced plans to issue a new rule that would propose a more modest increase to the salary threshold.

Exempt Employees

The minimum wage and overtime requirements of the FLSA do not apply to every worker whom the law covers. Some workers, called *exempt employees*, are not entitled to minimum wage or overtime, although they are still protected by the rest of the FLSA's provisions.

Employers of exempt workers remain covered by the FLSA as far as the rest of their workforce is concerned; they have to pay minimum wage and overtime to their nonexempt employees (those who do not fall within one of the exceptions listed below). They must also follow the FLSA's record-keeping and child labor requirements.

The following workers are exempt from the FLSA's minimum wage and overtime rules:

- executive, administrative, and professional employees who are paid on a salary basis (see "Salaried Executive, Administrative, and Professional Employees," below)
- independent contractors
- outside salespeople

- certain computer specialists—systems analysts, programmers, and software engineers who earn at least $27.63 an hour or $455 a week
- employees of seasonal amusement or recreational businesses, like ski resorts or county fairs
- employees of organized camps or religious and nonprofit educational conference centers that operate fewer than seven months a year
- employees of certain small newspapers and newspaper deliverers
- workers engaged in fishing operations
- seamen on international vessels
- employees who work on small farms
- certain switchboard operators, and
- casual domestic babysitters and persons who provide companionship to those who are unable to care for themselves. (This exemption applies only to those who are employed directly by the family—not by a third-party agency, for example—and whose duties are limited to companionship, such as watching television together, engaging in hobbies, or taking walks. Although the exemption still applies to companions who spend a limited amount of time helping with personal care, such as dressing and bathing, these activities may not take up more than 20% of the companion's time. And, someone who performs medical tasks or does chores that benefit other members of the household—such as laundry, preparing meals, or cleaning—are not covered by the exemption.

In addition, certain workers are exempt from the FLSA's overtime provisions only. (For details, see "Overtime," below.)

Salaried Executive, Administrative, and Professional Employees

Probably the most commonly used and most confusing exemptions to the FLSA's overtime and minimum wage requirements are for "white collar workers"—executive, administrative, and professional employees who are paid on a salary basis. To fall within one of these exemptions, an employee must meet two tests: a salary test and a job duties test.

Salary Test. To qualify as exempt administrative, executive, or professional employees, workers must earn a minimum weekly amount. The minimum threshold is currently $455 per week (or $23,660 per year). In 2015, the Department of Labor (DOL) passed a rule nearly doubling this threshold amount to $970 per week, which would have made millions of additional workers eligible for overtime. However, there was political opposition to the rule, and a federal court blocked it from taking effect in 2016. The DOL has since announced plans to propose a new rule that would increase the salary threshold by a more modest amount. The DOL is still in the rulemaking process, so until a final rule is passed, the weekly threshold remains at $455 per week.

Workers must also be paid on a salary basis in order to qualify for the exemption. Workers are paid on a salary basis if they receive their full salary for any week in which they perform any work, regardless of how many hours they work or the quality or amount of work they do.

An employer may not dock an exempt worker's pay for absences of less than a full week except under the following circumstances:

- for one or more full days when an employee is absent for personal reasons (other than sickness or disability)
- for one or more full days when an employee is absent due to sickness or disability, but only if the employer has a plan that compensates employees for this time off (such as disability insurance or a sick leave policy)
- to offset amounts that an employee receives in jury fees, witness fees, or military pay
- as a penalty imposed in good faith for violations of safety rules of major significance (that is, rules that prevent serious danger in the workplace), and
- for one or more full days when an employee has been suspended without pay due to a violation of workplace conduct rules (the disciplinary suspension must be imposed in good faith).

An employer may also make deductions for less than a full day's absence in the following circumstances:

- during the employee's first or last week of employment, and
- during weeks in which the employee takes unpaid leave under the Family and Medical Leave Act.

If an employer improperly docks a worker's pay (that is, the employer docks the worker's pay for reasons that don't fall within one of the exceptions listed above), the employer might have to pay overtime to all workers who (1) are in the job classification for which the improper deductions were made, and (2) report to the same manager who made the deductions. However, an employer will not face these consequences if either of the following is true:

- any improper deductions were isolated or inadvertent, and the employer reimburses the employees for the money improperly withheld, or
- the employer has a clearly communicated policy prohibiting improper deductions (including a complaint procedure), reimburses employees for the money improperly withheld, and makes a good-faith effort to comply with the law in the future.

Job Duties Test. An employee must perform certain job duties to qualify as an administrative, executive, or professional employee.

Administrative employees. An administrative employee's primary duty must be performing office or other nonmanual work directly related to the management of general business operations of the employer or the employer's customers. This work must include the exercise of discretion and independent judgment regarding matters of significance.

Executive employees. An executive employee must meet all of the following requirements:

- The employee's primary duty must be managing the company or a recognized department or subdivision of the company.
- The employee must customarily and regularly supervise at least two full-time employees (or the equivalent in part-time employees).
- The employee must have the authority to hire and fire, or the employee's recommendations as to hiring, firing, promotions, or any other change in employee status must be given particular weight.

Professional employees. There are two types of professional employees: learned professionals and creative professionals.

Learned professionals must meet all of these requirements:

- The employee's primary duty is performing work that requires advanced knowledge, is predominantly intellectual in nature, and requires the consistent exercise of discretion and judgment.
- The advanced knowledge is in a field of science or learning.
- The advanced knowledge is customarily acquired through a prolonged course of instruction.

Creative professionals must have the primary duty of performing work that requires invention, imagination, originality, or talent in a recognized artistic or creative field.

Did You Know ...

- The FLSA was enacted as part of President Franklin D. Roosevelt's New Deal. One purpose of the law was to create an incentive for employers to spread their work among more employees, which lawmakers thought would help the country recover from the Great Depression.
- The original minimum wage when the FLSA was enacted was 25 cents an hour.
- Under the National Industrial Recovery Act, which preceded the FLSA, businesses that voluntarily agreed to abolish child labor, pay a minimum wage, and limit work hours were allowed to display a "Blue Eagle" poster with the motto, "We Do Our Part."

Major Provisions of the FLSA

Minimum Wage

The FLSA sets the minimum wage for all covered employees. It includes special rules for workers who receive tips, younger workers, and workers who can be paid less than the minimum wage pursuant to certificates issued by the DOL.

Key Facts: Minimum Wage

- The federal minimum wage is $7.25. Most states impose a higher minimum wage.
- You can pay a lower minimum wage to certain workers, including teenagers, apprentices, and messengers, in some circumstances.
- In many states, you can pay tipped employees less than the minimum wage, as long as the tips they actually earn bring their hourly wage up to at least the minimum wage.

Covered Employers

All covered employers are subject to these provisions with regard to covered workers.

Covered Workers

All covered, nonexempt workers are subject to these provisions.

What's Required

Basic Minimum Wage Requirement

Employers must pay covered employees at least the federal minimum wage, which is $7.25 per hour. Employers are not required to pay employees by the hour, however. Employers may pay a salary, commission, or piece rate, for example, as long as the total amount paid divided by the total number of hours worked is equal to the minimum wage.

Each state is free to impose a higher minimum wage requirement, and most have done so. Many local governments have also passed minimum wage laws. The employer must pay whichever amount is higher, the federal, state, or local minimum wage. (See "State Laws Relating to Wages and Hours," below, for information on your state's law.) Some states also have additional rules for employers that pay by commission or piece rate.

Youth Minimum Wage

Employers may pay workers under the age of 20 a lower minimum wage for a few months. Employers must pay youth workers at least $4.25 an hour for the first 90 calendar days of their employment. Once the worker reaches the age of 20, the employer must pay the regular minimum wage ($7.25), even if the worker has not yet worked 90 days for the employer. Employers may not displace other employees or reduce their hours, wages, or benefits in order to hire workers who qualify for this lower wage.

Some states do not recognize or allow a separate minimum wage for younger workers. Employers doing business in such states must pay younger workers the same minimum wage as they pay everyone else.

Subminimum Wage Certificates

Employers may apply to the DOL for a certificate allowing them to pay certain workers a subminimum wage. The DOL can issue such a certificate only if necessary to prevent the curtailment of employment opportunities for these workers. Employers can apply for a certificate for the following employees:

- **messengers:** those employed primarily in delivering letters and messages for a company whose principal business is providing these delivery services
- **apprentices:** employees who are at least 16 years old and are employed to learn a skilled trade
- **full-time students:** students who are employed in retail, a service industry, or agriculture, or who work for the institution in which they are enrolled
- **student learners:** students who are receiving instruction in an accredited school and working part-time in a vocational training program
- **learners:** employees being trained for certain occupations for which skill, dexterity, and judgment must be learned, and who produce little or nothing of value when initially employed, and
- **disabled employees:** workers whose earning or productive capacity is impaired by a physical or mental disability. (For more on disability, see Chapter 2.)

Tipped Employees

If an employee makes at least $30 per month in tips, the employer may take a tip credit and pay that employee as little as $2.13 an hour. However, the employee's wage plus the tips the employee actually earns must add up to the minimum wage. Otherwise, the employer must make up the difference. Employers must give employees notice that they will take a tip credit, which includes:

- the hourly cash wage the employer will pay the employee
- the amount of tips that the employer will take as a tip credit (that is, the amount the employer will count toward the employee's wages, to meet the minimum wage requirement)
- that the employee is entitled to retain all tips received except any amount the employee is required to contribute to a valid tip pooling arrangement, and
- that the tip credit won't apply to any employee who has not been informed of these requirements.

This notice can be made orally, but the better practice is to put it in writing. Employers can require employees to participate in a tip pool under the FLSA. However, employers, managers, and supervisors cannot participate in the pool or keep any portion of the tips. For many years, federal regulations also prohibited employers from including "back of house" staff—such as dishwashers and cooks—from taking part in the tip pool. However, in 2018, the FLSA was amended to override this prohibition. Now, as long as the employer does not take a tip credit and pays employees the full hourly minimum wage, it may include back-of-house employees in a tip pool. Employers that take a tip credit and pay employees less than the full minimum wage per hour may not. Some states have more restrictive rules for tip pools, however, so check with your state's labor department. (See Appendix A for contact information.)

Several states do not allow employers to take a tip credit at all. Employers doing business in such states must pay tipped employees the same minimum wage as they pay everyone else. Other states allow employees to take a tip credit, but it is smaller than the federal tip crdit. In other words, the employer must pay more than $2.13 per hour but less than the regular minimum wage. (See "State Laws Relating to Wages and Hours," below, for information on each state's laws regarding tips.)

Deductions

The FLSA allows employers to withhold money from a worker's paycheck to satisfy a debt the worker owes the employer or to cover the cost of certain employment expenses (such as uniforms or tools). However, the employer may not deduct so much that the employee's earnings for the pay period drop below the minimum wage.

The FLSA makes an exception for deductions for room and board. An employer may deduct the reasonable cost of meals and housing provided to a worker, even if these deductions cause the worker's pay to fall below minimum wage. However, the employer can make such deductions only if all of the following requirements are met:

- The employer customarily pays the expenses.
- The items are provided for the benefit of the employee.
- The employee is told, in advance, about the deductions.
- The employee voluntarily agrees to accept less than the minimum wage in exchange for the food and lodging provided.

Some states do not allow employers to deduct certain expenses from an employee's paycheck.

Hours Worked

For purposes of the minimum wage and overtime rules, the FLSA requires employers to pay employees for any of their time that benefits the employer and that the employer controls. The rules for several common situations are set forth below, in "What's Required."

Key Facts: Hours Worked

- Although the FLSA doesn't require meal or rest breaks, many state laws do; some states also require employers to pay employees for this time.
- Whether an employee is entitled to pay for time spent on call depends on a number of factors, including where the employee must spend this time, how often the employee has to respond to calls, and what restrictions the employer places on the employee's use of this time.
- Employers don't have to pay for time an employee spends commuting to work but must pay for travel during the workday (for example, time spent traveling from one work site to another).

Covered Employers

All covered employers are subject to these provisions with regard to covered workers.

Covered Workers

All covered, nonexempt workers are subject to these provisions.

What's Required

Employers must pay employees for time that the employer controls. Conversely, employees are not entitled to be paid for time that they can spend as they wish. The FLSA does not provide much guidance on what constitutes work time, but the DOL and the courts have addressed some of the most common questions.

On-Call Time

Employers must pay employees for all of the time they spend on site waiting for work, even if they do not spend that time actually working. If employees are on call elsewhere, an employer must pay for those hours if the employees have little or no control over how they spend that time. The more restrictions an employer places on an employee on call, the more likely that employee is entitled to be paid. Courts will consider a number of factors to determine whether on-call time should be paid, including:

- **How many calls an employee gets while on call.** The more calls an employee has to respond to, the more likely he or she is entitled to pay, particularly if any of the calls require the employee to report to work or give advice or guidance over the phone.
- **How long an employee has to respond after a call.** If an employer requires employees to report in immediately after being paged, for example, such employees have a better argument that they should be paid for their time.
- **Where the employee can go while on call.** Employees who must stay within a limited distance from work are more likely to be entitled to compensation.
- **What the employee may do while on call.** If an employer sets a lot of rules for on-call workers, such as a ban on alcohol or a requirement that they respond quickly and in person to calls (which can be difficult if the employee is out running or taking the kids to school), the employer may have to pay for this time.

Meals and Breaks

Employers are not required to provide employees with any meal or rest breaks under the FLSA. However, if employers choose to offer breaks, they must follow certain rules. If an employer provides breaks of 20 minutes or less, employees must be paid for this time. Bona fide meal periods (typically 30 minutes or longer) can be unpaid, as long as the employee is relieved of all work duties during that time. For example, if an employee is required to sit by the phone to take calls, the meal period must be paid.

Many states require employers to provide workers with specified breaks or meal periods during the workday, and some states require that this time be paid. (For more information on state meal and rest break laws, see "State Laws Relating to Wages and Hours," below.)

Lactation Breaks

The FLSA requires employers to provide employees with reasonable breaks to express breast milk, for up to one year after the child's birth. These breaks may be unpaid. Employers must provide a private space, other than a restroom, for such purposes. Several states have laws regulating lactation breaks, which might be more beneficial to employees. (See "State Laws Relating to Wages and Hours," below.)

Sleeping Breaks

Employers must pay employees for any time during which they are allowed to sleep during a shift. However, if an employee has to be on duty for more than 24 hours at a time, the employer and employee may agree that eight of those hours will be for meals and sleep periods and will not be paid. If the employee has to actually work during that period, or is unable to get at least five hours of sleep because of work conditions, the eight hours must be paid.

Travel and Commuting

Commuting time—the time it takes a worker to get from home to the workplace—does not count as work time. However, an employer must pay employees for travel time that is part of the job—for example, if employees are required to go out on service or sales calls or have to drive from one work site to another during the workday.

Changing Clothes

Time employees spend putting on protective clothing or safety gear—such as hard hats, sanitary outer clothing, work boots, and so on—counts as work time, as does the time it takes an employee to walk from the changing area to the work area.

Overtime

Certain employees are entitled to overtime pay (time and a half) for each additional hour worked if they work more than 40 hours a week.

Key Facts: Overtime

- Nonexempt employees must be paid overtime if they work more than 40 hours in a week; a few states have stricter requirements, such as requiring overtime pay when employees work more than eight hours in one day.
- Compensatory time is generally illegal for private employers; however, employers can rearrange an employee's hours during the workweek to stay under the overtime threshold.

Covered Employers

All covered employers are subject to these provisions with regard to covered workers (see below).

Covered Workers

All covered, nonexempt workers are entitled to these protections, with the following exceptions:

- rail, air, and motor carrier employees
- employees who work as outside buyers of poultry, eggs, cream, or milk in their unprocessed state
- those who sell cars, trucks, farm implements, trailers, boats, or aircraft
- mechanics or parts persons who service cars, trucks, or farm implements
- announcers, news editors, and chief engineers of certain broadcasting stations
- local delivery drivers or drivers' helpers who are compensated on a trip rate plan
- agricultural workers
- taxi drivers
- movie theater employees, and
- domestic service workers who live in the employer's home. (This exemption applies only to workers who are employed directly by the family with whom they live, not to those employed by third-party agencies. Employers must still comply with record-keeping requirements for live-in domestic workers.)

What's Required

Employers must pay an overtime premium to covered employees who work more than 40 hours in a work week. Some states have more restrictive requirements, such as a daily overtime standard (when an employee works more than eight hours in a workday). (For information on your state's law, see "State Laws Relating to Wages and Hours," below).

The overtime premium is 50% of the employee's regular rate of pay. In other words, the employee is entitled to 1.5 times his or her regular rate of pay (also called "time-and-a-half") for any overtime hours worked. The employee's regular rate of pay includes all payments made by the employer, except for expense reimbursements, premium payments for overtime or weekend or holiday work, discretionary bonuses, gifts, and payments for occasional times when the employee performs no work (for example, for vacation, sick leave, or holidays).

Compensatory Time

Private employers may not give employees straight compensatory time (one hour off for every overtime hour worked) instead of overtime. Private employers that wish to provide time off rather than overtime pay have only two options. The first option is to adjust an employee's hours within each workweek so that the employee does not earn overtime (for example, by allowing an employee who has worked four ten-hour days to take the rest of the week off). However, this won't be legal in states that have a daily overtime standard.

The other option is to allow the employee to work overtime in week one, but reduce the employee's hours in the second week, in order to keep the employee's paycheck consistent. To do this, an employer would give the employee 1.5 hours off for every overtime hour worked. For example, if an employee worked 50 hours in the first week (10 of which were overtime hours), the employee would take 15 hours off in the second week.

Some state and local government employees are entitled to compensatory time; check with your state's department of labor for more information. (For contact information, see Appendix A.)

Child Labor

The FLSA regulates the employment of workers under the age of 18 by limiting the types of work they are legally allowed to do and the hours during which they can work.

Key Facts: Child Labor

- Employers may hire teenagers who are at least 16 to do any type of work that has not been deemed "hazardous" by the secretary of labor.
- Workers who are 14 or 15 may be hired to do certain types of work, but they can only work limited hours, particularly during the school year.
- The child labor laws don't apply to certain younger workers, including newspaper deliverers, child actors, and children who work for their parents.

Covered Employers

All covered employers are subject to these provisions.

Covered Workers

All covered workers are subject to these provisions.

What's Prohibited

The FLSA limits the types of jobs younger workers can do. These restrictions differ depending on whether the work is hazardous or agricultural.

Hazardous Work

The secretary of labor has the authority to designate certain occupations as hazardous for minors. These occupations include:

- mining
- driving or being an outside helper on a motor vehicle (those who are at least 17 may do certain jobs that require incidental or occasional driving, provided that the teens are properly licensed, have no moving violations, and meet a number of other requirements)
- working with explosives
- logging and sawmilling
- working with radioactive substances
- working with power-driven woodworking or paper products machines; hoisting equipment; and metal-forming, punching, and shearing machines
- slaughtering and meat packing
- manufacturing tile and brick

- working with power-driven bakery machines
- working with power-driven circular saws, band saws, or guillotine shears
- wrecking, demolition, and shipbreaking operations
- excavation operations, and
- roofing and other activities that take place on a roof, such as installing satellite dishes or working on gutters and downspouts.

Agricultural Work

Employers that own or operate a farm or another agricultural business must follow these rules:

- Children aged 16 and older may be hired to do any type of work, for unlimited hours.
- Children aged 14 or 15 may be hired to do any nonhazardous work, outside of school hours.
- Children aged 12 or 13 may be hired to do any nonhazardous work outside of school hours, but only if the child's parents work on the same farm or have consented in writing to the arrangement.
- Children aged ten or 11 may be hired to harvest crops by hand for no more than eight weeks per calendar year, but only if the DOL has granted the employer a waiver.
- Children of any age may be hired by their own parents or by a person standing in the place of their parents to do any type of agricultural work, if the parents own or operate the business.

Nonagricultural Work

Employers seeking younger workers for nonagricultural work must follow these rules:

- Children aged 16 and 17 may be hired to do any nonhazardous work, for unlimited hours.
- Children aged 14 and 15 may be hired to do certain retail, food service, and service station jobs; the regulations specify which types of jobs are acceptable. However, they may not work more than three hours per school day, 18 hours per school week, eight hours on a nonschool day, and 40 hours in a nonschool week. Also, they cannot begin work before 7 a.m. or end after 7 p.m. (except during the summer, when they can work until 9 p.m.).

Exceptions

Certain employees are not covered by the child labor laws. Such workers include:

- child actors or performers
- newspaper carriers
- children younger than 16 who are employed by their parents in an occupation other than mining, manufacturing, or another hazardous job, and
- children younger than 16 who are engaged in certain training and apprenticeship programs.

How the FLSA Is Enforced

Individual Complaints

An employee who wishes to file a complaint regarding the FLSA's minimum wage and overtime requirements has two choices. The employee may make a complaint to the Wage and Hour Division of the DOL (see "Agency Enforcement," below), or the employee may file a lawsuit in state court. A lawsuit must be filed within two years of the date the employer violated the law, or within three years if the employer committed a *willful violation*.

Only the DOL may enforce the FLSA's restrictions on child labor. This means that individual employees do not have the right to file a lawsuit alleging child labor violations.

Agency Enforcement

If an employee files a complaint with the DOL, the agency may choose to investigate the employer. Although the agency can also conduct random audits, investigations are much more likely following a complaint.

A DOL investigator may contact the employer ahead of time or may simply show up at the workplace. The investigator will examine the employer's records and interview employees who may have information relevant to the complaint. Once the investigation is complete, the investigator will meet with the employer to try to resolve any problems the investigation uncovered. The investigator will tell the employer whether it has violated the law, and how it can correct those violations—for example, by paying overdue wages to its workers.

If the employer refuses to comply, the secretary of labor can file a lawsuit in federal district court on behalf of the employees whose rights were violated. However, if the secretary of labor files a lawsuit on behalf of one or more employees, the employee no longer has the right to sue the company on his or her own. The secretary may also impose civil penalties against the employer; these penalties are assessed in an administrative hearing process, not a lawsuit, and they are paid to the government, not to the employee.

Complying With the FLSA

Reporting Requirements

The FLSA has no general reporting requirements. However, employers that apply for a subminimum wage certificate (see "Minimum Wage," above) or a waiver from the child labor laws (see "Child Labor," above) may have to provide certain information to the DOL.

Posting Requirements

All employers subject to the FLSA are required to post a notice (created by the DOL) describing the law's provisions. A copy of the notice must be posted conspicuously in each of the employer's establishments, where every employee can readily see it. This notice is available for free at the DOL's website. (See "Agency Resources," below.)

Employers that hire disabled workers at a subminimum wage pursuant to a certificate issued by the DOL (see "Minimum Wage," above) must post an official DOL notice about this program. This notice is available from the DOL free of charge. (See "Agency Resources," below.)

Record-Keeping Requirements

Employers must keep specified wage and hour records for each worker. Employers are not required to create or keep the records in any particular format, though.

The following records must be kept for three years:

- payroll records showing each employee's name, address, occupation, sex, birth date (if the worker is under the age of 19), hour and day when the workweek begins, total wages paid each pay period, and the date of the payment for each pay period
- plans, trusts, collective bargaining agreements, and individual employment contracts
- all certificates or notices required by the FLSA, and
- records showing the total dollar volume of the business and the total volume of goods purchased or received.

For employees who are entitled to overtime and/or the minimum wage, employers must keep these additional records for each employee for three years:

- total hours worked each day and week
- total daily or weekly earnings
- regular hourly pay rate in any week when the employee works overtime
- total overtime pay for each week, and
- any deductions from or additions to pay for each pay period.

For exempt employees, employers must keep records sufficient to calculate the employee's total compensation per pay period, including fringe benefits. These records, which must be kept for two years, include:

- time cards or other records showing workers' daily stop and start times
- records showing the amount of work accomplished by individual employees on a daily, weekly, or pay period basis, if those amounts affect the employees' wages (for example, if they are paid on commission or by piece rate)
- wage rate tables or other documents that show the rates used to compute piecework pay, straight time earnings wages, salary, or overtime pay
- order, shipping, and billing records, and
- records of additions to, or deductions from, wages paid, including records used by the employer to determine the original cost, operating cost, maintenance cost, depreciation, and interest charges, if these amounts are used to determine additions to or deductions from wages.

The regulations require employers to keep different types of records or additional records for certain types of employees, such as local delivery workers, seamen, and tipped employees. For more information on these requirements, see 29 C.F.R. § 516, which sets forth the FLSA's record-keeping requirements in detail.

Remedies

If a court finds that an employer has violated the FLSA, it may order the employer to pay the employee:

- Retroactive wages (called back pay), equal to the difference between what the employee actually earned and what the employee should have earned if the employer had followed the law, plus interest. An employee can collect up to two years' worth of back pay, or three years' worth if the employer committed a willful violation of the statute.
- An additional penalty (known as "liquidated damages"), equal to the entire back pay award, if the employer willfully violated the statute.

For violations of the child labor laws, employers may face penalties of over $55,000, depending on the type of violation. These penalties are assessed in an administrative hearing and paid to the government.

Agency Resources

- A guide to the FLSA's requirements
  Elaws—Fair Labor Standards Act Advisor
  www.dol.gov/elaws/flsa.htm

- The rules on employing minors in nonagricultural jobs
  Child Labor Bulletin 101
  www.dol.gov/whd/regs/compliance/childlabor101.pdf

- A fact sheet on calculating overtime pay
  Overtime Pay Requirements of the FLSA
  www.dol.gov/whd/regs/compliance/whdfs23.pdf

- A fact sheet on what types of activities count as work
  Hours Worked Under the Fair Labor Standards Act (FLSA)
  www.dol.gov/whd/regs/compliance/whdfs22.pdf

- A fact sheet on employees exempt from overtime and minimum wage laws
  Exemption For Executive, Administrative, Professional, Computer & Outside Sales Employees Under the Fair Labor Standards Act (FLSA)
  www.dol.gov/whd/overtime/fs17a_overview.pdf

- A guide to the FLSA's record-keeping rules
  Recordkeeping Requirements under the Fair Labor Standards Act (FLSA)
  www.dol.gov/whd/regs/compliance/whdfs21.pdf

- Poster on the FLSA that employers are required to display
  Employee Rights Under the Fair Labor Standards Act
  www.dol.gov/whd/regs/compliance/posters/minwagebw.pdf

- Poster employers must display if they employ disabled workers at subminimum wage
  Employee Rights for Workers with Disabilities Paid at Subminimum Wages
  www.dol.gov/regs/compliance/posters/disabc.pdf

- A list of the addresses and telephone numbers of local offices of the Wage and Hour Division
  Wage and Hour Division (WHD): WHD Local Offices
  www.dol.gov/whd/local

State Laws Relating to Wages and Hours

Most states have their own wage and hour laws, and some of them are almost as extensive as the FLSA. Here, you'll find the state rules on minimum wage, tip credits, overtime, and meal and rest breaks. However, to find out whether your state has rules on child labor, exempt versus nonexempt employees, or other wage and hour issues, contact your state labor department.

State Minimum Wage Laws for Tipped and Regular Employees

The chart below gives the basic state minimum wage laws. Depending on the occupation, the size of the employer's business, or the conditions of employment, the minimum wage may vary from the one listed here. Minimum wage rates in a number of states change from year to year; to be sure of your state's current minimum, contact your state department of labor or check its website. (See Appendix A for contact information.) Also, several local governments have enacted ordinances that set a higher minimum wage—contact your city or county government for more information. "Maximum Tip Credit" is the highest amount of tips that an employer can credit towards the employee's hourly wage. The "Minimum Cash Wage" is the lowest amount per hour that an employer can pay a tipped employee. A tipped employee's hourly wages plus actual tips cannot be less than the state minimum wage.

State and Statute	Notes	Basic Minimum Hourly Rate (*=tied to federal rate)	Maximum Tip Credit	Minimum Cash Wage for Tipped Employee	Minimum Tips to Qualify as a Tipped Employee (monthly unless noted otherwise)
United States 29 U.S.C. § 203; 29 U.S.C. § 206		$7.25	$5.12	$2.13	More than $30
Alabama	No minimum wage law				
Alaska Alaska Stat. § 23.10.065	Adjusts annually for inflation, posted at http://labor.alaska.gov/lss/whact.htm	$9.89	No tip credit	$9.89	N/A
Arizona Ariz. Rev. Stat. § 23-363	Adjusts annually for inflation, posted at www.azica.gov/labor-minimum-wage-main-page; does not apply to small businesses (those with gross revenue of less than $500,000 that are exempt from federal minimum wage laws)	$11 ($12 on January 1, 2020)	$3.00	$8 ($9 on January 1, 2020)	
Arkansas Ark. Code Ann. §§ 11-4-210 and 11-4-212	Applies to employers with 4 or more employees	$9.25 ($10 on January 1, 2020; $11 on January 1, 2021)	$6.82 (increases as minimum wage increases)	$2.63	More than $20

State Minimum Wage Laws for Tipped and Regular Employees (continued)

State and Statute	Notes	Basic Minimum Hourly Rate (*=tied to federal rate)	Maximum Tip Credit	Minimum Cash Wage for Tipped Employee	Minimum Tips to Qualify as a Tipped Employee (monthly unless noted otherwise)
California *Cal. Lab. Code § 1182.12*		Employers with 25 or fewer employees: $11 ($12 on January 1, 2020; $13 on January 1, 2021; $14 on January 1, 2022). Employers with 26 or more employees: $12 ($13 on January 1, 2020; $14 on January 1, 2021; $15 on January 1, 2022).	No tip credit	Same as for non-tipped employees	N/A
Colorado *Colo. Const. Art. 18, § 15; 7 Colo. Code Regs. § 1103-1:3*	Adjusted annually for inflation, posted at www.coworkforce.com	$11.10 ($12 on January 1, 2020)	$3.02	$8.08 ($8.98 on January 1, 2020)	More than $30
Connecticut *Conn. Gen. Stat. Ann. §§ 31-58(j), 31-60; Conn. Admin. Code § 31-61-E2*		$10.10	36.8% for wait staff in hotel and restaurant industries; 18.5% for bartenders	$6.38 for wait staff in hotel and restaurant industries; $8.23 for bartenders (increases as minimum wage increases)	$10 per week (full-time employees); $2 per day (part-time employees)

State Minimum Wage Laws for Tipped and Regular Employees (continued)

State and Statute	Notes	Basic Minimum Hourly Rate (*=tied to federal rate)	Maximum Tip Credit	Minimum Cash Wage for Tipped Employee	Minimum Tips to Qualify as a Tipped Employee (monthly unless noted otherwise)
Delaware *Del. Code Ann. tit. 19, § 902(a)*		$8.75 ($9.25 on October 1, 2019)	$6.02 (increases as minimum wage increases)	$2.23	More than $30
District of Columbia *D.C. Code Ann. § 32-1003*	Adjusted for inflation annually beginning in 2021	$13.25 ($14 on July 1, 2019; $15 on July 1, 2020)	$9.17 (increases as minimum wage increases)	$3.89 ($4.45 on July 1, 2019; $5 on July 1, 2020)	Not specified
Florida *Fla. Const., Art. X § 24; Fla. Stat. Ann. § 448.110*	Adjusted annually for inflation, posted at www.floridajobs.org	$8.46	$3.02	$5.44	More than $30
Georgia *Ga. Code Ann. § 34-4-3*	Applies to employers with 6 or more employees and more than $40,000 per year in sales	$5.15 if not covered by Federal Regulations, otherwise Federal Minimum Wage	Minimum wage does not apply to tipped employees	N/A	N/A
Hawaii *Haw. Rev. Stat. §§ 387-1 to 387-2*		$10.10	75¢ in 2016 and beyond, but only if the employee makes at least $7 more than minimum wage with tips	$9.35	More than $20
Idaho *Idaho Code §§ 44-1502; 44-1503*		$7.25	$3.90	$3.35	More than $30

State Minimum Wage Laws for Tipped and Regular Employees (continued)

State and Statute	Notes	Basic Minimum Hourly Rate (*=tied to federal rate)	Maximum Tip Credit	Minimum Cash Wage for Tipped Employee	Minimum Tips to Qualify as a Tipped Employee (monthly unless noted otherwise)
Illinois *820 Ill. Comp. Stat. § 105/4; Ill. Admin. Code tit. 56, § 210.110*	Applies to employers with 4 or more employees (and all employers with respect to domestic workers)	$8.25	40%	$4.95	At least $20
Indiana *Ind. Code Ann. § 22-2-2-4*	Applies to employers with 2 or more employees	$7.25*	$5.12	$2.13	Not specified
Iowa *Iowa Code § 91D.1*		$7.25	40%	$4.35	At least $30
Kansas *Kan. Stat. Ann. § 44-1203*	Applies to employers not covered by the FLSA	$7.25	$5.12	$2.13	Not specified
Kentucky *Ky. Rev. Stat. Ann. § 337.275*		$7.25*	$5.12	$2.13	More than $30
Louisiana	No minimum wage law				
Maine *Me. Rev. Stat. Ann. tit. 26, §§ 663(8), 664*	Indexed annual increases begin on January 1, 2021	$11 ($12 on January 1, 2020)	50%	$5.50 ($6 on January 1, 2020)	More than $30
Maryland *Md. Code Ann., [Lab. & Empl.] §§ 3-413, 3-419*		$10.10	$6.47 (increases as minimum wage increases)	$3.63	More than $30
Massachusetts *Mass. Gen. Laws ch. 151, § 1; Mass. Regs. Code tit. 454, § 27.03*		$12 ($12.75 on January 1, 2020; $13.50 on January 1, 2021; $14.25 on January 1, 2022)	$7.65 ($7.80 on January 1, 2020; $7.95 on January 1 2021; $8.10 on January 1, 2022)	$4.35 ($4.95 on January 1, 2020; $5.55 on January 1, 2021; $6.15 on January 1, 2022)	More than $20

State Minimum Wage Laws for Tipped and Regular Employees (continued)

State and Statute	Notes	Basic Minimum Hourly Rate (*=tied to federal rate)	Maximum Tip Credit	Minimum Cash Wage for Tipped Employee	Minimum Tips to Qualify as a Tipped Employee (monthly unless noted otherwise)
Michigan *Mich. Comp. Laws §§ 408.931 and following*	Applies to employers with 2 or more employees. Adjusted for inflation annually beginning in 2023.	$10 ($10.65 on January 1, 2020; $11.35 on January 1, 2021; $12 on January 1, 2022)	$5.20 (decreases as minimum cash wage increases, see next column)	48% of the minimum wage, which is $4.80 (percentage increases to 60% of the minimum wage in 2020, 70% in 2021, and 80% in 2022)	Not specified
Minnesota *Minn. Stat. Ann. § 177.24*	Indexed annual increases began on January 1, 2018	$9.89 for large employers; $8.04 for small employers (businesses with annual gross volume of sales of less than $500,000)	No tip credit	Same as for non-tipped employees	N/A
Mississippi	No minimum wage law				
Missouri *Mo. Rev. Stat. §§ 290.502, 290.512*	Adjusted annually according to cost of living	$8.60 ($9.45 on January 1, 2020; $10.30 on January 1, 2021; $11.15 on January 1, 2022)	50% of the minimum wage	$4.30 (increases as minimum wage increases)	Not specified
Montana *Mont. Code Ann. §§ 39-3-404, 39-3-409; Mont. Admin. R. 24.16.1508 & following*	Adjusted annually; posted at http://erd.dli.mt.gov/labor-standards/ wage-and-hour-payment-act/minimum-wage-history	$8.50 ($4.00 for businesses with gross annual sales of $110,000 or less)	No tip credit	$8.50	N/A

State Minimum Wage Laws for Tipped and Regular Employees (continued)

State and Statute	Notes	Basic Minimum Hourly Rate (*=tied to federal rate)	Maximum Tip Credit	Minimum Cash Wage for Tipped Employee	Minimum Tips to Qualify as a Tipped Employee (monthly unless noted otherwise)
Nebraska *Neb. Rev. Stat. § 48-1203*	Applies to employers with 4 or more employees	$9.00	$6.87	$2.13	Not specified
Nevada *Nev. Rev. Stat. Ann. §§ 608.100, 608.160, 608.250; Nev. Admin. Code § 608.100; Nev. Const. Art. 15 § 16*	Adjusted annually, posted at labor.nv.gov	$7.25 if employer provides health benefits; $8.25 if no health benefits provided	No tip credit	$7.25 if employer provides health benefits; $8.25 if no health benefits provided	N/A
New Hampshire *N.H. Rev. Stat. Ann. § 279:21*		$7.25*	55%	45%	More than $30
New Jersey *N.J. Stat. Ann. § 34:11-56a4*	Adjusted annually based on consumer price index; posted at http://lwd.dol.state.nj.us/labor	$8.85*	$6.72	$2.13 (suggested, not required)	Not specified
New Mexico *N.M. Stat. Ann. § 50-4-22*		$7.50	$5.37	$2.13	More than $30
New York *N.Y. Lab. Law § 652*	Indexed Annual Increases from 12/31/2018 to $12.50 by 12/31/2020. (Beginning January 1, 2021, the rate will be adjusted annually for inflation until it reaches $15 an hour.)	$11.10 ($11.80 on December 31, 2019)	Depends on occupation. See www.labor.ny.gov/legal/counsel/pdf/tips-frequently-asked-questions.pdf	Depends on occupation	Depends on occupation

State Minimum Wage Laws for Tipped and Regular Employees (continued)

State and Statute	Notes	Basic Minimum Hourly Rate (*=tied to federal rate)	Maximum Tip Credit	Minimum Cash Wage for Tipped Employee	Minimum Tips to Qualify as a Tipped Employee (monthly unless noted otherwise)
North Carolina *N.C. Gen. Stat. §§ 95-25.2(14), 95-25.3*		$7.25	$5.12	$2.13	More than $20
North Dakota *N.D. Cent. Code § 34-06-22; N.D. Admin. Code R. 46-02-07-01 to -03*		$7.25	33% of minimum wage	$4.86	More than $30
Ohio *Ohio Rev. Code Ann. § 4111.02; Ohio Const. art. II § 34a*	Adjusted annually, posted at www.com. ohio.gov/dico	$8.55 ($7.25 for employers with gross income under $314,000)	50%	$4.30	More than $30
Oklahoma *Okla. Stat. Ann. tit. 40, §§ 197.2, 197.4, 197.16*	Applies to employers that are not covered by the FLSA and that have more than 10 full-time employees or more than $100,000 in gross annual sales	$7.25	50% of minimum wage for tips, food, and lodging combined	$3.63	Not specified
Oregon *Or. Rev. Stat. §§ 653.025, 653.035(3)*	Adjusted annually; posted at www.boli. state.or.us	$10.75 ($11.25 on July 1, 2019; $12 on July 1, 2020; $12.75 on July 1, 2021; $13.50 on July 1, 2022)	No tip credit	$10.75 ($11.25 on July 1, 2019; $12 on July 1, 2020; $12.75 on July 1, 2021; $13.50 on July 1, 2022)	N/A

State Minimum Wage Laws for Tipped and Regular Employees (continued)

State and Statute	Notes	Basic Minimum Hourly Rate (*=tied to federal rate)	Maximum Tip Credit	Minimum Cash Wage for Tipped Employee	Minimum Tips to Qualify as a Tipped Employee (monthly unless noted otherwise)
Pennsylvania 43 Pa. Cons. Stat. Ann. §§ 333.103 and 333.104; 34 Pa. Code §§ 231.1 and 231.101		$7.25*	$4.42	$2.83	More than $30
Rhode Island R.I. Gen. Laws §§ 28-12-3 & 28-12-5		$10.50	$6.61	$3.89	Not specified
South Carolina	No minimum wage law				
South Dakota S.D. Codified Laws Ann. §§ 60-11-3 to -3.2	Adjusted annually based on cost of living; posted at http://dlr.sd.gov/employment_laws/minimum_wage.aspx	$9.10	50%	$4.55	More than $35
Tennessee	No minimum wage law				
Texas Tex. Lab. Code Ann. §§ 62.051 & 62.052		$7.25	$5.12	$2.13	More than $20
Utah Utah Code Ann. § 34-40-102; Utah Admin. R. 610-1		$7.25	$5.12	$2.13	More than $30
Vermont Vt. Stat. Ann. tit. 21, § 384(a); Vt. Code R. 24 090 003	Applies to employers with 2 or more employees; annual indexing began January 1, 2019, posted at www.vtlmi.info	$10.78	50% for employees of hotels, motels, restaurants, and tourist places	$5.39 (increases as minimum wage increases)	More than $120

State Minimum Wage Laws for Tipped and Regular Employees (continued)

State and Statute	Notes	Basic Minimum Hourly Rate (*=tied to federal rate)	Maximum Tip Credit	Minimum Cash Wage for Tipped Employee	Minimum Tips to Qualify as a Tipped Employee (monthly unless noted otherwise)
Virginia Va. Code Ann. §§ 40.1-28.9 and 28.10	Applies to employees not covered by FLSA	$7.25	Tips actually received	Minimum wage less tips actually received	Not specified
Washington Wash. Rev. Code Ann. § 49.46.020; Wash. Admin. Code § 296-126-022	Adjusted annually; posted at www.lni. wa.gov	$12 ($13.50 on January 1, 2020)	No tip credit	$12 ($13.50 on January 1, 2020)	N/A
West Virginia W.Va. Code §§ 21-5C-1, 21-5C-2, 21-5C-4	Applies to employers with 6 or more employees at one location who are not covered by the FLSA	$8.75	70% of minimum wage	$2.62 (increases as minimum wage increases)	Not specified
Wisconsin Wis. Admin. Code DWD § 272.03		$7.25	$4.92	$2.33	Not specified
Wyoming Wyo. Stat. § 27-4-202		$5.15 if federal regulations do not apply	$3.02	$2.13	More than $30

State Overtime Laws

This chart covers private-sector employment only. The overtime rules summarized are not applicable to all employers or all employees. Occupations that generally are not subject to overtime laws include health care and attendant care, emergency medical personnel, seasonal workers, agricultural labor, camp counselors, nonprofits exempt under the FLSA, salespeople working on a commission, transit drivers, babysitters and other household workers, and many others. For more information, contact your state's department of labor and be sure to check its website, where most states have posted their overtime rules. (See Appendix A for contact details.)

Alabama

No state overtime rules that differ from FLSA.

Alaska

Alaska Stat. §§ 23.10.060 and following

Time and a half after x hours per DAY: 8

Time and a half after x hours per WEEK: 40

Employment overtime laws apply to: Employers of 4 or more employees; commerce or manufacturing businesses.

Notes: Voluntary flexible work hour plan of 10-hour day, 40-hour week, with premium pay after 10 hours is permitted.

Arizona

No state overtime rules that differ from FLSA.

Arkansas

Ark. Code Ann. §§ 11-4-203, 11-4-211

Time and a half after x hours per WEEK: 40

Employment overtime laws apply to: Employers of 4 or more employees.

Notes: Employees in retail and service establishments who spend up to 40% of their time on nonexempt work must be paid at least twice the state's minimum wage ($572 per week).

California

Cal. Lab. Code §§ 500 to 511; Cal. Lab. Code § 513; Cal. Lab. Code § 860; Cal. Code Regs. tit. 8, §§ 11010 and following

Time and a half after x hours per DAY: 8; after 12 hours, double time. Agricultural employees only: after 10 hours per day (from 2019 to 2022, this will gradually decrease to 8 hours per day).

Time and a half after x hours per WEEK: 40. On 7th day: time and a half for the first 8 hours; after 8 hours, double time. Agricultural employees only: after 60 hours per week (from 2019 to 2022, this will gradually decrease to 40 hours per week).

Notes: Employee may make written request to work makeup time for hours taken off for personal obligations. As long as total hours don't exceed 11 in a day or 40 in a week, employer won't owe daily overtime. Employer may not encourage or solicit employees to request makeup time. Employees may, by majority vote in a secret ballot election, opt for an alternative workweek of four 10-hour workdays, in which case the employer will not owe overtime.

Colorado

7 Colo. Code Regs. § 1103-1:4

Time and a half after x hours per DAY: 12 hours in one workday or 12 consecutive hours

Time and a half after x hours per WEEK: 40

State Overtime Laws (continued)

Employment overtime laws apply to: Employees in retail and service, commercial support service, food and beverage, health and medical industries.

Connecticut

Conn. Gen. Stat. Ann. §§ 31-76b and 31-76c; Conn. Admin. Code § 31-62-E1

Time and a half after x hours per WEEK: 40. On 7th consecutive workday, time and a half for all hours worked.

Notes: In restaurants and hotels, time-and-a-half pay required for the 7th consecutive day of work or for hours that exceed 40 per week.

Delaware

No state overtime rules that differ from FLSA.

District of Columbia

D.C. Code Ann. § 32-1003(c); D.C. Mun. Regs. tit. 7, § 906

Time and a half after x hours per WEEK: 40

Notes: Employees must be paid one hour minimum wage for each day a split shift is worked, but not if the employee lives on the premises.

Florida

No state overtime rules that differ from FLSA.

Georgia

No state overtime rules that differ from FLSA.

Hawaii

Haw. Rev. Stat. §§ 387-1; 387-3

Time and a half after x hours per WEEK: 40. Dairy, sugarcane, and seasonal agricultural work: 48 hours per week.

Notes: No employer shall employ any employee in split shifts unless all of the shifts within a period of twenty-four hours fall within a period of fourteen consecutive hours, except in case of extraordinary emergency.

Idaho

No state overtime rules that differ from FLSA.

Illinois

820 Ill. Comp. Stat. §§ 105/3(d), 105/4a

Time and a half after x hours per WEEK: 40

Employment overtime laws apply to: Employers with 4 or more employees (and all employers with respect to domestic workers)

Notes: Collective bargaining agreement ratified by Illinois Labor Relations Board may provide for different overtime provisions.

Indiana

Ind. Code Ann. § 22-2-2-4(k)

Time and a half after x hours per WEEK: 40

Notes: Collective bargaining agreements ratified by the NLRB may have different overtime provisions. Domestic service work is not excluded from overtime laws.

Iowa

No state overtime rules that differ from FLSA.

Kansas

Kan. Stat. Ann. § 44-1204

Time and a half after x hours per WEEK: 46

Kentucky

Ky. Rev. Stat. Ann. §§ 337.050, 337.285; 803 Ky. Admin. Regs. § 1:060

State Overtime Laws (continued)

Time and a half after x hours per WEEK: 40; also, time and a half on the seventh day worked in a workweek.

Louisiana

No state overtime rules that differ from FLSA.

Maine

Me. Rev. Stat. Ann. tit. 26, § 664(3)

Time and a half after x hours per WEEK: 40

Maryland

Md. Code Ann., [Lab. & Empl.] § 3-420

Time and a half after x hours per WEEK: 40; 48 hours for bowling alleys and residential employees caring for the sick, aged, intellectually disabled, or mentally ill in institutions other than hospitals; 60 hours for agricultural work that is exempt from the overtime provisions of the federal act.

Massachusetts

Mass. Gen. Laws ch. 151, § 1A

Time and a half after x hours per WEEK: 40. Time and a half for work on Sunday and certain holidays (for retail employees). Time and a half on Sundays will be reduced to time and four-tenths in 2019. (This premium will be reduced by 1/10 each year until it is eliminated in 2023.)

Employment overtime laws apply to: All employers for 40 hours a week; employers with more than 7 employees for Sunday and holiday overtime.

Michigan

Mich. Comp. Laws §§ 408.412 and 408.414a

Time and a half after x hours per WEEK: 40

Employment overtime laws apply to: Employers of 2 or more employees.

Minnesota

Minn. Stat. Ann. § 177.25

Time and a half after x hours per WEEK: 48

Mississippi

No state overtime rules that differ from FLSA.

Missouri

Mo. Rev. Stat. §§ 290.500 and 290.505

Time and a half after x hours per WEEK: 40; 52 hours for seasonal amusement or recreation businesses.

Montana

Mont. Code Ann. §§ 39-3-405 and 39-3-406

Time and a half after x hours per WEEK: 40; 48 hours for students working seasonal jobs at amusement or recreational areas.

Nebraska

No state overtime rules that differ from FLSA.

Nevada

Nev. Rev. Stat. Ann. § 608.018

Time and a half after x hours per DAY: 8, if (1) employee receives health benefits from employer and employee's regular rate of pay is less than 1.5 times the minimum wage, or (2) employee does not receive health benefits from employer and employee's rate of pay is less than $12.375 per hour.

Time and a half after x hours per WEEK: 40

Notes: Employer and employee may agree to flextime schedule of four 10-hour days.

State Overtime Laws (continued)

A live-in domestic worker and employer may agree in writing to exempt the domestic worker from the requirements of subsections 1 and 2.

New Hampshire

N.H. Rev. Stat. Ann. § 279:21(VIII)

Time and a half after x hours per WEEK: 40

New Jersey

N.J. Stat. Ann. §§ 34.11-56a4 and 34.11-56a4.1

Time and a half after x hours per WEEK: 40

New Mexico

N.M. Stat. Ann. § 50-4-22(d)

Time and a half after x hours per WEEK: 40

New York

N.Y. Lab. Law §§ 160(3), 161; N.Y. Comp. Codes R. & Regs. tit. 12, § 142-2.2

Time and a half after x hours per WEEK: 40 for nonresidential workers; 44 for residential workers.

Notes: In some industries, employees must be given 24 consecutive hours off per week. See N.Y. Lab. Law § 161.

North Carolina

N.C. Gen. Stat. §§ 95-25.14, 95-25.4

Time and a half after x hours per WEEK: 40

North Dakota

N.D. Admin. Code § 46-02-07-02(4)

Time and a half after x hours per WEEK: 40; 50 hours per week, cabdrivers.

Ohio

Ohio Rev. Code Ann. § 4111.03

Time and a half after x hours per WEEK: 40

Employment overtime laws apply to: Employers who gross more than $150,000 a year.

Oklahoma

No state overtime rules that differ from FLSA.

Oregon

Or. Rev. Stat. §§ 652.020, 653.261, 653.265

Time and a half after x hours per WEEK: 40

Notes: Employees in manufacturing establishments are entitled to time-and-a-half based on a daily rate (more than 10 hours per day) or a weekly rate (more than 40 hours per week), whichever results in greater wages.

Live-in domestic workers must receive time-and-a-half for hours in excess of 44 per workweek.

Pennsylvania

43 Pa. Cons. Stat. Ann. § 333.104(c); 34 Pa. Code § 231.41

Time and a half after x hours per WEEK: 40

Rhode Island

R.I. Gen. Laws §§ 28-12-4.1 and following, 5-23-2(d)

Time and a half after x hours per WEEK: 40

Notes: Time and a half for Sunday and holiday work is required for most retail businesses (these hours are not included in calculating weekly overtime).

South Carolina

No state overtime rules that differ from FLSA.

State Overtime Laws (continued)

South Dakota

No state overtime rules that differ from FLSA.

Tennessee

No state overtime rules that differ from FLSA.

Texas

No state overtime rules that differ from FLSA.

Utah

No state overtime rules that differ from FLSA.

Vermont

Vt. Stat. Ann. tit. 21, §§ 382, 384(b)

Time and a half after x hours per WEEK: 40

Employment overtime laws apply to:
Employers of 2 or more employees; doesn't apply to retail or service establishments, hotels, motels, or restaurants (among other industries).

Virginia

No state overtime rules that differ from FLSA.

Washington

Wash. Rev. Code Ann. § 49.46.130

Time and a half after x hours per WEEK: 40

West Virginia

W.Va. Code §§ 21-5c-1(e), 21-5c-3

Time and a half after x hours per WEEK: 40

Employment overtime laws apply to:
Employers of 6 or more employees at one location.

Wisconsin

Wis. Stat. Ann. §§ 103.01, 103.02, 103.03; Wis. Admin. Code DWD §§ 274.01, 274.03, 274.04, 274.15

Time and a half after x hours per WEEK: 40

Employment overtime laws apply to:
Manufacturing, mechanical, or retail businesses; beauty parlors, laundries, restaurants, hotels; telephone, express, shipping, and transportation companies.

Wyoming

No state overtime rules that differ from FLSA.

State Meal and Rest Break Laws

Some states are not listed in this chart because they do not have laws or regulations on rest and meal breaks for adults employed in the private sector. Many states also exclude exempt professional, administrative, and executive employees from these rules.

Other exceptions may apply. For example, many states have special break rules for specific occupations or industries, which are beyond the scope of this chart. Check the statute or check with your state department of labor if you need more information. (See Appendix A for contact list.)

Alabama

Breast-feeding: No employment-specific laws. However, breast-feeding is allowed in any public or private location where the mother's presence is authorized.

Arizona

Breast-feeding: No employment-specific laws. However, breast-feeding is allowed in any public place or place of public accommodation where the mother is lawfully present.

Arkansas

Ark. Stat. Ann. § 11-5-116

Applies to: All employers.

Breast-feeding: Reasonable unpaid breaks to express breast milk; if possible, break time to run concurrently with other breaks.

California

Cal. Lab. Code §§ 512, 1030; Cal. Code Regs. tit. 8, §§ 11010–11170

Applies to: Employers in most industries.

Exceptions: Motion picture and other occupations. See wage orders, Cal. Code Regs. tit. 8, §§ 11010 to 11160, for additional exceptions.

Meal Break: 30 minutes, unpaid, after 5 hours, except employer and employee can agree to waive meal period if employee works 6 hours or less. Second 30-minute unpaid meal period when employee works more than 10 hours a day, except employer and employee can agree to waive the second meal period if the employee works 12 hours or less and took the first meal period. On-duty paid meal period permitted when nature of work prevents relief from all duties and parties agree in writing.

Rest Break: Paid 10-minute rest period for each 4 hours worked or major fraction thereof; as practicable, in the middle of the work period; not required for employees whose total daily work time is less than 3½ hours.

Breast-feeding: Reasonable unpaid breaks to express breast milk; if possible, break time to run concurrently with other breaks. Employer must make reasonable efforts to provide a private location, other than a bathroom, for the employee to express milk.

Colorado

C.R.S.A. §§ 8-13.5-101 through § 8-13.5-104; Colo. Code Regs. tit. 7 §§ 1103-1:7 and 1:8

Applies to: Retail and service, food and beverage, commercial support service, and health and medical industries.

Exceptions: Numerous exceptions are listed in the regulation.

Meal Break: 30 minutes, unpaid, after 5 hours of work. On-duty paid meal period permitted when nature of work prevents break from all duties.

State Meal and Rest Break Laws (continued)

Rest Break: Paid 10-minute rest period for each 4 hours or major fraction worked; if practical, in the middle of the work period.

Breast-feeding: Reasonable unpaid time and private space to express breast milk for up to two years after child's birth.

Connecticut

Conn. Gen. Stat. Ann. §§ 31-40w, 31-51ii

Applies to: All employers, except as noted.

Exceptions: Employers who pay for rest breaks as described below, those with a written agreement providing other break rules, and those granted an exemption for reasons listed in statute.

Meal Break: 30 minutes, unpaid, after first 2 hours of work and before last 2 hours for employees who work 7½ or more consecutive hours.

Rest Break: As alternative to meal break, a total of 30 minutes paid in each 7½-hour work period.

Breast-feeding: Employee may use meal or rest breaks for breast-feeding or expressing breast milk. Reasonable efforts to provide private space.

Delaware

Del. Code Ann. tit. 19 §§ 707, 710–711

Applies to: All employers, except as noted.

Exceptions: Employers with alternative written agreement and those granted exemptions specified in statute. Law does not apply to teachers.

Meal Break: 30 minutes, unpaid, after first 2 hours and before the last 2 hours, for employees who work 7½ consecutive hours or more.

Breast-feeding: Reasonable accommodations for limitations of a person related to pregnancy, childbirth, or a related condition may include break time and appropriate facilities for expressing breast milk, unless accommodation imposes an undue hardship.

District of Columbia

D.C. Code Ann. §§ 2-1402.82, 32-1231.01 to 32-1231.03

Applies to: All employers.

Breast-feeding: Reasonable unpaid time to express breast milk; runs concurrently with other paid or unpaid breaks provided by employer. Employer must make reasonable efforts to provide a private, sanitary location (other than a toilet stall) for expressing breast milk. Employer must provide reasonable accommodations to nursing mothers, unless it would cause an undue hardship.

Florida

Breast-feeding: No employment-specific laws. However, breast-feeding is allowed in any public or private location where the mother's presence is authorized.

Georgia

Ga. Code Ann. § 34-1-6

Applies to: All employers.

Breast-feeding: Reasonable unpaid break time to express breast milk. Employer is not required to provide break time if unduly disruptive to workplace operations. Breast-feeding is allowed in any public or private location where the mother's presence is authorized.

State Meal and Rest Break Laws (continued)

Hawaii

Haw. Rev. Stat. §§ 378-2, 378-91 to 93

Applies to: All employers.

Breast-feeding: Reasonable break time to express milk for nursing child for one year after birth each time the employee has a need to express breast milk, in a location, other than a bathroom, that is sanitary, shielded from view, and free from intrusion. Employers with fewer than 20 employees exempt if requirements impose undue hardship.

Illinois

820 Ill. Comp. Stat. §§ 140/3, 140/3.1, 260/10, 260/15

Applies to: All employers.

Exceptions: Employees whose meal periods are established by collective bargaining agreement. Employees who monitor individuals with developmental disabilities or mental illness, or both, and who are required to be on call during an entire 8-hour work period; these employees must be allowed to eat a meal while working.

Meal Break: 20 minutes, no later than 5 hours after the beginning of the shift, for employees who work 7½ or more continuous hours. Hotel room attendants are entitled to a 30-minute meal break if they work at least 7 hours.

Rest Break: In addition to meal break, hotel room attendants must receive two paid 15-minute rest breaks, if they work at least 7 hours.

Breast-feeding: Reasonable unpaid break time to express breast milk and reasonable efforts to provide a room or other location, other than a toilet stall, where an employee can express her milk in privacy for up to one year after the child's birth.

Indiana

Ind. Code §§ 22-2-14-1, 22-2-14-2

Applies to: Employers with 25 or more employees.

Breast-feeding: Employer must make reasonable efforts to provide a private space, other than a restroom, for an employee to express breast milk.

Iowa

Breast-feeding: No employment-specific laws. However, breast-feeding is allowed in any public or private location where the mother's presence is authorized.

Kansas

Kan. Admin. Reg. 49-30-3

Applies to: Employees not covered under FLSA.

Meal Break: Not required, but if less than 30 minutes is given, break must be paid.

Breast-feeding: No employment-specific laws. However, breast-feeding is allowed in any public or private location where the mother's presence is authorized.

Kentucky

Ky. Rev. Stat. Ann. §§ 337.355, 337.365; 803 KAR 1:065

Applies to: All employers, except as noted.

Exceptions: Written agreement providing different meal period; employers subject to Federal Railway Labor Act.

Meal Break: Reasonable off-duty period close to the middle of the shift; cannot be required to take it before the third or after

State Meal and Rest Break Laws (continued)

the fifth hour of work. Coffee breaks and snack time do not count toward the meal break.

Rest Break: Paid 10-minute rest period for each 4-hour work period; rest period must be in addition to regularly scheduled meal period.

Breast-feeding: No employment-specific laws. However, breast-feeding is allowed in any public or private location where the mother's presence is authorized.

Louisiana

Breast-feeding: No employment-specific laws. However, breast-feeding is allowed in any public or private location where the mother's presence is authorized.

Maine

Me. Rev. Stat. Ann. tit. 26, §§ 601, 604

Applies to: All employers, except those with fewer than 3 employees on duty who are able to take frequent breaks during the workday.

Exceptions: Collective bargaining or other written agreement between employer and employee may provide for different breaks.

Meal and Rest Break: 30 minutes after 6 consecutive hours of work, except in cases of emergency. Time may be unpaid if employee is completely relieved of duty.

Breast-feeding: Adequate unpaid time to express breast milk, or employee may use rest or meal time, for up to 3 years following childbirth.

Maryland

Md. Code Ann., Lab. & Empl. § 3-710

Applies to: Retail establishments with 50 or more retail employees.

Exceptions: Employees who work in an office or who work at a single location with 5 or fewer employees are not covered.

Meal Break: 30 minutes, unpaid, after 6 consecutive hours of work.

Rest Break: 15 minutes, unpaid, when working 4 to 6 consecutive hours. (This may be waived if the employee works less than 6 hours). Employees working 8 or more consecutive hours must receive a 15-minute unpaid break for every additional 4 consecutive hours after a meal break.

Breast-feeding: No employment-specific laws. However, breast-feeding is allowed in any public or private location where the mother's presence is authorized.

Massachusetts

Mass. Gen. Laws 149 §§ 100, 101; Mass. Gen. Laws 151B § 4

Applies to: All employers, except as noted.

Exceptions: Excludes iron works, glass works, paper mills, letterpresses, print works, and bleaching or dyeing works. Attorney general may exempt businesses that require continuous operation if it won't affect worker safety. Collective bargaining agreement may also provide for different breaks.

Meal Break: 30 minutes, if work is for more than 6 hours.

Minnesota

Minn. Stat. Ann. §§ 177.253, 177.254, 181.939

Applies to: All employers.

State Meal and Rest Break Laws (continued)

Exceptions: Excludes certain agricultural and seasonal employees. A collective bargaining agreement may provide for different rest and meal breaks.

Meal Break: Sufficient unpaid time for employees who work 8 consecutive hours or more.

Rest Break: Paid adequate rest period within each 4 consecutive hours of work to utilize nearest convenient restroom.

Breast-feeding: Reasonable unpaid break time to express milk. Employer must make reasonable efforts to provide a private room, other than a bathroom, for expressing breast milk.

Mississippi

Miss. Ann. Code § 71-1-55

Breast-feeding: Employee may use meal or rest break for expressing breast milk.

Missouri

Breast-feeding: No employment-specific laws. However, breast-feeding is allowed in any public or private location where the mother's presence is authorized.

Montana

Breast-feeding: No private employment-specific laws. However, breast-feeding is allowed in any public or private location where the mother's presence is authorized.

Nebraska

Neb. Rev. Stat. §§ 48-212, 48–1102

Applies to: Meal break provisions: assembly plant, workshop, or mechanical establishment.

Breast-feeding provisions: employers with 15 or more employees.

Exceptions: Other written agreement between employer and employees.

Meal Break: 30 minutes off premises for each 8-hour shift.

Breast-feeding: Employer with 15 or more employees must provide reasonable accommodation to nursing mothers, unless it would cause an undue hardship. Accommodation may include breaks and an appropriate location for breast-feeding or expressing breast milk.

Nevada

Nev. Rev. Stat. Ann. §§ 608.019, 608.0193

Applies to: Employers with two or more employees.

Exceptions: Employees covered by collective bargaining agreement; exemptions for business necessity.

Meal Break: 30 minutes for 8 continuous hours of work.

Rest Break: Paid 10-minute rest period for each 4 hours or major fraction worked; as practicable, in middle of the work period. Not required for employees whose total daily work time is less than 3½ hours.

Breast-feeding: Employer must provide reasonable break time with or without compensation to express breast milk as needed; and a place, other than a bathroom, reasonably free from dirt or pollution, protected from the view of others, and free from intrusion by others. Employer with less than 50 employees exempt if requirements constitute undue hardship. Certain licensed contractors are not required to comply with regard to employees who work at a construction job site located at least 3 miles from the employer's regular place of

State Meal and Rest Break Laws (continued)

business. If employer believes complying will cause an undue hardship, the employer and employee must engage in a timely, good faith and interactive process to determine an effective, reasonable accommodation. If the parties cannot reach an agreement, the employer can require the employee to accept the reasonable alternative selected by the employer, subject to the employee's right to appeal the decision to the appropriate authorities.

New Hampshire

N.H. Rev. Stat. Ann. § 275:30-a

Applies to: All employers.

Meal Break: 30 minutes after 5 consecutive hours, unless the employer allows the employee to eat while working and it is feasible for the employee to do so.

Breast-feeding: No employment-specific laws. However, restricting or limiting the right of a mother to breast-feed her child is discriminatory.

New Jersey

N.J. Stat. Ann. § 10:5-12

Applies to: All employers.

Breast-feeding: Employer must provide reasonable break time and a suitable private location, other than a toilet stall, unless it would cause undue hardship on the employer.

New Mexico

N.M. Stat. Ann. § 28-20-2

Breast-feeding: Flexible unpaid breaks to use breast pump in the workplace. Employer must provide a private space, other than a bathroom, for expressing breast milk.

New York

N.Y. Lab. Law §§ 162, 206-c

Applies to: Factories, workshops, manufacturing facilities, mercantile (retail and wholesale) establishments.

Meal Break: Factory employees, 60 minutes between 11 a.m. and 2 p.m.; mercantile employees, 30 minutes between 11 a.m. and 2 p.m. If a shift starts before 11 a.m. and ends after 7 p.m., every employee gets an additional 20 minutes between 5 p.m. and 7 p.m. If a shift starts between 1 p.m. and 6 a.m., a factory employee gets 60 minutes, and a mercantile employee gets 45 minutes, in the middle of the shift. Labor commissioner may permit a shorter meal break; the permit must be in writing and posted conspicuously in the main entrance of the workplace.

Breast-feeding: Reasonable unpaid break time to express breast milk for up to three years after child's birth. Employers must make reasonable efforts to provide a private room or other location for expressing breast milk.

North Carolina

Breast-feeding: No employment-specific laws. However, breast-feeding is allowed in any public or private location where the mother's presence is authorized.

North Dakota

N.D. Admin. Code § 46-02-07-02; N.D. Cent. Code § 23-12-17

Applies to: Applicable when two or more employees are on duty.

Exceptions: Waiver by employee or other provision in collective bargaining agreement.

State Meal and Rest Break Laws (continued)

Meal Break: 30 minutes for each shift over 5 hours. Unpaid if employee is completely relieved of duties.

Breast-feeding: Breast-feeding is allowed in any public or private location where the mother's presence is authorized. Employers may use the designation "infant friendly" by adopting voluntary workplace breastfeeding policies.

Oklahoma

Okla. Stat. Ann. tit. 40, § 435

Breast-feeding: Reasonable unpaid breaks to breast-feed or express breast milk. Breaks run concurrently with other breaks already provided to the employee, if possible. Employers may make reasonable efforts to provide a private room, other than a toilet stall, for expressing milk or breast-feeding. Employers are not required to provide breaks if it would cause undue hardship.

Oregon

Or. Rev. Stat. 653.077; Or. Admin. R. §§ 839-020-0050, 839-020-0051

Applies to: All employers except as noted.

Exceptions: Agricultural workers and employees covered by a collective bargaining agreement.

Meal Break: 30 minutes for employees who work at least six hours, unpaid if relieved of all duties; paid time to eat if employee cannot be relieved of duty; a shorter paid break (but no less than 20 minutes), if employer can show that it is industry practice or custom. If shift of 7 hours or less, meal break must occur between hours 2 and 5; if shift longer than 7 hours, meal break must be between hours 3 and 6.

Rest Break: Paid 10-minute rest period for each 4 hours or major fraction worked; if practical, in the middle of the work period. Rest period must be in addition to usual meal break and taken separately; can't be added to meal period or deducted from beginning or end of shift to reduce length of total work period. Rest period is not required for certain solo adult employees serving the public, although they must be allowed to use restroom.

Breast-feeding: Employer with 25 or more employees must provide a 30-minute unpaid break for every 4 hours worked to express breast milk, for up to 18 months after child's birth. If possible, breaks should run concurrently with other breaks already provided to the employee. Employers must make reasonable efforts to provide a private location, other than a bathroom, for expressing milk. Employers are not required to provide breaks if it would cause undue hardship.

Pennsylvania

43 P.S. § 1301.207

Applies to: Employers of seasonal farmworkers.

Meal and Rest Break: Seasonal farmworkers are entitled to a 30-minute meal or rest break if they work at least 5 hours.

Breast-feeding: No employment-specific laws. However, breast-feeding is allowed in any public or private location where the mother's presence is authorized.

State Meal and Rest Break Laws (continued)

Rhode Island

R.I. Gen. Laws §§ 28-3-8, 28-3-14, 28-5-7.4, 23-13.2-1

Applies to: Meal break provisions: employers with 5 or more employees. Breast-feeding provisions: employers with 4 or more employees.

Exceptions: Employers of health care facility or employers with fewer than 3 employees on any shift.

Meal Break: 20 minutes, unpaid, within a 6-hour shift or 30 minutes, unpaid, within an 8-hour shift.

Breast-feeding: Reasonable unpaid break time to breast-feed infant or express breast milk. Employers with 4 or more employees must provide reasonable accommodations to nursing mothers, which may include break time and private space for expressing breast milk, other than a restroom.

South Carolina

Breast-feeding: No employment-specific laws. However, breast-feeding is allowed in any public or private location where the mother's presence is authorized.

South Dakota

Breast-feeding: No employment-specific laws. However, breast-feeding is allowed in any public or private location where the mother's presence is authorized if the mother is in compliance with all other laws.

Tennessee

Tenn. Code Ann. §§ 50-1-305, 50-2-103(h)

Applies to: Employers with 5 or more employees.

Meal Break: 30 minutes unpaid for employees scheduled to work 6 consecutive hours or more, unless workplace environment provides ample opportunity for appropriate meal break. Tipped employees who work in food or beverage service may waive right to meal break if employee requests waiver, knowingly and voluntarily, in writing, and employer consents. Employer may not coerce employee into waiving right to meal break. Employer must post waiver policy that includes a form stating the employee's right to a break, how long the waiver will last, and how the employee or employer may rescind the waiver.

Breast-feeding: Reasonable unpaid break time to express breast milk. Breaks should run concurrently with any breaks already provided to the employee, if possible. Employers must make reasonable efforts to provide a private room, other than a toilet stall, for expressing breast milk. Employers are not required to provide breaks if it would unduly disrupt business operations.

Texas

Breast-feeding: Public employees only (V.T.C.A., Gov't Code § 619.005). However, breast-feeding is allowed in any public or private location where the mother's presence is authorized. Employers voluntarily implementing policies supporting worksite breast-feeding may designate themselves "mother-friendly."

Utah

Utah Code Ann. § 34A-5-106

Applies to: Employers with 15 or more employees.

State Meal and Rest Break Laws (continued)

Breast-feeding: Employer must provide reasonable accommodations related to breast-feeding unless employer demonstrates accommodations create an undue hardship on employer.

Vermont

Vt. Stat. Ann. tit. 21 §§ 304, 305

Applies to: All employers.

Meal and Rest Break: Employees must be given a "reasonable opportunity" to eat and use toilet facilities during work periods.

Breast-feeding: Reasonable time to express breast milk for up to three years after the child's birth. Breaks can be paid or unpaid. Employer must make reasonable efforts to provide a private location (other than a bathroom stall) for expressing breast milk. Employer not required to provide breaks or a private space if it would substantially disrupt its operations.

Virginia

Breast-feeding: Breast-feeding is allowed in any public or private location where the mother's presence is authorized. Employers with more than five but fewer than fifteen employees may not terminate a female employee on the basis of lactation.

Washington

Wash. Admin. Code §§ 296-126-092, 286-131-020

Applies to: All employers except as noted.

Exceptions: Newspaper vendor or carrier, domestic or casual labor around private residence, sheltered workshop; separate provisions for agricultural labor.

Meal Break: 30-minute break, if work period is more than 5 consecutive hours, not less than 2 hours or more than 5 hours from beginning of shift. This time is paid if employee is on duty or is required to be at a site for employer's benefit. Employees who work 3 or more hours longer than regular workday are entitled to an additional half hour, before or during overtime.

Agricultural employees: 30 minutes if working more than 5 hours; additional 30 minutes if working 11 or more hours in a day.

Rest Break: Paid 10-minute rest break for each 4-hour work period, scheduled as near as possible to midpoint of each work period. Employee cannot be required to work more than 3 hours without a rest break. Scheduled rest breaks not required where nature of work allows employee to take intermittent rest breaks equivalent to required standard.

Breast-feeding: Employer may use the designation "infant-friendly" on its promotional materials by voluntarily providing approved accommodations including flexible scheduling, breaks and work patterns that provide time for expression of breast milk; convenient, sanitary, safe, and private locations, other than a restroom, allowing privacy for breast-feeding or expressing breast milk, etc.

West Virginia

W.Va. Code § 21-3-10a

Applies to: All employers.

Meal Break: At least 20-minute break for each 6 consecutive hours worked, unless employees are allowed to take breaks as needed or to eat lunch while working.

State Meal and Rest Break Laws (continued)

Rest Break: Rest breaks of 20 minutes or less must be counted as paid work time.

Wisconsin

Wis. Admin. Code § DWD 274.02; Wis. Stat. Ann. § 103.935

Applies to: All employers.

Meal Break: For most workers, 30-minute meal period is recommended but not required. Meal period should be close to usual meal time or near middle of shift. Shifts of more than 6 hours without a meal break should be avoided. If employee is not free to leave the workplace or relieved of all duties for at least 30 minutes, meal period is considered paid time.

For migrant workers employed exclusively in agricultural labor, 30-minute meal period required after 6 continuous hours of work, unless the shift can be completed in an additional hour.

Rest Break: For migrant workers not employed exclusively in agricultural labor, rest period of at least 10 minutes within each 5 hours of continuous employment.

Breast-feeding: No employment-specific laws. However, breast-feeding is allowed in any public or private location where the mother's presence is authorized.

Family and Medical Leave Act (FMLA)

Statute: 29 U.S.C. §§ 2601 and following
To view the statutes, visit http://uscode.house.gov and select "Title 29" and "Chapter 28."

Regulations: 29 C.F.R. §§ 825.100 and following
To view the regulations, visit www.govinfo.gov and search "29 CFR 825."

Overview of the FMLA

O riginally passed in 1993, the Family and Medical Leave Act (FMLA) requires covered employers to allow eligible employees to take up to 12 weeks of unpaid leave during a 12-month period for the arrival of a new child through birth, adoption, or *foster care*, to care for a family member who is suffering from a *serious health condition*, or to deal with the employee's own serious health condition. Employees are entitled to continue their health benefits while on leave. Once their leave is over, employees are entitled to be reinstated to their jobs.

The FMLA also provides leave rights relating to military service:
- Employees may take FMLA leave for a qualifying exigency relating to a family member's *covered active duty*. This leave counts toward the employee's 12-week total entitlement for all types of FMLA leave.
- Employees may take up to 26 weeks of leave in a single 12-month period to care for certain family members who are *covered servicemembers*. If employees use this leave and regular FMLA leave during the year, they are entitled to a maximum of 26 weeks, and no more than 12 of those weeks may be used for regular FMLA leave (including qualifying exigency leave).

The FMLA has special rules for employees of public and private schools, which are not covered here.

Covered Employers

The following employers must comply with the FMLA:
- private employers with 50 or more employees
- the federal government
- state and local governments, and
- public and private elementary schools and secondary schools.

Definitions

Terms that appear in italics throughout this chapter are defined below:

Authentication: To give a health care provider a copy of the *certification* and request verification that the information was completed or authorized by the provider who signed the document. No additional medical information may be requested.

Certification: A document that employers may require employees to provide when they want to take leave for their own *serious health condition*, a family member's serious health condition, a *qualifying exigency*, or leave to care for a *covered servicemember* with a *serious illness or injury*.

Clarification: To contact a health care provider to understand the handwriting or the meaning of a response on a certification. No additional information may be sought beyond that required by the certification form.

Continuing treatment by a health care provider: A period of incapacity of more than three full consecutive days that also involves (1) treatment two or more times within 30 days of the first day of incapacity by a health care provider or a nurse or other provider of health care services under orders of, or on referral by, a health care provider; or (2) at least one treatment by a health care provider that results in a regimen of continuing treatment under the health care provider's supervision.

Covered active duty: For a member of a regular component of the armed forces, duty during deployment to a foreign country. For a member of the National Guard or reserves, duty during deployment to a foreign country under call or order to active duty.

Covered servicemember: (1) A current member of the armed forces, the National Guard, or reserves, who is undergoing medical treatment, recuperation, or therapy; is otherwise in outpatient status; or is otherwise on the temporary disability retired list, for a serious injury or illness.

(2) A veteran who is undergoing medical treatment, recuperation, or therapy, for a serious injury or illness and who was a member of the armed forces (including a member of the National Guard or reserves) at any time in the previous five years.

Essential duties: The fundamental, as opposed to marginal, duties of a job.

Definitions (continued)

Fitness for duty certification: A document from the employee's health care provider stating that the employee is able to resume work; employers may require employees who take FMLA leave for their own *serious health condition* to provide such a certification before returning to work.

Foster care: The 24-hour care for children as a substitute for, and away from, their own parents or guardians. Informal care arrangements don't constitute foster care, which arises only when the government is involved in taking children away from their families and placing them in another's home.

Intermittent leave: Leave that is not taken all at once, but is instead taken in increments or results in a reduced work schedule.

Key employee: A salaried eligible employee who is among the highest paid 10% of the employer's employees within a 75-mile radius of the site where the employee works.

Next of kin: A covered servicemember's nearest blood relative, other than a parent, child, or spouse, in the following order of priority: (1) blood relatives who have been granted legal custody of the servicemember; (2) siblings; (3) grandparents; (4) aunts and uncles; and (5) first cousins. If the covered servicemember has designated a blood relative as next of kin, that designation must be followed. If not, all blood relatives within the same level of the highest-priority relationship are considered the servicemember's next of kin.

Reasonable safety concerns: A reasonable belief of significant risk or harm to the employee or others, considering the nature, severity, and likelihood of the potential harm, which gives the employer a right to require more frequent fitness for duty certifications from an employee using intermittent leave.

Serious health condition: An illness, injury, impairment, or a physical or mental condition that involves (1) inpatient care (an overnight stay) in a medical facility; (2) incapacity for at least three full, consecutive days with *continuing treatment by a health care provider*; (3) incapacity due to pregnancy or prenatal care; (4) incapacity or treatment for a chronic serious health condition; (5) permanent or long-term incapacity for a condition for which treatment may not be effective

Definitions (continued)

(such as a terminal illness); or (6) absence for multiple treatments for either restorative surgery following an injury or accident or a condition that would require an absence of more than three days if not treated.

Serious illness or injury: In the case of a current member of the armed forces, National Guard, or reserves, an illness or injury that was incurred in the line of duty on active duty, or that existed before the member's active duty and was aggravated by service in the line of duty on active duty, which may render the member medically unfit to perform the duties of his or her office, grade, rank, or rating. In the case of a veteran, a serious injury or illness that was incurred in the line of duty on active duty, or that existed before the member's active duty and was aggravated in the line of duty on active duty, and that manifested itself before or after the member became a veteran, and that is any of the following:

- a continuation of a serious injury or illness that happened in the line of duty on active duty, or was aggravated in the line of duty on active duty, and that left the member unable to perform the duties of his or her office, grade, rank, or rating

- a physical or mental condition for which the veteran has a disability rating of 50% or higher from the U.S. Department of Veterans Affairs (and the veteran needs care for that condition)

- a physical or mental condition that substantially impairs—or would substantially impair without treatment—the veteran's ability to work because of a disability related to military service, or

- a physical or psychological injury that has led the veteran to enroll in the Department of Veterans Affairs Program of Comprehensive Assistance for Family Caregivers.

Total monthly guarantee: The minimum number of hours for which an employer has agreed to schedule a flight attendant or flight crew member in a given month, or the number of hours for which an employer has agreed to pay a flight attendant or flight crew member who is on reserve status in a given month, as established by the collective bargaining agreement or in the employer's policies.

Legal Developments

- **Department of Labor passes regulations expanding military family leave.** In 2013, the Department of Labor passed a set of regulations clarifying military family leave under the FMLA. Among other things, the final regulations added a new parental leave category for qualifying exigency leave; extended the maximum leave for qualifying exigency leave from five days to 15 days; clarified what counts as a serious illness or injury for a veteran; and modified the certification requirements for military family leave.
- **Same-sex spouses are now covered by the FMLA.** The history of same-sex couples and the FMLA has been a complicated one. When Congress passed the Defense of Marriage Act (DOMA), defining marriage as between one man and one woman, the Department of Labor issued an opinion letter stating that same-sex spouses were not covered by the FMLA. This was the general practice until 2013, when the Supreme Court held that DOMA was unconstitutional. (*U.S. v. Windsor*, 133 S. Ct. 2675 (2013).) After this decision, the Department of Labor issued a new rule, stating that an employee could take FMLA leave for a same-sex spouse, but only if the employee lived in a state that recognized same-sex marriage. In 2015, the Supreme Court legalized same-sex marriage in all 50 states. (*Obergefell v. Hodges*, 135 S. Ct. 2584 (2015).) As a result, employees may take FMLA leave for a same-sex spouse regardless of what state they live in.

Covered Workers

To be eligible to take FMLA leave, an employee must:

- have worked for a covered employer for at least 12 months (these months do not have to be consecutive, but the employer does not have to count time worked prior to a break in service of seven years or more in most cases)
- have worked at least 1,250 hours for the employer in the 12 months immediately preceding the leave (flight attendants and flight crew members are covered if they have worked at least 60% of their *total*

monthly guarantee or worked or been paid for at least 504 hours—
not including leave, vacation, or commute time—during the previous
12 months), and
- work at a location with 50 or more employees within a 75-mile radius.

Employees who take leave to serve in the U.S. military are entitled to count
that time as hours worked for all purposes, including eligibility for the FMLA.
(See Chapter 19, on the Uniformed Services Employment and Reemployment
Rights Act, for more information.)

Did You Know ...

- A 2012 survey commissioned by the Department of Labor revealed that 16% of
FMLA-eligible employees (about 14 million employees) took FMLA leave in the
previous year. The most common reason for taking leave was the employee's
own health condition (55%), followed by bonding with a new child (21%) and a
family member's serious health condition (18%).
- Between September 11, 2001 and October 2012, more than 850,000 Guard
members and reservists were mobilized.
- Almost a quarter of the employees who take FMLA leave use at least some of
it intermittently.

Major Provisions of the FMLA

12-Week FMLA Leave Provisions

The FMLA gives an eligible employee the right to take leave to bond with a
new child, recover from a serious health condition, care for a family member
with a serious health condition, or attend to a qualifying exigency relating to a
family member's *covered active duty.*

Covered Employers

All covered employers are subject to these provisions.

Covered Workers

All covered workers are subject to these provisions.

What's Prohibited

Employers may not prevent employees from exercising their FMLA rights, nor may they discriminate or retaliate against employees for exercising their FMLA rights (including taking or requesting FMLA leave).

Employers may not interfere with court proceedings or investigations pertaining to the FMLA. Prohibited interference includes firing or discriminating against someone who plans to testify or give information.

What's Required

Employers must grant leave to an eligible employee in the following circumstances, all discussed in "Reasons Employees May Take Leave," below:
- to bond with a newborn child, newly adopted child, or a child placed with the employee for *foster care*
- to care for a family member with a serious health condition
- for the employee's own serious health condition that makes the employee unable to work, or
- for a qualifying exigency relating to a family member's covered active duty.

Amount of Leave

Eligible employees are entitled to a maximum of 12 workweeks of unpaid leave for every 12-month period of employment. This limit applies to an employee's total leave for all covered situations. For example, an employee who uses eight weeks of leave to care for a new child has only four weeks of leave left in that 12-month period for all types of leave. Special time limits apply to certain types of leave for a qualifying exigency; see "Reasons Employees May Take Leave," below.

An employer can choose any one of the following methods for determining when the 12-month period begins and ends:
- the calendar year

- any fixed 12-month period, such as a fiscal year, a year required by state law, or a year starting on an employee's anniversary date
- a 12-month period beginning on the date the employee first takes FMLA leave, or
- a "rolling" 12-month period measured backward from the date the employee uses any FMLA leave.

The employer must use the same method of measuring the 12-month period for all employees. An employee who takes leave to bond with a new child must complete that leave within the 12-month period after the child arrives—that is, the day the child is born or placed for adoption or foster care.

The amount of leave that flight attendants and airline flight crew employees are entitled to is measured differently. These employees may take 72 days of leave, instead of 12 workweeks, for any FMLA-qualifying reason other than military caregiver leave.

Employees are entitled to take *intermittent leave* for certain types of FMLA leave. When an employee takes intermittent leave, the employer cannot require the employee to take more leave than necessary. For example, if an employee needs two hours of leave to attend a doctor's appointment, the employer cannot require the employee to take four hours of leave. For an in-depth discussion of how to calculate and track FMLA leave, see *The Essential Guide to Family & Medical Leave*, by Lisa Guerin and Deborah England (Nolo).

Substitution of Paid Leave

FMLA leave is unpaid. However, an employee may choose, or an employer may require an employee, to use accrued paid leave at the same time as FMLA leave. This rule applies only if the employee meets the criteria for the employer's paid leave plan and follows the employer's procedures for taking leave. For example, if the employer generally allows employees to use sick leave to care for an ailing family member, an employee may use that leave to get paid during FMLA leave to care for a family member with a serious health condition. If the employer allows employees to use sick leave only for their own illnesses, however, an employee may not use that leave when caring for a family member.

The employee must also meet the procedural requirements of the employer's paid leave plan. For example, if the employer's vacation policy requires two weeks' notice, an employee must follow that rule to use paid vacation time during FMLA leave. If the employee is unable to follow the rule—for example, because the employee is in an accident and needs FMLA leave immediately—the employee would not be entitled to vacation pay until the third week of FMLA leave.

Sometimes, an employee on FMLA leave also receives some wage replacement in the form of disability or workers' compensation benefits. In this situation, an employee is not entitled to substitute paid leave and an employer cannot require it. However, the employee and employer may mutually agree that the employee can use paid leave to make up the difference between the employee's benefit and the employee's usual salary. For example, if an employee is receiving two-thirds of his or her usual salary in workers' compensation benefits during the FMLA-protected leave, the employer and employee could agree that the employee may use vacation pay to make up the remaining third of the employee's wages.

Benefits While on Leave

Employees are entitled to keep their health benefits while on FMLA leave, and the employer must continue to pay whatever premiums it would pay if the employee were not on leave. If the employee voluntarily chooses not to return from leave, however, the employer may require the employee to repay the cost of the health care premiums it paid while the employee was on leave. The employer may not seek reimbursement if the employee fails to return to work for reasons beyond the employee's control (for example, a serious health condition that does not improve enough to allow the employee to return to work).

The employee accrues earned benefits such as seniority or paid time off while on FMLA leave in the same manner as employees who take other types of unpaid leave (according to the employer's policies).

Reasons Employees May Take Leave

For a New Child

A mother and a father have an equal right to take FMLA leave to bond with a new child, whether the child arrives by birth, adoption, or foster care.

If an employee is unable to work because of pregnancy, she may take FMLA leave before the child is born. However, she still gets a total of 12 weeks of FMLA leave, so the amount of time she takes off before the birth will count against the amount of time off she may take after the birth if both occur within the same 12-month period. Some states, such as California, provide separate leave for pregnancy-related disabilities, which is in addition to the 12 weeks of FMLA leave. For information about such laws, see "State Laws Relating to Family and Medical Leave," at the end of this chapter, and consult your state fair employment agency or labor department (see Appendix A for contact information).

Employees who are expecting a child through adoption or foster care may take some FMLA leave before the child arrives if the leave is needed to arrange for the child's placement. For example, some courts order parents to undergo counseling before receiving a foster child. The FMLA covers time off from work for that counseling.

Parents can take intermittent leave (that is, leave taken in separate increments) for the arrival of a new child only if the employer agrees.

For a Family Member With a Serious Health Condition

An employee may take FMLA leave to care for a family member who is suffering from a serious health condition. Employers may ask an employee to provide *certification* from a health care provider that the family member is suffering from a serious health condition. (For more information, see "Certification," below.)

If an employee needs leave to care for a family member, the employee may do so on an intermittent schedule—for example, hours, days, or weeks at a time. The employee can take intermittent leave both when the family member's health condition is intermittent and when the employee's need to take leave is intermittent (for example, when the employee shares care responsibilities with other people). If the leave is for planned medical treatment, the employer may temporarily assign the employee to a different position with equal pay and benefits to accommodate the intermittent schedule.

For purposes of this provision, a "family member" is a spouse, parent, or child:

- A spouse must be someone whom state law recognizes as being married to the employee. Until recently, whether an employee could take FMLA leave for a same-sex spouse depended largely on where the marriage took place. However, in a landmark decision in 2015, the U.S. Supreme Court held that all states must allow same-sex couples to marry and must recognize same-sex marriages from other states. (*Obergefell v. Hodges*, 135 S. Ct. 2584 (2015).) Because of this ruling, same-sex spouses are now covered by the FMLA in all 50 states.

- A parent must be a biological parent, adoptive parent, stepparent, or foster parent, or a person who acted as a parent (that is, someone who had the day-to-day responsibility of caring for or financially supporting the employee as a child). For example, an aunt who took in an employee as a child when the employee's parents were killed could qualify as a parent.
- A son or daughter is a biological child, adopted child, foster child, stepchild, legal ward, or a child for whom the employee acts as a parent (that is, a child for whom the employee takes day-to-day responsibility for care and financial support). For this provision of the FMLA, the child must be either under the age of 18, or if 18 and older, incapable of caring for himself or herself.

For Employee's Own Serious Health Condition

An employee may take FMLA leave for a serious health condition, as long as the employee is unable to perform one or more of the essential duties of his or her job. An employee can be considered unable to perform his or her job duties because he or she is absent from work for medical treatment.

The employer may require the employee to provide certification from a health care provider that the employee is indeed unable to perform an essential duty of the job. (For more, see "Certification," below.)

If medically necessary, an employee may take FMLA leave on an intermittent schedule for his or her own serious illness. If intermittent leave is necessary for planned medical treatment, the employee must make a reasonable effort to schedule the treatment so as not to unduly disrupt the employer's operations. The employer may temporarily assign the employee to a different position with equal pay and benefits to accommodate the intermittent schedule.

For a Qualifying Exigency

Employees may take FMLA leave for a qualifying exigency while the employee's spouse, child, or parent is on covered active duty. For purposes of this provision, the employee's child may be any age; in other words, children 18 and older are covered even if they can care for themselves.

This leave is available for exigencies relating to regular members of the armed forces as well as members of the National Guard or reserves and, in certain circumstances, retired members of the regular armed forces or reserves.

The FMLA establishes nine categories of qualifying exigencies, as explained below. For some of these exigencies, the amount of leave is limited. The categories of qualifying exigencies are:

- **Short-notice deployment.** Leave is available to address any issue arising from the fact that a covered family member is notified of the order or call to active duty within seven calendar days of the date of deployment. Leave may be used for seven calendar days starting on the date the covered family member is notified.

- **Military events and related activities.** Leave may be taken to attend any official ceremony, program, or event sponsored by the military and attend family support and assistance programs and information briefings sponsored or promoted by the military, military service organizations, or the American Red Cross, related to the family member's covered active duty.

- **Child care and school activities.** The employee may take leave to arrange alternative child care if a family member's covered active duty requires a change; to provide child care on an urgent, immediate need basis (not regularly); to enroll in or transfer the child to another school; and to attend meetings with school or day care staff.

- **Financial and legal arrangements.** Leave is available to deal with financial or legal matters necessary to address the family member's absence, such as creating financial and health care powers of attorney; transferring bank account signature authority; enrolling in the Defense Enrollment Eligibility Reporting System (DEERS); getting military ID cards; preparing a will or living trust; or acting as the family member's representative before a government agency regarding military service benefits, for up to 90 days after termination of the member's active duty status.

- **Counseling.** The employee may take leave to attend counseling for oneself, the family member, or the family member's child, relating to covered active duty.

- **Rest and recuperation.** The employee may take leave to spend time with the family member who is on short-term, temporary rest and recreation leave during deployment. The employee may take up to 15 days off for each of the family member's rest and recuperation periods.

- **Postdeployment activities.** Leave may be taken to attend arrival ceremonies, reintegration briefings and events, and any other official military ceremony or program for up to 90 days after termination of the family member's active duty. Leave is also available to address issues arising from the member's death, such as recovering the member's body and making funeral arrangements.

- **Parental care leave.** Leave may be taken when a military family member's parent is incapable of caring for himself or herself and the care is necessitated by the member's covered active duty. Covered activities include providing care on an immediate need basis (not regularly), making arrangements for other care, admitting the parent to a care facility, or attending meetings with the staff of a care facility.
- **Other qualifying exigencies.** An employer and employee may agree that other activities relating to a family member's military service are qualifying exigencies, as long as they also agree on the timing and duration of the leave.

Qualifying exigency leave may be taken intermittently or on a reduced leave schedule. Employers may require employees to submit a certification regarding their qualified exigency leave; see "Certification," below.

Required Notice From the Employer

There are four types of notice an employer may have to give under the FMLA: general notice, eligibility notice, rights and responsibilities notice, and designation notice.

General Notice

An employer must post a notice in its workplace explaining the FMLA. Employers can obtain this notice from the DOL's website. (See "Agency Resources," below, for details.) The notice can be posted electronically, as long as it is large enough to be easily read, contains fully legible text, and can readily be seen by employees and applicants for employment.

If an employer has any written materials, such as an employee handbook, that explain employee benefits, the employer must include the general notice in those materials or distribute a copy of the general notice to each new employee upon hire. In either situation, the notice may be distributed electronically.

Eligibility Notice

When an employee requests FMLA leave or the employer becomes aware that an employee's leave may qualify for FMLA protection, the employer must notify the employee of his or her eligibility to take FMLA leave. The employer has five business days to provide this eligibility notice, absent extenuating circumstances. This notice may be written or oral. If the employee is not eligible for leave, the notice must state at least one reason for the employee's ineligibility.

All FMLA absences for the same qualifying reason are considered a single leave, and the employee's eligibility to take leave for that reason doesn't change during the applicable 12-month period. If the employee requests leave for a second qualifying reason, and the employee's eligibility has not changed, the employer need not provide a second eligibility notice. However, if the employee's eligibility has changed, the employer must provide notice of the change within five business days, absent extenuating circumstances.

Rights and Responsibilities Notice

The employer must also give employees written notice of their rights and responsibilities under the FMLA. This notice must be provided each time the eligibility notice is provided. This notice must state:

- that the employee's leave may be designated as FMLA leave and counted against his or her entitlement
- whether the employer will require the employee to provide certification (and the consequences of failing to provide the certification)
- the employee's right to use accrued paid time off during the unpaid FMLA leave, whether the employer will require the employee to use accrued paid time off during leave, the conditions related to using accrued paid time off, and the employee's right to take unpaid FMLA leave if the employee doesn't meet the conditions for using paid leave
- how health benefit premiums will be paid and the consequences of failing to pay them
- whether the employee is a key employee and the consequences of that classification (see "Exceptions," below, for more about key employees)
- the employee's right to restoration of benefits and reinstatement to the same or an equivalent job upon return from leave, and
- the employee's potential liability for any health insurance premiums the employer pays while the employee is on FMLA leave, if the employee fails to return to work after FMLA leave.

The DOL has created prototype notice forms that employers may adapt as appropriate to meet their notice requirements; see "Agency Resources," below. The employer may distribute this notice electronically.

Designation Notice

When the employer has enough information to determine whether an employee is taking leave for an FMLA-qualifying reason, the employer must notify the employee whether leave will be designated and counted as FMLA leave. The employer must provide this notice within five business days, absent extenuating circumstances. The employer need provide only one designation notice per qualifying reason per 12-month leave year, whether the leave will be taken intermittently or all at once. If the information in the notice changes, the employer must notify the employee of the change within five business days after receiving the employee's first notice of need for leave following the change, absent extenuating circumstances.

If the employer requires the substitution of paid leave or will count paid leave taken under an existing plan against the employee's FMLA entitlement, the employer must inform the employee in the designation notice. The employer must also inform the employee if it will require a fitness for duty certification prior to the employee's return to work. The employer may require that the fitness for duty certification address the employee's ability to perform the essential functions of his or her position. If the employer imposes this requirement, it must inform the employee in the designation notice and must include a list of the job's essential functions.

The notice must tell the employee how much leave will be counted against the employee's leave entitlement. If the amount of leave needed is known when the employer designates it as FMLA leave, the employer must include the number of hours, days, or weeks that will be counted against the employee's FMLA entitlement in the designation notice. If it isn't possible to provide this detail (typically, because the employee needs intermittent leave on an unforeseeable basis), the employer must notify the employee of how much leave has been counted against his or her entitlement upon the employee's request, but no more often than once in a 30-day period during which leave was taken. The employer may give this notice orally, but must confirm it in writing no later than the following payday or, if that payday falls less than a week after the oral notice, by the subsequent payday. This written notice may be in any form, including a notation on the employee's pay stub.

Required Notice From the Employee

The employee must give the employer at least 30 days' notice of his or her desire to take leave when the leave is foreseeable (for example, for a planned birth or operation) or as soon as practicable for an unforeseeable event (for example, a sudden heart attack) or for leave that is foreseeable less than 30 days in advance (for example, if the employee is scheduled for surgery the following week). An employee who does not give 30 days' notice must respond to the employer's request to explain why giving notice was not practicable. Whether it is practicable for an employee to give notice depends on the facts and circumstances; ordinarily, it will be practicable for an employee to give notice the same day or following day after learning of the need for leave.

For qualifying exigency leave, the 30-day requirement doesn't apply; employees need only give as much notice as is practicable.

Absent unusual circumstances, employers may require employees to comply with usual notice and other requirements for requesting leave, such as making requests in writing or notifying a particular person; failure to comply may result in delay of leave, unless the employer's policy requires more notice than the FMLA and the employee's notice was timely under the FMLA.

Calling in "sick" without more information is not sufficient notice. The employee must provide enough details so the employer can determine whether the leave is for an FMLA-qualifying reason. The employee must respond to the employer's questions geared toward determining whether the leave is protected by the FMLA. Employees seeking more leave for a qualifying reason for which they have already taken leave must specifically refer to either the qualifying reason or the need for FMLA leave.

In addition to the initial notice, the employer can require an employee who is on FMLA leave to report periodically on his or her status and intent to return to work.

Reasons to Delay Leave

An employer may delay an eligible employee's leave in the following circumstances:

- If an employee could have given 30 days' notice, but failed to do so, the employer can delay the leave until 30 days have passed from the date the employee told the employer about the leave.
- If the employee fails to give notice as soon as practicable, the employer may delay the leave for the number of days between when the employee gave notice and when the employee should have given notice.
- If an employee doesn't provide certification, the employer can delay the leave until the employee does provide certification.

Certification

Medical Certification

If an employee requests FMLA leave for his or her own serious health condition or for a family member's serious health condition, the employer may ask the employee to provide documentation from a health care provider certifying the existence of the serious health condition. The employer must make this request within five business days after (1) the employee requests to take leave, or (2) the employee's unforeseeable leave begins. When the employer requests the certification, the employer must also inform the employee of the consequences of failing to provide certification.

The employee has 15 calendar days to provide the certification, unless it is not practicable to do so under the circumstances despite the employee's good-faith efforts. After an employee provides certification, the employer must tell the employee if it thinks the certification is incomplete or insufficient, and state in writing what additional information is necessary. The employer must give the employee at least seven calendar days to cure the problem, or more time if it is not practicable to do so under the circumstances, despite the employee's good-faith efforts.

After giving the employee the opportunity to cure any deficiencies in the certification, the employer may contact the health care provider for purposes of *authentication* or *clarification*. This contact must be made through a health care provider, human resources professional, leave administrator, or management official; the employee's direct supervisor may not contact the employee's health care provider.

The employee may submit a certification from a health care provider from another country if the employee is visiting there when his or her serious health condition develops, or in the case of a family member's serious health condition, the family member is living or visiting there. If the certification is not in English, the employee must provide a written translation upon the employer's request.

Certifications must contain very specific and detailed information. The DOL provides two forms that employees can use when obtaining medical certifications, one for the employee's own serious health condition and one for a family member's health condition. Although use of these forms is optional, they are helpful to employers and medical providers because they request the specific information that the FMLA requires. (For more information on how to find these forms, see "Agency Resources," below.)

If an employer doubts the validity of a certification, the employer can request a second opinion at its expense. Although the employer can choose the second health care provider, that person may not be someone who works for the employer on a regular basis. If the first and second opinions differ, the employer can request a third certification—again at the employer's expense. This third health care provider must be someone whom both the employer and the employee agree upon. This third opinion is final and binding.

The employer may also request recertification—a follow-up certification from the same health care provider. The employer may request recertification no more often than every 30 days, and only in connection with an employee's absence, with some exceptions. The employer must wait longer than 30 days to request recertification if the original certification indicates that the serious health condition is expected to last more than 30 days. In this situation, the employer must wait until the estimated duration of the health condition has passed. However, the employer is entitled to request recertification every six months, even if the health condition is expected to last longer than that.

An employer may request a recertification before 30 days have passed if any of the following are true:

- The employee requests an extension of leave.
- The circumstances described in the previous certification have changed significantly (for example, the employee is taking quite a bit more intermittent leave than the certification indicated would be necessary).
- The employer receives information casting doubt on the employee's stated reason for the absence or the continuing validity of the certification.

As part of the recertification process, the employer may give the health care provider a record of the employee's absence pattern and ask whether the serious health condition and need for leave is consistent with that pattern.

Certification of a Qualifying Exigency

When an employee first requests leave for a qualifying exigency, the employer may require the employee to provide a copy of the active duty orders or other documentation issued by the military indicating the family member's covered active duty and the dates of service. The employee need not supply this documentation again unless leave is necessary because of a subsequent active duty or a different family member. If the qualifying exigency leave is for rest and recuperation, the employer can require the employee to produce a copy of the military member's Rest and Recuperation leave orders.

The employer may also require the employee to submit a certification that includes specified information about the exigency and leave. The DOL has developed an optional form employers can use to request this information; see "Agency Resources," below.

If the certification is complete, the employer may not request more information. The employer may contact third parties identified in the certification to verify a meeting or an appointment schedule and to find out the nature of the meeting; no additional information may be requested, and the employee's permission is not required. The employer may also contact the Department of Defense (DOD) to request verification that the employee is on covered active duty; no additional information may be requested, and the employee's permission is not required.

An employer may not request recertification of the employee's need for qualifying exigency leave.

Fitness for Duty Certification

If an employee takes FMLA leave for his or her own serious health condition, the employer may require the employee to provide a fitness for duty certification from his or her doctor before returning to work. The employer may request that the fitness for duty certification specifically address the employee's ability to perform the essential functions of the job. To do so, the employer must notify the employee of the requirement and provide the employee with a list of those functions at the time of the designation notice.

The employer may seek authentication or clarification of the fitness for duty certification, but the employee's return to work may not be delayed while the employer contacts the provider.

The employer may not require a fitness for duty certification for each absence taken intermittently, but may require one every 30 days for such absences if *reasonable safety concerns* exist regarding the employee's ability to perform his or her duties relating to the serious health condition for which leave was taken.

Reinstatement

Following FMLA leave, an employee has the right to be returned to the same position the employee held before or to an equivalent position—one that is nearly identical to the employee's former position in terms of pay, benefits, and working conditions, including privileges, seniority, and status. The equivalent position must involve the same or substantially similar duties, which must require substantially equivalent skill, effort, responsibility, and authority.

Equivalent pay includes any bonuses or payments that occurred while the employee was on FMLA leave, if those payments were unconditional. Pay increases that depend on seniority, length of service, or work performed must be handled the same way for employees who take other types of leave. A bonus or payment based on the employee's achievement of a goal such as hours worked, products sold, or perfect attendance need not be paid to employees who missed the goal because of FMLA leave, unless such bonuses are paid to employees who missed the goal due to leave that is not FMLA-qualified.

An employee who accepts a light-duty position while recovering from a serious health condition retains the right to reinstatement to the employee's former position until the end of the leave year.

An employer can delay or deny an employee's return to work in any of the following circumstances:

- The employer can delay reinstatement until the employee provides a fitness for duty certification.
- If the employee could have been legitimately fired or laid off while not on leave, an employer may fire or lay off the employee while he or she is on FMLA leave. In such a situation, the employee has no right to reinstatement, continued leave, or continued benefits. For example, if an employee goes on FMLA leave to have a baby and, while the employee is on leave, the employer eliminates the employee's entire department, the employee does not have a right to reinstatement, because her job no longer exists. However, because it is illegal to fire or otherwise retaliate against an employee for taking FMLA leave, employers that rely on this provision must make very certain that their reasons for termination are beyond reproach. It's best to consult with a lawyer before firing or laying off an employee who has requested or taken FMLA leave.

- If an employee clearly tells the employer that he or she does not intend to return to work, the employee has no right to reinstatement, continued leave, or continued health benefits. Employers that rely on this provision should have documentation from the employee.
- If an employee is a key employee, the employer may deny reinstatement in certain circumstances. (See "Exceptions," below, for more about key employees.)
- If an employee obtains FMLA leave fraudulently (for example, by falsely claiming that a family member is seriously ill in order to take an extended vacation), the employee has no right to leave, reinstatement, or continued benefits.

Exceptions

Spouses Working for the Same Employer

If two spouses work for the same employer, the employer has the right to limit the total amount of leave the couple can take for the arrival of a new child or to care for a parent with a serious health condition. For those two types of leave, the employer can limit the employees to a combined total of 12 workweeks of unpaid leave during a 12-month period. For example, if one spouse takes four weeks to care for a new child, then the employer may limit the second spouse to eight weeks to care for the new child. Each spouse may use the remaining weeks of his or her leave for any other FMLA-qualifying reason that is not subject to the 12-week combined limit. For example, the first spouse may use the remaining eight weeks to care for the second spouse who has a serious health condition.

This limitation does not apply when married employees take leave for their own serious health conditions or for the serious health condition of a family member other than a parent. For example, if a married couple has a child with a serious health condition, each parent can take 12 workweeks of unpaid leave to care for the child.

Key Employees

If an employee is a key employee (see "Definitions," above), the employer may refuse to reinstate the employee if the employee's return would cause "substantial and grievous" economic injury to the employer. This is intended to be a difficult standard to meet (for example, more difficult than proving that a requested accommodation for a disabled employee would be an "undue hardship" on the employer—see Chapter 2).

In the rights and responsibilities notice, the employer must state whether it considers the employee to be a key employee and the consequences of that designation. The employer must also notify the employee if and when it decides not to reinstate the employee based on the key employee exception. This notice must explain the basis for the employer's finding that substantial and grievous economic injury will result from reinstatement and, if the employee is already on leave, must give the employee a reasonable time in which to return to work, taking into account the circumstances (for example, why the employee took leave and why the company needs the employee to return).

If the employee does not return to work in response to this notice, he or she is still entitled to take FMLA leave and receive continued health benefits. An employee who has been notified that he or she will not be reinstated pursuant to the key employee exception can still request reinstatement at the end of his or her leave. If the employee makes this request, the employer must once again determine whether reinstating the employee would cause substantial and grievous economic injury, based on the circumstances at that time.

26-Week Military Caregiver Leave

The FMLA also allows eligible employees to take up to 26 weeks of leave in a single 12-month period to care for a covered servicemember with a serious injury or illness. Although many of the rules for military caregiver leave are similar to the rules for other types of FMLA leave, there are also some important differences. This section covers those differences; issues that aren't included here are handled in the same manner as they are for 12-week FMLA leave, explained above.

Covered Employers

All covered employers are subject to these provisions.

Covered Workers

As for other types of FMLA leave, the employee must have worked for the employer for at least a year, and worked at least 1,250 hours in the year preceding the leave, to be eligible. For this type of leave, the employee must also be the covered servicemember's spouse, child, parent, or *next of kin*. A "child" of the servicemember may be any age; in other words, children 18 and older are covered even if they can care for themselves.

What's Prohibited

The same prohibitions that apply to the 12-week provisions of FMLA leave also apply to military caregiver leave.

What's Required

Employers must allow eligible employees to take up to 26 weeks of leave in a single 12-month period to care for a covered servicemember who has a serious injury or illness. For those who are current members of the armed forces, National Guard, or reserves, a serious illness or injury is one that was incurred in the line of duty on active duty and may render the member medically unfit to perform the duties of his or her office, grade, rank, or rating. Serious illnesses or injuries that preexisted the member's active duty and were aggravated by service in the line of duty on active duty are also covered.

Coverage also extends to veterans who are undergoing medical treatment, recuperation, or therapy, for a serious injury or illness and who were members of the armed forces (including a member of the National Guard or reserves) at any time in the previous five years (as long as the veteran was not dishonorably discharged).

In the case of a veteran, a serious illness or injury is one that was incurred in the line of duty on active duty, or that existed before the member's active duty and was aggravated in the line of duty on active duty, and that meets any of the following conditions:

- a continuation of a serious injury or illness that happened in the line of duty on active duty, or was aggravated in the line of duty on active duty, and that left the member unable to perform the duties of his or her office, grade, rank, or rating
- a physical or mental condition for which the veteran has received a disability rating of 50% or higher from the U.S. Department of Veterans Affairs (and the veteran needs care for that condition)
- a physical or mental condition that substantially impairs—or would substantially impair without treatment—the veteran's ability to work because of a disability related to military service, or
- a physical or psychological injury that has led the veteran to enroll in the Department of Veterans Affairs Program of Comprehensive Assistance for Family Caregivers.

The illness or injury may manifest itself before or after the member became a veteran.

Amount of Leave

Eligible employees may take up to 26 weeks of leave in a single 12-month period. This leave is available once per servicemember, per injury; it does not automatically renew each year. Any part of the 26 weeks the employee doesn't take during the 12-month period is lost; it doesn't carry over to the following year. The amount of leave for flight attendants and airline flight crew employees is slightly different; these employees may take up to 156 days of military caregiver leave, instead of 26 workweeks.

The employee is entitled to only one 26-week leave entitlement unless another covered servicemember for whom the employee is eligible to take leave suffers a serious injury or illness or the same covered servicemember suffers another serious injury or illness during a different 12-month period. The employee is also entitled to two separate 26-week leave periods for the same family member: one leave period when the family member is a current servicemember and another leave period when the family member becomes a veteran. For example, if an employee takes 26 weeks of leave for a current servicemember with a serious illness or injury, the employee may take another 26 weeks of leave when that servicemember becomes a veteran and needs care for the same serious illness or injury.

However, even if an employee has a right to more than one 26-week leave entitlement, the employee may not take more than 26 total weeks of leave in a 12-month period. This is true even if the leave entitlements overlap.

The 12-month period begins on the first day the employee takes military caregiver leave, regardless of how the employer measures the leave year for other types of FMLA leave.

The 26-week entitlement applies to all types of FMLA leave combined. Up to 12 of those weeks my be used for any FMLA-qualifying reason. For example, an employee may take 14 weeks of military caregiver leave and 12 weeks to bond with a new child. Or the employee can use all 26 weeks for military caregiver leave.

Whenever possible, the employer must designate FMLA leave as military caregiver leave. For example, if an employee takes time off to care for a covered servicemember who is the employee's spouse, that leave would likely otherwise count as both military caregiver leave and leave to care for a spouse with a serious health condition. The employer may not designate it as both, however; instead, the employer must designate any leave that qualifies for the military caregiver provision as that type of leave.

Military caregiver leave may be taken intermittently or on a reduced schedule if medically necessary.

Certification

The employer may require the employee to submit a certification. Until recently, part of the certification had to be completed by a health care provider who was affiliated with the military health care system, including:

- a DOD health care provider
- a Department of Veterans Affairs (VA) health care provider
- a DOD TRICARE network authorized private health care provider, or
- a DOD nonnetwork TRICARE authorized private health care provider.

However, the certification can now be filled out by private health care providers as well.

The health care provider may be asked to provide specified information about the serious injury or illness, treatment, and need for care. In addition, the employee or covered servicemember must provide information about the servicemember, the care and leave required, and the relationship between the employee and the servicemember. The DOL has created optional certification forms employers can use for this purpose—one for current servicemembers and one for veterans; see "Agency Resources," below.

The employer may seek authentication or clarification, for any certification. However, the employer may request a second or third opinion only when the certification is completed by a health care provider that is not affiliated with the DOD, VA, or TRICARE. Employers may not request recertifications for military caregiver leave. Employers may, however, require the employee to provide confirmation of the employee's relationship to the covered servicemember.

In lieu of certification, an employer must accept an invitational travel order or invitational travel authorization. For the time specified in that document, the employer may not require additional or separate certification. The employee need not be named in the document. If the time on the document expires, the employer may request certification. The employer may seek authentication or clarification of the document, but not recertification. The employer may ask for a second or third opinion only if the health care provider is not affiliated with the military.

Exceptions

Spouses Working for the Same Employer

Spouses who work for the same employer can be limited in how much combined leave they may take. The employer has the right to limit the amount of leave the couple can take to 26 weeks total for the following reasons:
- to bond with a new child
- to care for an employee's parent with a serious health condition, and
- to care for a covered servicemember with a serious illness or injury.

This limitation does not apply to leave that married employees take for their own serious health conditions or for the serious health condition of a family member other than a parent.

How the FMLA Is Enforced

Individual Complaints

Employees who believe their employers have violated their FMLA rights can file complaints with the Department of Labor (DOL) within two years of the violations, or they can file private lawsuits. They are not required to file complaints with the DOL before pursuing lawsuits. An employee may file a private lawsuit within two years of the employer's FMLA violation, or within three years if the violation was willful.

Agency Enforcement

The Wage and Hour Division of the DOL investigates FMLA complaints. The DOL can also file lawsuits against employers in court to compel compliance.

Complying With the FMLA

Deadlines

- Employers must give an employee an eligibility notice and a rights and responsibilities notice within five business days after an employee requests leave or after the employer learns that the employee's leave may be FMLA qualifying. If the employee's eligibility changes, the employer must notify the employee within five business days of the change.
- Employers must give an employee a designation notice within five business days after receiving enough information to determine whether an employee's leave is FMLA qualifying. If the information in the designation notice changes, the employer must notify the employee within five business days of the employee's first request for leave after the change.
- Employers that will require an employee to submit a certification must inform the employee of this requirement within five business days after (1) the employee requests to take leave, or (2) the employee's unforeseeable leave begins.

Reporting Requirements

The FMLA imposes no reporting requirements.

Posting Requirements

All covered employers must post a notice approved by the DOL that explains employee rights and responsibilities under the FMLA. To find out how to obtain a copy of that notice, see "Agency Resources," below.

Record-Keeping Requirements

Employers must keep records pertaining to their FMLA obligations. These records include:

- payroll information for each employee, including name, address, job title, rate or basis of pay, terms of compensation, daily and weekly hours worked per pay period, additions to wages, deductions from wages, and total compensation paid (unless the employee is exempt from the Fair Labor Standards Act's record-keeping requirements; see Chapter 7)

- dates the employee has taken FMLA leave
- if the employee has taken less than a day of FMLA leave, the number of hours of leave taken
- copies of all written notices the employee has given the employer about FMLA leave
- copies of all written notices the employer has given the employee about FMLA leave
- documents describing employee benefits
- documents showing employer policies regarding paid and unpaid leave
- documents showing employer-paid health insurance premiums, and
- records of any disputes between the employer and the employee regarding FMLA leave.

Employers of airline flight crews must also keep on file, with the secretary of labor, information regarding the applicable total monthly guarantee for each category of employee to whom such a guarantee applies, as well as scheduled work hours for these employees.

Employers must follow the confidentiality requirements set forth in the Genetic Information Nondiscrimination Act (GINA); see Chapter 9 for details.

Remedies

If an employee prevails in a lawsuit against an employer, the employee might be entitled to any or all of the following remedies:

- lost wages
- lost employment benefits
- cost of providing care (for example, the cost of paying a home care provider to care for a seriously ill family member for the period of time when an employee was illegally denied the right to take leave)
- interest on damages
- money damages set by the statute (called liquidated damages)
- reinstatement
- promotion
- attorneys' fees, and
- legal costs.

If an employer fails to post required notices, the DOL can impose a civil fine of up to $169 for each offense. An employer that fails to post required notices cannot deny an employee FMLA leave if the employee fails to give the employer advance notice of his or her intent to take FMLA leave.

Agency Resources

- The poster that employers must display alerting employees to their FMLA rights and obligations

  Employee Rights Under the Family and Medical Leave Act (FMLA) Poster
  www.dol.gov/whd/regs/compliance/posters/fmlaen.pdf

- An optional form that employees may use to obtain a medical certification from a health care provider regarding their own serious health condition

  Form WH-380-E: Certification of Health Care Provider for Employee's Serious Health Condition
  www.dol.gov/whd/forms/WH-380-E.pdf

- An optional form that employees may use to obtain a medical certification from a health care provider regarding a family member's own serious health condition

  Form WH-380-F: Certification of Health Care Provider for Family Member's Serious Health Condition
  www.dol.gov/whd/forms/WH-380-F.pdf

- An optional form that employees may use to obtain a certification from a health care provider regarding a current servicemember's serious illness or injury

  Form WH-385: Certification for Serious Injury or Illness of a Current Servicemember—for Military Family Leave
  www.dol.gov/whd/forms/WH-385.pdf

- An optional form that employees may use to obtain a certification from a health care provider regarding a veteran's serious illness or injury

  Form WH-385V: Certification for Serious Injury or Illness of a Veteran for Military Caregiver Leave
  www.dol.gov/whd/forms/wh385V.pdf

- An optional form that employees may use to provide certification of their need for qualifying exigency leave

  Form WH-384: Certification of Qualifying Exigency for Military Family Leave
  www.dol.gov/whd/forms/WH-384.pdf

- An optional form employers may use to provide the eligibility notice and rights and responsibilities notice

  Form WH-381: Notice of Eligibility and Rights & Responsibilities
  www.dol.gov/whd/fmla/forms/WH-381.pdf

- An optional form employers may use to provide designation notice

  Form WH-382: Designation Notice
  www.dol.gov/whd/forms/WH-382.pdf

The DOL has more information and publications available online. For a complete list, visit www.dol.gov/whd/fmla.

State Laws Relating to Family and Medical Leave

Some states also have laws that require employers to provide family and medical leave. These laws may be more extensive than the FMLA—for example, they may apply to smaller employers, allow employees to take leave to care for a broader range of family members (such as siblings or domestic partners), or provide time off to attend a child's school function or take a family member to medical appointments. In recent years, several states have also passed laws requiring employers to provide some paid sick leave or paid family leave, or both.

The chart below provides basic information about these state laws, but does not address every aspect of the law, such as notice requirements, medical certification rules, or reinstatement procedures. For more information, contact your state's department of labor (see Appendix A for contact information).

State Laws Relating to Family and Medical Leave

Arizona

A.R.S. § 23-371 and following

Paid Sick Leave: All employers must provide one hour paid sick time for every 30 hours worked. Employers with 15 or more employees may cap accrual and use at 40 hours per year; employers with fewer than 15 employees may cap accrual and use at 24 hours per year. Sick leave may be used for the employee's illness, to care for an ill family member, to seek assistance relating to domestic violence, or due to the closure of the employee's work or a child's school due to a public health emergency.

Arkansas

Ark. Code Ann. §§ 9-9-105, 11-3-205

Family and Medical Leave: Employers that allow employees to take leave for the birth of a child must give the same leave to employees adopting a child no older than 18 (does not apply to stepparent or foster parent adoptions).

Organ and Bone Marrow Donation: All employers must provide up to 90 days of unpaid leave for organ or bone marrow donation to employees who are not eligible for FMLA leave.

California

Cal. Gov't. Code §§ 12945, 12945.2, and 12945.6; Cal. Lab. Code §§ 230 and following; Cal. Unemp. Ins. Code §§ 3300 and following; Cal. Lab. Code §§ 245.5, 246, and 246.5

Family and Medical Leave: Employers with 50 or more employees must provide up to 12 weeks of leave each year to care for seriously ill family member, for employee's own serious illness, or to bond with new child.

Employees are eligible if they have worked for the employer for at least 12 months, have worked 1,250 hours in the year prior to the start of leave, and work at a location within a 75-mile radius of 50 more employees. Employers with 20 to 49 employees must provide up to 12 weeks of leave each year for employees to bond with a new child only. The same eligibility requirements apply, except the employee must work within a 75-mile radius of 20 employees.

Pregnancy Disability Leave: Employers with 5 or more employees must provide up to 4 months of pregnancy disability leave to employees who are unable to work due to pregnancy or childbirth. This time is in addition to 12 weeks of bonding leave under state family leave law.

School Activities: Employers with 25 or more employees must provide up to 40 hours per year, but not more than 8 hours per calendar month, to enroll a child in a school or a licensed child care provider or to participate in activities related to the school or licensed child care provider.

Domestic Violence: Employers with 25 or more employees must provide employees with a reasonable amount of time off to obtain medical treatment counseling, take safety measures, or deal with other issues related to domestic violence, stalking, or sexual assault.

Paid Sick Leave: All employers must provide employees with one hour of sick leave for every 30 hours worked. Employers may cap sick leave at 24 hours per year. Employees are eligible if they have worked at least 30 days for the employer. Employees may use sick leave for their own illnesses,

State Laws Relating to Family and Medical Leave (continued)

to care for an ill family member, or to deal with the effects of domestic violence.

Paid Family Leave: Employees may receive 6 weeks of paid family leave benefits from the state when taking leave to bond with a new child or care for a seriously ill family member. As of January 1, 2021, paid family leave is also available for qualifying exigencies related to the employee's covered active duty in the U.S. armed forces or the covered active duty of the employee's spouse, domestic partner, child, or parent.

Temporary Disability Insurance: Employees may receive up to 52 weeks of short-term disability from the state when unable to work due to disability (including pregnancy).

Colorado

Colo. Rev. Stat. §§ 19-5-211; 24-34-402.7

Family and Medical Leave: Employers that offer leave for the birth of a child must give the same leave for adoption (doesn't apply to stepparent adoption).

School Activities: Colorado's previous law requiring employers to provide time off to employees for a child's school activities expired in 2015.

Domestic Violence: Employers with 50 or more employees must provide up to 3 days in a year to seek a restraining order, obtain medical care or counseling, relocate, or seek legal assistance relating to domestic violence, sexual assault, or stalking. Employees are eligible if they have worked for the employer for one year.

Connecticut

Conn. Gen. Stat. Ann. §§ 31-51kk to 31-51qq; §§ 31-57r to 31-57t; 46a-60

Family and Medical Leave: Employers with 75 or more employees must provide up to 16 weeks during any 24-month period for childbirth, adoption, the employee's serious health condition, a family member's serious health condition, bone marrow or organ donation, or a qualifying exigency arising out of a family member's active duty in the military.

Employee may take up to 26 weeks in a 12-month period for a family member who is a current member of the armed forces and is undergoing medical treatment for a serious illness or injury. Employees are eligible if they have worked for the employer for one year and have worked 1,000 hours in the last year.

Pregnancy Disability Leave: Employers with 3 or more employees must provide a reasonable amount of leave to employees who are unable to work due to pregnancy.

Paid Sick Leave: Employers in the service industry with 50 or more employees must provide employees with one hour of paid sick leave for every 40 hours worked, but may cap accrual at 40 hours per year. Employees may use leave for their own illness or to care for an ill family member.

District of Columbia

D.C. Code Ann. §§ 32-501 and following; 32-1202, 32-131.01 and following

Family and Medical Leave: Employers with 20 or more employees must provide up to 16 weeks in a 24-month period for the birth of a child, adoption, foster care, placement of a child with the employee for whom the employee permanently assumes and discharges parental responsibility, or to care for family member with a serious health condition. Employees may take an additional

State Laws Relating to Family and Medical Leave (continued)

16 weeks in a 24-month period for their own serious health conditions. Employees must have worked for the employer for at least one year and worked at least 1,000 hours in the year before the start of leave.

School Activities: All employers must provide up to 24 hours of unpaid leave per year for an employee to attend a child's school activities.

Domestic Violence: Leave described under "Paid Sick Leave," may also be used for employee or family member who is a victim of stalking, domestic violence, or abuse to get medical attention, get services, seek counseling, relocate, take legal action, or take steps to enhance health and safety.

Paid Sick Leave: All employers must provide paid sick leave for employees to use for their own illness or to care for a family member. Amount of paid leave ranges from three days to seven days per year, depending on size of the employer. Sick leave may be used for the employee's illness, to care for an ill family member, or to deal with the effects of stalking, domestic violence, or abuse against the employee or a family member.

Paid Family Leave: Beginning on July 1, 2020, employees will be eligible to receive paid family leave benefits from the district when taking leave for their own serious health conditions (2 weeks), to care for a family member with a serious health condition (6 weeks), or to bond with a new child (8 weeks).

Florida

Fla. Stat. § 741.313

Domestic Violence: Employers with at least 50 employees must provide up to 3 days of unpaid leave each year to employees who are the victims of domestic violence or sexual abuse or whose family members are victims. Employees are eligible if they have worked for the employer for at least 3 months.

Georgia

Ga. Code § 34-1-10

Family and Medical Leave: No requirement to provide sick leave, but employers with 25 or more employees that choose to do so must allow up to five days each year to be used to care for a sick immediate family member.

Hawaii

Haw. Rev. Stat. §§ 378-1; 378-71 to 378-74; 392-23; 398-1 to 398-11

Family and Medical Leave: Employers with 100 or more employees must provide up to 4 weeks of unpaid leave each year for the birth of a child or adoption, or to care for a family member with a serious health condition. (If employer provides paid sick leave, up to 10 days may be used for these purposes.) Employees are eligible if they have worked for the employer for six months.

Pregnancy Disability Leave: All employers must provide a reasonable period of time off for disability resulting from pregnancy, childbirth, or a related condition.

Domestic Violence: All employers must provide domestic violence leave. Employers with 50 or more employees must allow up to 30 days' unpaid leave per year for employee who is a victim of domestic or sexual violence or if employee's minor child is a victim. Employer with 49 or fewer employees must allow up to 5 days' leave.

Organ and Bone Marrow Donation: Employers with 50 or more employees

State Laws Relating to Family and Medical Leave (continued)

must provide up to 7 days of unpaid leave for bone marrow donation and 30 days' unpaid leave for organ donation.

Temporary Disability Insurance: Eligible employees who are temporarily unable to work because of illness or injury (including pregnancy) may collect up to 26 weeks of benefits through the state disability insurance program.

Illinois

820 Ill. Comp. Stat. §§ 147/1 and following; 180/1 and following

School Activities: Employers with 50 or more employees must provide 8 hours per year, but not more than 4 hours in a day, for employees to participate in a child's school activities. Employees are eligible if they have worked for the employer at least half time for 6 months and have no paid leave available.

Domestic Violence: All employers must provide unpaid leave each year to an employee who is a victim of domestic violence or sexual assault or whose family or household member is a victim. Employers with 50 or more employees must provide 12 weeks of leave; employers with 15 to 49 employees must provide 8 weeks of leave; and employers with 14 or fewer employees must provide 4 weeks of leave.

Iowa

Iowa Code § 216

Pregnancy Disability Leave: Employers with 4 or more employees must provide 8 weeks of leave for disability due to pregnancy, childbirth, or related conditions.

Kentucky

Ky. Rev. Stat. Ann. § 337.015

Family and Medical Leave: All employers must provide 6 weeks of leave to employees adopting a child under 7 years old.

Louisiana

La. Rev. Stat. Ann. §§ 23:341 to 23:342; 23:1015 and following; 40:1263.4

Pregnancy Disability Leave: Employers with 25 or more employees must provide a reasonable period of time off for disability due to pregnancy and childbirth, not to exceed 6 weeks for normal pregnancy or 8 weeks for complicated pregnancy.

School Activities: All employers must provide 16 hours of leave each year to attend a child's school or daycare activities.

Organ and Bone Marrow Donation: Employers with 20 or more employees must provide 40 hours of paid leave each year for employees to donate bone marrow. Employees are eligible if they work at least 20 hours per week.

Maine

Me. Rev. Stat. Ann. tit. 26, §§ 843 and following; tit. 26, § 850

Family and Medical Leave: Employers with 15 or more employees at one location must provide 10 weeks of leave in a two-year period for the birth of a child, adoption (for child 16 or younger), the employee's serious health condition, a family member's serious health condition, organ donation, or the death or serious health condition of a family member incurred while on active military duty. Employees are eligible if they

State Laws Relating to Family and Medical Leave (continued)

have worked for the employer for at least one year.

Domestic Violence: All employers must provide reasonable and necessary leave to an employee who is the victim of domestic violence, sexual assault, or stalking, or whose parent, spouse, or child is a victim. Leave may be used to prepare for and attend court, for medical treatment, and for other necessary services.

Maryland

Md. Code Ann., [Lab. & Empl.] §§ 3-1301 to 3-1311, 3-801, 3-802, 3-803

Family and Medical Leave: Employers with 15 or more employees must provide the same leave for adoption as allowed for the birth of a child. Employers with 50 or more employees must give employees a day off when an immediate family member leaves for or returns from active military duty outside the United States. Employees are eligible if they have worked for the employer for at least 12 months and worked at least 1,250 hours in the last year.

Paid Sick Leave: Employers with 15 or more employees must provide sick leave; smaller employers must provide unpaid sick leave. Employees accrue one hour of sick leave for every 30 hours worked. However, employers may cap accrual at 40 hours per year and use at 64 hours per year. Employees may use sick leave for their own illnesses, to care for an ill family member, for preventative medical care for the employee or a family member, for maternity or paternity leave, or to deal with the effects of domestic violence.

Massachusetts

Mass. Gen. Laws ch. 149, §§ 52D, 105D, 148C; ch. 151B, § 1(5)

Family and Medical Leave: Employers with 6 or more employees must provide eight weeks of unpaid leave to employees for the birth of a child or the adoption of a minor. Employees are eligible once they have completed their initial probationary period of employment, as long as it doesn't exceed three months.

Employers with 50 or more employees must provide 24 hours of leave each year to take a minor child or relative who is 60 or older to medical or dental appointment (combined with school activities leave). Employees must meet the same eligibility requirements of the FMLA.

School Activities: Employers with 50 or more employees must provide 24 hours of leave each year for an employee to attend a child's school activities (combined with family and medical leave for medical appointments). Employees must meet the same eligibility requirements of the FMLA.

Domestic violence: Employers with 50 or more employees must provide 15 days of unpaid leave in a 12-month period if the employee, or the employee's family member, is a victim of abusive behavior. Leave may be used to seek medical attention or counseling, obtain a protective order from a court, attend child custody proceedings, and other related purposes. Employees must meet the same eligibility requirements of the FMLA.

Paid Sick Leave: All employers must provide one hour of sick leave for every thirty hours worked, although employers may cap annual accrual at 40 hours. Employers with 11 or more employees must provide paid time off; employers with 10 or fewer

State Laws Relating to Family and Medical Leave (continued)

employees may provide unpaid time off. Employees may use leave for their own illnesses, to care for an ill family member, or domestic violence reasons.

Michigan

Mich. Comp. Laws Ann. §§ 408.961 and following

Paid Sick Leave: Beginning around April 1, 2019, employees will accrue one hour of sick leave for every 30 hours worked. Employers with 10 or more employees may cap use of paid sick leave at 72 hours per year. Employers with fewer than 10 employees may cap use of paid sick leave at 40 hours per year and unpaid sick leave at 32 hours per year. Employees may use sick leave for their own illnesses or preventative care; a family member's illness or preventative care; to deal with the effects of domestic violence or sexual assault; to attend meetings at a child's school regarding health, disability, domestic violence, or sexual assault; or due to the closure of the employee's workplace or a child's school due to a public health emergency.

Minnesota

Minn. Stat. Ann. §§ 181.940 and following.

Family and Medical Leave: Employers with 21 or more employees at one site must provide 12 weeks of leave for the birth of a child or adoption. Employees may also use accrued sick leave to care for an ill family member. Employees are eligible if they have worked at least half time for one year.

School Activities: All employers must provide 16 hours in a 12-month period to attend a child's activities related to child care, preschool, or special education.

Employees are eligible if they have worked half time for at least one year.

Domestic violence: Employers with 21 or more employees must allow accrued sick leave to be used to seek assistance due to sexual assault, domestic violence, or stalking.

Organ and Bone Marrow Donation: Employers with 20 or more employees must provide 40 hours of paid leave each year to donate bone marrow. Employees are eligible if they work at least 20 hours per week.

Montana

Mont. Code Ann. §§ 49-2-310, 49-2-311

Pregnancy Disability Leave: All employers must provide a reasonable leave of absence for pregnancy disability and childbirth.

Nebraska

Neb. Rev. Stat. § 48-234

Family and Medical Leave: Employers that allow employees to take leave for the birth of a child must give the same leave for adoption of a child no older than 8, or a child no older than 18 if the child has special needs (does not apply to stepparent or foster parent adoptions).

Nevada

Nev. Rev. Stat. Ann. §§ 392.920, 392.4577, 608.0198, 613.4383

Pregnancy Disability Leave: Employers that provide sick or disability leave to employees with other medical conditions must provide the same leave for pregnancy, miscarriage, childbirth, and related medical condition.

State Laws Relating to Family and Medical Leave (continued)

School Activities: Employers with 50 or more employees must provide employees with a child in public school 4 hours of leave per school year to attend parent-teacher conferences, school-related activities during regular school hours, school-sponsored events, or to volunteer or be involved at the school. All employers may not fire or threaten to fire a parent, guardian, or custodian for attending a school conference or responding to a child's emergency.

Domestic Violence: All employers must provide 160 hours of unpaid leave within one year of an incident of domestic violence for the following purposes: to seek medical treatment, to obtain counseling, to participate in court proceedings, or to create a safety plan. Employees are eligible if they have worked for at least 90 days and if they are victims of domestic violence or have a family member who is a victim.

New Hampshire

N.H. Rev. Stat. Ann. § 354-A:7(VI)

Pregnancy Disability Leave: Employers with 6 or more employees must provide temporary disability leave for pregnancy, childbirth, or a related medical condition.

New Jersey

N.J. Stat. Ann. §§ 34:11B-1 and following; 34-11C1 and following; 34:11D-1 and following; 43:21-1 and following

Family and Medical Leave: Employers with 50 or more employees must provide 12 weeks of leave (or 24 weeks' reduced leave schedule) in any 24-month period for the birth or adoption of a child or to care for a family member with a serious health condition. Employees are eligible if they have worked for at least one year and at least 1,000 hours in previous 12 months.

Domestic violence: Employers with 25 or more employees must provide 20 unpaid days in one 12-month period for an employee who is (or whose family member is) a victim of domestic violence or a sexually violent offense. Employees are eligible if they have worked for at least one year and worked at least 1,000 hours in the last 12 months.

Paid Sick Leave: All employers must provide paid sick leave to their employees. Employees accrue one hour of paid sick leave for every 30 hours worked. However, employers may cap accrual and use at 40 hours per year. Employees may use sick leave for their own illnesses, to care for an ill family member, for preventative medical care for themselves or a family member, to attend a child's school events, to deal with the effects of domestic violence, or due to the closure of the employee's workplace or child's school due to a public health emergency.

Paid Family Leave: Employees may receive paid family leave benefits from the state for 6 weeks of leave per year to care for a seriously ill family member (including a registered domestic partner) or to bond with a new child.

Temporary Disability Insurance: Employees may receive temporary disability benefits from the state for up to 26 weeks when they are unable to work due to disability.

New Mexico

N.M. Stat. Ann. § 50-4A-1 and following

State Laws Relating to Family and Medical Leave (continued)

Domestic Violence: All employers must provide intermittent leave for up to 14 days each calendar year, but no more than eight hours in one day, to obtain an order of protection or other judicial relief from domestic abuse, to meet with law enforcement officials, to consult with attorneys or district attorneys' victim advocates, or to attend court proceedings related to the domestic abuse of an employee or an employee's family member.

New York

N.Y. Lab. Law §§ 201-c, 202-a; N.Y. Workers' Compensation Law § 200 and following

Family and Medical Leave: Employers that allow employees to take leave for the birth of a child must provide the same leave to employees adopting a child of preschool age or younger (or no older than 18 if disabled).

All employers must provide time off to employees to bond with a new child, take care of a family member with a serious health condition, or for qualifying exigencies arising out of a family member's call to active military duty. The maximum amount of leave in a 52-week period: 10 weeks in 2019 and 2020, and 12 weeks in 2021 and beyond. Full-time employees are eligible once they have been employed for 26 weeks; part-time employees are eligible once they have worked 175 days.

Organ and Bone Marrow Donation: Employers with 20 or more employees at one site must provide 24 hours' leave to donate bone marrow. Employees are eligible if they work at least 20 hours per week.

Paid Family Leave: Employees may also receive paid family leave benefits from the state when taking leave to care for a family member with a serious health condition, to bond with a new child, or for qualifying exigency arising out of a family member's call to active duty in the military. The maximum benefit in 2019 is 55% of employee's average weekly wage or state average weekly wage. This increases to 60% in 2020 and 67% in 2021.

Temporary Disability Insurance: Employees who have worked for a covered employer for at least 4 consecutive weeks may receive temporary disability insurance benefits from the state for up to 26 weeks while unable to work due to disability (including pregnancy).

North Carolina

N.C. Gen. Stat. §§ 50B-5.5, 95-28.3

School Activities: All employers must give employees 4 hours of leave per year to parents or guardians of school-aged children to participate in school activities.

Domestic Violence: All employers must provide reasonable time off to obtain or attempt to obtain relief from domestic violence and sexual assault.

Oregon

Or. Rev. Stat. §§ 659A.029, 659A.150 and following, 659A.270 and following, 659A.312, 653.601 and following

Family and Medical Leave: Employers with 25 or more employees must provide 12 weeks off per year for the birth or adoption of a child (parental leave), the employee's serious health condition, to care for a family member with a serious health condition, to care for a child with an illness or injury that requires home care (sick child leave), or to deal with the death of a family member

State Laws Relating to Family and Medical Leave (continued)

(bereavement leave). Bereavement leave is capped at 2 weeks. Employees can take 12 weeks of parental leave and an additional 12 weeks for sick child leave. Employees are eligible if they have worked 25 or more hours per week for at least 180 days (except parental leave, which only requires that the employee has worked 180 days).

Pregnancy Disability Leave: Employers with 25 or more employees must provide 12 weeks off per year for pregnancy disability. This is in addition to 12 weeks for parental leave and 12 weeks for sick child leave. Employees are eligible if they have worked 25 or more hours per week for at least 180 days.

Domestic Violence: Employers with 6 or more employees must provide reasonable leave to employee who is a victim of, or whose minor child is a victim of, domestic violence, harassment, sexual assault, or stalking. Leave may be used to seek legal treatment, medical services, counseling, or to relocate or secure existing home.

Organ and Bone Marrow Donation: All employers must allow the employee to use accrued leave or must provide the employee with 40 hours of unpaid leave, whichever is less, to donate bone marrow. Employees are eligible if they work at least 20 hours per week.

Paid Sick Leave: All employers must provide one hour of sick leave for every 30 hours worked, although employers may cap accrual and use at 40 hours per year. Up to 40 hours of accrued leave must carry over to the next year. Employers with 10 or more employees must provide paid time off; employers with 9 or fewer employees may provide unpaid time off. Employees may use leave for their own illnesses, to care for an ill family member, to deal with domestic violence issues, or for any purpose described under the "Family and Medical Leave" section.

Rhode Island

R.I. Gen. Laws §§ 28-48-1 and following; 28-41-34 through 28-41-42; 28-57-1 and following

Family and Medical Leave: Employers with 50 or more employees must provide 13 weeks of leave in a two-year period for the birth of a child, adoption of a child up to 16 years old, the employee's serious health condition, or to care for a family member with serious health condition. Employees must have worked an average of 30 or more hours a week for at least 12 consecutive months.

School Activities: Employers with 50 or more employees must provide up to 10 hours a year to attend a child's school conferences or other activities.

Paid Sick Leave: Employers with 18 or more employees must provide one hour of paid sick leave for every 35 hours worked, up to a maximum of 32 hours in 2019, and 40 hours in 2020 and beyond. Employers with fewer than 18 employees must provide the same amount of unpaid sick leave. Sick leave may be used for the employee's own illness, to care for an ill family member, for reasons relating to domestic violence, or due to the closure of the employee's work or a child's school due to a public health emergency.

Paid Family Leave: Employees who take time off to bond with a new child or care for a family member with a serious health condition may receive four weeks of temporary caregiver benefits from the state.

State Laws Relating to Family and Medical Leave (continued)

Temporary Disability Insurance: Employees who are unable to work due to illness, injury, or pregnancy may collect up to 30 weeks of benefits from the state through its short-term disability insurance program (temporary caregiver benefits are counted against the 30 weeks).

South Carolina

S.C. Code Ann. § 44-43-80

Organ and Bone Marrow Donation: Employers with 20 or more employees in the state at one site may—but are not required to—allow employees to take up to 40 hours' paid leave per year to donate bone marrow. Employees are eligible if they work at least 20 hours per week.

Tennessee

Tenn. Code Ann. § 4-21-408

Family and Medical Leave: Employers with 100 or more employees must provide up to 4 months of unpaid leave for pregnancy, childbirth, nursing, and adoption. Employees must give 3 months' notice unless a medical emergency requires the leave to begin sooner. Employees are eligible if they have worked full-time for the employer for 12 consecutive months.

Texas

Tex. Lab. Code Ann. § 21.0595

Family and Medical Leave: Employers with 15 or more employees that provide leave to care for a sick child must also allow leave to care for a sick foster child.

Vermont

Vt. Stat. Ann. tit. 21, §§ 471 and following; 481 and following

Family and Medical Leave: Employers with 10 or more employees must provide unpaid leave for pregnancy, childbirth, or parental leave for the birth of a child or adoption of a child 16 or younger. Employers with 15 or more employees must also provide unpaid leave for the employee's serious health conditions or to care for a family member with a serious health condition. Employees may take up to 12 weeks each year for any of these purposes. Employers with 15 employees must provide an additional 4 hours of leave in a 30-day period, but not more than 24 hours per year, to take a family member to a medical, dental, or professional well-care appointment or respond to a family member's medical emergency (combined with school activities leave). Employees are eligible if they have worked an average of 30 hours per week for one year.

School Activities: Employers with 15 or more employees must provide employees with 4 hours of leave in a 30-day period, but not more than 24 hours per year, to participate in a child's school activities (combined with leave to take a family member to medical appointments). Employees are eligible if they have worked an average of 30 hours per week for one year.

Domestic Violence: Unpaid leave for victims of crime, including domestic violence and sexual assault, to attend certain legal proceedings.

Paid Sick Leave: All employers must provide one hour of paid sick leave for every 52 hours worked. Employers may cap accrual at 40 hours per year in 2019. Employees are eligible if they have worked for a covered employer for an average of 18 hours per week for at least 20 weeks.

State Laws Relating to Family and Medical Leave (continued)

Employees may use sick leave for their own illnesses, to care for an ill family member, for preventative medical care for themselves or a family member, to arrange long-term care for a family member, to deal with the effects of domestic violence on themselves or a family member, or to care for a family member when a school or business is closed due to a public health emergency.

Washington

Wash. Rev. Code Ann. §§ 49.12.265 and following; 49.12.350 and following; 49.46.200 and following; 49.76.010 and following, 49.78.010 and following

Family and Medical Leave: Employers with 50 or more employees must provide 12 weeks of leave during any 12-month period for the birth or placement of a child (through adoption or foster placement), the employee's serious health condition, or to care for a family member with a serious health condition. Employees are eligible if they have worked for the employer for at least 12 months and have worked at least 1,250 hours in the previous year. Employers must offer the same parental leave to adoptive parents and stepparents as biological parents.

Pregnancy Disability Leave: Employers with 8 or more employees must provide leave for the period of time when an employee is temporarily disabled due to pregnancy or childbirth. This is in addition to any leave available under federal FMLA and state family and medical leave laws.

Domestic Violence: All employers must provide reasonable leave from work to employees who are victims of domestic violence, sexual assault, or stalking—or whose family member is a victim—to prepare for and attend court, for medical treatment, and for other necessary services.

Paid Sick Leave: All employers must provide one hour of paid sick leave for every 40 hours worked. No annual cap on accrual, but employees may only carry over 40 hours of accrued leave from year to year. Employees may use sick leave for their own illness, the illness of a family member, the closure of a child's school or day care due to a public health emergency, and to seek services relating to domestic violence. Washington has a state-run paid family leave program, but benefits won't be available until January 2020.

Paid Family Leave: Beginning in January 2020, employees may receive 12 weeks of paid family leave benefits while taking time off to bond with a new child, recover from an illness, care for an ill family member, or attend to certain military-related events.

Wisconsin

Wis. Stat. Ann. § 103.10

Family Medical Leave: Employers with 50 or more employees must provide 6 weeks of leave per 12-month period for pregnancy, childbirth, and to bond with a baby arriving by birth or adoption. These employers must provide an additional 2 weeks off each year for the employee's own serious health condition and an additional 2 weeks each year to care for a family member with a serious health condition. Employees are eligible if they have worked for at least one year and have worked 1,000 hours in the preceding 12 months.

Genetic Information Nondiscrimination Act (GINA)

Statute: 42 U.S.C. §§ 2000ff and following

To view the statutes, visit http://uscode.house.gov and select "Title 42" and "Chapter 21F."

Regulations: 29 C.F.R. § 1635

To view the regulations, visit www.govinfo.gov and search "29 CFR 1635."

Overview of GINA

The most recent civil rights law on the books is the Genetic Information Nondiscrimination Act (GINA), enacted in 2008. GINA prohibits health insurers from using genetic information to deny insurance coverage or determine premiums. It also prohibits covered employers from making employment decisions based on an applicant or employee's genetic information, and it requires employers to keep employee genetic information confidential.

Covered Employers

The following employers must comply with GINA:
- private employers with 15 or more employees
- the federal government
- state governments
- private and public employment agencies
- labor organizations, and
- joint labor-management committees.

Did You Know ...

- Federal employees have been protected from discrimination based on genetic information since February 2000, when President Clinton signed Executive Order 13145.
- More than 30 states have laws that prohibit genetic discrimination. (To find out whether your state is one of them, see "State Laws Prohibiting Discrimination in Employment," in Chapter 18.)
- According to a survey conducted in 2007 by the Genetics and Public Policy Center, 93% of respondents said that employers should not be able to make employment decisions based on genetic information; 76% of respondents supported a law that would prohibit employers from doing so.

Definitions

Terms that appear in italics throughout this chapter are defined below.

Family medical history: Information about the manifestation of a disease or disorder in a person's family members. To be manifested, a disease or disorder must be capable of diagnosis by a health care professional with appropriate training and expertise in the field; if the diagnosis is based principally on genetic information, the condition is not manifested.

Family member: A dependent of an employee or applicant, or a first-degree, second-degree, third-degree, or fourth-degree relative of an employee, applicant, or the employee's or applicant's dependent.

Genetic information: Information about (1) a person's genetic tests, (2) the genetic tests of a person's family members, (3) the manifestation of a disease or disorder in the person's family members, (4) any requests for or receipt of genetic services, or participation in clinical research that includes genetic services, by the person or his or her family members, and (5) genetic information of a fetus the person or a family member is carrying or of any embryo legally held by the person or a family member using assisted reproductive technology. Genetic information does not include information about the sex or age of the person or family members, nor does it include information about the race or ethnicity of the person or family members that is not derived from a genetic test.

Genetic monitoring: The periodic examination of employees to evaluate acquired modifications to their genetic material, such as chromosomal damage or evidence of increased occurrence of mutations, caused by exposure to toxic substances in performing their jobs, in order to identify, evaluate, and respond to those effects or to control adverse environmental exposures in the workplace.

Genetic services: A genetic test, genetic education, or genetic counseling (including the gathering, interpretation, and assessment of genetic information).

Genetic test: An analysis of human DNA, RNA, chromosomes, proteins, or metabolites, that detects genotypes, mutations, or chromosomal changes.

Legal Developments

- **Genetic discrimination charges at the EEOC.** In 2017, the EEOC received 206 charges of discrimination under GINA. Most of the cases were resolved, netting $700,000 in monetary benefits (not including any damages awarded in litigation).
- **Workers win big in GINA case.** In 2015, two employees of a Georgia company were awarded $2.2 million in a GINA case dubbed the "devious defecator" case. In an attempt to identify who was leaving feces on the warehouse floor, the employer required the employees to submit to a DNA test by cheek swab. Both employees tested negative and promptly filed suit, arguing that this was a violation of GINA's prohibition against collecting genetic information from employees. The Georgia court agreed.

Covered Workers

GINA protects all prospective and current employees of a covered employer.

Major Provisions of GINA

Discrimination

Employers may not use *genetic information* as a basis for employment decisions.

Covered Employers

All covered employers are subject to GINA's antidiscrimination provisions.

Covered Workers

All covered workers are protected by GINA's antidiscrimination provisions.

Key Facts: Discrimination

- Employers may not make employment decisions based on genetic information about an employee, an applicant, or a family member of an employee or applicant.
- Employers may not retaliate against an employee or applicant who complains about a violation of GINA or participates in a hearing or investigation of such a violation.
- Disparate impact claims—in which an employee alleges that a seemingly neutral employment practice has had a disproportionately negative effect on a protected group—are not allowed under GINA.

What's Prohibited

Employers may not discriminate against any employee or applicant based on genetic information. Like Title VII (see Chapter 18), GINA prohibits discrimination in every aspect of employment, including hiring, firing, compensation, benefits, job classifications, and any other terms, conditions, or privileges of employment.

GINA also prohibits retaliation against an employee who has opposed any act the law prohibits or who has made a charge, testified, assisted, or participated in any other way in an investigation, proceeding, or hearing regarding a GINA violation.

Unlike Title VII, GINA does not allow disparate impact claims, in which an employee alleges that a neutral employment practice had a disproportionately negative effect on a protected group. (For more on Title VII and disparate impact claims, see Chapter 18.)

Exceptions

It is not a violation of GINA for an employer to make decisions based on genetic information if it is required to do so by a law or regulation that mandates *genetic monitoring*, such as certain OSHA regulations.

Acquisition of Genetic Information

With a few exceptions, GINA prohibits employers from requiring or asking workers to provide genetic information.

Key Facts: Acquisition of Genetic Information

- Employers may not require employees, applicants, or their family members to provide genetic information.
- Employers may not purchase genetic information about employees, applicants, or their family members.
- A handful of exceptions to this rule exist; if one of them applies, the employer is obligated to treat any genetic information it receives as a confidential medical record.

Covered Employers

All covered employers are subject to these provisions.

Covered Workers

All covered workers are subject to these provisions.

What's Prohibited

Employers may not ask or require employees to provide genetic information about themselves or a *family member*. For example, an employer may not require employees to take a *genetic test*. Employers also may not purchase genetic information about employees or their family members.

This prohibition applies to otherwise lawful medical examinations relating to employment, such as fitness for duty exams. In this case, the employer must tell the health care provider not to collect or provide genetic information, and it must take reasonable steps if it learns that such information is nonetheless being requested or provided, such as selecting a new provider to perform the exams.

An employer that lawfully requests, requires, or purchases information about a manifested disease, disorder, or pathological condition of an employee's family member who works for the same employer has not violated this prohibition. For example, it doesn't violate the law if an employee's sibling applies for a job and is asked to take a post-offer medical examination, or if the sibling works for the same employer and is receiving voluntary *genetic services*.

Exceptions

There are six exceptions to the general prohibition on acquiring genetic information from employees and their family members. Even if one of these exceptions applies, however, employers may not use the genetic information acquired as a basis for employment decisions. Employers must also safeguard the confidentiality of the information, as provided in "Confidentiality of Genetic Information," below.

It isn't illegal for an employer to obtain genetic information on an employee or family member in any of the circumstances described below.

1. **The employer inadvertently requests or requires genetic information from an employee or family member.** This might happen if a supervisor hears of genetic information during a casual conversation, in response to an expression of concern, or on a social networking site (if, for example, the supervisor and employee are Facebook friends and the employee posts that his family medical history includes colon cancer), as long as the supervisor didn't solicit the information. This exception doesn't apply if the employer seeks the information by, for example, searching online for genetic information about an employee, eavesdropping on conversations, searching someone's personal belongings, or asking pointed follow-up questions in a conversation about a family member's health.

If an employer receives genetic information in response to a lawful request for medical information, it will be considered inadvertent (and therefore be covered by this exception) as long as the employer told the health care provider not to disclose genetic information. This part of the exception applies to, for example, requests for documentation to support a request for reasonable accommodation under the ADA or other disability laws, a request pursuant to the FMLA or other leave laws, or a request for leave under the employer's own policies. The regulations provide the following suggested language, which may be provided in writing (or orally if the employer requests the medical information orally):

> The Genetic Information Nondiscrimination Act of 2008 (GINA) prohibits employers and other entities covered by GINA Title II from requesting or requiring genetic information of an individual or family member of the individual, except as specifically allowed by this law. To comply with this law, we are asking that you not provide any genetic information when responding to this request for medical information. "Genetic information" as defined by GINA, includes an individual's family medical history, the results of an individual's or family member's genetic tests, the fact that an individual or an individual's family member sought or received genetic services, and genetic information of a fetus carried by an individual or an individual's family member or an embryo lawfully held by an individual or family member receiving assistive reproductive services.

2. **The employer offers health or genetic services, for example, as part of a voluntary wellness program.** GINA allows employers to collect genetic information as part of a wellness program, as long as the disclosure is voluntary. In the past, EEOC regulations had a strict definition of "voluntary": Employers could not reward employees for providing genetic information or penalize employees for refusing to provide it. For example, a wellness program could not condition a financial incentive on an employee answering questions about his or her past or current health status.

However, in 2016, the EEOC passed a final rule allowing employers to offer a financial incentive of up to 30% of the total cost for self-coverage for the employee only (including premiums paid by both the employer and employee). Employers can offer the incentive to employees in connection with a wellness program that solicits a medical examination or disability-related information that would otherwise be prohibited under the Americans with Disabilities Act. (See Chapter 2 for more on the ADA.) Employers can also offer the same incentive to an employee's spouse who is covered under the group health plan without running afoul of GINA. The spouse may be asked to provide information about the manifestation of a disease or disorder as part of a health risk assessment. The spouse cannot, however, be asked to provide genetic information, including results of genetic tests. And, the assessment cannot ask about the manifestation of a disease or disorder in the employee's children.

In 2017, a federal district court held that the EEOC's rule was invalid because it failed to sufficiently demonstrate that a 30% incentive would not render participation in a wellness program involuntary. Although the court initially allowed the rule to remain in place until the EEOC could take further action, it subsequently declared the rules invalid as of January 1, 2019. The EEOC has since announced that it has no immediate plans to issue new proposed rules, creating legal uncertainty about how employers should proceed. Because this is a new and uncertain area of the law, you should consult with an employment lawyer to verify that your wellness program is in compliance with the law.

3. **The employer requests family medical history to comply with the certification requirements of the FMLA (see Chapter 8), state or local family medical leave laws, or employer policies that permit the use of leave to care for a sick family member.**

4. **The employer acquires genetic information from documents that are commercially and publicly available.** This exception applies if, for example, the employer reads a newspaper or magazine article about an employee's struggle with a genetic disorder. It does not apply if the employer gathers the information from medical databases, court records, or scientific research databases available to scientists on a restricted basis,

or through sources with limited access, such as social networking sites that require permission to access from a particular person or that allow access only to members of a particular group. It also doesn't apply if the employer accessed commercially and publicly available documents with the intent of gathering employee genetic information, or if the employer was likely to acquire genetic information from viewing them (for example, if an employer visits an online discussion group about genetic testing or discrimination).

5. **The information acquired is to be used for genetic monitoring of the biological effects of toxic substances in the workplace.** This exception applies only if all of the following are true:
   - The employer provides written notice of the monitoring to the employee.
   - The monitoring is required by federal or state law, or the employee gives prior knowing, voluntary, and written authorization to the monitoring on a form that is written so the employee is likely to understand it, that describes the type of genetic information that will be obtained and the restrictions on disclosure of genetic information.
   - The employee is informed of the results of individual monitoring.
   - The monitoring complies with either federal or state genetic monitoring regulations (depending on whether the state has its own genetic monitoring program under the authority of the OSH Act).
   - Other than any licensed health care professional or genetic counselor involved in the program, the employer receives results from the program only in aggregate form, which does not disclose the identity of individual employees.

6. **The employer conducts DNA analysis for law enforcement purposes as a forensic laboratory or to identify human remains, and requests or requires genetic information from employees only for analysis of DNA identification markers as a means of detecting sample contamination.**

Confidentiality of Genetic Information

Employers that have genetic information about an employee must keep it in separate files and treat it confidentially.

Covered Employers

All covered employers that possess genetic information about an employee are subject to these provisions.

Covered Workers

All covered workers are subject to these provisions.

What's Required

Employers that have genetic information about employees must keep it separately, and treat it as a confidential medical record. GINA provides that employers will comply with this requirement if they treat genetic information as they treat confidential medical records under the Americans with Disabilities Act (ADA). This means the information must be kept separate from regular personnel files and have restricted access.

An employer that receives genetic information orally (for example, in casual conversation with an employee) need not reduce it to writing, but still must keep it confidential. An employer need not go through its personnel files and remove genetic information that predates the effective date of GINA (November 21, 2009), but it may not use or disclose that information except in accordance with the law. Genetic information that an employer acquires through commercially and publicly available sources (in accordance with an exception to the prohibition on acquiring genetic information discussed above) need not be treated as confidential, but the employer may not discriminate based on that information.

Exceptions

An employer may disclose genetic information about an employee in the following circumstances:

- to the employee or a family member, upon the employee's written request
- to an occupational or health researcher, for research conducted in compliance with Part 46 of Title 45 of the Code of Federal Regulations (the Department of Health and Human Service's rules for conducting research involving human subjects)
- in response to a court order, but only the genetic information expressly authorized by that order; the employee (or a family member to whom the court order pertains) must be notified of the order and any genetic

information that was disclosed as a result, if the court order was obtained without the employee's (or family member's) knowledge
- to government officials investigating compliance with GINA, if the information is relevant to the investigation
- in connection with the employee's compliance with the certification requirements of the FMLA or a similar state law, or
- to a federal, state, or local public health agency, but only information about the manifestation of a disease or disorder in an employee's family member that concerns a contagious disease that presents an imminent hazard of death or life-threatening illness; the employer must notify the employee of the disclosure.

How GINA Is Enforced

Individual Complaints

The enforcement provisions of Title VII apply to GINA. (See Chapter 18.)

Agency Enforcement

The enforcement provisions of Title VII apply to GINA. (See Chapter 18.)

Complying With GINA

Posting Requirements

Employers must post a notice about federal laws prohibiting discrimination, including GINA. See Chapter 18 for information on getting the required poster from the EEOC.

Remedies

The remedies for violating GINA are the same as those for violating Title VII. (See Chapter 18.)

Agency Resources

- Information for employers on genetic information discrimination
  Genetic Information Discrimination
  www.eeoc.gov/laws/types/genetic.cfm
- FAQs for small businesses regarding GINA
  Questions and Answers for Small Businesses: EEOC Final Rule on Title II of the Genetic Information Nondiscrimination Act of 2008
  www.eeoc.gov/laws/regulations/gina_qanda_smallbus.cfm

State Laws Relating to Genetic Discrimination

See "State Laws Prohibiting Discrimination in Employment," in Chapter 18, for information on state laws relating to all forms of employment discrimination, including discrimination on the basis of genetic information.

Immigration Reform and Control Act of 1986 (IRCA)

Statute: 8 U.S.C. §§ 1324a and 1324b

To view the statutes, visit http://uscode.house.gov and select "Title 8," "Chapter 12," and "Subchapter II."

Regulations: 8 C.F.R. § 274a

To view the regulations, visit www.govinfo.gov and search "8 CFR 274a.1."

28 C.F.R. § 44

To view the regulations, visit www.govinfo.gov and search "28 CFR 44."

Overview of IRCA

When the Immigration Reform and Control Act of 1986 (IRCA) was passed, it was the most sweeping immigration law enacted by Congress in more than 35 years. IRCA addresses many immigration issues, but this chapter focuses only on the law's regulation of the employment relationship. This discussion does not cover the rules that apply to agricultural workers, nor does it cover the steps potential employers can take to secure temporary employment visas (such as H-1B visas) for foreign workers whom they wish to hire.

The IRCA has three major provisions affecting nonagricultural employment:

- **Verification.** Employers must verify that all employees are legally *authorized to work in the United States*. IRCA makes it illegal for an employer to knowingly hire, recruit, or refer for employment an unauthorized alien.
- **Record-keeping requirements.** Employers must keep forms verifying that employees are legally authorized to work in the United States.
- **Antidiscrimination.** Employers may not discriminate based on citizenship status or national origin.

The United States Citizenship and Immigration Services (USCIS) is responsible for the administrative aspects of IRCA, including processing and granting applications for citizenship or authorization to work in the United States. The U.S. Immigration and Customs Enforcement (ICE) is the agency responsible for enforcing IRCA, including investigating, detaining, and deporting aliens who are not authorized to be in the United States.

Covered Employers

The verification and record-keeping provisions of IRCA cover all employers regardless of size, including:

- private employers
- the federal government
- state governments
- local governments, and
- persons or entities that refer workers to employers for a fee.

The antidiscrimination provision of IRCA applies to the following employers only:

- private employers with four or more employees
- the federal government
- state governments, and
- local governments.

Definitions

Terms that appear in italics throughout this chapter are defined below.

Authorized to work in the United States: Legally permitted to hold a job in the United States. The following categories of people are authorized to work in the United States:

- U.S. citizens
- lawful permanent resident aliens
- lawful temporary resident aliens
- aliens paroled into the United States as refugees (but only for the specified period)
- aliens granted asylum (but only for the specified period)
- aliens admitted into the United States as nonimmigrant fiancées and fiancés (but only for the specified period)
- citizens of Micronesia and the Marshall Islands
- aliens granted suspension of deportation, and
- aliens granted extended voluntary departure as members of certain nationality groups, by request of the secretary of state.

Date of hire: The date on which the employee actually starts working for wages or other remuneration. The date of hire is not necessarily the date a job offer is made or accepted (although it can be, if the employee starts work that same day).

Independent contractor: Someone who carries on an independent business, contracts to do a piece of work according to his or her own means or methods, and is subject to the control of the person or business who contracted for the work only as to results (and not the manner of performing the work). Other federal and state laws have somewhat different definitions, but those do not apply here.

Unauthorized alien: A person who is not a U.S. citizen and who is neither (1) an alien lawfully admitted into the United States for permanent residence, nor (2) an alien authorized to be employed in the United States.

Legal Developments

- **Employers can check work authorization online.** A USCIS program called E-Verify allows employers to use the Internet to verify that new hires are authorized to work in the United States. Employers can check Social Security Administration and Department of Homeland Security databases to verify the employment authorization of new hires. Although the program is voluntary for most employers, federal contractors are required to use it. In addition, some states require private employers to use E-Verify.
- **Changes to the I-9 Form.** In 2017, the USCIS updated Form I-9, which is used to verify an individual's authorization to work in the United States. Employers have been required to use this version of the form for all new hires and for reverifications since September 18, 2017. The form is accessible at the USCIS website; see "Agency Resources," below, for more information.

Covered Workers

The verification and record-keeping provisions of IRCA cover all employees of covered employers, including:

- U.S. citizens and nationals, and
- aliens who are legally authorized to work in the United States.

The antidiscrimination provision of IRCA covers the following workers:

- citizens and nationals of the United States
- aliens lawfully admitted for permanent residence
- aliens lawfully admitted for temporary residence
- aliens admitted as refugees, and
- aliens granted asylum.

None of IRCA's employment-related provisions cover *independent contractors* or people who provide domestic services (for example, babysitting or housecleaning) in a private home and whose service is sporadic, irregular, or intermittent. If, however, the domestic worker's service is regular (for example, once a week or twice a month), then the worker is covered by IRCA.

Did You Know ...

- In 2017, ICE announced its plan to step up workplace efforts, employing I-9 audits, workplace investigations, civil fines, criminal arrests of employers that knowingly break the law, and administrative arrests of unauthorized workers.
- On May 4, 2018, ICE reported that it had already doubled workplace investigations over the previous year (3,510 compared to 1,716). The agency also reported conducting 2,282 I-9 audits and 594 criminal arrests related to worksite enforcement, both significant increases from the previous year.

Major Provisions of IRCA

Verification

Employers must verify that the people who work for them are legally authorized to work in the United States.

Covered Employers

All covered employers are subject to these provisions.

Covered Workers

All covered workers are subject to these provisions.

What's Prohibited

Employers may not:
- knowingly hire, recruit, or refer for a fee an *unauthorized alien* for employment in the United States
- continue to employ a person after discovering that he or she is an unauthorized alien, or
- ask an employee for additional identity and work authorization documents if the documents the employee presents reasonably appear genuine and reasonably appear to refer to the person who presented them (see "Record-Keeping Requirements," below, for a list of acceptable documents that establish identity and work authorization).

Key Facts: Verification

- Employers may not knowingly hire, recruit, or refer unauthorized aliens for employment in the United States or continue to employ someone after discovering that he or she is an unauthorized alien.
- To verify the employee's work authorization, employers must examine certain documents within three days of hiring an employee, or if the employee will work for fewer than three days, by the end of the employee's first day of work. If the employee's authorization to work in this country has an expiration date, the employer must reverify the employee's work eligibility when that authorization has expired.
- If the documents the employee presents reasonably appear genuine and to refer to the person who presented them, the employer may not ask the employee for additional identification and work authorization documents.
- Employers that fail to properly verify work authorization face civil and criminal penalties and fines.

What's Required

Employers must do all of the following:

- Within three business days of the employee's *date of hire*, the employer must physically examine documents presented by the employee to establish the employee's identity and authorization to work in the United States. (See "Record-Keeping Requirements," below, for a list of acceptable documents.)
- If the employer is hiring the employee for fewer than three days total, the employer must examine the documents before the end of the employee's first day of work.
- If the employee's authorization to work in the United States is temporary, the employer must reverify the employee's employment eligibility on or before the date when the original authorization expires. The employer may do this by completing Section 3 of the original Form I-9, or by completing a new Form I-9. A new Form I-9 must be filled out if the original I-9 was completed on the pre-2017 version of the form.

Record-Keeping Requirements

Employers must keep records to prove that they verified the legality of their workers.

Covered Employers

All covered employers are subject to these provisions.

Covered Workers

All covered workers are subject to these provisions.

What's Prohibited

Employers may copy any of the documents presented by the employee for verification purposes, but only if copies are made for all employees and kept with the I-9 Forms. Employers are not required to make photocopies of verification documents, however, unless they participate in the E-Verify program. Employers that participate in the E-Verify program must keep copies of certain documents if presented by the employee, including U.S. passports or passport cards, green cards, and work permits. Employers that make copies of verification documents may not use them for any purpose other than for compliance with IRCA. (See "What's Required," below, for more about Form I-9.)

Key Facts: Record Keeping

- After examining the necessary documents to verify work authorization, employers must complete Form I-9 for each employee they hire, including their own relatives.
- Only certain documents are acceptable to verify employment authorization. (See "Acceptable Documents," below.)
- Employers must keep an employee's Form I-9 for three years after the date of hire or one year after the employee's termination, whichever is later. Employers need not file the forms with any agency but must keep them and make them available for inspection by federal agencies.

What's Required

Employers must do all of the following:

- Within three business days of the date of hire, the employer must verify under penalty of perjury that the employee is a U.S. citizen or an authorized alien by completing Form I-9. Employers must do this for all employees, including employees who are relatives or personal acquaintances.
- If the employer is hiring the employee for fewer than three days, then the employer must complete Form I-9 before the end of the employee's first day of work.
- The employer must make sure that the employee completes his or her portion of Form I-9 within one day of the date of hire.
- The employer may complete "Section 3: Updating and Reverification" of the employee's original Form I-9, rather than generating a new Form I-9, if:
  - the employee changes his or her name
  - the employee is rehired within three years of the date the original form was completed, and continues to be eligible for employment on the same basis, or
  - the employee's original work authorization has expired or will soon expire.
- Employers must keep the Form I-9 for three years after the date of hire or one year after the date of termination, whichever is later. Employers may store these forms electronically.
- Employers must make all I-9 forms available for inspection by the USCIS, ICE, the Office of the Special Counsel for Immigration-Related Unfair Employment Practices (OSC), or the U.S. Department of Labor (DOL).

Acceptable Documents

To satisfy the law's verification and record-keeping requirements, employers may view one document or a combination of documents, depending on the nature of the document.

Documents that are acceptable under IRCA fall into one of three categories:

- those that verify both identity and authorization to work in the United States (see List A, below)
- those that verify identity only (see List B, below), and
- those that verify employment authorization only (see List C, below).

If an employee submits a document from List A, no other documents are necessary. Otherwise, an employee must submit one document each from List B and List C. To get the most up-to-date information regarding acceptable documents, visit the USCIS website. (See Appendix A for contact information.)

List A. The following documents establish both identity and employment authorization:

- U.S. passport or passport card
- permanent resident card or alien registration receipt card (Form I-151 or I-551)
- foreign passport with a temporary I-551 stamp or temporary I-551 printed notation on a machine-readable immigrant visa
- employment authorization document that includes a photograph (Form I-766)
- for a nonimmigrant alien authorized to work for a particular employer incident to status, a foreign passport with Form I-94 or Form I-94A bearing the same name as the passport and containing an endorsement of the holder's nonimmigrant status, as long as the endorsement period has not expired and the proposed employment does not conflict with any restrictions or limitations listed on the form, or
- a passport from Micronesia (FSM) or the Marshall Islands (RMI) with Form I-94 or Form I-94A indicating nonimmigrant admission under the Compact of Free Association Between the United States and the FSM or RMI.

List B. The following documents establish identity only:

- driver's license or identification card issued by a state or outlying possession of the United States, as long as it contains a photograph or identifying information such as name, date of birth, sex, height, eye color, and address
- identification card issued by a federal, state, or local government agency or entity, provided it contains a photograph or identifying information such as name, date of birth, sex, height, eye color, and address
- school identification card with a photograph
- voter's registration card
- U.S. military card or draft record
- military dependent's identification card
- U.S. Coast Guard Merchant Mariner card

- Native American tribal document
- driver's license issued by a Canadian government authority, or
- for those younger than 18 who can't present any of the documents above, a school report or report card; a clinic, doctor, or hospital record; or a day care or nursery school record.

List C. The following documents establish work authorization only:

- U.S. Social Security card issued by the Social Security Administration (other than a card stating that it is not valid for employment)
- certification of birth abroad issued by the Department of State (Form FS-545 or Form DS-1350)
- original or certified copy of a birth certificate issued by a state, county, municipal authority, or outlying possession of the United States bearing an official seal
- Native American tribal document
- U.S. citizen identification card (Form I-197)
- identification card of a resident citizen in the United States (Form I-179), or
- unexpired employment authorization document issued by the Department of Homeland Security (other than those listed under List A, above).

In certain circumstances, an employer may accept a document called a receipt in place of one of the acceptable documents listed above—for example, when the employee presents a receipt showing application for a replacement document. For details on when receipts are an acceptable substitute for the specified documents, refer to USCIS's publications and website. (See "Agency Resources," below.)

Antidiscrimination

IRCA protects certain workers from discrimination based on citizenship or national origin.

Covered Employers

All covered employers are subject to these provisions.

Covered Workers

All covered workers are subject to these provisions.

What's Prohibited

Employers may not discriminate against employees on the basis of citizenship status or national origin, unless a federal law explicitly allows them to do so because U.S. citizenship has been declared an essential requirement of the job. This prohibition applies to all aspects of the employment relationship, including hiring, promotion, pay, job assignment, discipline, and termination. An employer may not refuse to hire a worker because the worker's authorization document has a future expiration date.

Employers may not retaliate against workers for asserting their rights under IRCA.

Exceptions

IRCA's antidiscrimination provisions do not protect the following types of aliens:
- one who fails to apply for naturalization within six months of the date he or she first becomes eligible to apply for naturalization, or
- one who has applied on a timely basis, but who has not been naturalized as a citizen within two years after the date of the application (excluding the time government agencies spend processing the application), unless the alien can establish that he or she is actively pursuing naturalization.

If two applicants are equally qualified for a position, an employer may give preference to a citizen or national of the United States. However, an employer may not institute a blanket policy of preferring U.S. citizens for all job openings.

Key Facts: Antidiscrimination

- Employers may not discriminate in any aspect of employment based on citizenship status or national origin unless a federal law specifically allows them to do so.
- Employers that discriminate can be investigated by the Office of the Special Counsel for Immigration-Related Unfair Employment Practices (OSC) and/or the EEOC and face fines and lawsuits.

How IRCA Is Enforced

Individual Complaints

Anyone may file a complaint with the USCIS on the belief that an employer has violated the record-keeping or verification provisions of the law. Employees who want to complain about discrimination can complain to either the OSC or the EEOC, depending on the type of discrimination and the size of the employer:

- Employees who think that they are being discriminated against on the basis of citizenship status—and who work for an employer with four or more employees—can file a charge with the OSC.
- Employees who think that they are being discriminated against on the basis of national origin—and who work for an employer with four to 14 employees—can file a charge with the OSC.
- Employees who think that they are being discriminated against on the basis of national origin—and who work for an employer with 15 or more employees—can file a charge with the EEOC. (For more about the EEOC and national origin discrimination, see Chapter 18.)

Agency Enforcement

The Department of Homeland Security (DHS), which includes USCIS and ICE, has the authority to investigate discrimination complaints and inspect employers' I-9 forms.

The OSC has the authority to investigate an employee's or applicant's complaint that an employer has violated IRCA. The OSC may file a complaint against the employer before an administrative law judge. The OSC also has the power to initiate independent investigations of an employer based on information obtained in other investigations or on information provided by members of the public.

The EEOC has the authority to investigate charges and file complaints against employers in a court of law. Like the OSC, the EEOC also has the power to initiate independent investigations.

Complying With IRCA

Reporting Requirements

IRCA imposes no reporting requirements.

Posting Requirements

IRCA imposes no posting requirements.

Record-Keeping Requirements

IRCA's record-keeping requirements are discussed in "Record-Keeping Requirements," above.

Penalties

The penalties for violating IRCA depend on the provision violated.

Employers that knowingly hire an unauthorized alien or that knowingly continue to employ an unauthorized alien face both criminal and civil penalties:

- **Criminal penalties.** Employers can be fined up to $3,000 for each unauthorized worker or imprisoned for up to six months, or both.
- **Civil penalties.** Employers can be ordered to cease violating the law and to pay a fine according to the following schedule:
  - first offense: $559 to $4,473 for each unauthorized alien
  - second offense: $4,473 to $11,181 for each unauthorized alien, and
  - more than two offenses: $6,709 to $22,363 for each unauthorized alien.

Employers that fail to comply with IRCA's verification or record-keeping requirements must pay a fine of $224 to $2,236 for each unauthorized alien whose identity and work authorization they fail to verify.

Employers that refuse to honor acceptable documents presented to them, or ask for more documents than necessary to follow the law, must pay a civil penalty of between $185 and $1,848 for each violation.

Employers that violate IRCA's antidiscrimination provisions may face a hearing in front of an administrative law judge or a civil trial in federal court and may be assessed the following penalties:

- an order to reinstate the aggrieved employee(s) with or without back pay (wages lost because of the discrimination)
- if the employer has never been found guilty before, a civil fine of between $461 and $3,695 for each aggrieved employee or applicant
- if the employer has been found guilty once before, a civil fine of between $3,695 and $9,239 for each aggrieved employee or applicant
- if the employer has previously been found guilty two or more times, a civil fine of between $5,543 and $18,477 for each aggrieved employee or applicant, and
- an order to pay the attorneys' fees of the employee(s) or applicant(s) who brought suit.

Employers that have 15 or more employees and have been found guilty of national origin discrimination also face penalties under Title VII. (For more, see Chapter 18.)

Agency Resources

- USCIS Form I-9
  www.uscis.gov/i-9
- Guide for employers on completing the I-9 form
  How Do I Complete Form I-9, Employment Eligibility Verification?
  www.uscis.gov/sites/default/files/USCIS/Resources/E3en.pdf
- A comprehensive manual on completing and storing I-9 forms
  Handbook for Employers: Guidance for Completing Form I-9
  www.uscis.gov/i-9-central/handbook-employers-m-274

State Laws Relating to Immigration

To find out if your state has a law relating to immigration, contact your state fair employment practices agency and/or state labor department. (See Appendix A for contact details.)

National Labor Relations Act (NLRA)

Statute: 29 U.S.C. §§ 151–169
To view the statutes, visit http://uscode.house.gov and select "Title 29,"
"Chapter 7," and "Subchapter II."

Regulations: 29 C.F.R. §§ 100.101–103.100 (National Labor Relations Board)
To view the regulations, visit www.govinfo.gov and search "29 CFR 100.101."

29 C.F.R. §§ 1400 and following (Federal Mediation and Conciliation Service)
To view the regulations, visit www.govinfo.gov and search "29 CFR
1400.735–12."

Overview of the NLRA

The National Labor Relations Act (NLRA) establishes what unions and management can and can't do in their dealings with each other and with individual employees. When it became law in 1935, the NLRA voiced strong support for workers' rights to organize and bargain collectively with their employer. The law outlawed certain employer efforts to prevent union organizing or bust up existing unions. Subsequent amendments to the NLRA (particularly the Labor Management Relations Act, commonly known as the Taft-Hartley Act) are more supportive of employers, declaring certain union actions to be illegal and upholding a worker's right not to support a union.

The law includes provisions on:

- **Organizing and representation elections.** The NLRA sets the guidelines for employer and union conduct during organizing campaigns and elections held to determine whether a union should represent a group of workers.
- **Unfair labor practices.** The NLRA prohibits employers and unions from engaging in certain acts toward each other and toward individual employees.

This book does not cover the Labor Management Reporting and Disclosure Act, commonly known as the Landrum-Griffin Act (29 U.S.C. §§ 401–531), which imposes a number of procedural requirements on unions and establishes certain rights that unions must provide to their members.

Definitions

Terms that appear in italics throughout this chapter are defined below.

Bargaining unit: A group of employees whom a union represents (or seeks to represent) in its dealings with an employer. Workers in a bargaining unit must have similar job duties, skills, or working conditions and must have common concerns about wages and hours. Usually, professional and nonprofessional employees will not be combined in a single bargaining unit. A single workplace may contain more than one bargaining unit (for example, the butchers, checkers, and janitors in a grocery store might all have their own bargaining units). A bargaining unit can include workers from different facilities (for example, all of the cashiers in a chain of retail stores).

Definitions (continued)

Collective bargaining agreement: The contract between the union (on behalf of the bargaining unit it represents) and the employer that governs the terms and conditions of the workers' employment.

Federal Mediation and Conciliation Service: An agency of the federal government that helps parties to a labor dispute reach a resolution through negotiation and mediation.

Health care institution: A hospital, convalescent hospital, health maintenance organization, health clinic, nursing home, extended care facility, or another institution devoted to providing care for the sick, infirm, or aged.

Hot cargo agreement: An agreement between an employer and a union in which the employer promises to stop doing business with another employer, typically one with whom the union has a dispute.

Manager: A worker who represents the company's interests by taking or recommending actions that control or implement company policy.

Protected concerted activities: Action taken by two or more employees to improve, protest, or otherwise change the terms and conditions of their employment (such as wages, benefits, work environment, supervision, productivity requirements, or workplace rules). Workers may not be disciplined or retaliated against for engaging in protected concerted activities, whether they are in a union or not.

Supervisor: An employee who has the authority, in the interests of the employer, to hire, transfer, suspend, lay off, recall, promote, discharge, assign, reward, discipline, responsibly direct, or adjust the grievances of other employees, or to effectively recommend any of those actions. The authority granted to the supervisor must require the exercise of independent judgment: it may not be merely routine or clerical. Supervisors may spend most of their time doing the same work as the employees they supervise, as long as they spend 10% to 15% of their time on the supervisory tasks described above.

Covered Employers

The NLRA applies to all private employers whose operations affect interstate commerce—that is, whose employees handle, sell, produce, or otherwise work on goods or materials that have come from or will go to another state, or whose employees use the mail, telephone, or other equipment to communicate across state lines. The law would reach virtually every employer if not for the jurisdictional limits noted below.

The NLRA does not apply to:
- federal, state, or local governments
- religious schools, and
- any employer subject to the Railway Labor Act (45 U.S.C. §§ 151–188), which governs labor relations in the railroad and airline industries.

Jurisdictional Limits

Although the National Labor Relations Board (NLRB) has the right to act to enforce the NLRA whenever the employer's enterprise affects interstate commerce, the NLRB has decided to intervene only in larger disputes. In its discretion, the NLRB has set minimum business volume requirements, which it calls "jurisdictional requirements," that an employer's business must meet before the NLRB will step in. Jurisdictional limits for some common industries are as follows:

- **Nonretail businesses:** at least $50,000 in direct sales of goods or services to consumers in other states, in indirect sales (through other sellers), in direct purchases of goods or services from suppliers in other states, or in indirect purchases (through other purchasers)
- **Retail enterprises:** at least $500,000 in total gross annual business volume
- **Management and operation of office buildings and shopping centers:** at least $100,000 in total annual revenue, of which $25,000 or more must come from organizations that meet any of the other jurisdictional standards (except the indirect sale or purchase of goods standards for nonretail businesses)
- **Newspapers:** at least $200,000 in total annual business volume
- **Radio, telegraph, television, and telephone companies:** at least $100,000 in total annual business volume

- **Hotels, motels, and residential apartment buildings:** at least $500,000 in total annual business volume
- **Private health care and child care institutions:** at least $250,000 in total annual business volume for hospitals, medical and dental offices, and child care centers; $100,000 for nursing homes, visiting nurses associations, and related facilities
- **Private universities and colleges:** at least $1,000,000 in gross annual revenue from all sources (except contributions not available for operating expenses at the grantor's request)
- **Law firms and legal assistance programs:** at least $250,000 in gross annual revenue
- **Employers that provide social services (such as groups that solicit and distribute charitable contributions):** at least $250,000 in gross annual revenue, and
- **National defense:** any enterprise affecting commerce whose operations have a substantial impact on national defense.

This is not an exhaustive list: The NLRB has standards for a variety of enterprises, including taxi companies, symphony orchestras, casinos, and cemeteries.

If an employer won't give the NLRB the information it needs to figure out whether the employer meets one of these standards, the NLRB can disregard the standards altogether and intervene in a dispute involving that employer.

 Legal Developments

- **NLRB passes new "speedy election" rules.** In 2015, the NLRB issued new regulations intended to streamline the process of union elections. The new rules would shorten the timeframe for election proceedings by, among other things, limiting the legal challenges that parties may bring before the election is held and limiting written briefs. However, in December 2017, the NLRB—under new leadership—published a request for information regarding the "speedy election" rules, typically the first step in modifying or rescinding a rule.

Legal Developments (continued)

- **Social media policies in the spotlight—and on the hot seat.** Employers may not adopt "business only" work email policies. In the past, the NLRB took the position that employers could prohibit employees' use of work email for personal purposes, as long as the rule applied equally to all types of non-work communications and didn't single out union-related messages. However, in December of 2014, the NLRB overruled its own decision. (*Purple Communications, Inc.*, 361 NLRB No. 126 (2014).) Under the new rule, employers cannot prohibit employees from using work email for activities protected by the NLRA on nonworking time. For example, employees may use work email to organize a union or to discuss the terms and conditions of their employment, during meal breaks, rest breaks, or the time before or after work hours. In 2018, the NLRB requested briefs from interested parties on the rule established by *Purple Communications*, indicating that changes might be ahead. The Office of the General Counsel for the NLRB submitted a brief recommending reversal of the rule; however, no decisions have been made.

Covered Workers

The NLRA generally covers all employees of a covered employer, except:
- agricultural workers
- domestic service workers
- anyone employed by a parent or spouse
- independent contractors
- *managers*
- *supervisors*
- government employees, and
- workers whose employers are subject to the Railway Labor Act.

Did You Know ...

- The NLRA applies even to nonunion companies. For example, a nonunion company must follow the legal rules for union elections, employee discussions or actions regarding the terms and conditions of their employment, and work rules that could inhibit employee rights to organize and act collectively.
- When the NLRA was passed in 1935, fewer than 14% of American workers were union members. Five years after the NLRA became law, that number had doubled. Today, union membership has once again declined, to 10.7% of all employees in 2017. More than a third (34.4%) of public employees belong to a union, compared to only 6.5% of the private sector workforce.
- For 2014, the median weekly earnings for a union member were $212 more than for an employee who was not represented by a union. This adds up to a wage differential of more than $11,000 a year.

Major Provisions of the NLRA

Organizing and Representation Elections

The NLRA establishes workers' basic right to organize—to form, join, or assist a union; to choose their own representatives to negotiate with their employer about terms and conditions of employment; and to engage in other collective efforts to improve their work situations. The law also establishes procedures for determining whether a particular union should have the right to represent a group of workers.

Key Facts: Organizing and Elections

- Employers may not use threats or coercion to influence the outcome of a union election, nor may they unfairly influence their workers' decision to join or form a union.
- Employers may not adopt policies or take actions that unfairly inhibit their employees' rights to discuss the terms and conditions of their employment or union issues. However, employers have the right to prohibit nonwork discussions at certain times and places.
- In some states, an employer and a union may enter into a union security agreement, which requires all workers—even those who choose not to join the union—to pay agency fees to the union as a condition of getting or keeping a job. However, other states have prohibited these types of agreements. Also, employees who object to paying these fees on religious or political grounds are entitled to pay the same amount to certain types of charity organizations instead of the union.

The Election Process

In order to represent workers in negotiations with an employer, a union must have the support of a majority of workers in an appropriate *bargaining unit*. Unions generally demonstrate this support by asking workers to sign authorization cards, which are forms that each worker signs to indicate a desire to be represented by the union in dealings with the employer.

If the union gets the support of a majority of bargaining unit workers, it will often ask the employer to recognize the union voluntarily. If the employer agrees, the union will be the official bargaining representative of the unit, and employer and union can begin negotiating a *collective bargaining agreement*.

If the employer refuses to recognize the union—for example, if the employer believes the bargaining unit is improper or believes the union's support is not genuine—the workers or the union can file a petition with the NLRB, asking it to hold an election. The petition must be supported by authorization cards or other signed statements of union support from at least 30% of the workers in the proposed bargaining unit. After the NLRB investigates and tries to resolve any disputes between the parties over the scope of the bargaining unit and the time and place of the election, the NLRB will hold a secret election. If the union receives a majority of the votes cast, it will be certified as the bargaining representative of the unit.

An employer may also petition the NLRB for an election if one or more individuals or unions claims the right to represent a particular bargaining unit.

In 2011, the NLRB issued a final rule proposing changes to the election process. Sometimes referred to as the "speedy election" rule or "ambush election" rule, these regulations have been very controversial, in part because they provide less time and fewer opportunities for an employer to try to legitimately defeat a union organizing campaign. Some of the changes simply bring the agency up to technological speed or otherwise streamline the election process. However, a number of changes also significantly speed up the process, both by shortening existing time periods and eliminating or postponing certain procedures or challenges until after the election is over. For example, the new rules would do away with the automatic delay of 25 to 30 days before an election is held, as well as postpone oral arguments and challenges to voter eligibility until after the election is held. Under the previous rules, the NLRB aimed to hold an election within 42 days after a petition was filed. Under the new rules, the timeline could be as short as two or three weeks.

The speedy election rules have undergone legal challenges and other setbacks. In 2012, a federal judge held that the rules were invalid because the NLRB lacked the requisite number of board members to pass new rules. The NLRB passed the rule again when it regained full board membership. However, by 2017, the NLRB—under new leadership—questioned the soundness of the new rules. The NLRB issued a request for information, seeking comments from the public about whether the rule should be modified or rescinded. This is generally the first step in the rulemaking process, which is still ongoing.

Covered Employers

All covered employers are subject to these provisions.

Covered Workers

All covered workers are subject to these provisions.

What's Prohibited: Employers

The NLRA prohibits employers from unfairly influencing their workers' decision to join or form a union and from using threats or other coercive tactics to influence the outcome of an election. However, employers still have free speech rights. Many of the tactics that the NLRA prohibits employers from using during an election process are discussed as unfair labor practices, below.

If the NRLB finds that an employer has unfairly influenced the outcome of an election, it can set aside a vote rejecting the union or declare the union the victor by default. Here are some examples of prohibited employer conduct:

- **Punishing union supporters.** An employer may not retaliate or discriminate against workers who support the union.
- **Threats.** An employer cannot threaten to fire, demote, or take any other negative job action against workers because they support a union, nor can it threaten to shut down or move the business if the union wins the election.
- **Inducements.** An employer cannot promise or give benefits to workers who oppose the union. Once an organizing campaign has begun, an employer may not increase workers' benefits to discourage them from forming or joining a union.
- **Infiltration.** An employer may not conduct surveillance or otherwise spy on union meetings or on employees who support the union.
- **Interrogation.** An employer may not question workers about their union membership, union meetings, or their support for the union; nor may it ask employees to report back on union activities or their coworkers' union views.

What's Prohibited: Unions

Like employers, unions are prohibited from unfairly influencing a worker's decision to support or join the union or the outcome of an election. The list of prohibited actions for unions is similar to the list for employers. Here are some examples:

- **Threats.** A union may not threaten workers with job loss or other negative job actions for failing to support the union, nor may a union cause an employer to take negative job actions against such workers.

- **Takeovers.** A union may not enter into an agreement with an employer that recognizes the union as the exclusive bargaining representative of a bargaining unit if it does not have the support of a majority of unit employees.
- **Inducements.** A union may not promise or grant benefits to workers for supporting the union.
- **Violence.** A union may not use or threaten physical violence against workers to influence their votes.

Exceptions

Union Security Agreements

The NLRA protects a worker's right to refuse to join or support a union. However, it also allows a union and an employer to enter into a contract, called a union security agreement, requiring workers to make certain payments (called "agency fees") to the union as a condition of getting or keeping a job. If a union and an employer have entered into a union security agreement, all workers must either join the union or pay agency fees to the union as a condition of employment. If a worker refuses to pay up or join, the employer must fire the worker. The United States Supreme Court recently held that it is illegal to require government employees to pay agency fees when they decide not to join the union. However, the ruling does not apply to private sector employment.

The NLRA does allow states to prohibit union security agreements, and many have. In these states (called "right-to-work" states), workers who decide not to join the union cannot be required to pay any fees to the union and can't be fired or otherwise penalized for failing to do so. (See "State Right-to-Work Laws," at the end of this chapter, for a list of states that have adopted these laws.)

Dues Objectors

Workers who are subject to a union security agreement—but who object to paying agency fees on religious, political, or other grounds—may make alternative arrangements.

Workers who object to joining a union on religious grounds are exempt from paying union dues. However, they can be required to pay the same amount to a nonlabor, nonreligious charity group instead.

Workers who object to the union's use of their fees for political or other purposes are entitled to a refund of the portion of their dues spent for those purposes. However, they still have to pay their fair share of union money spent on representing the bargaining unit's workers. In some states, unions are required to get workers' permission before collecting any fees for activities other than representing workers.

Unfair Labor Practices

In addition to the rules governing union organizing campaigns and elections, the NLRA prohibits a number of activities—called unfair labor practices—by employers and unions. Some of these rules apply to the interactions between employer and union; others protect individual workers from unfair treatment by an employer or a union.

Covered Employers

All covered employers are subject to these provisions.

Covered Workers

All covered workers are subject to these provisions.

What's Prohibited: Employers

In addition to the prohibitions discussed in "Organizing and Representation Elections," above, the NLRA prohibits employers from:

- interfering with an employee's right to organize, join, or assist a union; to engage in collective bargaining; or to engage in *protected concerted activities* (see "Banning Union Discussions in the Workplace," below)
- dominating or providing illegal assistance or support to a labor union (see "Company Unions," below)

- discriminating against employees to encourage or discourage member-ship in a labor organization, or replacing workers who strike to protest an unfair labor practice (see "Replacing Workers During a Protected Strike," below)
- retaliating against an employee for filing a charge with or testifying before the NLRB
- refusing to engage in good-faith collective bargaining (see "What's Required: Employers and Unions," below), and
- making a *hot cargo agreement* with a union.

Key Facts: Unfair Labor Practices

- The NLRA prohibits employers from taking certain actions tending to inhibit employees' right to organize, including:
  - banning workplace discussions about union issues or working conditions (for example, wages) while allowing workplace conversations about other nonwork topics
  - retaliating against an employee for filing a complaint with the NLRB
  - refusing to bargain collectively with a union
  - unilaterally changing a workplace rule or policy that covers a topic that the employer is required to bargain over with the union, and
  - dominating a union or creating a sham union.
- The NLRB has found that certain voluntary workplace committees composed of workers and management might be sham unions, if the group is dominated by management and deals with issues that must be collectively bargained.
- Strikes are protected under the NLRA only if employees are striking over issues of wages, hours, or terms and conditions of employment, or to protest an unfair labor practice by the employer. However, a strike will not be protected under the NLRA if it violates a no-strike clause in the collective bargaining agreement, regardless of the reason for the strike.

Banning Union Discussions in the Workplace

An employer may not completely prohibit union discussions—including discussions that occur before workers are unionized, such as conversations about whether to form or join a union—in the workplace. Instead, employers must treat union-related communications like any other matter not related to work. The following rules apply:

- An employer may prohibit workers from talking about union matters in work areas during work hours, but only if the employer prohibits workers from talking about all other nonwork issues as well.
- An employer must allow workers to talk about union matters outside of work hours in nonwork areas (like a lunchroom or locker room).
- An employer may prohibit union discussions outside of work hours in work areas only if such a rule is necessary to maintain productivity or discipline and the rule applies to all nonwork topics.
- An employer may prohibit distribution of union literature (such as pamphlets or fact sheets) in work areas at all times, as long as the ban applies to all nonwork literature.
- An employer may not prohibit workers from wearing clothing bearing a pro-union message or logo, unless that apparel creates a safety hazard or other special circumstances override the workers' right to communicate their support for the union.

These rules apply equally to union and nonunion workplaces, and they cover discussions that are explicitly about unions or unionizing, as well as discussions aimed at improving wages, working conditions, or other terms and conditions of employment. (Such discussions are protected concerted activities under the NLRA.) Employers may not prevent employees from exercising these rights by, for example, prohibiting employees from talking about their wages.

Email is subject to a different set of rules. As explained in "Legal Developments," above, the NLRB recently addressed the issue of whether employers can adopt "business only" email policies, which prohibit employees from using work email to discuss nonwork topics—including those related to union organizing or other activities protected by the NLRA. The NLRB held that employers cannot prohibit employees from using work email to engage in these protected activities on nonworking time. Employees must be allowed to use work email during meal or rest breaks, or before or after established work hours, for the purpose of discussing union-related activities or trying to improve the terms and conditions of their employment.

Social Media Policies and Practices

For several years, the NLRB was extremely active in going after employers who fired or disciplined employees for posting critical comments about the company on social media sites or blogs. For example:

- A collections agency was found to have illegally fired an employee for Facebook posts complaining about her transfer. The employee used profanity and said she was done being a good employee; her coworkers who were Facebook friends posted comments expressing support, criticizing the employer, and suggesting a class action lawsuit. Because the employees were discussing taking action regarding the terms of their employment, the NLRB concluded that they were engaged in protected concerted activity.

- An employee at a veterinary hospital complained on Facebook that she was denied a promotion. Several coworkers responded to the post, complaining about the person who received the promotion, the company's practices regarding raises and reviews, and so on. The NLRB held that this was protected activity and that the employer had illegally fired and disciplined the employees.

- A former employee took to Facebook to complain about her former employer's mistakes in withholding taxes from her paycheck. A current employee posted a similar complaint in response, including derogatory remarks about the manager responsible for the miscalculations. A second employee "liked" the original post, but didn't comment. The NLRB held that the employees were engaged in protected activity.

As part of these enforcement actions, the NLRB often found that the employer's social media and posting policy was too broad, because it would discourage employees from exercising their right to engage in protected, concerted activities (known as Section 7 activities). The Board has objected to policies that prohibit disparagement or criticism of the company, management, or others; policies that require employees not to post "confidential" or "non-public" information (unless the policy illustrates the types of information covered, so as not to dissuade employees from discussing wages or other terms of employment); policies that require employees to avoid picking fights or discussing topics that are objectionable or inflammatory; and policies that require employees to check with a supervisor before posting.

However, the NLRB no longer appears to have the same agenda to closely regulate and restrict employer social media policies. In fact, in a 2017 decision, the NLRB changed the standard for evaluating employer handbook policies, making it easier for them to withstand legal challenges. Under the previous standard, the NLRB focused on whether employees would reasonably construe the rule to restrict their rights under the NLRA. However, in *The Boeing Co.*, 365 NLRB No. 154 (2017), the board criticized past decisions as being overinclusive and improperly prohibiting any rule that "could" be interpreted as covering NLRA-protected activity. The General Counsel for the NLRB issued a memo on Handbook rules afterwards, making it clear that rules should not be interpreted against the drafter (that is, the employer) and that provisions should not be interpreted as banning all activity that could possibly be covered by the NLRA.

Company Unions

Employers may not establish, dominate, or interfere with any labor organization. This rule exists to outlaw so-called sham unions—company groups that appear to represent employees' interests but are really controlled by the employer. To figure out whether an employer unfairly controls a particular workplace group, the NLRB looks at all the circumstances, including:

- whether the employer started the group
- whether the employer played a role in organizing the group and deciding how it will function
- whether management actually attends the group's meetings or otherwise tries to set the group's agenda
- the group's purpose, and
- how the group makes decisions.

The NLRB has held that workplace employee-management committees—informal groups in which workers and management meet to resolve workplace problems—violate this rule if they are dominated by management and if they resolve topics that must be collectively bargained, such as wages, hours, or working conditions (see "What's Required: Employers and Unions," below).

Replacing Workers During a Protected Strike

The NLRA limits an employer's right to replace workers who go out on strike for a protected purpose. Generally, a strike has a protected purpose if workers are striking over wages, hours, or terms and conditions of employment or to protest an unfair labor practice by the employer (like discriminating against union members or refusing to bargain with the union). Strikes that don't fall within these categories are not protected by the NLRA, nor are strikes for any reason that violate a no-strike provision in a collective bargaining agreement or strikes in which the strikers engage in serious misconduct. (See "Unlawful Strikes," in "What's Prohibited: Unions," below, for examples.)

An employer may not fire, or hire permanent replacements for, workers who strike to protest an unfair labor practice. These workers are entitled to reinstatement once the strike is over.

However, workers who strike for other protected reasons can be replaced permanently. Once the strike is over, the workers are entitled to their former jobs only if the employer did not hire permanent replacements. If the employer hired permanent replacements, the workers who went on strike are only entitled to be called back for job openings as those jobs become available, and only if they are unable to find regular and substantially similar work elsewhere.

What's Prohibited: Unions

In addition to the rules discussed in "Organizing and Representation Elections," above, the NLRA prohibits unions from:

- restraining or coercing employees in the free exercise of their right not to support a union (for example, by threatening employees who don't want a union or expelling members for crossing an illegal picket line)
- restraining or coercing an employer in its choice of a bargaining representative (by insisting on meeting only with a particular management employee or refusing to bargain with the representative the employer chooses)
- causing or trying to cause an employer to discriminate against an employee for the purpose of encouraging union membership (for example, convincing an employer to penalize employees who engage in antiunion activities)

- refusing to engage in good-faith collective bargaining (for example, refusing to come to the bargaining table or listen to any of the employer's proposals) (see "What's Required: Employers and Unions," below)
- engaging in strikes, boycotts, or other coercive action for an illegal purpose (see "Unlawful Strikes," below)
- charging excessive or discriminatory membership fees
- getting or trying to get an employer to agree to pay for work that is not performed (this practice is called featherbedding)
- for a union that is not certified to represent a group of workers, picketing or threatening to picket an employer in order to force the employer to recognize or bargain with the union or force the workers to accept the union as their representative if (1) another union already represents the workers, (2) a valid representation election was held in the past year, or (3) the union does not file a petition for an election with the NLRB within 30 days after the picketing starts
- making a *hot cargo agreement*, and
- striking, picketing, or otherwise engaging in a collective work stoppage at any *health care institution* without giving at least ten days' written notice both to the institution and the *Federal Mediation and Conciliation Service*.

Unlawful Strikes

A union may not strike, boycott, or use other means of persuasion or coercion for prohibited purposes. Such prohibited purposes include:

- forcing or requiring an employer to assign particular work to employees in a particular union, trade, craft, or class
- forcing or requiring an employer to recognize or bargain with a particular union if another union has been duly certified as the representative of its employees
- forcing or requiring any person to stop doing business with any other business or to stop using, selling, or transporting the products of any other business (such strikes or boycotts against a business other than the employer are called secondary strikes), and
- forcing or requiring an employer or self-employed person to join any labor or employer organization or to enter into a *hot cargo agreement*.

Even a strike with a lawful purpose might not be protected under the NLRA if the workers strike in violation of a no-strike provision in the collective bargaining agreement or if the strikers engage in serious misconduct (like violence).

What's Required: Employers and Unions

Once a union has been elected, the NLRA requires employer and union to engage in collective bargaining. Collective bargaining is the negotiation process between the union (on behalf of the bargaining unit it represents) and the company to work out an agreement that will govern wages, work hours, and other terms and conditions of the workers' employment. These topics are called mandatory subjects of bargaining. The two sides don't have to reach an agreement, but they have to bargain in good faith.

Before an employer changes a workplace rule or policy that affects a mandatory subject of bargaining, it must ask the union to negotiate the issue—even if the change will provide an overall benefit to workers. An employer that makes unilateral changes regarding mandatory bargaining issues commits an unfair labor practice.

How the NLRA Is Enforced

Individual Complaints

An employee, an employer, or a union that believes an unfair labor practice has been committed may file a charge with the NLRB. Unfair labor practice charges must be filed within six months of the incident alleged to be unfair.

If a dispute arises over whether employees want a particular union to represent them, then an employee, an employer, or a union may file a petition asking the NLRB to hold an election. The NLRB's procedures for handling charges and petitions are described below.

The NLRA cannot be enforced through private lawsuits; violations of the NLRA must be challenged through the NLRB.

Agency Enforcement

The NLRB handles two issues: representation questions (disputes over whether employees want a union) and unfair labor practices.

Representation Questions

Representation questions are brought to the NLRB when an employee, an employer, or a union files a petition with the agency. If a union or an employee files the petition, it must show that at least 30% of the affected workers want an election. An employer may petition the NLRB for an election only if one or more individuals or unions claim the right to represent a particular bargaining unit.

Once a petition is filed, the NLRB will investigate if the employer in question meets the NLRB's jurisdictional requirements (see "Jurisdictional Limits," above). If it finds that the petition has merit, it will try to hammer out an agreement between the employees and employer regarding election issues like the scope of the bargaining unit and the time and place of the election. The NLRB will then order an election by secret ballot and certify a union if it receives a majority of votes cast. If a union is certified, it becomes the workers' representative and is entitled to bargain with the employer. If a union is not certified, it does not have the right to represent the workers.

Unfair Labor Practices

Unfair labor practices come to the NLRB when an employee, an employer, or a union files a charge with the agency. The NLRB will investigate the charge if the employer in question meets the NLRB's jurisdictional requirements. (See "Jurisdictional Limits," above.) If the NLRB finds reason to believe that the NLRA has been violated, the agency will try to get the parties to settle their differences. If this fails, the NLRB will hold a hearing before an administrative law judge, who will issue a written decision. This decision may be appealed within the NLRB, and if either party is dissatisfied with the NLRB's final decision, it may appeal the matter to the federal courts.

Complying With the NLRA

Reporting Requirements

The NLRA imposes no reporting requirements. However, employers and unions have reporting requirements under the Labor Management Reporting and Disclosure Act. These reports, which must be made to the Office of Labor-Management Standards (OLMS), are beyond the scope of this book.

Posting Requirements

Once the NLRB gets involved in a representation dispute or an unfair labor practice complaint, it can require employers to post various notices relating to elections or the resolution of a particular charge of unfair labor practices.

Under an executive order, federal contractors and subcontractors must post a notice informing employees of their rights under the NLRA. All other private employers may, but are not required to, post the notice at the workplace. (See "Agency Resources," below, for a link to the poster.)

Record-Keeping Requirements

The NLRA does not impose record-keeping requirements.

Remedies

If an employer, a union, or an employee files a petition seeking an election, there are no penalties awarded. The NLRB simply holds an election and certifies the results.

If the NLRB finds that an employer has committed an unfair labor practice during an organizing campaign or at any other time, the employer may be required to do any or all of the following:

- pay any compensation, benefits, or other monetary losses, plus interest, that employees suffered as a result of the unfair practice
- take action to remedy the problem by reinstating employees, changing workplace rules, stopping an illegal practice, or recognizing a union
- pay attorneys' fees and costs (with some limitations), and/or
- post a notice in the workplace regarding the unfair practice.

Agency Resources

- A tool to help you find local NLRB offices
  Regional Offices
  www.nlrb.gov/who-we-are/regional-offices
- A comprehensive resource on the NLRA's provisions
  Basic Guide to the National Labor Relations Act
  www.nlrb.gov/sites/default/files/documents/224/basicguide.pdf
- Mandatory poster for federal contractors and subcontractors; optional for other employers
  Employee Rights Under the National Labor Relations Act
  www.dol.gov/olms/regs/compliance/EmployeeRightsPoster11x17_Final.pdf
  (available in other languages at www.dol.gov/olms/regs/compliance/
  EO13496.htm)
- NLRB General Counsel's memorandum on employee handbook policies
  post-*Boeing*
  Visit www.nlrb.gov/news-outreach and select "NLRB Memoranda,"
  "General Counsel Memos," and "Guidance on Handbook Rules Post-Boeing."

State Right-to-Work Laws

As noted under "Exceptions" in "Organizing and Representation Elections," above, the NLRA allows states to prohibit union security agreements. In these states (called "right-to-work" states), workers who decide not to join the union cannot be required to pay any fees to the union and cannot be fired or otherwise penalized for failing to do so. The chart below lists the states that have prohibited union security agreements and provides a citation to the relevant state statute.

State Right-to-Work Laws

Alabama	Ala. Code §§ 25-7-30 to 25-7-36; Ala. Const. art. I, § 36.05
Alaska	No right-to-work law
Arizona	Ariz. Const. art. 25; Ariz. Rev. Stat. §§ 23-1301 to 23-1307
Arkansas	Ark. Const. amend. 34 § 1; Ark. Code Ann. §§ 11-3-301 to 11-3-304
California	No right-to-work law
Colorado	No right-to-work law
Connecticut	No right-to-work law
Delaware	No right-to-work law
District of Columbia	No right-to-work law
Florida	Fla. Const. art. 1, § 6; Fla. Stat. Ann. §§ 447.01, 447.03, 447.17
Georgia	Ga. Code Ann. §§ 34-6-20 to 34-6-28
Hawaii	No right-to-work law
Idaho	Idaho Code §§ 44-2001 to 44-2011
Illinois	No right-to-work law
Indiana	Ind. Code Ann. § 22-6-6-8
Iowa	Iowa Code §§ 731.1 to 731.9
Kansas	Kan. Const. art. 15 § 12; Kan. Stat. Ann. §§ 44-808(5), 44-831
Kentucky	Ky. Rev. Stat. Ann. §§ 336.130, 336.132, 336.135, 336.180, 336.990
Louisiana	La. Rev. Stat. Ann. §§ 23:981 to 23:987 (all workers) and 23:881 to 23:889 (agricultural workers)
Maine	No right-to-work law
Maryland	No right-to-work law
Massachusetts	No right-to-work law
Michigan	Mich. Comp. Laws §§ 423.1, 423.8, 423.14, 423.17
Minnesota	No right-to-work law
Mississippi	Miss. Const. art. 7, § 198-A; Miss. Code Ann. § 71-1-47

State Right-to-Work Laws (continued)	
Missouri	No right-to-work law
Montana	No right-to-work law
Nebraska	Neb. Const. art. XV, §§ 13 to 15; Neb. Rev. Stat. § 48-217 to 48-219
Nevada	Nev. Rev. Stat. Ann. §§ 613.230 to 613.300
New Hampshire	No right-to-work law
New Jersey	No right-to-work law
New Mexico	No right-to-work law
New York	No right-to-work law
North Carolina	N.C. Gen. Stat. §§ 95-78 to 95-84
North Dakota	N.D. Cent. Code §§ 34-01-14
Ohio	No right-to-work law
Oklahoma	Okla. Const. Art. 23, § 1A
Oregon	No right-to-work law
Pennsylvania	No right-to-work law
Rhode Island	No right-to-work law
South Carolina	S.C. Code Ann. §§ 41-7-10 to 41-7-130
South Dakota	S.D. Const. art. VI, § 2; S.D. Codified Law Ann. §§ 60-8-3 to 60-8-8
Tennessee	Tenn. Code Ann. §§ 50-1-201 to 50-1-208
Texas	Tex. Lab. Code Ann. §§ 101.051 to 101.053
Utah	Utah Code Ann. §§ 34-34-1 to 34-34-17
Vermont	No right-to-work law
Virginia	Va. Code Ann. §§ 40.1-59 to 40.1-69
Washington	No right-to-work law
West Virginia	W. Va. Code §§ 21-1A-3, 21-5G-1 through 21-5G-7
Wisconsin	Wis. Stat. Ann. §§ 111.02, 111.04, 111.06, 947.20
Wyoming	Wyo. Stat. Ann. §§ 27-7-108 to 27-7-115

Occupational Safety and Health Act (OSH Act)

Statute: 29 U.S.C. §§ 651 and following
To view the statutes, visit http://uscode.house.gov and select "Title 29"
and "Chapter 15."

Regulations: 29 C.F.R. §§ 1900 and following
To view the regulations, visit www.govinfo.gov and search "29 CFR 1902.1,"
"29 CFR 1911.1," "29 CFR 1926.1," "29 CFR 1928.1."

Overview of the OSH Act

Congress passed the Occupational Safety and Health Act (the OSH Act) in 1970 to ensure safe working conditions for all American workers. The act requires employers to provide working conditions that are free of hazards likely to cause serious injury or death. Employers that fail to do so are subject to stiff penalties.

The OSH Act has four main provisions:

- **Compliance.** Employers must comply with standards issued by the Occupational Safety and Health Administration (OSHA) or, if they are in a *state plan state*, by the state agency.
- **Safety.** Employers must keep their workplaces free of *recognized hazards*.
- **Inspection.** Employers must submit to inspections from OSHA inspectors or, if they are in a state plan state, from OSHA-approved state inspectors.
- **Employee rights.** The OSH Act gives employees the right to request information about workplace hazards, refuse to work in hazardous environments, and otherwise get involved in workplace safety issues without employer retaliation.

In addition, employers must maintain accurate records of all work-related accidents and diseases and inform employees of their rights and obligations under the law.

The OSH Act has literally thousands of pages of regulations, covering everything from proper use of ladders to handling radioactive substances. The type of business a company engages in will determine which of these regulations it must follow. This discussion addresses only general employer duties under the OSH Act; it cannot begin to cover all of the industry-specific regulations that may apply to a particular company. To find out about these rules, refer to the "Agency Resources" section, below.

Issues relating to multiemployer responsibility are also not covered here.

Covered Employers

The OSH Act covers virtually all private businesses, regardless of size, as long as they employ at least one person and are located in one of the 50 states, the District of Columbia, the Virgin Islands, American Samoa, Puerto Rico, the Trust Territory of the Pacific Islands, the Canal Zone, the Outer Continental Shelf, Wake Island, or Johnson Island.

Definitions

Terms that appear in italics throughout this chapter are defined below.

Imminent danger: Any condition or practice that could reasonably be expected to cause death or serious physical harm either immediately or before the danger can be eliminated through OSHA enforcement procedures.

Longshoring: The loading, unloading, moving, or handling of a ship's cargo, stores, gear, and so on.

Recognized hazard: A workplace hazard that an employer is, or should be, aware of and that is likely to cause death or serious physical harm. Recognized hazards encompass not only working conditions and the workplace environment, but also workplace practices.

State plan state: A state that has submitted a workplace safety plan to the secretary of labor for approval. If the secretary approves the plan, the state can retain control of work-related health and safety issues within its borders.

The OSH Act allows states to enact their own occupational health and safety laws, and many states have done so. Employers in these states (called state plan states) must follow state regulations instead of OSH Act regulations. (See "State Laws Relating to Occupational Safety and Health," below, for more about this issue.)

The OSH Act does not apply to businesses regulated under the Atomic Energy Act or under job safety rules of federal agencies other than the U.S. Department of Labor (DOL). For example, the Federal Aviation Administration has its own regulations on how to transport radioactive materials on airplanes. Those rules supersede OSHA regulations about radioactive hazards for airline workers. There has been much dispute over which federal regulations fit within this exception and which do not; because these rules are quite complicated, they aren't covered here.

The OSH Act does not apply to local governments and their political subdivisions. It also does not apply to state governments and their political subdivisions. However, if a state wants to take advantage of the state plan option, its plan must cover state employers. Thus, in all of the state plan states, state employers are subject to the state's equivalent of the OSH Act.

Legal Developments

- **OSHA proposes rule to modify electronic reporting of injuries and illnesses.** An Obama-era final rule, scheduled to take effect on July 1, 2018, would have required employers with 250 or more employees, and employers in certain high-risk industries, to electronically submit Form 300A (summary of workplace injuries and illnesses for the year), Form 300 (log of injuries and illnesses), and Form 301 (incident reports for injuries and illnesses). However, in 2018, OSHA delayed the implementation of the rule and proposed a new rule that would only require these employers to electronically submit Form 300A. OSHA is still in the rulemaking process, which will likely continue into 2019.

The OSH Act does not apply to the federal government and its political subdivisions. However, it does require each federal agency to devise health and safety standards that are consistent with the OSH Act. In addition, an executive order issued by President Carter protects federal workers by requiring federal agencies to comply with OSH Act standards, provide workplaces free of recognized hazards, and submit to inspections from the DOL. The order also protects workers from retaliation for filing reports about unsafe working conditions. OSHA does not have authority to impose fines on federal agencies, but it does respond to complaints from federal government employees.

Covered Workers

The OSH Act applies to any employee of a covered employer, regardless of the employee's title, status, or classification. Thus, the law applies to managers, supervisors, partners, stockholders, officers, and family member employees as well as to rank-and-file employees.

The OSH Act does not apply to independent contractors or to the immediate family members of a farm operator.

Did You Know ...

- Workplace fatalities are on the rise. In 2016, there were 5,190 fatal work injuries according to the Bureau of Labor Statistics.
- Some of the most common causes of fatal workplace injuries are transportation incidents (such as car crashes or being struck by a vehicle); violent acts (by people or animals); machine-related injuries; falls, slips, or trips; machine-related injuries; and exposure to harmful substances or environments.
- OSHA offers Voluntary Protection Programs (VPP) to promote health and safety at company worksites. VPP invites companies to apply to be assessed against its criteria for managed safety and health systems. Approval requires application review, vigorous inspection, annual self-evaluation, and periodic reevaluation. But OSHA claims that participating in VPP reduces injuries and illnesses among employees, leading to lower workers' compensation premiums and other costs. For more information, visit www.osha.gov/dcsp/vpp/index.html.

Major Provisions of the OSH Act

Compliance

Since its inception in 1970, OSHA has been issuing workplace safety standards. These standards fall into four broad categories: general industry, maritime and *longshoring*, construction, and agricultural. Covered employers must follow the safety standards that apply to their businesses. This is referred to as "pre-inspection compliance," because employers must comply with the safety regulations before they are specifically told to do so by an OSHA inspector. Failure to comply may result in fines and penalties.

If an employer operates in a state plan state, then it must follow its state plan standards rather than the OSH Act standards. (See "State Laws Relating to Occupational Safety and Health," below, for information about state plan states.)

Key Facts: Compliance

- Employers must determine which standards—under the federal OSH Act or an applicable state plan—apply to their industry, their specific business, and their operations, and then strictly comply with those standards.
- Employers must train and supervise their employees appropriately and adequately under the OSH Act or an applicable state plan.
- Employers must provide safe tools and equipment, as well as proper safety equipment, for all of their workers.

Covered Employers

All covered employers are subject to these provisions.

Covered Workers

All covered workers are subject to these provisions.

What's Required

Employers must follow the standards that apply to their industries:

- **General industry.** As a general rule, all covered employers must follow the general industry standards, unless the standard itself specifies the type of workplace to which it applies. (For example, one set of general industry standards applies only to bakeries.) The general industry standards cover such things as safe operation of machinery, exit routes, fire safety, how materials must be handled and stored, walkways and work surfaces, ventilation, exposure to noise, use of forklifts, and personal protective gear.
- **Construction.** As the name suggests, construction standards apply to covered employers with employees who do construction work, including construction, alteration, repair, painting, and decorating.

- **Maritime and longshoring.** These standards apply to covered employers with employees involved in ship repairing, shipbuilding, shipbreaking, and longshoring.
- **Agricultural.** These standards apply to covered employers with employees involved in growing or harvesting crops, raising livestock or poultry, or related activities on sites such as farms, ranches, orchards, or dairies.

Within each broad category are additional categories and levels of standards—and sometimes, two or more standards may apply to the same activity. Thus, finding out which standards apply to any one business or to any one operation can be daunting. OSHA and the state plan states provide resources to help employers understand which standards they must follow. (To find out more, see "Agency Resources" and "State Laws Relating to Occupational Safety and Health," below.)

The standards are meant to be taken literally. Whether or not an accident has occurred is irrelevant to determining whether a covered employer has violated the compliance provision. An employer can have no accidents for decades and still violate the OSH Act (or its state equivalent) if it doesn't follow the standard. Similarly, an employer can have a number of accidents and be in full compliance as long as it follows the standard (although workplace accidents may place the employer in violation of the OSH Act's safety provisions or the safety provisions of its state equivalent; see "Safety," below).

The OSH Act requires employers to train employees adequately for their jobs. Some of the standards specify the type of training employees must receive. In addition, covered employers must adequately supervise their employees.

Employers have a general duty to provide employees with tools and equipment that are in safe condition. Many of the standards require that employers provide their employees with specific types of safety equipment; with very few exceptions, employers have to pay for this equipment. Some of the standards require employers to protect employees from health hazards, such as asbestos and lead.

There are a number of defenses that employers can raise if they are accused of failing to follow the standards. Those are beyond the scope of this discussion.

Safety

Covered employers have a general duty to provide their employees with a workplace free of *recognized hazards*. Congress enacted this provision to cover serious hazards to which no OSHA standard applies. If an OSHA standard does cover a hazard, then that hazard does not fall under the general safety provision.

If an employer operates its business in a state plan state, then it must follow its state plan standards, not the OSH Act standards. (See "State Laws Relating to Occupational Safety and Health," below, for information about state plan states.)

Key Facts: Safety

- Employers must provide their employees with work and a workplace free of recognized hazards that could cause death or serious physical injury.

Covered Employers

All covered employers are subject to these provisions.

Covered Workers

All covered workers are subject to these provisions.

What's Required

Covered employers must provide work and a place of employment free of recognized hazards that have caused or are likely to cause death or serious physical injury to employees. This duty extends beyond the four walls of a company's business to any location where an employee performs work for an employer.

It can be difficult to determine which hazards are recognized hazards. Obviously, a hazard that an employer knows about is recognized, as is one that is common knowledge in the employer's industry. A hazard will also be a recognized hazard if the employer could easily detect it simply by walking through the workplace and using the five senses. Many courts have also held that hazards that the employer could detect through instruments are recognized hazards.

Inspections

The chief way in which OSHA enforces the OSH Act is through on-site inspections. These inspections may be conducted at random, or OSHA may inspect a particular worksite because it has received a complaint of unsafe conditions.

Employers that operate their businesses in state plan states face inspection from state inspectors, not OSHA inspectors.

Key Facts: Inspections

- OSHA inspectors (or state plan inspectors, where applicable) enforce the OSH Act (or state law) through random on-site inspections or inspections in response to complaints.
- Employers can demand that an inspector have or obtain a warrant before conducting an inspection. But once the investigator provides a warrant, an employer must allow the inspection.

Covered Employers

All covered employers are subject to these provisions.

Covered Workers

All covered workers are subject to these provisions.

What's Required

If OSHA presents an employer with an inspection warrant, the employer must submit to the inspection. If OSHA appears without a warrant, however, the employer can either consent to the inspection or demand that OSHA get a warrant before entering the worksite.

Employee Rights

The OSH Act gives employees various ways to take action to ensure that their workplace is safe. If an employee works for an employer that operates in a state plan state, the employee's rights may be slightly different from the ones described in this section.

Key Facts: Employee Rights

- Under the OSH Act, employees have the right to ensure that their workplaces are safe in a variety of ways, including participating in setting safety standards and complaining to authorities about unsafe working conditions or OSH Act violations.
- Employees also have a right to get information about hazards in their workplaces.
- Employees may refuse to work when they face an imminent danger in the workplace that the employer refuses to correct, but only if the condition is so dangerous that it could harm the employee before OSHA is able to respond to an employee's request for an investigation.

The OSH Act gives employees a number of important rights, including the right to:
- petition OSHA to adopt a safety standard
- file a complaint with OSHA about unsafe working conditions or other OSH Act violations
- where an *imminent danger* exists, seek a court order compelling the secretary of labor to conduct an inspection
- participate in the inspection and conferences relating to the inspection
- oppose settlements and withdrawals of contested cases
- inspect their employer's log of occupational injuries and illnesses, and
- request a government determination as to whether there are any toxic substances in the workplace.

The Act also gives employees the right to receive or request certain information about workplace hazards. For example, employers whose operations require them to monitor employee exposure to toxic substances must:

- inform employees of the presence of certain toxic substances in the workplace
- allow employees to participate in the monitoring
- give employees all of the information obtained in the monitoring
- inform employees when they are being exposed to dangerous levels of toxins, and
- give employees access to exposure records and their own medical records.

Although the OSH Act does not expressly allow employees to refuse to work in dangerous conditions, OSHA regulations do allow it when employees are faced with imminent danger. An employer may not discipline an employee for refusing to work if all of the following are true:

- The employee has a reasonable and good-faith belief that performing the work presents a real danger of death or serious physical injury.
- The employer will not correct the danger.
- There isn't enough time to eliminate the danger through other channels, such as requesting an OSHA inspection.

In the case of a toxic substance or another health hazard, the worker must reasonably believe that the toxic substance or hazard is present and will shorten life or substantially reduce physical or mental efficiency. The harm itself does not have to happen immediately.

State plan states and unionized workplaces with collective bargaining agreements may have different rules about when employees can refuse to work because of workplace hazards.

How the OSH Act Is Enforced

Individual Complaints

Employees can complain to OSHA, or to the OSHA-approved agency in their state if they work in a state plan state, about safety hazards and violations. Employees cannot sue their employers directly for violations of the OSH Act.

Agency Enforcement

Except in state plan states, the OSH Act is enforced by OSHA, a division of the Department of Labor. (See Appendix A for information on how to contact OSHA.) In state plan states, the law is enforced by an OSHA-approved state equivalent.

The principal enforcement method is inspections by federal OSHA inspectors or by OSHA-authorized state inspectors in state plan states. Often, the agency will not inspect in person, but instead will call the employer and follow up with a letter describing the unsafe conditions that have been alleged. If the employer responds quickly and provides detailed facts showing either that the hazard does not exist or that it will be remedied soon, that might end the matter.

If, however, the employer's response does not satisfy the agency, or the agency decides that the allegations are serious enough to warrant an on-site inspection (for example, because an imminent danger is alleged or because the employer has a history of OSH Act violations), the company can expect visitors. If the inspectors find violations, they will issue a citation to the employer along with a proposed penalty. Usually, the citation will also order the employer to cure the violation within a certain time period.

If the employer disagrees with the citation or wants to do something different from what the citation orders, the employer must respond within 15 days. If the employer doesn't act within 15 days, the citation becomes final. If the employer disputes the citation, it doesn't have to pay penalties or cure the alleged violation until an administrative law judge decides the matter.

Complying With the OSH Act

Reporting Requirements

All covered employers must report to OSHA, *within eight hours,* any accident that results in one or more deaths. Workplace injuries that result in the hospitalization of one or more employees, the amputation of an employee's limb, or the loss of an employee's eye must be reported to OSHA within 24 hours. These requirements apply even to employers that are exempt from OSHA's record-keeping requirements (see "Record-Keeping Requirements," below).

Posting Requirements

All covered employers must post:

- an OSHA poster informing employees of their rights and obligations under the OSH Act (see "Agency Resources," below)
- a log and summary of occupational illnesses and injuries (unless the employer is not required to keep these records—see "Record-Keeping Requirements," below)
- current citations that OSHA inspectors have issued to the employer, and
- any petitions that the employer has filed for modification or abatement.

Employers may be required to post additional industry-specific notices, depending on the type of businesses that they run. Employers that operate in a state plan state may have different posting responsibilities than the ones described above.

Record-Keeping Requirements

The OSH Act has numerous record-keeping regulations. Generally speaking, however, covered employers must maintain:

- records of their efforts to comply with the law and to prevent occupational injuries and illnesses
- records of work-related deaths, injuries, and illnesses, and
- records of employee exposure to potentially toxic substances or harmful physical agents.

Not all covered employers have to keep all of these records, however. Employers with ten or fewer employees do not have to keep OSHA illness and injury records, nor do employers in certain low-hazard retail and service industries, such as art galleries, advertising agencies, banks, computer and data processing companies, insurance agencies, and restaurants.

Employers must allow OSHA inspectors access to their logs and records and must transmit certain information about workplace health and safety to OSHA. Employers must use OSHA forms to keep their records.

Employers must also participate in any surveys that the Bureau of Labor Statistics sends to them.

Companies that operate in state plan states may have to follow different record-keeping rules. Those employers should contact their state agencies (see "State Laws Relating to Occupational Safety and Health," below, for more information).

Penalties

Employers face civil penalties and criminal prosecution for violating the OSH Act. These penalties can be as high as $129,336 for each willful or repeated violation.

In addition, some state prosecutors have charged employers with crimes such as manslaughter, murder, and aggravated assault when employees have been severely injured or killed by unsafe working conditions. Sometimes, prosecutors introduce OSH Act violations as evidence in these prosecutions.

In addition, workers and their families can sometimes sue employers outside of the workers' compensation system for injuries and deaths caused by unsafe workplaces.

Agency Resources

- Workplace safety poster that employers are required to display
  Job Safety and Health: It's the Law!
  www.osha.gov/Publications/osha3165.pdf

- A concise summary of employer responsibilities under the OSH Act
  Employer Responsibilities
  www.osha.gov/as/opa/worker/employer-responsibility.html

- Information about OSHA's consultation program for small businesses
  On-Site Consultation
  www.osha.gov/dcsp/smallbusiness/consult.html

- FAQs on the OSH Act's record-keeping requirements
  Detailed Guidance for OSHA's Injury and Illness Recordkeeping Rule
  www.osha.gov/recordkeeping/entryfaq.html

- A list of the industries, by SIC (Standard Industrial Classification) code number, that are exempt from OSHA's record-keeping requirements

  Partially Exempt Industries

  www.osha.gov/recordkeeping/ppt1/RK1exempttable.html

The National Institute for Occupational Safety and Health (NIOSH) is part of the Centers for Disease Control and Prevention in the U.S. Department of Health and Human Services. It researches health and safety problems and develops criteria that OSHA can use when promulgating standards designed to cure those problems. As part of its research, NIOSH can inspect workplaces, issue subpoenas, and interview employers and workers. NIOSH also conducts training and educational programs. The NIOSH website (www.cdc.gov/niosh) offers lots of information about workplace hazards and safety strategies.

State Laws Relating to Occupational Safety and Health

When it was passed, the OSH Act preempted all state job safety and health laws. Each state then had the option of submitting a plan to the secretary of labor for approval. If the secretary found the plan acceptable, then the state's law could stand. Below is a list of states that have exercised this state plan option for state and local government workplaces and private workplaces as of November 2018. For the most up-to-date list and contact information for each of the state plan organizations, visit www.osha.gov/dcsp/osp/index.html.

State Plan States

Alaska	Kentucky	North Carolina	Vermont
Arizona	Maryland	Oregon	Virginia
California	Michigan	Puerto Rico	Washington
Hawaii	Minnesota	South Carolina	Wyoming
Indiana	Nevada	Tennessee	
Iowa	New Mexico	Utah	

In addition, Connecticut, Illinois, Maine, New Jersey, New York, and the Virgin Islands have state plans that cover state and local government employment only.

If a state has an approved state plan, that state can govern workplace health and safety with its own laws, regulations, and standards.

If a state does not have an approved plan, the federal law preempts state laws, regulations, and standards relating to job health and safety—except in cases where the federal law doesn't cover an issue. For example, the federal law does not have standards relating to elevators. Therefore, states can have their own standards relating to elevators, even if they did not exercise the state plan option.

In addition, all states—even those that aren't state plan states—can enforce laws, such as fire codes, that protect a wider class of people than just employees. All states can also train and educate and consult on job safety and health issues. And all states can have laws protecting state and local government employees.

Older Workers Benefit Protection Act (OWBPA)

Statute: 29 U.S.C. §§ 621 and following

To view the statutes, visit http://uscode.house.gov and select "Title 29" and "Chapter 14."

Regulations: 29 C.F.R. §§ 1625 and following

To view the regulations, visit www.govinfo.gov and search "29 CFR 1625."

Overview of OWBPA

Passed in 1990, the Older Workers Benefit Protection Act (OWBPA) gives guidance to courts that have to decide whether the benefits employers offer to workers 40 and older are equal to the benefits offered to younger workers, which is required by the Age Discrimination in Employment Act (ADEA). (See Chapter 1 for more information on the ADEA.) OWBPA also requires employers to take certain steps to make sure that *waivers* of rights under the ADEA are knowing and voluntary.

The OWBPA includes provisions on:

- **Benefits.** Employers must offer older workers (those 40 and older) benefits that are equal to or, in some cases, cost the employer as much as, the benefits offered to younger workers. The rules for determining whether benefits are equal depend on the type of benefit offered.
- **Waivers.** A waiver of the right to sue for age discrimination is valid only if it meets certain standards designed to ensure that the waiver is knowing and voluntary.

Although technically an amendment to the ADEA, OWBPA addresses issues that were not covered in the original ADEA. For this reason, human resources professionals and lawyers generally refer to it by its own name as a separate law—as do we.

Definitions

Terms that appear in italics throughout this chapter are defined below.

Applicable defined benefit plan: A defined benefit plan in which the accrued benefit, or any portion of it, is calculated as the balance of a hypothetical account maintained for the participant or as an accumulated percentage of the participant's final average compensation.

Bona fide employee benefit plan: A benefit plan that has been accurately described, in writing, to all employees and that actually provides the benefits promised.

Definitions (continued)

Defined benefit plan: A type of pension plan in which participants do not receive an individual account and benefits are not based solely on contributions to that account. Instead, a defined benefit plan guarantees participants a specified pension benefit defined either as a particular dollar amount or as a set formula (for example, 1% of final average salary per year of service).

Early retirement incentive plan: A voluntary program in which employers offer employees the opportunity to retire early—before they reach normal retirement age under the employer's pension or other retirement plan—in exchange for additional benefits to which they would not otherwise have been entitled. Many employers credit employees who agree to retire early with additional years of service for purposes of pension accrual, so the employee will be eligible to receive an immediate *unreduced pension*.

Exit incentive program: A voluntary program offered to a group or class of at least two employees, whereby the employees are offered something of value (such as enhanced benefits or compensation) in exchange for their decision to resign and sign a *waiver*.

Other employment termination program: A program by which a group or class of at least two employees are terminated involuntarily (through a layoff or reduction in force, for example) and are offered something of value in exchange for their decision to sign a *waiver*.

Unreduced pension: The full pension amount an employee will receive under an employer's pension plan if the employee works until normal retirement age.

Waiver: A legal agreement or contract between an employer and an employee in which the employee gives up ("waives") the right to sue the employer for specified claims. A waiver may cover every potential legal claim an employee might have against an employer or may be limited to only certain claims. The requirements of the OWBPA apply only to waivers of claims for age discrimination under the Age Discrimination in Employment Act (ADEA). A waiver is sometimes also referred to as a "release" or "release of claims."

Covered Employers

OWBPA applies to all employers covered by the ADEA. (See Chapter 1.)

Legal Developments

- **EEOC guidance for employees on waivers and releases.** In 2009, the EEOC issued enforcement guidance for employees with questions about releases and severance agreements. As the guidance states, the economic downturn led to an increase in employee reductions and terminations, which have led more employees to question their rights when asked to sign a waiver. Although the guidance is written for employees, it includes good information on the OWBPA's waiver requirements, along with a sample release to be used in a group layoff situation that meets the OWBPA's requirements. (See "Agency Resources," below, for a link to the EEOC publication.)

- **Pension system may benefit younger employees in certain situations.** In 2008, the Supreme Court upheld Kentucky's pension system for employees in hazardous positions who suffer a disability on the job. An employee who had not yet served enough years to qualify for retirement received credit for the additional years necessary upon suffering a disability. Because of the way the system was set up, it could result in younger workers being credited with more years—and, therefore, receiving higher pension payments—than older employees. The Court nonetheless upheld the system, finding that Kentucky did not intend to discriminate based on age. (*Kentucky Retirement Systems v. Equal Employment Opportunity Commission*, 128 S.Ct. 2361 (2008).)

Covered Workers

OWBPA protects all employees and job applicants covered by the ADEA. (See Chapter 1.) Like the ADEA, it applies only to those who are at least 40 years old. For ease of reference, we sometimes refer to this protected group as "older workers" throughout this chapter. Workers under 40 are referred to as "younger workers."

Did You Know ...

Congress passed the OWBPA to overturn a U.S. Supreme Court case called *Public Employees Retirement System of Ohio v. Betts* (492 U.S. 158 (1989).) In *Betts*, the Supreme Court found that bona fide employee benefit plans were not covered by the ADEA—that is, employees could not claim that such a plan was discriminatory—unless the plan was a subterfuge for illegal age discrimination in some other aspect of employment. (As an example, the Court said that a company that cut all employee salaries while simultaneously providing substantially increased benefits only to younger workers might be using its benefit plan as a subterfuge for age discrimination.) Congress found that this interpretation ignored its intent to prohibit discrimination in the provision of benefits except when justified by "significant cost considerations."

Major Provisions of OWBPA

Benefits

Congress passed OWBPA not only to prohibit age discrimination in the provision of fringe benefits (such as life insurance, health insurance, disability benefits, pensions, and retirement benefits) but also to allow employers to reduce benefits to older workers when justified by significant cost considerations. In most situations, employers must provide equal benefits to older and younger workers. For some types of benefits, however, employers can meet this nondiscrimination requirement by spending the same amount on the benefit provided to each group, even if older workers receive lesser benefits. Employers are also allowed, in some circumstances, to provide lesser benefits to older workers if the older workers receive additional benefits (from the employer or the government) to make up the difference.

As you'll see, these rules are detailed, and applying them can be fairly complicated. If you need help determining whether your company's plans offer equal benefits to older and younger workers, consult with an employee benefits lawyer or an enrolled actuary.

Key Facts: Benefits

- In some situations, an employer may count other benefits older workers receive, from the employer or from the government, toward the equal benefit obligation. As long as the older workers' total benefits are equal to the total benefits younger workers receive, the employer has not violated OWBPA. However, this rule applies only to certain benefits.
- Special rules apply to some early retirement incentive plans, pension plans, hybrid pension plans, long-term disability plans, and employee contribution plans.

Covered Employers

All covered employers are subject to these provisions.

Covered Workers

All covered employees are subject to these provisions.

What's Prohibited

Employers may not rely on the provisions of a benefit plan to:
- refuse to hire anyone based on the person's age, or
- require anyone to retire involuntarily because of that person's age.

What's Required

Employers are not always required to provide precisely the same benefits to workers 40 and older as they provide to younger workers. In some cases, an employer may comply with OWBPA by showing that although the benefits to each group aren't identical, the employer paid the same amount for benefits to both groups. This is called the "equal cost defense." In some other cases, employers may comply with OWBPA by showing that any shortfall in benefits to older workers was made up (offset) by additional benefits from the employer or the government.

Below, we explain how these defenses work and a few special rules that apply to certain types of benefits.

The Equal Cost Defense

An employer may offer a lesser benefit to older workers if it costs the same as the benefit offered to younger workers. However, this rule applies only to certain types of benefits and is subject to several conditions. An employer may use the equal cost defense only if all of the following are true:

- **The benefit is one that becomes more costly to provide as workers grow older.** This is often true of life insurance, health insurance, and disability insurance, for example. As workers age, it becomes more likely that they will use these benefits, and insurers often charge more for coverage to guard against this possibility. Because benefits such as severance pay or paid vacations do not cost more to provide to older workers, the equal cost defense does not apply to these benefits.

- **The benefit is not a retirement benefit (to which the equal cost defense does not apply).**

- **The benefit is provided as part of a *bona fide employee benefit plan*.**

- **The benefit plan explicitly requires lower benefits for older workers.** An employer cannot use the equal cost defense if the benefit plan gives the employer discretion to provide lower benefits to older workers if it chooses; the plan must require benefits to diminish for older workers.

- **The employer pays the same amount to provide for coverage for older and younger workers.** This is the "equal cost" requirement. For example, the employer may pay the same amount in premiums for older and younger workers, even though younger workers will receive more in benefits.

- **Benefit levels for older workers have not been reduced more than is necessary to achieve equal cost for coverage of older and younger workers.**

- **When comparing coverage costs, the employer has not used age brackets of more than five years.** That is, an employer that wishes to reduce a benefit for workers ages 61 through 65 must compare the cost of covering those workers to the cost of covering workers ages 56 through 60—not the cost of covering workers in their 20s or 30s.

Offsets

In some cases, employers may offer older employees lesser benefits if those employees receive additional benefits from the employer or the government that make up the difference. The employer may use these additional benefits to offset the shortfall and bring the older workers' benefits up to the same level offered to younger employees.

Offsets may be used only in the following circumstances:

- Employers can use government-provided disability benefits to offset disability benefits or disability retirement benefits provided by the employer. For example, if a disabled employee collects workers' compensation or Social Security disability payments, the employer can count that money toward the total disability benefit it offers older workers for purposes of the equal benefit rule.

- Employers can use the portion of an older worker's pension benefit that is attributable to employer contributions to offset long-term disability benefits if:
  - the worker voluntarily elects to receive the pension (at any age), or
  - the worker has reached age 62 or the pension plan's normal retirement age—whichever is later—and is eligible for an *unreduced pension.*

- Employers can use retiree health benefits provided to an employee to offset severance benefits if (1) the retiree actually receives the health benefit coverage (if an employer offers the benefit but the retiree turns it down, this requirement has not been met), (2) the retiree health benefits are at least comparable to Medicare benefits in type and value, or if the retiree is 65 or older, at least comparable to one-fourth the value of Medicare benefits, and (3) the retiree is eligible for an immediate pension. If these requirements are met, the employer may take the following offsets:
  - For health benefits provided for an unlimited time period (for example, for the rest of the employee's lifetime), the employer may offset $48,000 if the employee is younger than 65, or $24,000 if the employee is 65 or older at the time of retirement.
  - For benefits of limited duration, the employer may deduct $3,000 per year of benefits paid before the employee reaches the age of 65, and $750 per year once the employee reaches 65.

- Employers can use additional pension benefits to offset severance benefits if both of the following are true:
  - The additional pension benefits are made available solely because of the employee's separation from employment.
  - Counting the additional pension benefit, the employee is eligible for an immediate and unreduced pension.

- Employers that increase the value of a pension benefit for employees who work beyond normal retirement age may use that increased value to offset the employee's pension accrual. For example, if a pension accrues a benefit of $50 per year of service but pays employees $75 for each year of work beyond normal retirement age, the employer is not required to pay both amounts. The $75 increased value offsets the $50 benefit.
- Employers that begin pension payments while an employee is still working may use the actuarial value of those payments to offset the employee's pension accrual. For example, if an employee works for one year beyond normal retirement age and receives $10,000 in pension payments during that time, the employer may use the actuarial value of those payments (what that amount would be worth to the employee per month over the course of the employee's lifetime) to offset pension accrual (how much the employee is entitled to earn per year of service).
- Employers may use Social Security Old Age benefits to offset pension benefits, in some cases.

Special Rules for Certain Benefits

OWBPA places special requirements on certain types of benefits.

Employee Contribution Plans. If an employee contributes a portion of the costs of a required benefit (for example, an employee pays part of a health insurance or life insurance premium for a benefit that all employees are required to have), the employer may not require an older employee, as a condition of employment, to pay a higher contribution than a younger employee. However, the employer may require an older employee to contribute more to participate in a voluntary benefit plan, as long as that higher contribution is justified by the equal cost defense. The employer may also allow older workers to pay more to maintain their benefits at the same level provided to younger employees.

Benefit Packages. The equal cost approach applies to benefit packages as well as to individual benefits. An employer may offer a different total benefit package to older employees than to younger employees, as long as the difference is justified by the equal cost defense. However, all of the following requirements apply:

- Only those benefits that become more costly to provide with increasing age may be included in the benefits to which the equal cost defense is applied. Retirement or pension plans may not be included.

- Employers may not use the benefit package approach to reduce health benefits beyond what would be allowed under an individual benefit comparison. Any reductions in health insurance must be justified by the increased cost to the employer of providing that benefit alone.
- If an older worker is deprived of a particular benefit because of the increased cost of providing that benefit as workers age, the worker must receive additional benefits in exchange. Considered as a whole, the entire benefit package for older workers must be no worse than they would have received had the employer compared benefits individually under the equal cost defense.

Long-Term Disability Benefits. OWBPA provides a safe harbor for employers that offer long-term disability benefits, as long as they follow this schedule:

- For workers who became disabled at age 60 or younger, benefits stop at age 65.
- For workers who became disabled at age 61 or older, benefits stop five years after the employee became disabled.

Retiree Health Benefits. Employers that provide health benefits to retirees may alter, reduce, or eliminate those benefits once the recipient is eligible for Medicare health benefits. These employers are exempt from the equal cost/equal benefit rules that would otherwise apply. This exemption is intended to encourage employers to provide retiree health benefits by allowing them to coordinate those benefits with Medicare (and thereby reducing the costs of providing such benefits).

Pension Benefits. An employer that offers pension benefits is legally allowed to:

- set a normal or early retirement age for receipt of benefits
- require a specified number of years of service before an employee will be eligible to retire and receive benefits, and
- limit the total amount of benefits provided or the total number of years of service that will be credited in calculating pension benefits.

However, employers may not:

- prevent an employee from participating in a pension plan solely because that employee is near the plan's normal retirement age when hired
- discontinue benefit accrual based on an employee's age, or
- stop contributing to an employee's pension account because of the employee's age.

Early Retirement Incentive Plans. *Early retirement incentive plans* sometimes provide a greater benefit to younger employees: If the plan offers an unreduced pension benefit to employees who have not yet reached normal retirement age, the youngest employees benefit the most from such a plan. Nevertheless, an early retirement incentive plan that doesn't provide equal benefits to older and younger employees is legal if it is voluntary (that is, it does not require any employee to retire) and it meets at least one of these additional requirements:

- The incentive plan subsidizes a retirement plan by paying employees who agree to retire early additional pension benefits. An employer may pay retiring employees an additional sum to bring their retirement benefits up to the level of an unreduced pension.
- The incentive plan provides Social Security supplements to retiring employees who are not yet eligible for Social Security, as long as the payments do not exceed the amount that would be paid if the employee received Social Security. Such payments must stop when the employee becomes eligible for Social Security.
- The plan is offered by an institution of higher education to tenured faculty, as long as the plan does not reduce or eliminate other benefits or repackage benefits that were already offered to the retiring employees during the year prior to the incentive.
- The plan otherwise treats employees equally without regard to age. For example, an employer may offer employees additional compensation to retire (a set dollar amount, additional money based on years of service, a percentage or set dollar increase in pension benefits, or credit for additional years of service) as long as the same benefits are offered to all employees eligible for the retirement incentive.

Applicable Defined Benefit Plans. The Pension Protection Act of 2006 creates special rules for *applicable defined benefit plans*, which can be less beneficial to older employees because of the way benefits are calculated. In a cash balance hybrid plan, for example, an employee's benefit is expressed as the balance in a hypothetical individual account. Each year, the employee's "account" receives a pay credit, based on the employee's compensation for that year, and an interest credit, representing the earnings of the entire account balance for the year based on a stated interest rate. Because younger employees will earn interest on their account balances for a longer period of time, their benefit might be more valuable than an older employee's benefit. This issue has led to litigation, particularly by older employees whose employers converted, during their employment, from a traditional *defined benefit plan* to a cash balance plan.

The Pension Protection Act amends the OWBPA to provide that defined benefit plans in which the benefit is calculated as the balance of a hypothetical account for a participant, or as an accumulated percentage of the participant's final average compensation, won't be considered discriminatory if a participant's accrued benefit under the plan is at least equal to the accrued benefit of any other younger participant who is similarly situated except for age. These plans must also meet all of the following requirements to pass muster under the OWBPA and the ADEA (additional requirements may apply under ERISA):

- Any "interest credit" portion of the benefit must be calculated at an interest rate that is no greater than the market rate of return. An interest rate of less than zero may not reduce the account value below the total amount of contributions credited to the account.
- If an employer converts to a hybrid plan, a participant's benefit may not be less than his or her total benefit under the old plan before the conversion plus his or her total benefit under the new plan since the conversion.
- If the plan uses a variable rate to calculate interest credits, and the plan terminates, it must calculate interest using the average rate used by the plan over the five years preceding its termination.

Waivers

Under OWBPA, a *waiver* of the right to sue for age discrimination is valid only if it is knowing and voluntary.

Covered Employers

All covered employers must comply with these provisions when seeking waivers of ADEA claims from their employees.

Key Facts

- Although an employer generally is required to give employees 21 days to consider a waiver and seven days to revoke the waiver after signing it, these requirements do not apply if the employee has already filed an EEOC charge or a lawsuit alleging age discrimination.
- If the waiver is offered as part of an exit incentive program or another employment termination program, the employer must provide specific information to the employee about the program and the employees to whom it was offered.
- The employer may not stop providing any continuing benefits (for example, severance payments or health insurance benefits) because an employee files a lawsuit despite the waiver.

Covered Workers

These provisions protect all covered workers whose employers ask them to waive ADEA claims.

What's Required

A waiver is valid only if it is knowing and voluntary. Because these terms are open to interpretation, Congress decided that a waiver will not be considered knowing and voluntary unless it meets certain minimum requirements. (See "Requirements for a Knowing and Voluntary Agreement," below.)

Waivers that do not meet these requirements are invalid. This means that a court will not enforce the waiver, and the worker will be able to sue for age discrimination despite having signed the waiver.

Even if a waiver meets these minimum standards, a court still might find it invalid if other evidence demonstrates that the worker did not knowingly and voluntarily agree to the waiver. For example, if the waiver is misleading or omits important information, a court might throw out the waiver, even if it meets the specifications listed below.

Requirements for a Knowing and Voluntary Agreement

A waiver will be considered knowing and voluntary only if it:

- is part of a written agreement between the employer and the employee
- is written in language understandable to the employee (or, in the case of an offer made to a group, understandable to the average employee eligible to participate)
- specifically refers to the worker's rights or claims under the ADEA
- does not require the employee to waive any rights or claims that may arise after the agreement is signed, and
- gives the employee something of value (such as cash or continued benefits) in exchange for the waiver, over and above anything to which the employee is already entitled. For example, if all employees receive a set amount of severance pay when they leave the company, the employer must give an employee who signs an ADEA waiver something in addition to that pay.

In addition, employers must:

- advise the employee, in writing, to consult with an attorney before signing the agreement
- give the employee at least 21 days to consider the agreement, or 45 days if the waiver is requested in connection with an *exit incentive program* or *another employment termination program* offered to a group of employees (the employee can accept the agreement after a shorter period of deliberation, as long as the employee had the opportunity to take as long as the law allows), and
- give the employee at least seven days after signing to revoke the agreement.

Additional Rules for Exit Incentive or Other Employment Termination Programs

If the waiver is requested in connection with an exit incentive program or another employment termination program offered to a group of employees, the employer must also inform the employee, in writing, of:

- any class, unit, or group of individuals covered by the program, any eligibility rules for the program, and any time limits applicable to the program, and
- the job titles and ages of all individuals eligible or selected for the program, and the ages of all individuals in the same job classification or organizational unit who are not eligible or selected for the program.

Rules for Waivers to Settle an EEOC Charge or Lawsuit

If an employee has already filed a charge of age discrimination with the EEOC or filed a lawsuit against the employer for age discrimination, the rules for waivers are less strict. In these situations, the employer does not have to provide 21 (or 45) days for the employee to consider the agreement, allow a revocation period of seven days, or give the additional information on eligible employees (their ages and so on) required for a group exit program.

However, the waiver must meet the other requirements listed above. In addition, the employee must be given a reasonable period of time to consider the settlement.

Lawsuits Filed After a Waiver: The Tender-Back Rule

If a worker tries to sue an employer after signing a waiver, traditional legal principles require that worker to first give back whatever he or she received (for example, severance pay or continued benefits) in exchange for giving up the right to sue. This requirement, referred to as the "tender-back rule," requires workers to put their money where their mouths are: In order to argue that the waiver is invalid and should not prevent a lawsuit, the worker must give up the benefit received under the waiver.

However, the tender-back rule does not apply to workers who file age discrimination lawsuits. Older workers may keep the severance (or other benefit) and file an ADEA claim. However, if the worker wins a damages award in the lawsuit, the award can be reduced to account for the money already paid by the employer. The reduction is either the amount of the severance pay or the amount of the worker's award, whichever is less. For example, if the employer paid $5,000 in severance and the employee receives an award of $4,000, the award will be reduced to zero.

The waiver may not include any penalty for filing a lawsuit. For example, some waivers require an employee to pay the employer's attorneys' fees if the employee files a lawsuit—such a requirement is illegal for ADEA waivers. Employers also may not stop fulfilling their obligations under a waiver if a lawsuit is filed. For example, many waivers provide that an employee will be paid a monthly severance check or receive certain retirement benefits for a period of time. The employer cannot stop making payments simply because the employee files a lawsuit claiming the waiver is invalid.

How OWBPA Is Enforced

Individual Complaints

Employees may file a complaint (also called a charge) of age discrimination with the EEOC. The deadlines for filing a charge depend on whether the state in which the discrimination charge will be filed has its own antidiscrimination law. In states without antidiscrimination laws, an employee has 180 days from the date of the discriminatory act to file a charge. In states with an antidiscrimination law, this deadline is extended to 300 days. (See Chapter 18 for information on state antidiscrimination laws.)

An employee may also file a lawsuit for age discrimination under the OWBPA. However, the employee must file a charge of discrimination with the EEOC (or a state agency) and get a "right to sue" letter first. An employee must file the lawsuit within 90 days of receiving a right to sue letter from the EEOC.

Agency Enforcement

The federal agency responsible for investigating OWBPA complaints is the EEOC. An employee usually initiates the process by filing a charge with the EEOC, although the agency can also act on its own initiative. The EEOC has the power to investigate, negotiate with employers, and bring lawsuits against employers to stop discriminatory practices.

Complying With OWBPA

Reporting Requirements

OWBPA imposes no reporting requirements.

Posting Requirements

OWBPA has no posting requirements separate from those required by the ADEA, which are covered in Chapter 1.

Record-Keeping Requirements

OWBPA has no record-keeping requirements separate from those required by the ADEA, which are covered in Chapter 1.

Remedies

The remedies available under OWBPA are the same as those available under the ADEA, which are covered in Chapter 1.

Agency Resources

- Information on waivers of ADEA and other discrimination claims
  Understanding Waivers of Discrimination Claims in Employee Severance Agreements
  www.eeoc.gov/policy/docs/qanda_severance-agreements.html

- Detailed explanations and examples of OWBPA's benefits rules
  EEOC Compliance Manual: Employee Benefits
  www.eeoc.gov/policy/docs/benefits.html

State Laws Relating to Age Discrimination

At the end of Chapter 18, you'll find a chart of state laws relating to fair employment, which includes laws prohibiting age discrimination.

Personal Responsibility and Work Opportunity Reconciliation Act (PRWORA)

Statute: 42 U.S.C. §§ 651 and following
To view the statutes, visit http://uscode.house.gov and select "Title 42," "Chapter 7," and "Subchapter IV."

Regulations: 45 C.F.R. §§ 301 and following
To view the regulations, visit www.govinfo.gov and search "45 CFR 301."

Overview of PRWORA

Passed in 1996 as part of former President Clinton's welfare reform effort, the Personal Responsibility and Work Opportunity Reconciliation Act (PRWORA) enlists employers in the effort to help parents collect child support. The law requires employers to report all new hires to a state registry, which uses this information to track down parents who aren't meeting their child support obligations.

PRWORA is a broad welfare law, with provisions on nutrition programs, teen pregnancy prevention, welfare-to-work requirements, and more. The discussion in this book is limited to employers' responsibilities under the law's child support collection provision.

Definitions

Terms that appear in italics throughout this chapter are defined below.

Date of hire: The first day on which an employee performs services for wages; in other words, an employee's first actual workday. The date of hire is not the same as the day on which a job offer is made or accepted, unless the employee begins work that day.

Independent contractor: Someone who performs services for another person or business under contract, rather than as an employee. PRWORA uses the Internal Revenue Service's definitions of employee and independent contractor. Under these rules, a worker will usually be classified as an independent contractor if the person paying the worker has the right to control or direct only the result of the work, not the means or methods by which the work is performed.

Multistate employer: An employer that has employees working in more than one state.

Covered Employers

The law covers:

- state and local governments
- the federal government
- all private employers
- union hiring halls, if they retain an employment relationship with the workers whom they refer for jobs (for example, if the union rather than the company pays the worker's wages)
- unions that employ workers for wages (as paid organizers or administrative workers, for example), and
- temporary or placement agencies that retain an employment relationship with the workers whom they place (for example, agencies that collect an hourly rate from the companies in which workers are placed, then pay a portion of that rate to the workers as wages).

Employers on Native American reservations and lands are not required to comply with the law, unless the tribe has entered into an agreement with the state to do so.

Did You Know ...

- More than $32 billion was collected for child support in 2014; 75% of those dollars were submitted by employers through wage withholding.
- As of April 2017, total child support arrearages—child support that was owed and not paid—exceeded $114 billion.

Covered Workers

PRWORA applies to all newly hired employees, including:

- former employees who are rehired, if the employee has been separated from the company for at least 60 days or is required to complete a new IRS W-4 form

- agricultural and domestic workers (housekeepers and child care workers, for example), and
- short-term employees (workers who quit or are fired before the 20-day deadline for reporting new hires has passed; see "What's Required," below, for more on this deadline).

PRWORA does not cover any of the following:

- **Employees acquired through a merger or reorganization.** For example, if one company buys another company and acquires its workers, the purchasing company usually does not have to report those employees as new hires. However, if the employees complete new IRS W-4 forms after the merger, then the company must report them as new hires.
- **Independent contractors.** Some states require employers to report *independent contractors*, but PRWORA does not.
- **Employees working outside of the United States.** PRWORA does not cover employees that work in another country, even if they work for an American employer.
- **Employees of a federal or state agency who perform intelligence or counter-intelligence functions.** Such employees are not covered if the head of the agency determines that reporting them as new hires could endanger the employees' safety or compromise an ongoing investigation or intelligence mission.

Key Facts

- Employers must report new hires to a state agency, which uses the information to find parents who are not fulfilling their child support obligations.
- Some states require employers to provide more information on new hires than PRWORA requires or to submit information on workers who are not covered by PRWORA.
- Employers that do business in more than one state can designate one state to which they will send all new hire reports, even for employees who do not work in that state.

What's Required

Employers must report all new hires to a state agency called the State Directory of New Hires (PRWORA requires each state to establish such an agency). Employers must submit this information to the state agency in the state where the employee works, except that *multistate employers* may designate one state as the recipient of all new hire reports. (See "Exceptions," below).

Required Information

The employer must submit the following information every time it hires a new employee:

- employee's name, address, Social Security number, and *date of hire*, and
- employer's name, address, and federal employer identification number.

The employer may comply with this requirement by submitting the employee's IRS W-4 form or by supplying the information in a different format.

PRWORA allows states to require employers to submit additional information on new hires, such as the employee's birth date.

Deadlines for Submitting Information

Employers must submit the required information within 20 days after a new employee's date of hire. Employers that choose to report new hire information electronically or by magnetic tape must report at least twice a month. These reports must be no less than 12, and no more than 16, days apart.

Information Requested for Employees Called to Active Duty

In addition to the required information on new hires, the federal Office of Child Support Enforcement (OCSE) asks employers to submit additional information for current employees who are called to active military duty. This is a request, not a requirement: Employers are not legally obligated to submit this information.

For employees serving in the reserves, employers are asked to:

- contact the child support agency that issued the wage withholding order
- tell the agency that the employee has been called to active duty, and
- provide the date of the employee's activation.

This will allow the agency to issue a new withholding order to the military, so the employee's child support payments will continue uninterrupted while he or she is on active duty.

Exceptions

The law does not require multistate employers to report each new hire to the state agency where the employee works. Instead, a multistate employer can designate one state agency as the recipient of all new hire reports, regardless of where these employees actually work. To use this exception, the multistate employer must:

- choose a state where it employs workers
- submit its new hire information electronically or by magnetic tape
- follow that state's reporting laws for all employees (for example, if the state requires employers to report information for independent contractors, then the employer must submit information on all independent contractors, including contractors who work in other states), and
- tell the office of the Secretary of Health and Human Services, in writing, which state it has designated to receive new hire reports.

How PRWORA Is Enforced

Under PRWORA, state agencies are responsible for policing an employer's compliance with PRWORA's reporting requirement. Although the federal Office of Child Support Enforcement (OCSE), a division of the Administration for Children and Families (ACF), which is part of the Department of Health and Human Services, oversees the entire program, each state is responsible for making sure that employers within its borders comply with PRWORA. (See Appendix A for information on how to contact the OCSE.)

Individuals may not sue an employer for failing to comply with PRWORA.

Complying With PRWORA

Deadlines

- Employers must report new hires within 20 days after their date of hire.
- Employers that report new hire information electronically or by magnetic tape must report at least twice a month, no less than 12 days apart and no more than 16 days apart.

Reporting Requirements

The law is essentially a reporting requirement. (See "What's Required," above, for details.)

Record-Keeping Requirements

PRWORA imposes no special record-keeping requirements on employers. There is no requirement that employers keep a copy of the information they send to the state directory of new hires for any length of time, for example.

Penalties

PRWORA authorizes states to impose penalties on employers that fail to report new hires as required by the law. If a state chooses to impose such a penalty, it may not exceed:

- $25 for each new hire whom the employer fails to report, or
- $500 for each new hire, if the employer and employee conspire in the failure to report (for example, if an employer agrees to an employee's request that it not file the report so that the employee can evade child support obligations).

Agency Resources

- A list of regional offices of the Administration for Children and Families
  Offices
  www.acf.hhs.gov/about/offices
- An employer's guide to complying with PRWORA's reporting requirements
  New Hire Reporting
  www.acf.hhs.gov/programs/css/employers/employer-responsibilities/new-hire-reporting
- A list of each state's new hire reporting requirements, including contact information and websites for state child support enforcement offices
  State New Hire Reporting Contacts and Program Requirements
  www.acf.hhs.gov/css/resource/state-new-hire-reporting-contacts-and-program-requirements

- A form multistate employers can use to designate the state to which they will submit new hire information
  Multistate Employer Notification Form for New Hire Reporting
  www.acf.hhs.gov/sites/default/files/programs/css/mse_form.pdf
- Information on how to respond to a wage-withholding order
  Processing an Income Withholding Order or Notice
  www.acf.hhs.gov/programs/css/resource/processing-an-income-withholding-order-or-notice

State Laws Relating to New Hire Reporting

PRWORA gives states the leeway to impose stricter requirements on employers. For example, although the federal law doesn't require it, states may choose to enact laws requiring employers to:

- report independent contractors as well as employees
- submit new hire information sooner than the 20 days allowed under PRWORA
- provide more information about new hires than the federal law requires, and
- pay penalties for failing to comply with the law.

You can find information on each state's requirements, as well as citations to your state's law and the address of your state's enforcement agency, at the OCSE's website; see "Agency Resources," above.

Pregnancy Discrimination Act (PDA)

Statute: 42 U.S.C. § 2000e(k)

To view the statutes, visit http://uscode.house.gov and select "Title 42," "Chapter 21," and "Subchapter VI."

Regulations: 29 C.F.R. § 1604 and Appendix to Part 1604

To view the regulations, visit www.govinfo.gov and search "29 CFR 1604."

Overview of the Pregnancy Discrimination Act

The Pregnancy Discrimination Act (PDA) prohibits discrimination on the basis of pregnancy, childbirth, and related medical conditions in employment, health insurance plans, disability insurance plans, and sick leave plans. Under the PDA, discrimination based on pregnancy, childbirth, and/or related medical conditions is impermissible sex-based discrimination under Title VII of the Civil Rights Act of 1964 (Title VII). (Chapter 18 covers Title VII in detail.)

Definitions

Definitions for the Pregnancy Discrimination Act are the same as those for Title VII. (See "Definitions," in Chapter 18.)

Covered Employers

The PDA covers:
- private employers with 15 or more employees
- the federal government
- state and local governments
- private and public employment agencies
- labor organizations, and
- joint labor/management committees.

Covered Workers

The PDA protects all prospective and current employees of a covered employer.

What's Prohibited

The PDA prohibits employers from discriminating against prospective and current employees on the basis of pregnancy, childbirth, or related medical conditions. The PDA applies to all terms and benefits of employment, including:

- hiring
- firing
- compensation and benefits
- job assignment
- employee classification
- transfer
- promotion
- layoff or recall
- training and apprenticeship programs
- use of company facilities
- retirement plans, and
- time off.

Legal Developments

- **Supreme Court clarifies duty to accommodate pregnant employees.** In 2015, the Supreme Court settled the long-standing question of exactly what the PDA requires when it comes to reasonable accommodation. It is well established that an employer cannot offer reasonable accommodations to all nonpregnant workers while denying the same accommodations to pregnant workers. However, until recently, it wasn't clear if employers are required to offer accommodations to pregnant employees if they offer accommodations to some—but not all—nonpregnant workers (for example, accommodating workers with on-the-job injuries, but not accommodating pregnant workers or workers with off-the-job injuries). According to the Supreme Court, employers are permitted to treat pregnant employees differently from a group of nonpregnant workers. However, the employer must be able to show a legitimate, nondiscriminatory reason for doing so. (*Young v. United Parcel Service*, 135 S. Ct. 1338 (2015).)
- **Congress considers the Pregnant Workers Fairness Act.** In recent years, Congress has considered the Pregnant Workers Fairness Act, a bill that would require employers to accommodate pregnant employees, regardless of whether they accommodate other workers. The bill has been introduced multiple times since 2012, but has yet to pass. However, similar laws have been passed at the state level in recent years. (See "State Laws Relating to Pregnancy Discrimination," below.)

The PDA also prohibits employers from retaliating against those who complain or otherwise assert their rights under the law. For example, an employer cannot fire someone for filing a charge of pregnancy discrimination with the EEOC. (For more, see "Retaliation," in Chapter 18.)

Did You Know ...

- Congress passed the PDA in 1978 in direct response to the U.S. Supreme Court's ruling in the case of *General Electric Co. v. Gilbert*, 429 U.S. 125 (1976), in which the Court held that pregnancy-related discrimination was not necessarily sex discrimination—and, therefore, was not necessarily illegal under Title VII.
- There were 3,174 pregnancy discrimination claims filed with the U.S. Equal Employment Opportunity Commission in 2017. Not including cases that actually went to court, the EEOC obtained $15 million in compensation for workers whose pregnancy discrimination claims it settled in 2017.
- In the ten years before the advent of the PDA, more than half of employed women quit their jobs when they became pregnant. That number dropped to 26.9% by the early 1990s.

Key Facts

- Under the PDA, discrimination based on pregnancy, birth, or related medical conditions in any aspect of employment is illegal sex-based discrimination under Title VII of the Civil Rights Act of 1964. (See Chapter 18 for more on Title VII.)
- The PDA is part of Title VII; as such, the PDA's requirements, prohibitions, and complaint and enforcement procedures are the same as those for Title VII.
- Employers must treat workers with pregnancy-related disabilities the same as they treat nonpregnant workers who are temporarily unable to work.

Related Medical Conditions

Unfortunately, the PDA does not define the term "related medical condition," so the task of giving this term meaning has been left to the courts. Although courts define the term differently, there are a few bright-line rules. If, as a direct result of pregnancy or childbirth, a woman suffers from a medical complication or disability that requires medical treatment, that qualifies as a related medical condition. For example, recovery from childbirth (even if the birth was uneventful) and recovery from miscarriage or abortion fall within this category.

Women are also protected from discrimination based on their potential to become pregnant or intention to become pregnant. Employers also may not discriminate against women because of the potential risk for reproductive harm. For example, an employer cannot exclude all women of childbearing years from jobs that require contact with toxic chemicals or other substances that could lead to birth defects.

Lactation and breast-feeding are considered pregnancy-related medical conditions that are protected by the PDA. Federal law, and the laws of many states also require employers to accommodate their employees' desire to provide breast milk to their children by providing lactation breaks. (See Chapter 7.)

Whether infertility is a pregnancy-related medical condition depends on the context. Several courts have held that penalizing female employees who are seeking fertility treatment in order to become pregnant is impermissible under the PDA. Yet other courts have held that, because infertility can affect both men and women, denying health care coverage for infertility treatments cannot give rise to a claim of sex discrimination under the PDA. Infertility may also qualify as a disability under the Americans with Disabilities Act (see Chapter 2) or a serious health condition under the Family and Medical Leave Act (see Chapter 8). Because this area of law is unsettled, it's best to consult with an attorney before denying time off or accommodations to an employee undergoing fertility treatments.

What's Required

Unlike the Americans with Disabilities Act (see Chapter 2), the PDA does not impose an affirmative duty on employers to accommodate pregnant employees, for example, by providing light-duty work, schedule changes, or time off. Instead, employers must only treat pregnant employees the same as nonpregnant employees who are "similar in their ability or inability to work." In other words, if an employer doesn't offer reasonable accommodations to employees who are temporarily disabled for other reasons, it doesn't have to accommodate pregnant employees either. But what if the employer provides accommodations to only some of those nonpregnant employees? Must it do the same for pregnant workers?

The U.S. Supreme Court recently settled this issue in *Young v. United Parcel Service*, 135 S. Ct. 1338 (2015). In that case, a driver named Peggy Young was placed on an unpaid leave of absence after her employer refused to accommodate her pregnancy-related lifting restriction. Young filed suit under the PDA, arguing that UPS was required to accommodate her because it accommodated nonpregnant workers, including those who had suffered on-the-job injuries. However, UPS argued that it was not required to accommodate Young because it did not accommodate other groups of nonpregnant workers—such as those who suffered injuries off the job.

The Supreme Court resolved the dispute by holding that employers are not required to accommodate pregnant employees any time they accommodate a subset of nonpregnant employees. However, the employer must be able to show a legitimate, nondiscriminatory reason for the different treatment. The fact that it is more costly or inconvenient to accommodate pregnant women is not a legitimate reason.

These rules also apply to benefit accrual, seniority, vacation calculation, pay increases, and other benefits. Pregnant employees cannot be singled out for worse treatment than nonpregnant employees who are temporarily disabled for other reasons.

Employers must allow pregnant employees to work for as long as they are able to do their jobs. For example, an employer cannot require a pregnant employee to go on leave—whether paid or unpaid—prior to the baby's birth if the employee is able to work and does not want to go on leave.

If the male spouses or partners of a company's employees get comprehensive medical benefits as dependents of employees, then the female spouses or partners must also get comprehensive medical benefits as dependents—including benefits for pregnancy, childbirth, and related medical conditions.

If the employer provides health insurance as a benefit to employees, the policy must cover expenses for pregnancy, childbirth, and related medical conditions to the same extent that it covers expenses for other medical conditions. However, employer-provided benefits do not have to cover an abortion unless the life of the mother would be endangered if she carried the fetus to term. If a woman does have an abortion, the employer's health benefits must cover any medical complications arising from that abortion, whether or not the benefits paid for the abortion in the first place.

Because the Pregnancy Discrimination Act also applies to a woman's potential to become pregnant, the EEOC has stated that the PDA applies to contraceptives as well. According to enforcement guidelines issued by the EEOC in 2014, employers must include coverage for prescription contraceptives in their health plans to the same extent that they provide drugs, devices, or services that are intended to prevent other medical conditions from occurring. The EEOC takes a broad view of preventative drugs and services, which includes vaccinations, blood pressure medication, mammograms and other screening tests, and even physical examinations. In other words, most employer health plans need to include coverage for contraceptives.

However, there may be an exemption for religious employers. In *Burwell v. Hobby Lobby Stores, Inc.*, the religious owners of a craft store refused to comply with a mandate of the Affordable Care Act, which requires covered employers to provide access to contraceptives in their health plans. The owners objected to coverage for contraceptives that prevent implantation of an already fertilized egg, which they considered to be forms of early abortion. They argued that forcing them to comply with the mandate would violate their right to exercise their religious beliefs under the Religious Freedom Restoration Act of 1993. The Supreme Court agreed. (*Burwell v. Hobby Lobby Stores, Inc.*, 134 S. Ct. 2751 (2014).) While this ruling was limited to the Affordable Care Act mandate, employers could make similar challenges to contraceptive mandates under the PDA.

Employees who are pregnant or new parents may also have rights under the Family and Medical Leave Act. (See Chapter 8 for more information.) Employees who develop pregnancy-related complications (such as gestational diabetes) may also be protected under the ADA (see Chapter 2) as having a disability.

Exceptions

The exceptions to the PDA are the same as those for Title VII. (See Chapter 18.)

How the Pregnancy Discrimination Act Is Enforced

Individual Complaints

The enforcement provisions of Title VII apply to the PDA. (See Chapter 18.)

Agency Enforcement

The enforcement provisions of Title VII apply to the PDA. (See Chapter 18.)

Complying With the Pregnancy Discrimination Act

Reporting Requirements

The reporting requirements for the PDA are the same as those for Title VII. (See Chapter 18.)

Posting Requirements

The PDA is among the laws covered in the general antidiscrimination poster required by Title VII. (See Chapter 18 for information on how to access this poster.)

Record-Keeping Requirements

The record-keeping requirements for the PDA are the same as those for Title VII. (See Chapter 18.)

Penalties

The penalties for violating the PDA are the same as those for violating Title VII. (See Chapter 18.)

Agency Resources

- Information about pregnancy discrimination
  Pregnancy Discrimination
  www.eeoc.gov/laws/types/pregnancy.cfm

- A fact sheet on the relationship between the Family and Medical Leave Act, the Americans with Disabilities Act, and Title VII's protections against pregnancy and sex discrimination
  The Family and Medical Leave Act, the Americans with Disabilities Act, and Title VII of the Civil Rights Act of 1964
  www.eeoc.gov/policy/docs/fmlaada.html

State Laws Relating to Pregnancy Discrimination

Many states have laws that protect pregnant workers from discrimination. (See "State Antidiscrimination Laws," in Chapter 18, for information.) In recent years, more states have passed laws imposing an affirmative duty on employers to provide reasonable accommodations to pregnant employees. Around 20 states and the District of Columbia have pregnancy accommodation laws that apply to private employers.

Sarbanes-Oxley Act of 2002 (SOX)

Statute: 15 U.S.C. §§ 78j-1(m); 18 U.S.C. § 1514A

To view the statutes, visit http://uscode.house.gov and select "Title 15" and "Chapter 2B;" and "Title 18" and "Chapter 73."

Regulations: 17 C.F.R. § 240.10A-3; 29 C.F.R. § 1980

To view the regulations, visit govinfo.gov and search "17 CFR 240-10A-1" and "29 CFR 1980-100."

Overview of SOX

n the wake of corporate scandals involving WorldCom, Enron, and other large companies accused of defrauding shareholders, Congress passed the Sarbanes-Oxley Act of 2002 (SOX). The stated purpose of SOX is to protect investors by improving the accuracy and reliability of corporate disclosures. Much of the law seeks to further this goal by imposing strict rules for audits and auditors of publicly traded companies, by preventing insider trading and deals, by requiring companies to adopt strict internal controls, and by increasing the penalties for white-collar crimes relating to investor fraud. Because these provisions don't directly implicate employment issues, they aren't covered here.

SOX also creates employee whistle-blower protections: Employees who complain of, or provide information about, actions they believe to be shareholder fraud are protected from discrimination and retaliation. The law also obligates covered companies to create procedures by which employees can report concerns about audits or accounting procedures.

In 2010, Congress passed the Dodd-Frank Act, also called the Wall Street Reform and Consumer Protection Act, a response to the financial collapse that began in late 2007. The Dodd-Frank Act amends SOX in several important aspects, all of which are covered in this chapter. The Dodd-Frank Act also adds a number of whistle-blower protections for those who raise concerns about the conduct of financial firms, rating agencies, and so on; however, these rules are not covered in this book.

Covered Employers

SOX generally applies only to *public companies* (which includes their subsidiaries and affiliates). However, its whistle-blower provisions also apply to *company representatives*, which could include people or businesses that haven't issued stock or gone public. For example, the whistle-blower provisions could apply to a private company that contracts to do work for public companies.

SOX creates personal liability for company representatives, including employees who are in a position to retaliate against other employees who raise concerns about corporate misfeasance. This means that managers and supervisors who violate SOX by retaliating against whistle-blowers may be held personally liable—and required to pay any judgment awarded to the employee.

Although SOX's prohibition on retaliation for whistle-blowing and the penalties for violating that provision apply only to public companies and their representatives, SOX also includes a criminal provision that applies more broadly. Anyone who intentionally harms someone else for providing truthful information to a law enforcement officer relating to the commission of any federal offense faces up to ten years in prison. (18 U.S.C. § 1513(e).) Because the law defines harm to include interference with the employment or livelihood of the informant, this provision could apply to anyone who retaliates against a whistle-blower, whether or not the perpetrator works for or has any association with a public company.

Definitions

Terms that appear in italics throughout this chapter are defined below.

Audit committee: A committee of members of the board of directors of a *public company*, formed to oversee the company's audits and accounting and financial reporting processes. The audit committee has a number of legal obligations under SOX. If a public company does not establish a separate audit committee, the entire board of directors is responsible for seeing that these obligations are met.

Company representative: Any officer, contractor, subcontractor, agent, or employee of a company.

Public company: Any company that has a class of securities registered with the Securities and Exchange Commission (SEC) under 15 U.S.C. § 78l or that is required to file periodic reports with the SEC under 15 U.S.C. § 78o(d). As amended by the Dodd-Frank Act, this includes any subsidiary or affiliate whose financial information is included in the consolidated financial statements of such a company.

Legal Developments

- **Whistle-blowers can receive a bounty.** Someone who reports possible violations of federal security laws directly to the Securities and Exchange Commission (SEC) may be entitled to a share of what the agency recovers. To qualify, the whistle-blower must voluntarily provide the SEC with original information that leads to a successful enforcement action resulting in an award of more than $1 million in monetary sanctions. The bounty payment ranges from 10% to 30% of the sanctions collected. From 2011 to 2017, the Commission received 22,818 whistle-blower tips and issued awards totaling more than $300 million. The largest single award was for $50 million.
- **OSHA's pilot ADR program extended to all regions.** In October of 2012, OSHA—the agency responsible for enforcing SOX's whistle-blower protections—introduced a voluntary alternative dispute resolution (ADR) pilot program in two of its regions. The pilot program was a success and is now fully implemented in all regions. The program uses mediation to try to help the parties resolve complaints outside of the formal legal system.

Covered Workers

All employees who work for public companies are covered by SOX's whistle-blower provisions. Not every employee qualifies as a whistle-blower, however. To be protected, an employee must either:

- make a complaint to specific people or groups about certain types of misconduct, or
- participate in certain types of proceedings relating to shareholder misconduct.

Protected Complaints

To qualify as a protected whistle-blower, an employee must provide information, cause information to be provided, or assist in an investigation or a proceeding regarding conduct that the employee reasonably believes violates (1) 18 U.S.C. §§ 1341, 1343, 1344, or 1348 (statutes that criminalize mail fraud, wire fraud, bank fraud, and shareholder fraud); (2) any rule or regulation of the SEC; or (3) any federal law relating to shareholder fraud. The employee must raise these concerns with particular people or organizations in order to be protected.

Did You Know ...

- Human resources professionals are finding themselves responsible for SOX compliance in areas outside of their traditional employee relations function. For example, many HR experts are responsible for—or assist in—implementing Section 404 of the law, which requires companies to have strict internal controls to ensure the accuracy of their financial numbers. Because salaries, benefits, recruiting, and other costs of hiring and managing employees are the largest component of many companies' budgets, HR experts are often involved in developing and implementing ways to verify that the company—and, more importantly for purposes of SOX, its shareholders—are getting their money's worth.

Conduct Relating to Shareholder Fraud

An employee is protected under SOX only for providing information about conduct that he or she reasonably believes violates the federal laws enumerated above, SEC regulations, or federal laws against shareholder fraud. Employees who complain of violations of state law are not protected under SOX, nor are employees who complain of violations of internal company policies or procedures (unless the violation also could mislead shareholders).

There is some uncertainty over what types of complaints are covered. Clearly, if an employee complains that the company failed to disclose material information to its shareholders, the complaint would be protected. The rules are less clear, however, if the employee complains of other allegedly illegal activities that could potentially affect the company's bottom line.

There is also some uncertainty about whether an employee has to specifically state, when reporting concerns or making a complaint, that he or she believes the law was violated. Some judges have found that an employee who only questions certain conduct or complains about the conduct without raising the possibility of shareholder fraud is not protected by SOX.

The employee's claim of shareholder fraud does not have to be correct. Rather, the employee must show only that he or she had a reasonable belief that the conduct constituted fraud. An employee whose complaint is based on a feeling or hunch, in the absence of any evidence, is not protected. However, an employee who reasonably believes that the company has overstated income, filed false reports, or engaged in accounting fraud is protected, even if the company's actions turn out to be perfectly legal.

Recipients of the Complaint or Assistance

An employee cannot claim the protections of SOX unless he or she provides information to, causes information to be provided to, or assists in an investigation conducted by:

- a federal regulatory or law enforcement agency (such as the SEC)
- a member or committee of Congress, or
- a person who either has supervisory authority over the employee or has the authority to investigate, discover, or terminate the alleged misconduct.

Key Facts:

- SOX prohibits retaliation against an employee who provides information or assists in an investigation regarding conduct that the employee reasonably believes to be a violation of specified federal statutes that prohibit mail fraud, wire fraud, bank fraud, and securities fraud; any rule or regulation of the Securities and Exchange Commission (SEC); or any federal law relating to shareholder fraud.
- To be protected, the employee must provide the information to, or assist in an investigation by, a federal agency, a member or committee of Congress, or a person who either supervises the employee or has the authority to investigate or put a stop to the alleged misconduct.
- The law also prohibits retaliation against an employee who files or participates in an enforcement proceeding relating to shareholder fraud.
- SOX requires companies to adopt procedures for receiving, handling, and retaining complaints about their accounting, auditing, or internal controls. Companies must also establish a way for employees to submit confidential, anonymous complaints of questionable accounting or auditing practices.

Protected Proceedings

There are two types of proceedings that are protected under SOX: investigations and legal proceedings.

Employees are protected if they assist in an investigation into conduct that they reasonably believe constitutes shareholder fraud by any of the complaint recipients listed in "Recipients of the Complaint or Assistance," above. An employee does not have to provide the information that leads to the investigation; an employee who acts as a witness in or provides information to an ongoing investigation is also protected.

Employees are also protected if they file, cause to be filed, testify in, participate in, or otherwise assist in a proceeding that has been filed or is about to be filed relating to an alleged violation of SEC regulations or federal laws relating to shareholder fraud.

What's Prohibited

Public companies and company representatives may not retaliate against an employee in the terms or conditions of employment because the employee provided information, participated in an investigation, or participated in a proceeding relating to shareholder fraud.

SOX states that termination, demotion, suspension, threats, and harassment all constitute retaliation. However, judges are divided as to whether actions that don't cause a tangible job consequence qualify. Some cases have held that giving a negative performance evaluation, moving the employee to a work space with fewer amenities, or taking away the employee's "officer" status did not constitute retaliation, because they were unaccompanied by any tangible consequences such as a demotion or decrease in pay. On the other hand, other cases have held that taking away job responsibilities, changing the employee's performance improvement plan, and placing the employee on a layoff list (although he or she is never actually laid off) are all sufficient to constitute retaliation.

What's Required

The *audit committee* of a public company must establish procedures for:
- receiving, keeping, and handling complaints the company receives regarding its accounting, auditing, or internal accounting controls, and
- allowing employees to submit confidential, anonymous complaints and concerns about questionable accounting or auditing matters.

The SEC regulations do not require companies to follow particular procedures for taking employee complaints (such as setting up an ethics hotline or a Web-based complaint system).

How SOX Is Enforced

Individual Complaints

An employee who wishes to bring a lawsuit claiming that he or she was discriminated or retaliated against in violation of SOX's whistle-blower protections must first file a complaint with the Occupational Safety and Health Administration (OSHA) within 180 days. (See Appendix A for information on how to contact OSHA.) If OSHA does not issue a final decision on the employee's complaint within 180 days after the complaint is filed, the employee can file a lawsuit in federal district court.

However, 15 days before filing the lawsuit, the employee must file a notice with the administrative law judge assigned to the original complaint (or to the Administrative Review Board, if the case is pending before it) that the employee intends to file such a lawsuit. The employee must also serve this notice on the other parties to the dispute (the employer and any other companies or individuals whom the employee accuses of retaliation). (For more detailed information about OSHA's investigation and hearing procedures, see "Agency Enforcement," below.)

There is no avenue for employee complaints regarding a public company's failure to adopt an appropriate system for confidential employee complaints. This provision is enforced by the SEC only.

Agency Enforcement

Whistle-Blower Protections

The whistle-blowing provisions of SOX are enforced by OSHA, a division of the Department of Labor (DOL). After an employee files a complaint (as described in "Individual Complaints," above), OSHA will investigate if the complaint shows that:

- the employee engaged in protected activity (that is, made a protected complaint or participated in a protected proceeding)
- the person accused of retaliation knew of the activity
- the employee suffered an adverse employment action, and
- the circumstances create an inference that the adverse employment action was due, at least in part, to the employee's protected activity.

Even if the employee provides evidence of the points listed above, OSHA will not proceed if the company or person named in the complaint can show, by clear and convincing evidence, that it would have taken the same action against the employee even in the absence of the employee's protected activity. The company or person must present its evidence within 20 days after it receives notice of the complaint.

If OSHA investigates, it will issue findings and a preliminary order within 60 days after the complaint is filed. Either party may object to these findings and request a hearing within 30 days after receiving the findings and order. If a hearing is requested, it will be held before an administrative law judge, who will issue a decision and order. Either party may request a review of the judge's decision by filing a petition with the Administrative Review Board within ten days after the date on the judge's order. The board can either adopt the judge's decision as its own or conduct its own review of the case. Once the board issues its decision, the parties have 60 days to file an appeal with the U.S. Court of Appeals.

Internal Complaint Procedures

The requirement that public companies create procedures for anonymous employee complaints is enforced by the SEC. The SEC has issued rules requiring the national securities exchanges and associations to delist the stock of companies that fail to comply with this requirement (see "Remedies," below). This effectively enlists the securities exchanges and associations as the primary enforcers of this provision.

Complying With SOX

Deadlines

- The employer has 20 days to respond to an employee's complaint to OSHA.
- The employer has 30 days to object to the administrative law judge's findings and request a hearing.
- The employer has 60 days to appeal the board's decision to the U.S. Court of Appeals.

Reporting Requirements

The financial safeguards imposed by SOX include numerous reporting requirements, but there are no reporting requirements associated solely with its whistle-blower provisions.

The rules of the national securities exchanges and associations may require public companies to report on the complaint policies adopted by their audit committees.

Posting Requirements

SOX imposes no posting requirements relating to its whistle-blower provisions. However, posting could be one component of a company's complaint system.

Record-Keeping Requirements

SOX requires public companies to develop a system for retaining complaints regarding auditing or accounting procedures.

Remedies

Whistle-Blower Protections

Public companies and company representatives who violate the whistle-blower protections of SOX may be ordered to:

- reinstate the worker to the same position, with the same benefits, responsibilities, and seniority, that the worker would have had absent the retaliation
- pay the worker all compensation and benefits lost as a result of the retaliation, with interest, and
- pay the employee's attorneys' fees and court costs.

Courts and judges are divided as to whether SOX allows damages for reputational harm or pain and suffering.

Complaint Procedures

A public company that fails to adopt the complaint procedures mandated by SOX can have its stock delisted by the national securities exchanges and associations.

Differences Between SOX and Dodd-Frank Retaliation Claims

Both SOX and the Dodd-Frank Act protect whistle-blowers from retaliation, but the laws differ in certain ways, including the types of relief an employee may receive and the procedure for pursuing legal action. One major difference is that whistle-blowers seeking protection under the Dodd-Frank Act must report securities violations to the Securities and Exchange Commission. Although internal reporting—for example to a manager or company executive—is protected by SOX, it is not protected by the Dodd-Frank Act. (*Digital Realty Trust, Inc. v. Somers*, 138 S.Ct. 767 (2018).) Another important difference is that a whistle-blower seeking protection under Dodd-Frank may file a lawsuit directly in court without filing an OSHA complaint first.

Agency Resources

- A detailed discussion of SOX whistle-blower cases decided by the DOL
  Sarbanes-Oxley Act (SOX) Whistleblower Digest
  www.oalj.dol.gov/PUBLIC/WHISTLEBLOWER/REFERENCES/
  REFERENCE_WORKS/SOX_DIGEST_REMOVAL_TO_FEDERAL_
  DISTRICT_COURT.HTM

- A tool to help you find local OSHA offices
  Regional & Area Offices
  www.osha.gov/html/RAmap.html

- A page of links to newsletters, cases decided by administrative law judges, and other resource materials on SOX

  OALJ Whistleblower Collection
  www.oalj.dol.gov/LIBWHIST.HTM

State Laws Relating to Whistle-Blowers

Some states have laws that protect whistle-blowers from retaliation for reporting particular types of misconduct, such as dangerous work conditions or violations of child labor laws. In some states, courts recognize an employee's legal right to sue for wrongful termination "in violation of public policy" if he or she was fired in retaliation for reporting illegal or unethical conduct. The requirements for these types of claims vary from state to state. For information on your state's whistle-blower protections (if any), contact your state labor department. (You can find contact information in Appendix A.)

Civil Rights Act of 1866 (Section 1981)

Statute: 42 U.S.C. § 1981

To view the statutes, visit http://uscode.house.gov and select "Title 42" and "Chapter 21" and view "Subchapter I."

Overview of Section 1981

The Civil Rights Act of 1866 declares African Americans to be citizens, entitled to a series of rights previously reserved only to white men. This law is known as Section 1981 because of its location in the United States Code.

Section 1981 confers a number of rights, including the right to sue or be sued in court, to give evidence in a lawsuit, and to purchase property. This book discusses only one of the law's protections: the right to make and enforce contracts, which courts have found prohibits racial discrimination in the employment relationship.

Although the law's original purpose was to protect African Americans, courts have since interpreted it to protect people of all races from discrimination and harassment.

Definitions

Terms that appear in italics throughout this chapter are defined below.

At-will employee: An employee who can quit or be fired at any time, for any reason that is not illegal. In every state but Montana, a worker is employed at will unless he or she has an employment contract that limits the employer's right to fire. Such an employment contract may be written, oral, or implied from the conduct of the employer and employee.

Covered Employers

Section 1981 applies to:
- state and local governments, and
- private employers of any size.

Section 1981 also applies to some entities that are not employers in the legal sense, but have a contractual relationship with people performing work for them. For example, partners in a partnership are covered by Section 1981, but not by other federal antidiscrimination statutes, such as Title VII, the Age Discrimination in Employment Act, or the Americans with Disabilities Act.

Most courts have also found that firms hiring independent contractors are covered by Section 1981. (See "Covered Workers," below.)

Legal Developments

- **Supreme Court decides that retaliation is covered by Section 1981.** In 2008, the U.S. Supreme Court found that an employee may bring a retaliation claim under Section 1981. In that case, the employee had claimed race discrimination and retaliation under both Title VII and Section 1981, but his Title VII claims were dismissed. The Supreme Court found that its previous decision interpreting 42 U.S.C. § 1982, a provision similar to Section 1981 but dealing with the right to own property, had led most lower federal courts to conclude that retaliation was also prohibited under Section 1981. The Supreme Court agreed with this interpretation. (*CBOCS West, Inc. v. Humphries*, 553 U.S. 442 (2008).)
- **Employees have up to four years to file retaliation claims under Section 1981.** Because Section 1981 doesn't include its own statute of limitations (the time limit for filing lawsuits under the law), lower courts had traditionally applied the statute of limitations for similar claims in the state where the plaintiff brought the lawsuit. In 2004, however, the U.S. Supreme Court held that claims that were made possible by a post-1990 law should be governed by a four-year federal statute of limitations. (*Jones v. R.R. Donnelly & Sons*, 541 U.S. 369 (2004).) Because the Civil Rights Act of 1991 amended Section 1981 to include a retaliation claim, employees have four years to file a retaliation lawsuit. This ruling means that employees have much longer to file certain claims under Section 1981 than under other federal antidiscrimination statutes.

Covered Workers

All private employees and employees of state and local governments are covered by Section 1981. In addition, the law covers partners in a partnership.

At-Will Employees

Section 1981 protects the right to make and enforce contracts, including employment contracts. Most federal courts—including several federal courts of appeal—have decided that *at-will employees* may sue an employer for violating Section 1981, even though they do not have employment contracts limiting the employer's right to fire them. These courts reasoned that at-will employees still have very basic employment contracts (covering, for example, wages and work to be performed), even though those contracts offer no job protection. The Supreme Court has not yet considered this issue explicitly. However, the Court did find in favor of an employee claiming retaliation in violation of Section 1981 in the case of *CBOCS West, Inc. v. Humphries*, 553 U.S. 442 (2008); according to the federal Court of Appeals opinion in that case, Mr. Humphries was an at-will employee.

Independent Contractors

Section 1981 protects independent contractors from race discrimination by their hiring firm. However, at least one court has decided that this protection does not extend to claims of race harassment. The U.S. Supreme Court has not yet considered this issue.

Contractors who have incorporated their businesses cannot personally sue another company for race discrimination in contracting, however. In *Domino's Pizza v. McDonald*, 546 U.S. 470 (2006), the U.S. Supreme Court rejected a black contractor's Section 1981 claim that Domino's Pizza had broken several contracts with his corporation because of his race. Although the contractor was the sole shareholder of his corporation and entered into the contracts on its behalf, the Court found that he had no right to sue because the contracts were between Domino's and his corporation, not him personally.

Federal Employees

The Supreme Court has found that federal applicants and employees must use Title VII (and its separate enforcement scheme for federal agencies) to challenge any discriminatory conduct covered by that statute. Because Title VII prohibits employment discrimination on the bases of race and national origin (among other things), most courts have found that federal employees cannot use Section 1981 for employment-related claims.

Did You Know ...

- Section 1981 was passed over the veto of President Andrew Johnson. His opposition to this and other Reconstruction-era efforts to grant civil rights to the former slaves was one of the major issues that led to his eventual impeachment.
- A primary purpose of Section 1981 was to undermine the so-called Black Codes, state laws adopted after the Civil War that restricted the rights of newly freed slaves to own property, make contracts, or leave a job, among other things.
- Although Title VII of the Civil Rights Act of 1964 (see Chapter 18) also prohibits race discrimination, many workers prefer to sue under Section 1981, because it applies to all employers regardless of size, it does not require workers to file an administrative charge with the EEOC before bringing a lawsuit, it gives workers a longer deadline for filing cases, and it doesn't impose a limit on the money damages an employee can win in a successful lawsuit.

What's Prohibited

Section 1981 prohibits discrimination on the basis of race in the making or enforcement of employment contracts. This language has been interpreted broadly to prohibit any intentional workplace discrimination—including harassment—on the basis of race. Some courts have also found that Section 1981 prohibits discrimination and harassment on the basis of ethnicity, at least where that ethnicity has a racial component. (See "Race and Ethnicity," below.) Section 1981 also prohibits retaliation against those who complain of race discrimination.

Covered Employment Practices

Employers may not discriminate on the basis of race in any aspect of employment, including:
- hiring
- promotions
- employment benefits
- pay
- time off, and
- firing.

Key Facts

- Section 1981 prohibits discrimination on the basis of race and, in some cases, ethnicity in every aspect of employment. It also prohibits retaliation against those who assert their rights under the statute.
- Unlike Title VII (see Chapter 18), Section 1981 applies to all private employers, regardless of size.
- Employees do not have to file a charge of discrimination with the EEOC before bringing a lawsuit under Section 1981.

Racial Harassment

Today, it is undisputed that Section 1981 prohibits racial harassment. However, this issue was fiercely contested at one time, in a battle between Congress and the Supreme Court.

In 1989, the U.S. Supreme Court decided that Section 1981 covered only the right to enter into a contract in the first place and did not extend to any problems or issues—such as harassment—that might later arise in the employment relationship. (*Patterson v. McClean Credit Union*, 491 U.S. 164.) In response to this and several other Supreme Court decisions that narrowed employees' rights, Congress passed the Civil Rights Act of 1991. Among other things, this law overruled *Patterson* and amended Section 1981 so that it now clearly prohibits racial harassment.

An employee claiming racial harassment in violation of Section 1981 must show that he or she was subjected to unwelcome racial comments or offensive conduct that was severe or pervasive enough to alter the conditions of employment. This is the same test used under Title VII. (See Chapter 18 for more information on what constitutes harassment.)

Race and Ethnicity

Although Section 1981 was originally intended to protect newly freed slaves, courts have consistently interpreted the law to protect people of any race (including white people) from intentional race discrimination.

Some courts have also found that Section 1981 prohibits discrimination on the basis of ethnicity, but only if that discrimination is racial in character. For example, courts have held that discrimination against Latin Americans, Arab Americans, and Asian Americans violates Section 1981, but discrimination against persons of Slavic or Italian origin does not.

In deciding whether ethnic discrimination constitutes race discrimination under Section 1981, courts consider several factors, including:

- whether the discriminator perceived or characterized the victim as belonging to a separate race because of his or her ethnicity
- whether the victim belongs to an ethnicity that is perceived as "nonwhite"
- whether the victim belongs to an ethnicity that has traditionally been subject to discrimination, and
- whether the victim is claiming discrimination based on characteristics commonly associated with national origin (country of birth, language fluency, and surname, for example), which is not a violation of Section 1981; or on characteristics commonly associated with race (physical characteristics or skin color, for example), which is.

Exceptions

Other Types of Discrimination

Section 1981 prohibits only discrimination based on race or ethnicity. It does not prohibit discrimination based on sex, religion, disability, or age.

Unintentional Discrimination

Only intentional race discrimination violates Section 1981. Unintentional discrimination—such as the use of seemingly neutral hiring criteria that disproportionately weed out applicants of a particular race—does not violate the law. Lawsuits for unintentional discrimination (called "disparate impact" lawsuits) are allowed under other antidiscrimination laws, such as Title VII. (See Chapter 18.)

How Section 1981 Is Enforced

Individual Complaints

Employees or applicants who believe that their rights under Section 1981 have been violated may file a lawsuit in state court or in a federal district court.

No government agency takes complaints about violations of Section 1981. Therefore, an employee's only official avenue of redress is through the courts.

If an employer is covered by Title VII (see Chapter 18), the employee can also file a charge of race discrimination with the Equal Employment Opportunity Commission (EEOC). However, the EEOC will only enforce rights under Title VII, not Section 1981.

Agency Enforcement

Section 1981 is enforced only through private lawsuits, not through agency action.

Complying With Section 1981

Reporting Requirements

Section 1981 imposes no reporting requirements.

Posting Requirements

Posting is not required under Section 1981.

Record-Keeping Requirements

Section 1981 does not require employers to keep any particular records.

Remedies

If an employee wins a lawsuit for violation of Section 1981, the employer may be required to:

- pay the employee back pay and benefits lost as a result of the discrimination or harassment
- pay the employee compensatory damages for pain and suffering (the mental or physical effects of the discrimination or harassment)
- pay punitive damages, a sum of money intended to punish the employer for serious violations of the law
- take action to remedy the discrimination, such as promoting, hiring, or reinstating a worker who was discriminated against, and
- pay the employee's attorneys' fees and court costs.

State Laws Relating to Race Discrimination

You'll find a chart of state laws prohibiting discrimination, including race discrimination, at the end of Chapter 18.

Title VII of the Civil Rights Act of 1964 (Title VII)

Statute: 42 U.S.C. §§ 2000e and following

To view the statutes, visit http://uscode.house.gov and select "Title 42" and "Chapter 21" and view "Subchapter VI."

Regulations: 29 C.F.R. §§ 1600–1609

To view the regulations, visit www.govinfo.gov and search "29 CFR 1600."

Overview of Title VII

Signed by President Lyndon B. Johnson, the landmark Civil Rights Act of 1964 outlaws discrimination and segregation in public establishments, schools, and federally funded programs. Title VII of the Civil Rights Act —so named for its location in the law—prohibits employment discrimination based on race, color, religion, sex, and national origin.

Covered Employers

Title VII covers the following employers:
- private employers with 15 or more employees
- the federal government
- state and local governments
- private and public employment agencies
- labor organizations, and
- joint labor/management committees.

Title VII covers multinational employers with operations in the United States or its territories, unless the employer is covered by a treaty or another binding international agreement that dictates otherwise—for example, a treaty permitting the company to prefer its own citizens for specific jobs.

Title VII covers an employer with operations in other countries if the employer is incorporated in the United States, based in the United States, or controlled by a U.S. company. However, an employer is exempt from Title VII's requirements if complying with Title VII would violate a law of the country in which it operates.

Definitions

Terms that appear in italics throughout this chapter are defined below.

Bona fide occupational qualification (BFOQ): An exception to Title VII's general prohibition of discrimination, BFOQs allow employers to discriminate (except on the basis of race) when the nature of the job requires them to do so.

Disparate impact: A type of unlawful discrimination that occurs when a seemingly neutral policy disproportionately affects members of a *protected class*.

Harassment: Unwelcome comments or conduct based on a protected characteristic that an employee must put up with in order to keep the job or that is severe or pervasive enough to create a work environment that is hostile, intimidating, or offensive.

Protected class: A group specifically protected by Title VII. For example, because Title VII prohibits discrimination based on sex, both men and women fall within protected classes.

Quid pro quo: A Latin term meaning "this for that," which refers to a type of sexual harassment in which a supervisor demands sexual favors from a subordinate in exchange for a promotion, positive performance evaluation, or another job benefit, or in which a supervisor threatens an adverse employment action (such as termination or demotion) if the subordinate does not comply with a sexual demand.

Retaliation: Adverse action taken by an employer or someone who works for the employer against an employee for complaining, participating in an investigation or another proceeding, or otherwise opposing *harassment* or discrimination.

Sexual harassment: Any unwelcome sexual advance or conduct on the job that the employee must put up with in order to keep the job or that is severe or pervasive enough to create an intimidating, hostile, or offensive working environment.

Legal Developments

- **Courts split over whether sexual orientation discrimination is illegal under Title VII.** After the EEOC began accepting and pursuing complaints of sexual orientation discrimination, employers challenged these decisions in court. Multiple federal appeals courts have weighed in on whether Title VII's prohibition against "sex" discrimination includes sexual orientation discrimination, and they are not all in agreement. To learn more, see "Protected Classes," below.
- **Supreme Court clarifies the duty to accommodate.** In 2015, the U.S. Supreme Court held that an employer's duty to accommodate is triggered when it has reason to believe that an employee needs an accommodation for religious reasons. In other words, the employer does not need actual knowledge of the need for an accommodation. The Supreme Court case involved a Muslim woman named Samantha Elauf, who wore a hijab (a religious headscarf) to her interview for a sales position at Abercrombie & Fitch. During the interview, Elauf did not mention her religion or the need for a religious accommodation. However, unbeknownst to Elauf, the hijab violated Abercrombie's strict "look policy," which did not allow headwear of any kind. Rather than discuss the issue with Elauf and consider accommodations, Abercrombie simply rejected her application. Elauf sued for religious discrimination. In its defense, Abercrombie argued that it didn't have actual knowledge that Elauf wore the headscarf for religious reasons and would therefore need an accommodation. However, the Supreme Court held that it was enough that Abercrombie suspected that Elauf would need an accommodation and that this was the motivation behind its refusal to hire her. (*EEOC v. Abercrombie & Fitch Stores, Inc.*, 135 S. Ct. 2028 (2015).)

Covered Workers

Title VII protects all prospective and current employees of a covered employer, including foreign nationals working for a covered employer, even if the employee is not authorized to work in the United States. While such an employee still has rights under Title VII, his or her available remedies may be limited. For example, although reinstatement is usually an available remedy for an unlawfully fired employee, a foreign national may not be reinstated to a job in the United States if he or she is not authorized to work in the United States.

Title VII also protects U.S. citizens working outside the United States for employers that are incorporated in the United States, based in the United States, or controlled by a U.S. employer.

Did You Know ...

- Before it was passed in 1964, Title VII was the subject of the longest debate in Congressional history.
- Sexual harassment was not recognized as a form of sex discrimination until 1977 —13 years after Congress passed Title VII.
- In 2017, retaliation was the single most common allegation in EEOC charges, more common than any type of discrimination. More than 38% of all charges alleged retaliation.

What's Prohibited

Title VII prohibits employers from discriminating against prospective and current employees on the basis of race, color, religion, sex, and national origin. (For detailed information about each, see "Protected Classes," below.)

Title VII was amended in 1978 to add pregnancy as a *protected class*. To learn more about pregnancy discrimination, see Chapter 15, which covers the Pregnancy Discrimination Act (PDA).

Title VII prohibits discrimination and *harassment* in all aspects of employment, including:

- hiring
- firing
- compensation and benefits
- job assignments
- employee classification
- transfer
- promotion

- layoff or recall
- training and apprenticeship programs
- use of company facilities
- retirement plans, and
- time off.

Title VII also prohibits employers from retaliating against those who complain about discrimination or harassment, who participate in a legal proceeding regarding such violations, or who otherwise assert their rights under the law. (For more, see "Retaliation," below.)

Key Facts

- Title VII prohibits employment discrimination and harassment based on race, color, religion, sex, and national origin.
- An employer may not retaliate (take adverse action) against a prospective or current employee who complains in good faith of discrimination or harassment, even if the original complaint itself is found to be baseless.
- Seemingly neutral employment policies that have a disproportionately negative impact on members of a protected class may violate Title VII, even if the employer did not intend to discriminate.

Discrimination

Unlawful discrimination includes the following practices:
- giving some people preferential treatment over others based on their membership in a protected class
- treating some people worse than others based on their membership in a protected class
- harassing people because of their membership in a protected class (see "Harassment," below)
- physically isolating or segregating employees because of their membership in a protected class
- coding resumes or employment applications to indicate race, color, gender, national origin, or religion

- asking questions in an interview to elicit information about an applicant's race, color, gender, national origin, or religion
- making decisions based on stereotypes about people of a protected class (for example, refusing to hire a woman as a police officer because of a belief that women are too emotional and not tough enough to do the job), and
- treating people differently because of their marriage to or association with members of a protected class (for example, refusing to hire a white man because he is married to an Asian American woman).

Title VII outlaws both intentional discrimination and practices that have a discriminatory effect, even if the employer did not intend to discriminate. Called *disparate impact* cases, theses cases involve a seemingly neutral policy or practice that affects a protected class in a disproportionate and unfair way. Unless the employer has a legitimate and nondiscriminatory business reason for using that practice, the law will view it as unlawful. For example, if an employer refuses to hire people who don't meet minimum strength requirements, the employer could be discriminating against women, who will be disproportionately affected by this rule. The rule will pass legal muster only if the employer can show that it is clearly related to the physical demands of the particular job—heavy lifting in a warehouse, for example.

Harassment

Harassment occurs when employees are forced to endure unwelcome conduct based on a protected characteristic in order to keep the job or when that conduct is severe or pervasive enough to create a hostile work environment. Harassing acts can include:

- slurs
- offensive "jokes"
- offensive remarks based on a protected characteristic
- drawings or pictures that depict people with a protected characteristic in an unfavorable light
- threats
- intimidation
- hostile demeanor, and
- physical violence.

Sexual Harassment

Sexual harassment is a type of gender discrimination. It is unwelcome sexual conduct that affects the terms and conditions of the victim's employment—either because the victim's submission or failure to submit to the behavior is the basis for job-related decisions (this is sometimes referred to as *quid pro quo* harassment) or because the conduct is so severe or pervasive that it creates a workplace that is intimidating, hostile, or abusive. Examples of sexual harassment include unwelcome sexual advances, fondling, requests for sexual favors, making sexual remarks or jokes, sending sexually explicit emails, commenting on the employee's sex life, and posting pornographic images in the workplace.

The harasser can be the victim's supervisor, manager, or coworker. The harasser can even be a nonemployee—for example, a customer or vendor—if the person is on the premises with the employer's permission.

Both men and women can be sexual harassers, and both men and women can be the victims of sexual harassment. Women may sexually harass other women, and men may sexually harass other men. However, most allegations of sexual harassment are made by women against men.

Harassment based on gender can also constitute sexual harassment, even if it is not sexual in nature. In these cases, the harasser is not interested in having a sexual relationship with the victim or otherwise "sexualizing" the workplace, but instead wants to make the workplace hostile for workers of a particular gender (almost always women). The harassment in these claims, typically complained of by women working in traditionally male professions, might involve sabotaging the tools, vehicles, or work of female employees; defacing women's workspaces, lockers, or restroom facilities; subjecting women to dangerous working conditions; making comments about women's ability to do the job; or displaying cartoons or telling jokes that depict violence toward women.

Retaliation

An employer commits *retaliation* when it takes negative action against an employee for opposing harassment or discrimination—for example, by filing a complaint or giving evidence as a witness in a lawsuit, an administrative proceeding, or an internal investigation. Any action harmful enough to deter a reasonable worker from asserting his or her rights qualifies as illegal retaliation.

Any action an employer or manager takes against an employee because that employee has made a complaint could conceivably be illegal retaliation, even if the employer did not intend to harm the employee. For example:

- A female employee complains that her supervisor is sexually harassing her. In response, the employer moves the employee who complained from the day shift to the night shift, so she doesn't have to work with that supervisor anymore. Even though the employer didn't intend to hurt the employee, this action could be retaliatory if the employee preferred the day shift.
- An African American employee complains to his employer that his coworkers tell racial jokes and refer to him by racially derogatory names. In response, the employer transfers him to another store. This action could be retaliatory if the new store is farther from the employee's home or is less desirable in some other way.
- A male employee is fired after his fiancée, who works for the same company, files an EEOC charge alleging sex discrimination. This is illegal retaliation because it is likely to deter an employee from exercising her rights if she knew that her fiancé would be fired for it.

Protected Classes

Race

In addition to prohibiting race discrimination, Title VII forbids discrimination against people because they have certain physical characteristics associated with people of a certain race, such as skin color, hair texture, or other physical features.

Color

Discrimination based on color is prohibited by Title VII, even if that discrimination is not also race based. For example, it is illegal to favor a light-skinned employee over one with darker skin color, even if both employees are African American.

Religion

Title VII prohibits employers from making employment decisions based on a person's religion and requires employers to accommodate a person's religious beliefs. For example, the law prohibits employers from discriminating based on the fact of someone's religion (for example, because an employee is Jewish, Catholic, or Muslim), and it requires employers to make allowances for a person's religious practices and beliefs (for example, that an employee needs time after lunch to pray or needs Saturdays off to observe the Sabbath).

The first part is fairly simple. Employers can't refuse to hire someone because he or she is Jewish, and they can't promote someone because he or she is Muslim. Employers must make those decisions for nondiscriminatory reasons.

The second part is more complicated. Employers must work with their employees—within reason—to make it possible for the employees to practice their religious beliefs. This might mean agreeing not to schedule an employee to work on his or her Sabbath day or relaxing a dress code so that an employee can wear religious garments. In legal parlance, these allowances are called accommodations.

Employers must accommodate an employee's religious practice unless doing so would cause the business to suffer undue hardship. Although this term is used in other employment laws, such as the Americans with Disabilities Act (covered in Chapter 2) and the Uniformed Services Employment and Reemployment Rights Act (covered in Chapter 19), it is typically easier for an employer to show that a particular religious accommodation creates an undue hardship. For instance, an employer need not depart from its established seniority system to accommodate an employee's religious practice if doing so would deprive another employee of his or her rights under the system. Similarly, an employer doesn't have to pay more than minimal administrative costs—for example, the cost of adjusting its scheduling documents and payroll—to provide a religious accommodation.

In general, the applicant or employee will need to request a religious accommodation if he or she needs one. However, if the employer has reason to believe that the applicant or employee needs a religious accommodation (for example, because of a comment the person made in an interview), the employer must consider reasonable accommodations. (See "Legal Developments," above, for more information.)

National Origin

The prohibition against national origin discrimination generally means that employers cannot make employment decisions based on:

- birthplace
- ancestry
- culture
- native language
- English language proficiency (unless lack of proficiency affects the person's ability to perform the job)
- accent (unless it affects the person's ability to perform the job)
- marriage or association with people of a national ethnic group
- membership in or association with an ethnic cultural organization
- attendance or participation in schools, churches, temples, or mosques that are generally associated with a specific ethnic group, or
- a name that is associated with a specific ethnic group.

A rule requiring employees to speak only English at work will violate Title VII unless the employer can show that the rule is necessary for the safe or efficient operation of its business. For example, an employer may be able to prohibit employees from speaking other languages in the presence of English-speaking customers, but not in private areas of the workplace or during meal or rest breaks.

National origin and citizenship status discrimination are also prohibited by the federal Immigration Reform and Control Act (IRCA). (For more on IRCA, see Chapter 10.)

Sex

Title VII's prohibition against sex discrimination protects both men and women from discrimination and harassment based on gender. Title VII also prohibits discrimination against pregnant employees. (See Chapter 15 for information on the Pregnancy Discrimination Act, which amended Title VII to explicitly prohibit discrimination based on pregnancy and associated medical conditions.)

Sex discrimination includes decisions based on someone's failure to conform to gender stereotypes. For example, a restaurant may not refuse to hire a woman as a waitress or bartender because she isn't feminine enough. However, courts have upheld dress and grooming rules that require female employees to wear makeup and style their hair, as long as the rules have parallel dress and grooming requirements for men (for example, short hair styles, no facial hair, and trimmed fingernails). If dress codes and grooming rules impose unequal burdens on either men or women, however, they may violate Title VII.

Title VII does not explicitly prohibit discrimination based on sexual orientation or gender identity. However, over the years, there has been more legal support for interpreting Title VII's prohibition against "sex" discrimination to include both. Courts have generally held that discriminating on the basis of gender stereotypes is illegal under Title VII—for example, firing a female executive because she doesn't behave in ways expected of the female gender. Following this line of authority, the EEOC has taken the position that sexual orientation and gender identity discrimination are illegal under Title VII because they necessarily involve gender-based stereotypes of how men and women should act.

Some federal appeals courts have weighed in on the issue, but they are not all in agreement. The U.S. Court of Appeals for the Seventh and Second Circuits have held that sexual orientation is protected under Title VII, while the Eleventh Circuit has held the opposite. The Sixth Circuit has held that gender identity discrimination is illegal under Title VII. This is an unsettled area of law, which can only be resolved by the U.S. Supreme Court, or by new legislation from Congress. For now, however, the EEOC is accepting and pursuing sexual orientation and gender identity discrimination claims.

Many states have antidiscrimination laws that explicitly protect gender identity, sexual orientation, or both. (See "State Antidiscrimination Laws," below, for information on the types of discrimination each state prohibits.)

What's Required

Employers must provide their employees with a workplace free of unlawful discrimination and harassment. This means that employers must act when they learn that an employee, customer, vendor, manager, or supervisor is discriminating against or harassing another employee or group of employees. Employers must take effective and immediate action to stop such conduct. This action might include investigating the situation and disciplining (up to and including firing) the offender.

Exceptions

In a very rare and narrow exception to Title VII, employers can discriminate on the basis of gender, religion, and national origin (but not race or color) if the very nature of the job requires them to do so. This rule, called the *bona fide occupational qualification (BFOQ)* exception, reflects Congress's recognition that some jobs must be filled by people who have certain characteristics, even though the law would ordinarily prohibit the employer from discriminating on that basis.

In order to use this exception, the employer must prove that the discriminatory policy is reasonably necessary to the operation of its business—in other words, that the essence of the operation would be undermined if the employer had to do away with its discriminatory policy. The employer must also show that there is no reasonable alternative to its policy.

Although it can be very hard to defend, there are times when an employer has no choice but to use the BFOQ exception. Sometimes this is necessary for reasons of authenticity. For example, a director casting the role of Hamlet's mother could refuse to consider men for the part. Sex-based BFOQ exceptions have also been allowed for positions like bathroom attendants and prison guards, on the grounds of protecting privacy.

How Title VII Is Enforced

Individual Complaints

A person may file a complaint (also called a charge) of discrimination, harassment, or retaliation with the U.S. Equal Employment Opportunity Commission (EEOC). (For contact information, see Appendix A.) In states with their own antidiscrimination laws, the complaint must be filed with the EEOC within 300 days of the alleged incident. In states without an antidiscrimination law, the complaint must be filed within 180 days of the incident. (To find out about your state's law, see "State Antidiscrimination Laws," below.)

Individuals may also file a lawsuit. However, they must first file a complaint with the EEOC or their state fair employment office (if their state has one), and then receive what is called a "right to sue" letter. Once they receive that letter, they have 90 days to file suit.

Agency Enforcement

The EEOC may act on its own initiative or after receiving a complaint. It has the authority to investigate a complaint, negotiate a settlement, mediate the dispute, and bring a suit in federal court. The EEOC also issues regulations and other forms of guidance interpreting Title VII. Even if an aggrieved employee has signed an arbitration agreement limiting his or her right to sue, the EEOC may still sue on the employee's behalf (although this is very rare).

Complying With Title VII

Reporting Requirements

Large private employers (those with 100 or more employees) and certain companies with federal contracts must file annual reports with the EEOC. The requirements of these reports—called Standard Form 100, but commonly referred to as the EEO-1 Form—are beyond the scope of this chapter.

Posting Requirements

Employers must post a notice about federal laws prohibiting discrimination. The notices must be posted in locations easily accessible to employees. (For information on how to obtain a copy of the poster, see "Agency Resources," below.)

Record-Keeping Requirements

EEOC regulations require employers to keep personnel and employment records for at least one year. If an employee is involuntarily terminated, the employer must keep that employee's records for a year after the termination.

Remedies

If an employer is found guilty of discrimination, harassment, or retaliation, it might be required to do the following:
- pay lost wages and benefits
- hire the aggrieved applicant(s)

- promote the aggrieved employee(s)
- reinstate the aggrieved employee(s)
- pay for pain and suffering
- pay punitive damages
- pay the applicant or employee's out-of-pocket expenses (such as the cost of finding a new job)
- provide a reasonable accommodation
- take corrective and preventive measures to cure discrimination in the workplace, and/or
- pay attorneys' fees, expert witness fees, and court costs.

The maximum combined award that an applicant or employee can receive for pain and suffering, punitive damages, and out-of-pocket costs is capped by Title VII. The cap ranges from $50,000 to $300,000, depending on the size of the employer.

Agency Resources

The EEOC has a publications page on its website from which you can download many informative publications in multiple languages. You can also order copies of any publications not available online. Among the publications included are fact sheets on all types of discrimination and the laws the EEOC enforces. Visit www.eeoc.gov/eeoc/publications for the complete list.

Employers must display a poster informing employees of their rights under federal antidiscrimination laws. The poster is available online at www1.eeoc. gov/employers/poster.cfm.

State Antidiscrimination Laws

Almost every state has its own antidiscrimination law, and many of these laws are more restrictive than Title VII. For example, some state laws apply to smaller employers or prohibit additional types of discrimination. The chart below provides basic information on these state laws. If you need to know more, contact your state fair employment practices agency (see Appendix A for contact information).

State Laws Prohibiting Discrimination in Employment

Note: Federal law makes it illegal to discriminate on the basis of race, color, national origin, sex (including pregnancy, childbirth, and related medical conditions), age (40 and older), disability (including AIDS/HIV), religion, and genetic information. The following states have their own laws protecting certain classes from discrimination.

Alabama

Ala. Code §§ 25-1-20, 25-1-21

Law applies to employers with: 20 or more employees

Private employers may not make employment decisions based on:
- Age (40 and older)

Alaska

Alaska Stat. §§ 18.80.220, 18.80.300, 47.30.865

Law applies to employers with: One or more employees

Private employers may not make employment decisions based on:
- Age
- Ancestry or national origin
- Physical or mental disability
- Gender
- Marital status, including changes in status
- Pregnancy, childbirth, and related medical conditions, including parenthood
- Race or color
- Religion or creed
- Mental illness

Arizona

Ariz. Rev. Stat. §§ 41-1461, 41-1463, 41-1465

Law applies to employers with: 15 or more employees

Private employers may not make employment decisions based on:
- Age (40 and older)
- Ancestry or national origin
- Physical or mental disability
- AIDS/HIV
- Gender
- Race or color
- Religion or creed
- Genetic testing information

Arkansas

Ark. Code Ann. §§ 11-4-601, 11-5-403, 16-123-102, 16-123-107

Law applies to employers with: Nine or more employees

Private employers may not make employment decisions based on:
- Ancestry or national origin
- Physical, mental, or sensory disability
- Gender
- Pregnancy, childbirth, and related medical conditions
- Race or color
- Religion or creed
- Genetic testing information

California

Cal. Gov't. Code §§ 12920, 12926.1, 12940, 12941, 12945; Cal. Lab. Code § 1101

Law applies to employers with: Five or more employees

Private employers may not make employment decisions based on:
- Age (40 and older)
- Ancestry or national origin
- Physical or mental disability
- AIDS/HIV
- Gender

State Laws Prohibiting Discrimination in Employment (continued)

- Marital status
- Pregnancy, childbirth, and related medical conditions, including breast-feeding
- Race or color
- Religion or creed
- Sexual orientation
- Genetic testing information
- Gender identity
- Gender expression
- Medical condition
- Political activities or affiliations
- Status as victim of domestic violence, sexual assault, or stalking
- Military and veteran status

Colorado

Colo. Rev. Stat. §§ 24-34-301, 24-34-401, 24-34-402, 24-34-402.5, 27-65-115; Colo. Code Regs. 708-1:60.1, 708-1:80.8

Law applies to employers with: One or more employees; 25 or more employees (marital status only)

Private employers may not make employment decisions based on:
- Age (40 and older)
- Ancestry or national origin
- Physical, mental, or learning disability
- AIDS/HIV
- Gender
- Marital status (only applies to marriage to a coworker or plans to marry a coworker)
- Pregnancy, childbirth, and related medical conditions
- Race or color
- Religion or creed
- Sexual orientation, including perceived sexual orientation
- Lawful conduct outside of work

- Mental illness
- Transgender status

Connecticut

Conn. Gen. Stat. Ann. § 46a-51, 46a-60, 46a-81a, 46a-81c

Law applies to employers with: Three or more employees

Private employers may not make employment decisions based on:
- Age
- Ancestry or national origin
- Present or past physical, mental, learning, or intellectual disability
- Gender
- Marital status, including civil unions
- Pregnancy, childbirth, and related medical conditions
- Race or color
- Religion or creed
- Sexual orientation, including having a history of such a preference or being identified with such a preference
- Genetic testing information
- Gender identity or expression
- Arrests or convictions that have been erased, pardoned, or rehabilitated
- Veteran status

Delaware

Del. Code Ann. tit. 19, §§ 710, 711, 724

Law applies to employers with: Four or more employees

Private employers may not make employment decisions based on:
- Age (40 and older)
- Ancestry or national origin
- Physical or mental disability
- AIDS/HIV

State Laws Prohibiting Discrimination in Employment (continued)

- Gender
- Marital status
- Pregnancy, childbirth, and related medical conditions
- Race or color
- Religion or creed
- Sexual orientation
- Genetic testing information
- Gender identity
- Status as victim of domestic abuse, sexual offense, or stalking
- Family responsibilities
- "Reproductive health decisions"

District of Columbia

D.C. Code Ann. §§ 2-1401.02, 2-1401.05, 2-1402.82, 7-1703.03, 32-531.08

Law applies to employers with: One or more employees

Private employers may not make employment decisions based on:
- Age (18 and older)
- Ancestry or national origin
- Physical or mental disability
- Gender, including reproductive health decisions
- Marital status, including domestic partnership
- Pregnancy, childbirth, and related medical conditions, including parenthood and breast-feeding
- Race or color
- Religion or creed
- Sexual orientation
- Genetic testing information
- Enrollment in vocational, professional, or college education
- Family duties
- Personal appearance
- Political affiliation

- Gender identity or expression
- Status as unemployed
- Tobacco use
- Credit information

Florida

Fla. Stat. Ann. §§ 448.075, 760.01, 760.02, 760.10, 760.50

Law applies to employers with: 15 or more employees

Private employers may not make employment decisions based on:
- Age
- Ancestry or national origin
- "Handicap"
- AIDS/HIV
- Gender
- Marital status
- Pregnancy, childbirth, and related medical conditions
- Race or color
- Religion or creed
- Sickle cell trait

Georgia

Ga. Code Ann. §§ 34-1-2, 34-5-1, 34-5-2, 34-6A-1 and following

Law applies to employers with:
- 15 or more employees (disability)
- 10 or more employees (gender) (domestic and agricultural employees not protected)
- One or more employee (age)

Private employers may not make employment decisions based on:
- Age (40 to 70)
- Physical, mental, or learning disability
- Gender (wage discrimination only)

State Laws Prohibiting Discrimination in Employment (continued)

Hawaii

Haw. Rev. Stat. §§ 378-1 and following; Hawaii Admin. Rules § 12-46-182

Law applies to employers with: One or more employees

Private employers may not make employment decisions based on:
- Age
- Ancestry or national origin
- Physical or mental disability
- AIDS/HIV
- Gender
- Marital status
- Pregnancy, childbirth, and related medical conditions, including breast-feeding
- Race or color
- Religion or creed
- Sexual orientation
- Genetic testing information
- Arrest and court record (unless there is a conviction directly related to job)
- Credit history or credit report, unless the information in the individual's credit history or credit report directly relates to a bona fide occupational qualification
- Gender identity and gender expression
- Status as a victim of domestic or sexual violence (if employer has knowledge or is notified of this status)

Idaho

Idaho Code §§ 39-8303, 67-5902, 67-5909, 67-5910

Law applies to employers with: Five or more employees

Private employers may not make employment decisions based on:
- Age (40 and older)

- Ancestry or national origin
- Physical or mental disability
- Gender
- Pregnancy, childbirth, and related medical conditions
- Race or color
- Religion or creed
- Genetic testing information

Illinois

410 Ill. Comp. Stat. § 513/25; 775 Ill. Comp. Stat. §§ 5/1-102, 5/1-103, 5/2-101, 5/2-102, 5/2-103; 820 Ill. Comp. Stat. §§ 105/4, 180/30; Ill. Admin. Code tit. 56, § 5210.110

Law applies to employers with: 15 or more employees; one or more employees (disability only)

Private employers may not make employment decisions based on:
- Age (40 and older)
- Ancestry or national origin
- Physical or mental disability
- Gender
- Marital status
- Pregnancy, childbirth, and related medical conditions
- Race or color
- Religion or creed
- Sexual orientation
- Genetic testing information
- Citizenship status
- Military status
- Unfavorable military discharge
- Gender identity
- Arrest record
- Victims of domestic violence
- Order of protection status
- Lack of permanent mailing address or having a mailing address of a shelter or social service provider

State Laws Prohibiting Discrimination in Employment (continued)

Indiana

Ind. Code Ann. §§ 22-9-1-2, 22-9-2-1, 22-9-2-2, 22-9-5-1 and following

Law applies to employers with: Six or more employees; one or more employees (age only); 15 or more employees (disability only)

Private employers may not make employment decisions based on:

- Age (40 to 75)
- Ancestry or national origin
- Physical or mental disability
- Gender
- Race or color
- Religion or creed
- Off-duty tobacco use
- Status as a veteran
- Sealed or expunged arrest or conviction record

Iowa

Iowa Code §§ 216.2, 216.6, 216.6A, 729.6

Law applies to employers with: Four or more employees

Private employers may not make employment decisions based on:

- Age (18 or older)
- Ancestry or national origin
- Physical or mental disability
- AIDS/HIV
- Gender
- Pregnancy, childbirth, and related medical conditions
- Race or color
- Religion or creed
- Sexual orientation
- Genetic testing information
- Gender identity
- Wage discrimination

Kansas

Kan. Stat. Ann. §§ 44-1002, 44-1009, 44-1112, 44-1113, 44-1125, 44-1126, 65-6002(e)

Law applies to employers with: Four or more employees

Private employers may not make employment decisions based on:

- Age (40 or older)
- Ancestry or national origin
- Physical or mental disability
- AIDS/HIV
- Gender
- Race or color
- Religion or creed
- Genetic testing information
- Military service or status

Kentucky

Ky. Rev. Stat. Ann. §§ 207.130, 207.135, 207.150, 342.197, 344.010, 344.030, 344.040

Law applies to employers with: Eight or more employees

Private employers may not make employment decisions based on:

- Age (40 or older)
- Ancestry or national origin
- Physical or mental disability
- AIDS/HIV
- Gender
- Pregnancy, childbirth, and related medical conditions
- Race or color
- Religion or creed
- Occupational pneumoconiosis with no respiratory impairment resulting from exposure to coal dust
- Off-duty tobacco use

State Laws Prohibiting Discrimination in Employment (continued)

Louisiana

La. Rev. Stat. Ann. §§ 23:301 to 23:368

Law applies to employers with: 20 or more employees; 25 or more employees (pregnancy, childbirth, and related medical condition only)

Private employers may not make employment decisions based on:

- Age (40 or older)
- Ancestry or national origin
- Physical or mental disability
- Gender
- Pregnancy, childbirth, and related medical conditions
- Race or color
- Religion or creed
- Genetic testing information
- Sickle cell trait
- Being a smoker or nonsmoker

Maine

Me. Rev. Stat. Ann. tit. 5, §§ 19302, 4552, 4553, 4571 to 4576, 23; tit. 26, § 833; tit. 39-A, § 353

Law applies to employers with: One or more employees

Private employers may not make employment decisions based on:

- Age
- Ancestry or national origin
- Physical or mental disability
- AIDS/HIV
- Gender
- Pregnancy, childbirth, and related medical conditions
- Race or color
- Religion or creed
- Sexual orientation, including perceived sexual orientation
- Genetic testing information

- Gender identity or expression
- Past workers' compensation claim
- Past whistle-blowing
- Medical support notice for child

Maryland

Md. Code, [State Government], §§ 20-101, 20-601 to 20-608; Md. Code Regs. 14.03.02.02

Law applies to employers with: 15 or more employees

Private employers may not make employment decisions based on:

- Age
- Ancestry or national origin
- Physical or mental disability
- Gender
- AIDS/HIV
- Marital status
- Pregnancy, childbirth, and related medical conditions
- Race or color
- Religion or creed
- Sexual orientation
- Genetic testing information
- Civil Air Patrol membership
- Gender identity

Massachusetts

Mass. Gen. Laws ch. 149, § 24A, ch. 149 § 105A ch. 151B, §§ 1, 4 Code of Massachusetts Regulations 804 CMR 3.01

Law applies to employers with: Six or more employees

Private employers may not make employment decisions based on:

- Age (40 or older)
- Ancestry or national origin
- Physical or mental disability
- Gender

State Laws Prohibiting Discrimination in Employment (continued)

- Marital status
- Pregnancy, childbirth, and related medical conditions
- Race or color
- Religion or creed
- Sexual orientation
- Genetic testing information
- Military service
- Arrest record
- Gender identity
- Veteran status

Michigan

Mich. Comp. Laws §§ 37.1103, 37.1201, 37.1202, 37.2201, 37.2202, 37.2205a, 750.556

Law applies to employers with: One or more employees

Private employers may not make employment decisions based on:
- Age
- Ancestry or national origin
- Physical or mental disability
- AIDS/HIV
- Gender
- Marital status
- Pregnancy, childbirth, and related medical conditions
- Race or color
- Religion or creed
- Genetic testing information
- Height or weight
- Misdemeanor arrest record
- Civil Air Patrol membership

Minnesota

Minn. Stat. Ann. §§ 144.417, 181.81, 181.974, 363A.03, 363A.08

Law applies to employers with: One or more employees

Private employers may not make employment decisions based on:
- Age (18 to 70)
- Ancestry or national origin
- Physical, sensory, or mental disability
- Gender
- Marital status
- Pregnancy, childbirth, and related medical conditions
- Race or color
- Religion or creed
- Sexual orientation, including perceived sexual orientation
- Genetic testing information
- Gender identity
- Member of local commission
- Receiving public assistance
- Familial status (protects parents or guardians living with a minor child)

Mississippi

Miss. Code Ann. § 33-1-15

Law applies to employers with: One or more employees

Private employers may not make employment decisions based on:
- Military status
- No other protected categories unless employer receives public funding

Missouri

Mo. Rev. Stat. §§ 191.665, 213.010, 213.055, 375.1306

Law applies to employers with: Six or more employees

Private employers may not make employment decisions based on:
- Age (40 to 70)
- Ancestry or national origin

State Laws Prohibiting Discrimination in Employment (continued)

- Physical or mental disability
- AIDS/HIV
- Gender
- Race or color
- Religion or creed
- Genetic testing information
- Off-duty use of alcohol or tobacco

Montana

Mont. Code Ann. §§ 49-2-101, 49-2-303, 49-2-310

Law applies to employers with: One or more employees

Private employers may not make employment decisions based on:
- Age
- Ancestry or national origin
- Physical or mental disability
- Gender
- Marital status
- Pregnancy, childbirth, and related medical conditions
- Race or color
- Religion or creed

Nebraska

Neb. Rev. Stat. §§ 20-168, 48-236, 48-1001 to 48-1010, 48-1102, 48-1104

Law applies to employers with: 15 or more employees; 20 or more employees (age only)

Private employers may not make employment decisions based on:
- Age (40 or older)
- Ancestry or national origin
- Physical or mental disability
- AIDS/HIV
- Gender
- Marital status

- Pregnancy, childbirth, and related medical conditions
- Race or color
- Religion or creed
- Genetic testing information (applies to all employers)

Nevada

Nev. Rev. Stat. Ann. §§ 613.310 and following; 613.4353 and following; 2017 Nevada Laws Ch. 271 (A.B. 113), Ch. 496 (S.B. 361)

Law applies to employers with: 15 or more employees

Private employers may not make employment decisions based on:
- Age (40 or older)
- Ancestry or national origin
- Physical or mental disability
- AIDS/HIV
- Gender
- Pregnancy, childbirth, and related medical conditions, including breast-feeding
- Race or color
- Religion or creed
- Sexual orientation, including perceived sexual orientation
- Genetic testing information
- Use of service animal
- Gender identity or expression
- Opposing unlawful employment practices
- Credit report or credit information (with some exceptions)
- Requesting leave or reasonable accommodation due to status as victim of domestic violence (applies to all employers)

State Laws Prohibiting Discrimination in Employment (continued)

New Hampshire

N.H. Rev. Stat. Ann. §§ 141-H:3, 354-A:2, 354-A:6, 354-A:7

Law applies to employers with: Six or more employees

Private employers may not make employment decisions based on:

- Age
- Ancestry or national origin
- Physical or mental disability
- Gender
- Marital status
- Pregnancy, childbirth, and related medical conditions
- Race or color
- Religion or creed
- Sexual orientation
- Genetic testing information
- Victims of domestic violence, harassment, sexual assault, or stalking
- Gender identity
- Off-duty use of tobacco products

New Jersey

N.J. Stat. Ann. §§ 10:5-1, 10:5-4.1, 10:5-5, 10:5-12, 10:5-29.1, 34:6B-1, 43:21-49

Law applies to employers with: One or more employees

Private employers may not make employment decisions based on:

- Age (18 to 70)
- Ancestry or national origin
- Past or present physical or mental disability
- AIDS/HIV
- Gender
- Marital status, including civil union or domestic partnership status
- Pregnancy, childbirth, and related medical conditions, including breast-feeding)
- Race or color
- Religion or creed
- Sexual orientation, including affectional orientation and perceived sexual orientation
- Genetic testing information
- Atypical hereditary cellular or blood trait
- Accompanied by service or guide dog
- Military service
- Gender identity
- Unemployed status
- Liability for service in the U.S. Armed Forces
- Familial status

New Mexico

N.M. Stat. Ann. §§ 24-21-4, 28-1-2, 28-1-7, 50-4A-4; N.M. Admin. Code 9.1.1

Law applies to employers with:

- Four or more employees
- 50 or more employees (marital status only)
- 15 or more employees (sexual orientation and gender identity only)

Private employers may not make employment decisions based on:

- Age (40 or older)
- Ancestry or national origin
- Physical or mental disability
- Gender
- Marital status
- Pregnancy, childbirth, and related medical conditions
- Race or color
- Religion or creed
- Sexual orientation (including perceived sexual orientation)
- Genetic testing information

State Laws Prohibiting Discrimination in Employment (continued)

- Gender identity
- Serious medical condition
- Domestic abuse leave

New York

N.Y. Exec. Law §§ 292, 296; N.Y. Lab. Law § 201-d

Law applies to employers with: Four or more employees; all employers (sexual harassment only)

Private employers may not make employment decisions based on:

- Age (18 and over)
- Ancestry or national origin
- Physical or mental disability
- Gender
- Marital status
- Pregnancy, childbirth, and related medical conditions
- Race or color
- Religion or creed
- Sexual orientation, including perceived sexual orientation
- Genetic testing information
- Lawful recreational activities when not at work
- Military status or service
- Observance of Sabbath
- Political activities
- Use of service dog
- Arrest or criminal accusation
- Domestic violence victim status
- Familial status
- Gender identity
- Transgender status

North Carolina

N.C. Gen. Stat. §§ 95-28.1, 95-28.1A, 127B-11, 130A-148, 143-422.2, 168A-5

Law applies to employers with: 15 or more employees

Private employers may not make employment decisions based on:

- Age
- Ancestry or national origin
- Physical or mental disability
- AIDS/HIV
- Gender
- Race or color
- Religion or creed
- Genetic testing information
- Military status or service
- Sickle cell or hemoglobin C trait
- Use of lawful products off site and off duty

North Dakota

N.D. Cent. Code §§ 14-02.4-02, 14-02.4-03, 34-01-17

Law applies to employers with: One or more employees

Private employers may not make employment decisions based on:

- Age (40 or older)
- Ancestry or national origin
- Physical or mental disability
- Gender
- Marital status
- Pregnancy, childbirth, and related medical conditions
- Race or color
- Religion or creed
- Lawful conduct outside of work
- Receiving public assistance
- Keeping and bearing arms (as long as firearm is never exhibited on company property except for lawful defensive purposes)
- Status as a volunteer emergency responder

State Laws Prohibiting Discrimination in Employment (continued)

Ohio

Ohio Rev. Code Ann. §§ 4111.17, 4112.01, 4112.02

Law applies to employers with: Four or more employees

Private employers may not make employment decisions based on:

- Age (40 or older)
- Ancestry or national origin
- Physical, mental, or learning disability
- AIDS/HIV
- Gender
- Pregnancy, childbirth, and related medical conditions
- Race or color
- Religion or creed
- Military status
- Caring for a sibling, child, parent, or spouse injured while in the armed services

Oklahoma

Okla. Stat. Ann. tit. 25, §§ 1301, 1302; tit. 36, § 3614.2; tit. 40, § 500; tit. 44, § 208

Law applies to employers with: 1 or more employees

Private employers may not make employment decisions based on:

- Age (40 or older)
- Ancestry or national origin
- Physical or mental disability
- Gender
- Pregnancy, childbirth, and related medical conditions (except abortions where the woman is not in "imminent danger of death")
- Race or color
- Religion or creed
- Genetic testing information

- Military service
- Being a smoker or nonsmoker or using tobacco off duty

Oregon

Or. Rev. Stat. §§ 659A.030, 659A.122 and following, 659A.303

Law applies to employers with: One or more employees; 6 or more employees (disability only)

Private employers may not make employment decisions based on:

- Age (18 or older)
- Ancestry or national origin
- Physical or mental disability
- Gender
- Marital status
- Pregnancy, childbirth, and related medical conditions
- Race or color
- Religion or creed
- Sexual orientation
- Genetic testing information
- Parent who has medical support order imposed by court
- Domestic violence victim status
- Refusal to attend an employer-sponsored meeting with the primary purpose of communicating the employer's opinion on religious or political matters
- Credit history
- Whistle-blowers
- Off-duty use of tobacco products

Pennsylvania

Pa. Stat. Ann. tit. 43, §§ 954 to 955

Law applies to employers with: Four or more employees

State Laws Prohibiting Discrimination in Employment (continued)

Private employers may not make employment decisions based on:
- Age (40 to 70)
- Ancestry or national origin
- Physical or mental disability
- Gender
- Pregnancy, childbirth, and related medical conditions
- Race or color
- Religion or creed
- Relationship or association with a person with a disability
- GED rather than high school diploma
- Use of service animal
- Relationship or association with a person with a disability

Rhode Island

R.I. Gen. Laws §§ 12-28-10, 23-6.3-11, 28-5-6, 28-5-7, 28-6-18, 28-6.7-1

Law applies to employers with: Four or more employees; one or more employees (gender-based wage discrimination only)

Private employers may not make employment decisions based on:
- Age (40 or older)
- Ancestry or national origin
- Physical or mental disability
- AIDS/HIV
- Gender
- Pregnancy, childbirth, and related medical conditions
- Race or color
- Religion or creed
- Sexual orientation, including perceived sexual orientation
- Genetic testing information
- Domestic abuse victim
- Gender identity or expression
- Homelessness

South Carolina

S.C. Code §§ 1-13-30, 1-13-80

Law applies to employers with: 15 or more employees

Private employers may not make employment decisions based on:
- Age (40 or older)
- Ancestry or national origin
- Physical or mental disability
- AIDS/HIV
- Gender
- Pregnancy, childbirth, and related medical conditions
- Race or color
- Religion or creed

South Dakota

S.D. Codified Laws Ann. §§ 20-13-1, 20-13-10, 60-2-20, 60-12-15, 62-1-17

Law applies to employers with: One or more employees

Private employers may not make employment decisions based on:
- Ancestry or national origin
- Physical or mental disability
- Gender
- Pregnancy, childbirth, and related medical conditions
- Race or color
- Religion or creed
- Genetic testing information
- Preexisting injury
- Off-duty use of tobacco products

Tennessee

Tenn. Code Ann. §§ 4-21-102, 4-21-401 and following, 8-50-103, 50-2-201, 50-2-202

State Laws Prohibiting Discrimination in Employment (continued)

Law applies to employers with: Eight or more employees; one or more employees (gender-based wage discrimination only)

Private employers may not make employment decisions based on:

- Age (40 or older)
- Ancestry or national origin
- Physical, mental, or visual disability
- Gender
- Race or color
- Religion or creed
- Use of guide dog
- Volunteer rescue squad worker responding to an emergency

Texas

Tex. Lab. Code Ann. §§ 21.002, 21.051, 21.101, 21.106, 21.402

Law applies to employers with: 15 or more employees

Private employers may not make employment decisions based on:

- Age (40 or older)
- Ancestry or national origin
- Physical or mental disability
- Gender
- Pregnancy, childbirth, and related medical conditions
- Race or color
- Religion or creed
- Genetic testing information

Utah

Utah Code Ann. §§ 26-45-103, 34A-5-102, 34A-5-106

Law applies to employers with: 15 or more employees

Private employers may not make employment decisions based on:

- Age (40 or older)
- Ancestry or national origin
- Physical or mental disability
- AIDS/HIV
- Gender
- Pregnancy, childbirth, and related medical conditions (including breast-feeding)
- Race or color
- Religion or creed
- Sexual orientation
- Genetic testing information
- Gender identity

Vermont

Vt. Stat. Ann. tit. 21, §§ 305, 495, 495d; tit. 18, § 9333

Law applies to employers with: One or more employees

Private employers may not make employment decisions based on:

- Age (18 or older)
- Ancestry or national origin
- Physical, mental, or emotional disability
- AIDS/HIV
- Gender
- Pregnancy, childbirth, and related medical conditions
- Race or color
- Religion or creed
- Sexual orientation
- Genetic testing information
- Gender identity
- Place of birth
- Credit report or credit history
- Status as crime victim

State Laws Prohibiting Discrimination in Employment (continued)

Virginia

Va. Code Ann. §§ 2.2-3900, 2.2-3901, 40.1-28.6, 40.1-28.7:1, 51.5-41

Law applies to employers with: One or more employees

Private employers may not make employment decisions based on:

- Age
- Ancestry or national origin
- Physical or mental disability
- AIDS/HIV
- Gender
- Marital status
- Pregnancy, childbirth, and related medical conditions
- Race or color
- Religion or creed
- Genetic testing information

Washington

Wash. Rev. Code Ann. §§ 38.40.110, 49.002.011, 49.44.090, 49.44.180, 49.60.030, 49.60.040, 49.60.172, 49.60.180, 49.76.120; Wash. Admin. Code § 162-30-020

Law applies to employers with: Eight or more employees; one or more employees (gender-based wage discrimination only)

Private employers may not make employment decisions based on:

- Age (40 or older)
- Ancestry or national origin
- Physical, mental, or sensory disability
- AIDS/HIV
- Gender
- Marital status
- Pregnancy, childbirth, and related medical conditions, including breast-feeding
- Race or color
- Religion or creed

- Sexual orientation
- Genetic testing information
- Hepatitis C infection
- Member of state militia
- Use of trained service animal by person with a disability
- Gender identity
- Domestic violence victim

West Virginia

W.Va. Code §§ 5-11-3, 5-11-9, 16-3C-3, 21-5B-1, 21-5B-3

Law applies to employers with: 12 or more employees; one or more employees (gender-based wage discrimination only)

Private employers may not make employment decisions based on:

- Age (40 or older)
- Ancestry or national origin
- Physical or mental disability, or blindness
- AIDS/HIV
- Gender
- Race or color
- Religion or creed
- Off-duty use of tobacco products
- Membership in the Civil Air Patrol (for employers with 16 or more employees)

Wisconsin

Wis. Stat. Ann. §§ 111.32 and following

Law applies to employers with: One or more employees

Private employers may not make employment decisions based on:

- Age (40 or older)
- Ancestry or national origin
- Physical or mental disability
- Gender
- Marital status

State Laws Prohibiting Discrimination in Employment (continued)

- Pregnancy, childbirth, and related medical conditions
- Race or color
- Religion or creed
- Sexual orientation, including having a history of or being identified with a preference
- Genetic testing information
- Arrest or conviction record
- Military service
- Declining to attend a meeting or to participate in any communication about religious matters or political matters
- Use or nonuse of lawful products off duty and off site

Wyoming

Wyo. Stat. §§ 19-11-104, 27-9-102, 27-9-105

Law applies to employers with: Two or more employees

Private employers may not make employment decisions based on:

- Age (40 or older)
- Ancestry or national origin
- Disability
- Gender
- Pregnancy, childbirth, and related medical conditions
- Race or color
- Religion or creed
- Military service or status

Uniformed Services Employment and Reemployment Rights Act (USERRA)

Statute: 38 U.S.C. §§ 4301 and following

To view the statutes, visit uscode.house.gov and select "Title 38" and "Chapter 43" and "Subchapter I."

Regulations: 20 C.F.R. §§ 1002.1–1002.314

To view the regulations, visit www.govinfo.gov and search "20 CFR 1002."

Overview of USERRA

Since 1940, federal law has guaranteed certain employment rights to workers who are in the *uniformed services*. In 1994, following the Persian Gulf War, Congress substantially revised this law, now called the Uniformed Services Employment and Reemployment Rights Act (USERRA). The law includes provisions on:

- **Antidiscrimination.** Employers may not discriminate against members of the uniformed services.
- **Reinstatement.** Employers must reinstate employees upon their return from up to five years of leave for *service in the uniformed services*.
- **Benefits.** Employers must restore all benefits to returning servicemembers. For purposes of benefit eligibility, accrual of seniority-based benefits, and vesting (that is, rules providing that employees are not entitled to collect or use benefits until they have worked for a certain period of time), time spent on leave for service in the uniformed services must be treated as time worked.
- **Job security.** Employers may not fire returning service members except for *cause* for up to one year after they return from military duty.

Definitions

Terms that appear in italics throughout this chapter are defined below.

Cause: A legitimate, nondiscriminatory reason for firing or laying off an employee. There are two types of cause recognized by USERRA: misconduct by the employee (stealing from the employer, for example) and legitimate business reasons unrelated to the employee's military service (such as companywide layoffs).

Escalator position: The position an employee would have attained had he or she not taken time off to serve in the *uniformed services*. The escalator position includes any promotions, pay raises, increased responsibilities, and other benefits the employee ordinarily would have attained; it could also include demotion, transfer, or layoff, if those events would have occurred if the employee had not taken leave.

Service in the uniformed services: Voluntary or involuntary performance of duties in the *uniformed services*, including:
- active duty

Definitions (continued)

- active duty for training
- initial active duty for training
- inactive duty training
- full-time National Guard duty
- absence for an examination to determine a worker's fitness for any of the above types of duty
- funeral honors duty performed by National Guard or reserve members, or
- service as an intermittent, disaster response appointee of the National Disaster Medical System, when federally activated or attending authorized training.

For ease of reference, we sometimes refer to this as "military service."

Successor employer: A company that takes over or acquires the company for which the employee worked.

Undue hardship: An action requiring significant difficulty or expense for the employer, in light of:

- the nature and cost of the action
- the overall financial resources of the particular facility where the action would be taken
- the number of workers at the facility
- how the action would affect the facility's operation, including expenses and resources
- the overall financial resources and size of the employer, including the location, number, and nature of its facilities, and
- the type of operations in which the employer engages.

Uniformed services: The following branches of the U. S. military:

- Army
- Navy
- Marine Corps
- Air Force
- Coast Guard
- Reserves
- Army or Air National Guard, and
- Commissioned Corps of the Public Health Service.

Covered Employers

USERRA covers employers of all sizes, including:

- all private employers, including foreign employers doing business in the United States
- American businesses that operate either directly or through an entity under their control in a foreign county (unless complying with USERRA would violate the laws of that country)
- hiring halls operated by a union or an employer association, if they perform hiring and job assignment functions for the employer
- the federal government, and
- state and local governments.

USERRA also covers *successor employers*. If a company takes over another company through a merger or an acquisition, for example, the new company may be considered a successor to the former employer and have to comply with USERRA. This issue typically comes up when the original employer is acquired while an employee is serving in the military: If the new company is a successor employer, it will have to reinstate the employee according to USERRA's provisions. Whether a company is a successor depends on:

- whether there is substantial continuity in business operations from the former to the current employer
- whether the current employer uses the same or similar facilities, machinery, equipment, and methods of production
- whether the current employer uses many of the same employees, managers, and/or supervisors
- whether the jobs and working conditions are similar, and
- whether the products or services offered are similar.

Covered Workers

Everyone who performs or has performed service in the uniformed services has USERRA rights. However, only a person who is employed, was employed, or seeks initial employment as an applicant can invoke those rights. A company does not have USERRA obligations to those who perform services for the company as independent contractors.

Legal Developments

- **Time served is time worked.** The Department of Labor has issued guidance on the effect of military leave on an employee's rights under the Family and Medical Leave Act (FMLA). (See Chapter 8 for more information on the FMLA.) Because time an employee spends on military leave must be counted as hours worked for purposes of eligibility for and accrual of benefits (see "Benefits," below), such time also must be counted as hours worked for purposes of eligibility under the FMLA.

- **Courts are enforcing arbitration agreements for USERRA claims.** Several federal courts have found that employers can compel arbitration of USERRA claims if the employee has signed a valid agreement to arbitrate employment-related disputes rather than taking them to court. The courts in these cases generally found that requiring employees to arbitrate these claims did not violate their rights under USERRA, but instead merely required them to submit disputes over those rights to a different forum (that is, to an arbitrator rather than a federal court). (See, for example, *Landis v. Pinnacle Eye Care, LLC,* 537 F.3d 559 (6th Cir. 2008); *Ziober v. BLB Resources, Inc.,* 839 F.3d 814 (9th Cir. 2016).)

An employee's entitlement to the protections of USERRA's various provisions depends on several factors, including length of military service. (For details, see "Major Provisions of USERRA," below.)

An employee's entitlement to the reinstatement, benefits, and job security rights provided by USERRA terminates if the employee:

- is separated from a uniformed service under conditions other than honorable (such as a dishonorable discharge, a bad conduct discharge, or an "other than honorable" discharge), or
- in the case of a commissioned officer, is dropped from the military rolls because of an unauthorized absence of more than three months or imprisonment by a civilian court, is dismissed from the uniformed service in a court martial, or is dismissed by order of the president in time of war.

Did You Know ...

- According to a 2017 report to Congress, more than 900 USERRA claims were reviewed by the DOL for that year. However, many more problems were handled informally: The Employer Support for the Guard and Reserve (ESGR), a Department of Defense organization, reported that it received more than 10,700 contacts regarding USERRA in the same time frame, and that 1,801 of those contacts turned into USERRA cases for which ESGR provided ombudsman services.
- In 2017, 42% of USERRA complaints reviewed by the DOL involved discrimination based on the employee's past, present, or future military service or status.

Major Provisions of USERRA

Antidiscrimination

Employers may not discriminate against members of the uniformed services or retaliate against workers who exercise their rights under USERRA.

Key Facts: Antidiscrimination

- Members of the military and those who take leave under USERRA are protected from employment discrimination.
- Employers may not retaliate against employees for exercising their rights under USERRA or participating in a USERRA investigation or enforcement proceeding.

Covered Employers

All covered employers are subject to this provision.

Covered Workers

All members of, and applicants for membership in, the uniformed services are covered by this provision. In addition, any person who participates in a proceeding to enforce USERRA rights (a witness in an investigation, a hearing, or a lawsuit, for example) is protected from retaliation, whether or not the person is a member of the uniformed services.

What's Prohibited

Employers may not take any negative job action against an employee or job applicant based on that person's membership, or application for membership, in the uniformed services. Negative job actions include:

- firing
- demoting
- reducing pay or benefits
- transferring, and
- refusing to hire.

Employers also may not retaliate against any person who:

- takes action to enforce USERRA rights
- testifies or makes a statement in connection with any USERRA enforcement proceeding
- participates in an investigation of a USERRA violation, or
- exercises his or her rights under USERRA.

Reinstatement

Employers must reinstate employees when they return to work after up to five years of military leave.

Covered Employers

All covered employers are subject to these provisions.

Covered Workers

Reinstatement rights are available only to employees who have been absent from employment due to service in the uniformed services. In addition, employees are eligible for reinstatement only if all of the following are true:

- The employee gave the employer notice, before taking leave, that the leave was for military service. This notice may be oral or written. If military necessity prevented the employee from giving notice or it was otherwise impossible or unreasonable to give notice under the circumstances (for example, because the employee was ordered to report for service immediately), this requirement doesn't apply.
- The employee spent no more than five years, cumulatively, on leave for military service. This time limit may be extended in some circumstances. (See "Exceptions," below.)
- The employee was released from military service under honorable conditions.
- The employee reports back or applies for reinstatement within specified time limits. These limits vary depending on the length of the employee's leave and whether the employee suffered or aggravated a disability while serving. (See "What's Required," below.)

Key Facts: Reinstatement

- Employers must reinstate returning servicemembers to the positions they would have held had they been not been on leave (called the "escalator position"), unless the employers' circumstances have changed so much that reemployment is impossible or unreasonable.
- If an employee is not qualified for an escalator position, the employer must make reasonable efforts to help the employee qualify. If these efforts fail, the employer may reinstate the employee to the position he or she held before taking leave for military service.
- To be reinstated, the employee must:
  - notify the employer beforehand that the leave was for military service
  - spend no more than five years, total, on leave (with a few exceptions)
  - be released from military service under honorable conditions, and
  - report back to work within specified time limits.

What's Required

An employer must reinstate workers who have taken up to a total of five years of leave to serve in the uniformed services. Reinstated employees are entitled to be returned to the "escalator position": the position they would have held had they not taken leave. They are entitled to any promotions, raises, and other seniority-based benefits they would have received had they not taken leave. (See "Benefits," below.)

The employee is not entitled to be placed in a better position than he or she would have been in if he or she had not taken leave. If, for example, an employer transfers the employee's entire department to another facility while the employee is on leave, the employee is entitled only to that transferred position; the employee is not entitled to be reinstated at the original facility while the rest of the department works elsewhere.

Returning employees are entitled to "prompt" reinstatement. What constitutes prompt reinstatement will depend on the circumstances, such as how long the employee has been gone, whether the employee's return date was known to the employer, what staffing or other changes will be required to reinstate the employee, and so on. The Department of Labor regulations state that employees should be reinstated within two weeks of the employee's application for reinstatement, absent unusual circumstances.

Reinstatement of an Unqualified Worker

If the worker is not qualified for the *escalator position*, the employer must make reasonable efforts to help the employee qualify (by offering training, for example). If the employee still isn't qualified, the employer's obligations depend on the length of the employee's military service:

- If the employee served for up to 90 days, the employer may reinstate him or her to the position held prior to starting military service. If the employee is no longer qualified for the pre-service position, the employer may reinstate him or her to a position that nearly approximates the escalator position, or if that's not possible, one that nearly approximates the pre-service position.

- If the employee served for more than 90 days, the employer must reinstate him or her to a position of like seniority, status, and pay to the escalator position. If the employee isn't qualified for this position, the employer may reinstate the employee to his or her pre-service position or a position of like seniority, status, and pay. If the employee isn't qualified for these positions, the employer may reinstate the employee to a position that nearly approximates the escalator position, or if that's not possible, one that nearly approximates the pre-service position.

Time Limits for Reinstatement

Absent unusual circumstances, the employer must reemploy a returning servicemember within two weeks after he or she applies for reinstatement. The time limits for reporting back or applying for reinstatement depend on how long the worker was out on leave:

- **Workers who were on leave for 30 or fewer days** must report back on the first regularly scheduled workday after their service is complete, allowing for safe transportation home and an additional eight-hour period.
- **Workers who were on leave for 31 to 180 days** must submit an application for reemployment within 14 days of completing their service. If it is impossible or unreasonable for the employee to report within 14 days, through no fault of his or her own, the employee may report for work on the next calendar day when it becomes possible to do so.
- **Workers who were on leave for 181 days or more** must submit a written or oral application for reemployment within 90 days after their period of service is complete.
- **Workers who are injured or become ill while performing service** must report to the employer or submit an application for reemployment once they have recovered. This recovery period may not exceed two years.

Documentation

If an employee served for more than 30 days, the employer can ask the employee to provide documents showing that:

- The employee's application for reinstatement is timely.
- The employee's service did not exceed the five-year limit.
- The employee was separated or discharged from service under honorable conditions.

However, the employee's inability to provide this documentation doesn't relieve the employer of the obligation to return the employee to work. The employer must reinstate the employee pending availability of these documents. If the documents don't exist, the employee need not provide them. If, however, documentation later becomes available showing that the employee didn't meet one or more of the requirements for reinstatement, the employer may fire the employee.

Exceptions

Exceptions to the Reinstatement Right

An employer is not required to reinstate an employee in any of the following situations:

- The employer's circumstances have changed so much that reemployment is impossible or unreasonable.
- The job was for a brief, nonrecurrent period, and the worker had no reasonable expectation that the job would continue indefinitely or for a significant length of time.
- The employee is not qualified and helping the employee qualify for reinstatement would impose an *undue hardship* on the employer.

Exceptions to the Five-Year Service Limit

An employee who takes more than a total of five years of leave is still entitled to reinstatement if any of the following are true:

- The employee's initial service obligation exceeds five years. (For example, some military specialties require members to serve an initial term of more than five years.)
- The employee is unable to obtain a release from duty within five years. (This exception applies to service members who are involuntarily retained on active duty after their initial service obligation ends.)
- The employee takes time off for reserve or National Guard training, or for other training as determined and certified by a proper military authority as necessary to complete skill training, for retraining, or for the employee's professional development. This training does not count toward the five-year limit.
- The employee is ordered to remain or go on active duty during a domestic emergency, a national security situation, or a war or national emergency declared by the president or Congress.
- The employee performs service while ordered to, or retained on, active duty in the following capacities:
  - involuntary active duty by a military retiree or retired Coast Guard member
  - retention on active duty while held captive
  - involuntary active duty of a critical person in a time of crisis
  - voluntary active duty by a retired Coast Guard officer or enlistee

- involuntary active duty by the Coast Guard reserves during disasters, or
- involuntary retention of Coast Guard members on active duty.
- The employee volunteers for active duty in support of an operational mission for which members of the Selected Reserve have been involuntarily ordered to active duty. (Examples of this exception are workers who volunteered to support operational missions in Bosnia.)
- The employee volunteers for active duty in support of a critical mission or requirement (as certified by the secretary of the uniformed service involved), when no war or national emergency has been declared and no involuntary call-up is in effect.
- The employee is a member of the National Guard called into federal service by the president to suppress an insurrection, repel an invasion, or execute the laws of the United States.

Benefits

Employers must make certain employment benefits available to workers who take leave for service in the uniformed services. In addition, returning workers are entitled to have their benefits restored.

Key Facts: Benefits

- Employers are required to provide health insurance continuation for up to 24 months while an employee is on leave.
- Employees on leave are entitled to the same benefits that are provided to employees who take a leave of absence for other reasons.
- An employee who returns from military leave is entitled to the seniority and all rights and benefits based on seniority that he or she would have accrued if not for taking leave.
- An employee who has been on leave must be allowed to make up any missed employee contributions to a pension plan. An employer must match these contributions to the same extent that it matches contributions from other employees, and it must make any required contributions for the period when the employee was on leave.

Covered Employers

All covered employers are subject to these provisions.

Covered Workers

Workers who take leave from work for service in the uniformed services are eligible for benefits continuation while on leave. Only workers who are entitled to reinstatement following service in the uniformed services are eligible for benefits reinstatement. (See "Reinstatement," above.)

What's Required

Benefits During Leave

While a worker is on leave, the employer has the following obligations, depending on the type of benefit:

- **Health insurance.** Employers must continue to provide health insurance for up to 24 months after a worker goes on leave for service in the uniformed services. If the worker is absent for up to 30 days, the employer may not require the worker to pay more than the usual employee share (if any) for such coverage. If the worker is absent for more than 30 days, the employer may require the worker to pay up to 102% of the full premium for such coverage (including the employer's share).
- **Paid time off.** Employers must allow, but may not require, servicemembers to use accrued vacation time for military service, if they wish.
- **Other benefits.** The employer must give the worker the same benefits that are generally provided to a worker in a similar position who takes a leave of absence for other reasons. If such workers are required to continue to pay the employee cost of a funded benefit, workers on leave for military service may also be required to pay.

Benefits After Reinstatement

Once a worker is reinstated following leave for service in the uniformed services, all benefits must be restored. Additional obligations depend on the type of benefit.

Health Insurance. If the worker's health insurance coverage was terminated while he or she was on leave, this coverage must be reinstated without an exclusion or a waiting period for the worker and any others (spouse and dependents, for example) covered under the worker's insurance. However, the health plan can impose an exclusion or a waiting period as to illnesses or injuries that the Secretary of Veterans Affairs office determines were caused or aggravated by the employee's military service.

Seniority-Based Benefits. Reinstated workers are entitled to the seniority, and any rights and benefits based on seniority, that they would have attained had they been continuously employed. For example, time the employee spent on leave must be counted as time worked for purposes of determining whether the employee is eligible for FMLA leave. (For more on the FMLA's eligibility requirements, see Chapter 8.)

Benefits Not Based on Seniority. A reinstated worker is entitled to the same benefits not based on seniority that are generally provided to employees who take a leave of absence for nonmilitary reasons.

Pension Plans. USERRA provides detailed rules for the treatment of pension plans. A reinstated worker's time on leave must not be treated as a break in service for purposes of an employer-maintained pension plan. For purposes of vesting and benefit accrual, time the worker spends on military service and any time the worker is legally allowed to take off before applying for reinstatement must be considered service with the employer.

If the employee is not required or permitted to contribute to the pension plan (that is, if the plan is funded entirely by the employer), the employer must contribute the amount attributable to the time the employee spent on leave. This must be done either within 90 days after the employee is reinstated or when contributions are ordinarily made for the years in which the employee was on leave, whichever is later.

The employee must be allowed to make up any employee contributions he or she missed because of service in the uniformed services, and the employer must match these contributions to the same extent it matches contributions by other employees. The worker has up to three times the length of his or her military service, or five years, whichever is shorter, to make these contributions. If the employee received a distribution from the plan while on leave, the employee must be allowed to repay this amount, with interest.

Job Security

Employers may not fire an employee, except for *cause*, for a certain period of time after he or she returns to work after service in the uniformed services. The length of time of the job security provision depends on the length of the employee's military service.

Key Facts: Job Security

- Employers must have cause to fire an employee for a limited time after he or she returns from military service. An employer may fire an employee during this protected period for cause, but the employer must show that it acted reasonably and that the employee had notice that his or her conduct was cause for discharge.
- Employees are entitled to this protection only if they served for at least 31 days in the uniformed services.

Covered Employers

All covered employers are subject to these provisions.

Covered Workers

Only employees who served for at least 31 days in the uniformed services are covered by the job protection provision.

What's Prohibited

Employers are prohibited from firing an employee who returns to work after service in the uniformed services, except for *cause*, for:
- 180 days after the worker is reinstated, if the worker served in the uniformed services for 31 to 180 days, or
- one year after the worker is reinstated, if the worker served in the uniformed services for more than 180 days.

During USERRA's required period of job security, an employer that fires a protected employee must show that the discharge was reasonable and that the employee had notice that his or her conduct was cause for discharge. The employer bears the burden of proving that it acted legally.

How USERRA Is Enforced

Individual Complaints

An employee whose USERRA rights have been violated has several options. The employee may try to resolve the problem informally, with the assistance of the Department of Defense's Employer Support for the Guard and Reserve (ESGR) ombudsmen services. The ESGR offers information and mediation services to assist the employer and employee in resolving disputes.

The employee may also file a complaint with the Veterans Employment and Training Service (VETS), an agency within the Department of Labor, which will investigate and attempt to resolve the complaint. (For information on contacting VETS, see Appendix A.)

An employee does not have to complain to the ESGR or VETS, however. The employee can go directly to federal district court and file a lawsuit against the employer. USERRA does not specify a statute of limitations; this means that, in theory at least, employees may file a lawsuit no matter how much time has passed since their employer violated USERRA. However, some courts have applied a four-year statute of limitations to USERRA claims. Also, if the employee unreasonably delays bringing a lawsuit, and this delay prejudices the employer's ability to defend itself, a judge might throw out the case.

Agency Enforcement

VETS has the authority to investigate complaints of USERRA violations. Once it has investigated, it will attempt to resolve the complaint. However, VETS cannot force an employer to comply with the law, nor can it impose penalties or fines on an employer that refuses to comply. If VETS's efforts at resolution are unsuccessful, it will inform the complaining employee in writing of the results of the investigation and of the employee's right to continue to press the complaint. The employee can either file a lawsuit or ask VETS to refer the complaint to the U.S. attorney general's office.

If the attorney general's office decides that the complaint has merit, a lawyer from that office may bring a lawsuit against the employer to enforce the complaining employee's USERRA rights. If the attorney general's office decides not to take the case, the employee can still file a private lawsuit.

Complying With USERRA

Deadlines

Many of USERRA's deadlines apply to employees only—for example, the requirement that employees must report or return to work within a specified time (see "Reinstatement," above) and make up missed pension plan contributions within a specific timeframe.

Here are the deadlines that apply to employers:

- Employers generally must reemploy returning service members within *two weeks* after the employee reports or applies for reinstatement.
- Employers must make up their contributions to a pension plan for the period the employee spent in military service within *90 days* after the employee is reinstated or by the deadline for making contributions for the years when the employee was serving in the military, whichever is later.

Reporting Requirements

USERRA imposes no reporting requirements.

Posting Requirements

Employers are required to notify employees of their USERRA rights. They can meet this obligation by posting a notice created by the Department of Labor. (See "Agency Resources," below, for information on getting this poster.)

Record-Keeping Requirements

USERRA does not require employers to keep any particular records.

Remedies

Employers that violate USERRA may be required to:

- comply with the law (for example, by reinstating a worker or restoring a worker's benefits)

- pay the worker for any benefits or wages lost because of the employer's violation, and
- pay the worker's attorneys' fees and court costs.

If a court finds that the employer knew, or should have known, that its acts were against the law, the employer can also be ordered to pay twice the amount of the worker's lost benefits and wages.

Agency Resources

- A directory of VETS offices nationwide
  VETS Regional Offices
  www.dol.gov/vets/aboutvets/regionaloffices/map.htm

- A fact sheet about USERRA's basic provisions
  Employment Law Guide: Uniformed Service Members
  https://webapps.dol.gov/elaws/elg/userra.htm

- An interactive guide to USERRA
  Elaws—USERRA Advisor
  https://webapps.dol.gov/elaws/USERRA.htm

- The USERRA poster
  Your Rights Under USERRA
  www.dol.gov/vets/programs/userra/poster.htm

State Laws Relating to Military Service

Many states have laws that protect employees who take time off to serve in the state National Guard or militia. Some of these laws are similar to USERRA, in that they provide a right to reinstatement and prohibit discrimination against those in the military. Others provide additional rights, such as a minimum number of days off per year to attend training or educational activities.

The chart below provides some basic information about these state laws. If you need more information, contact your state labor department (you can find contact information in Appendix A).

State Laws on Military Leave

Alabama

Ala. Code §§ 31-12-1 to 31-12-4

Members of the Alabama National Guard, or the national guard of another state, called to active duty or for federally funded duty for service other than training have the same leave and reinstatement rights and benefits guaranteed under USERRA (doesn't apply to normal annual training, weekend drills, and required schools).

Alaska

Alaska Stat. § 26.05.075

Employees called to active service in the state militia or the National Guard of another state are entitled to unlimited unpaid leave and reinstatement to their former or a comparable position, with the pay, seniority, and benefits the employee would have had if not absent for service. Reinstatement is not required if it would pose an undue hardship on the employer or would be impossible or unreasonable due to the employer's changed circumstances. Employee must return to work on next workday, after time required for travel. Disabled employee must request reemployment within 30 days of release; if disability leaves the employee unable to do the job, employee must be offered a position with similar pay and benefits.

Arizona

Ariz. Rev. Stat. §§ 26-167, 26-168

Members of the national guard of Arizona or any other state, or the U.S. armed forces reserves, called to training or active duty have the same leave and reinstatement rights and benefits guaranteed under USERRA. When called to active duty or to attend camps, formations, maneuvers, or drills, military members are entitled to unlimited unpaid leave and reinstatement to their former or a higher position with the same seniority and vacation benefits. Employers may not dissuade employees from enlisting in state or national military forces by threatening economic reprisal.

Arkansas

Ark. Code Ann. § 12-62-413

Employees called to active state duty as a member of the armed forces (which includes the National Guard, militia, and reserves) of Arkansas or any other state have the same leave and reinstatement rights and benefits guaranteed under USERRA.

California

Cal. Mil. & Vet. Code §§ 394, 394.5, 395.06

Members of the California National Guard, or the national guard of any state, called to active duty are entitled to unlimited unpaid leave and reinstatement to their former position or to a position of similar seniority, status, and pay. Full-time employees must be reinstated (without loss of retirement or other benefits), unless the employer's circumstances have so changed as to make reinstatement impossible or unreasonable. Part-time employees must be reinstated if an open position exists. Reinstated employees cannot be terminated without cause for one year. Full-time employees must apply for reinstatement within 40 days of discharge, while part-time employees must apply for reinstatement within 5 days of discharge.

State Laws on Military Leave (continued)

Employees in the U.S. armed forces reserves, National Guard, or Naval Militia are entitled to 17 days' unpaid leave per year for military training, drills, encampment, naval cruises, special exercises, or similar activities. Employer may not terminate employee or limit any benefits or seniority because of a temporary disability resulting from duty in the National Guard, Naval Militia, State Military Reserve, or the federal reserve components of the U.S. Armed Forces (up to 52 weeks).

Employers may not fire or otherwise discriminate against employees because of their performance of any ordered military duty or training or due to their membership in the state military, state naval forces, or the federal reserve components of the U.S. Armed Forces.

Colorado

Colo. Rev. Stat. §§ 28-3-609, 28-3-610, 28-3-610.5

Members of the Colorado National Guard or U.S. armed force reserves are entitled to 15 days' unpaid leave per year for training. Employees called to active state duty in the Colorado National Guard are entitled to unlimited unpaid leave. Employees on leave for training and active duty must be reinstated to their former positions or a similar position with the same status, pay, and seniority, and they must receive the same vacation, sick leave, bonuses, benefits, and other advantages they would have had if not absent for service.

Connecticut

Conn. Gen. Stat. Ann. §§ 27-33a, 27-34a

Members of the Connecticut National Guard, or the national guard of any state, ordered into active state service by the governor are entitled to the same rights and benefits guaranteed under USERRA, except those pertaining to life insurance. Employees who are members of the state armed forces, any reserve component of the U.S. armed forces, or the national guard of any states, are entitled to take leave to perform ordered military duty, including meetings or drills, that take place during regular work hours, without loss or reduction of vacation or holiday benefits. Employer may not discriminate in terms of promotion or continued employment.

Delaware

Del. Code Ann. tit. 20 § 905

National Guard members who are called to state active duty shall be entitled to the same rights, privileges, and protections as they would have had if called for military training under federal law protecting reservists and National Guard members.

Florida

Fla. Stat. Ann. §§ 250.481, 250.482, 252.55, 627.6692(5)

Employees who are called to active duty in the National Guard, or into active duty by the laws of any other state, may not be penalized for absence from work. Upon return from service, employees are entitled to reinstatement with full benefits unless employer's circumstances have changed

State Laws on Military Leave (continued)

to make reinstatement impossible or unreasonable or it would impose an undue hardship. Reinstated employees may not be terminated without cause for one year.

If a member of the National Guard or Reserves is receiving COBRA benefits when called to active duty, the period of time when that servicemember is covered by TRICARE (military health benefits) won't count against his or her COBRA entitlement. Discrimination against members of the National Guard or reserves is prohibited.

Employers with 15 or more employees must provide up to 15 days of unpaid leave to members of the Civil Air Patrol. Employers must reinstate an employee after the leave, unless the employer's circumstances have changed such that it would be unreasonable or impossible or it would cause an undue hardship. Returning employees may not be fired without cause for one year.

Georgia

Ga. Code Ann. § 38-2-280

Discrimination against members of the U.S. military reserves or state militia is prohibited. Employees called to active duty in the U.S. uniformed services, the Georgia National Guard, or the national guard of any other state, are entitled to unlimited unpaid leave for active service and up to 6 months' leave in any 4-year period for service school or annual training. Employee is entitled to reinstatement with full benefits unless employer's circumstances have changed to make reinstatement impossible or unreasonable. Employee

must apply for reinstatement within 90 days of discharge or within 10 days of completing school or training.

Hawaii

Haw. Rev. Stat. § 121-43

Members of the National Guard are entitled to unlimited unpaid leave while performing ordered National Guard service and while going to and returning from service, and reinstatement to the same or a position comparable in seniority, status, and pay. If an employee is not qualified for his or her former position because of a disability sustained during service but is qualified for another position, the employee is entitled to the position that is most similar to his or her former position, unless employer's circumstances have changed to make reinstatement impossible or unreasonable. Employee cannot be terminated without cause for one year after reinstatement. Employer cannot discriminate against employee because of any obligation as a member of the National Guard.

Idaho

Idaho Code §§ 46-224, 46-225, 46-407, 46-409

Members of the Idaho National Guard, or the national guard of another state, who are called to active duty by the governor or president in time of war, armed conflict, or emergency, are entitled to the same protections as USERRA. Once their leave is over, employees are entitled to reinstatement to their former position or a comparable position with like

State Laws on Military Leave (continued)

seniority, status, and pay. If an employee is not qualified for his or her former position because of a disability sustained during service, the employee is entitled to the position that is most similar to his or her former position in terms of seniority, status, and pay (provided that the employee is qualified). Reinstated employees may not be fired without cause for one year.

Members of the National Guard and U.S. armed forces reserves may take up to 15 days' unpaid leave per year for training without affecting the employee's rights to vacation, sick leave, bonus, advancement, and other advantages of employment. Employees must give 90 days' notice of training dates.

Illinois

330 Ill. Comp. Stat. § 61/1-1 and following; 820 Ill. Comp. Stat. Ann. §§ 148/10, 148/15, 148/20

Members of the U.S. Armed Forces, Illinois State Guard, and national guard of any state are entitled to the same leave and reinstatement rights and benefits guaranteed under USERRA for military service. This includes service in a federally recognized auxiliary of the U.S. Armed Forces when performing official duties in support of military or civilian authorities in an emergency. Servicemembers are also protected while absent from work and receiving medical or dental treatment related to a condition incurred or aggravated during active service.

Employers with at least 15 employees must provide up to 15 days of unpaid Civil Air Patrol leave to employees performing a Civil Air Patrol mission. Employers with at least 50 employees must provide up to 30 days of unpaid leave for the same purposes. Employees must be reinstated to the same position with the same pay, benefits, and seniority.

Indiana

Ind. Code Ann. §§ 10-16-7-4 , 10-16-7-6, 10-16-7-23; 10-17-4-1 to 10-17-4-5

Members of the Indiana National Guard, or the national guard of any other state, who are called to state active duty have the same leave and reinstatement rights and benefits guaranteed under USERRA. Employers may not refuse to allow members of the Indiana National Guard to attend assembly for drills, training, or other duties.

Members of the U.S. armed force reserves may take up to 15 days' unpaid leave per year for training. Employees must provide evidence of dates of departure and return 90 days in advance, and proof of completion of the training upon return. Leave does not affect vacation, sick leave, bonus, or promotion rights. At the end of training, employee must be reinstated to former or a similar position with no loss of seniority or benefits.

Iowa

Iowa Code § 29A.43

Members of the Iowa National Guard, the national guard of any other state, the organized reserves of the U.S. armed forces, or the Civil Air Patrol who are called into temporary duty are entitled to reinstatement to former or a similar

State Laws on Military Leave (continued)

position. Leave does not affect vacation, sick leave, bonuses, or other benefits. Employee must provide evidence of satisfactory completion of duty and of qualifications to perform the job's duties. Employers may not discriminate against these employees or discharge them due to their military affiliations.

Kansas

Kan. Stat. Ann. §§ 48-222, 48-517

Employees called into active duty by the state of Kansas, or any other state, are entitled to unlimited leave and reinstatement to the same position or a comparable position with like seniority, status, and pay. Reemployment not required if employer's circumstances have changed so as to make reemployment impossible/unreasonable or if reemployment would impose undue hardship on employer. Reinstated employees may not be discharged without cause for one year. Members of the Kansas National Guard are entitled to 5 to 10 days' leave each year to attend annual muster and camp of instruction. Employer's failure to allow employee to attend or punishing employee who attends is a misdemeanor.

Kentucky

Ky. Rev. Stat. Ann. §§ 38.238, 38.460

Members of National Guard are entitled to unlimited unpaid leave for active duty or training and reinstatement to former position with no loss of seniority or benefits. Employer may not in any way discriminate against employee or use threats to prevent employee from enlisting in the Kentucky National Guard, the national guard of any other state, or active militia.

Louisiana

La. Rev. Stat. Ann. §§ 29:38, 29:38.1

Employees called into active duty in National Guard, state militia, or any branch of the state military forces of Louisiana or any other state are entitled to reinstatement to same or comparable position with same seniority, status, benefits, and pay. If employee is not qualified for former position because of disability sustained during active duty, but is otherwise qualified to perform another position, employer or successor shall employ person in other or comparable position with like seniority, status, benefits, and pay provided the employment does not pose a direct threat or significant risk to the health and safety of the individual or others that cannot be eliminated by reasonable accommodation. Employees on leave are entitled to the benefits offered to employees who take leave for other reasons. Employee must report to work within 72 hours of release or recovery from service-related injury or illness and cannot be fired, except for cause, for one year after reinstatement. Employer cannot discriminate against employee because of any obligation as a member of the state National Guard or U.S. reserves.

Maine

Me. Rev. Stat. Ann. tit. 37-B, § 342; tit. 26, §§ 811 to 813

Employer may not discriminate against employee for membership or service in National Guard or United States armed forces reserves. Employees in the National Guard or reserves are entitled

State Laws on Military Leave (continued)

to military leave in response to state or federal military orders. Upon completion of service, employees must be reinstated, at the same pay, seniority, benefits, and status, and must receive all other employment advantages as if they had been continuously employed.

For the first 30 days of an employee's military leave, the employer must continue the employee's health, dental, and life insurance at no additional cost to the employee. After 30 days, the employee may continue these benefits at his or her own expense (paying the employer's group rates).

Maryland

Md. Code Ann., [Public Safety], § 13-704; Md. Code Ann., Lab. & Empl., § 3-1001 to 3-1007

Members of the state National Guard and Maryland Defense Force ordered to military duty have the same leave and reinstatement rights and benefits guaranteed under USERRA. Maryland employers with 15 or more employees must allow employees who have been employed for at least 90 days to take at least 15 days off each year to respond to an emergency mission of the Maryland Wing of the Civil Air Patrol. Employees must give as much notice as possible of their need for this leave. After arriving at the emergency location, employees must notify their employer and estimate how long the mission will take. Employees are entitled to reinstatement upon their return from this type of leave. Employers may not penalize employees for exercising their rights under this law, nor may they retaliate against employees who complain that an employer has violated the law.

Massachusetts

Mass. Gen. Laws ch. 151B, § 4; ch 33 § 13

Employers may not discriminate against employees and applicants based on their membership in, application to perform, or obligation to perform military service, including service in the National Guard. Employees who are members of the armed forces are entitled to the same rights and protections granted under USERRA.

Michigan

Mich. Comp. Laws §§ 32.271 to 32.274

Employees who are called to active duty in the U.S. uniformed services, the National Guard, or the military or naval forces of Michigan or any other state, are entitled to take unpaid leave, and to be reinstated when their service has ended. Reinstatement is not required for military service that exceeds five years, except in certain cases. Employers may not discriminate against employees based on their military service, use threats to prevent employees from enlisting, or prevent employees from attending military encampments or other places of drills or instruction.

Minnesota

Minn. Stat. Ann. § 192.34

Employer may not discharge employee, interfere with military service, or dissuade employee from enlisting by threatening employee's job. Applies to employees who are members of the U.S., Minnesota, or any other state military or naval forces.

State Laws on Military Leave (continued)

Mississippi

Miss. Code Ann. §§ 33-1-15, 33-1-19

Employers may not discriminate against employees or applicants based on their current membership in the reserves of the U.S. armed forces or their former membership in the U.S. armed forces. Employers may not threaten employees to dissuade them from enlisting.

Members of the U.S. armed forces reserves or U.S. military veterans may take time off for state or federal military training or duty, with reinstatement to their former position (or a similar position) once their leave is over. Employees must provide evidence that they have completed their training.

Missouri

Mo. Rev. Stat. §§ 40.490, 41.730

Members of the Missouri military forces, the national guard of any other state, or a reserve component of the U.S. armed forces, who are called to active duty are entitled to the same leave and reinstatement rights provided under USERRA. Employers may not discharge employees, interfere with their military service, or use threats to dissuade employee from enlisting in the state organized militia.

Montana

Mont. Code Ann. §§ 10-1-1005, 10-1-1006, 10-1-1007

Employees who are ordered to federally funded military service are entitled to all rights available under USERRA. Members of the Montana National Guard, or the national guard of any other state, who are called to state military duty are entitled

to leave for duration of service. Leave may not be deducted from sick leave, vacation, or other leave, although employee may voluntarily use that leave. Returning employee is entitled to reinstatement to same or similar position with the same seniority, status, pay, health insurance, pension, and other benefits, provided that the employee told the employer of membership in the military at the time of hire, or if the employee enlisted during employment, at the time of enlistment. Employer may not in any way discriminate against employee or dissuade employee from enlisting in the state organized militia.

Nebraska

Neb. Rev. Stat. § 55-161

Employees who are called into active duty in the Nebraska National Guard, or the national guard of any other state, have the same leave and reinstatement rights and benefits guaranteed under USERRA.

Nevada

Nev. Rev. Stat. Ann. §§ 412.139, 412.606

Employers may not discriminate against members of the Nevada National Guard or the national guard of another state and may not discharge any employee because he or she assembles for training, participates in field training, is called to active duty, or otherwise meets as required for ceremonies, maneuvers, and other military duties.

New Hampshire

N.H. Rev. Stat. Ann. §§ 110-B:65, 110-C:1

Members of the state National Guard or militia called to active duty by the governor

State Laws on Military Leave (continued)

have the same leave and reinstatement rights and benefits guaranteed under USERRA. Employer may not discriminate against employee because of connection or service with state National Guard or militia; may not dissuade employee from enlisting by threatening job.

New Jersey

N.J. Stat. Ann. § 38:23C-20

An employee is entitled to take unpaid leave for active service in the U.S. or state military services. Upon return, employee must be reinstated to the same or a similar position, unless employer's circumstances have changed to make reinstatement impossible or unreasonable. If same or similar position is not possible, employer shall restore such person to any available position, if requested by such person, for which the person is capable and qualified to perform the duties. Employee must apply for reinstatement within 90 days of release from service. Employee may not be fired without cause for one year after returning from service. Employee is also entitled to take up to 3 months' leave in 4-year period for annual training or assemblies relating to military service, or to attend service schools conducted by the U.S. armed forces. Employee must apply for reinstatement within 10 days.

New Mexico

N.M. Stat. Ann. §§ 28-15-1, 28-15-2, 20-4-6

Members of the U.S. armed forces, organized reserves, or national guard of any state may take up to five years of unpaid leave for service, as long as they've given advance notice (unless that notice is impossible or unreasonable). Employees must request reinstatement within 90 days after being released from duty or discharged from up to two years of hospitalization and convalescence following duty. Employees who are still qualified must be reinstated in former or similar position with same status, seniority, and pay unless employers' circumstances have changed to make reinstatement impossible or unreasonable. Employees may not be fired without cause for one year after returning from service. Employers may not prevent employees from performing military service or discriminate against or discharge employees because of membership in national guard.

New York

N.Y. Mil. Law §§ 251, 252, 317, 318

Members of the U.S. armed forces or organized militia are entitled to unpaid leave for active service; reserve drills or annual training; service school; or initial full-time or active duty training. Returning employee is entitled to reinstatement to previous position, or to one with the same seniority, status, and pay, unless the employer's circumstances have changed and reemployment is impossible or unreasonable. Employee must apply for reinstatement within 90 days of discharge from active service, 10 days of completing school, reserve drills, or annual training, or 60 days of completing initial full-time or active duty training. Employee may not be discharged without cause for one year after reinstatement. Employers may not discriminate against persons subject to state or federal military duty.

State Laws on Military Leave (continued)

North Carolina

N.C. Gen. Stat. §§ 127A-201, 127A-202, 127A-202.1, 127B-14

Members of the North Carolina National Guard, or the national guard of any other state, who are called to active state duty by a state governor are entitled to take unpaid leave. Within five days of release from state duty, employee must be restored to previous position or one of comparable seniority, status, and salary, unless the employer's circumstances now make it unreasonable. Employees who are no longer qualified for their jobs must be placed in another position with appropriate seniority, status, and salary. For service of 30 days or less, the employee must apply for reinstatement in writing on the next regularly scheduled workday at least 24 hours after traveling home. For service of more than 30 days, the employee must apply in writing within 14 days of release from duty. (If the employee is hospitalized due to an injury or illness sustained in active duty, different rules apply.)

Employers may not discriminate against or fire an employee because of membership in the national guard of any state or fire an employee called up for emergency military service.

North Dakota

N.D.C.C. §§ 37-29-01, 37-29-03

Employers may not terminate, demote, or otherwise discriminate against volunteer members of the North Dakota National Guard or North Dakota Air National Guard, or volunteer civilian members of the civil air patrol. The employer must allow such employees to be absent or tardy from work for up to 20 days in a calendar year because they are responding to a disaster or national emergency (20-day limit does not apply to involuntarily activated members of the North Dakota National Guard). An employee who needs this leave must make a reasonable effort to notify the employer. Upon request, the employee must also provide written verification of the dates and times of service.

Ohio

Ohio Rev. Code Ann. §§ 5903.01, 5903.02

Employees who are members of the Ohio organized militia or National Guard or in the organized militia of another state called for active duty or training; members of the commissioned public health service corps; or any other uniformed service called up in time of war or emergency; have the same leave and reinstatement rights and benefits guaranteed under USERRA.

Oklahoma

Okla. Stat. Ann. tit. 44, §§ 71, 208.1

Employees in the Oklahoma National Guard who are ordered to state active duty or full-time National Guard duty have the same reinstatement rights and other benefits guaranteed by USERRA. Members of the state National Guard must be allowed to take time off to attend state National Guard drills, instruction, encampment, maneuvers, ceremonies, exercises, or other duties.

State Laws on Military Leave (continued)

Oregon

Or. Rev. Stat. §§ 659A.082, 659A.086

Members of Oregon or other states' organized militias called into active state service or state active duty may take unpaid leave for term of service. Returning employee is entitled to reinstatement with no loss of seniority or benefits including sick leave, vacation, or service credits under a pension plan. Employee must return to work within 7 calendar days of release from service.

Pennsylvania

51 Pa. Cons. Stat. Ann. §§ 7301 to 7309

Employees who enlist or are drafted during a time of war or emergency called by the president or governor, along with reservists or members of Pennsylvania National Guard called into active duty, are entitled to unpaid military leave. Leave expires 90 days after enlistment/draft period, 90 days after military duty for reservists, 30 days after state duty for Pennsylvania National Guard members. Returning employee must be reinstated to same or similar position with same status, seniority, and pay. If no longer qualified due to disability sustained during military duty, employer must restore to position with like seniority, status, and pay unless employer or successor's circumstances have changed so as to make it impossible or unreasonable to do so. Employers may not discharge or discriminate against any employee because of membership or service in the military. Employees called to active duty are entitled to 30 days' health insurance continuation benefits at no cost.

Rhode Island

R.I. Gen. Laws §§ 30-11-2 to 30-11-9, 30-21-1

Members of state military forces and the National Guard of Rhode Island or any other state who are called to active duty have the same leave and reinstatement rights and benefits guaranteed under USERRA. Members of the National Guard or U.S. armed forces reserves are entitled to unpaid leave for training and are entitled to reinstatement with the same status, pay, and seniority. Employees in the U.S. armed forces are entitled to reinstatement to the same position or a position with similar seniority, status, and pay unless the employer's circumstances make reinstatement impossible or unreasonable. Employee must request reinstatement within 40 days. Employer may not discriminate against or discharge employee because of membership in the state military forces or U.S. reserves, interfere with employee's military service, or dissuade employee from enlisting by threatening employee's job.

South Carolina

S.C. Code Ann. §§ 25-1-2310 to 25-1-2340, 25-1-2350

Members of the South Carolina National Guard or State Guard, or the national or state guard of any state, who are called to active duty by a state governor are entitled to unpaid leave for service. Upon honorable discharge from service, the employee must be reinstated to the same position or a position with similar seniority, status, and pay. Employee must apply for reinstatement in writing, within

State Laws on Military Leave (continued)

5 days of release from service or related hospitalization. Employer has no duty to reinstate if the employer's circumstances make reinstatement unreasonable.

South Dakota

S.D. Codified Laws Ann. § 33A-2-9

Members of the South Dakota National Guard, or the national guard of any state, ordered to active duty by the governor or president have the same leave and reinstatement rights and benefits guaranteed under USERRA.

Tennessee

Tenn. Code Ann. § 58-1-604

Employer may not terminate or refuse to hire an employee because of Tennessee National Guard membership or because employee is absent for a required drill, including annual field training.

Texas

Tex. Gov't. Code Ann. §§ 437.204, 437.213

Members of the state military forces are entitled to the same leave and reinstatement protections granted under USERRA. Employers may not discriminate against members of the Texas military forces, or the military forces of any other state, and have the right to be reinstated following a call to active duty or training. Employees are entitled to be reinstated to the same position they held before leaving, with no loss of time, efficiency rating, vacation time, or other benefits. An employee must give notice of his or her intent to return to work as soon as practicable after release from duty.

Utah

Utah Code Ann. § 39-1-36

Members of U.S. armed forces reserves who are called to active duty, active duty for training, inactive duty training, or state active duty may take up to 5 years of unpaid leave. Upon return, employee is entitled to reinstatement to previous employment with same seniority, status, pay, and vacation rights. Employer may not discriminate against an employee based on membership in armed forces reserves.

Vermont

Vt. Stat. Ann. tit. 21, § 491, Vt. Stat. Ann. tit. 20, § 608

Employees who are members of U.S. armed forces reserves, an organized unit of the National Guard of Vermont or any other state, or the ready reserves are entitled to 15 days per year of unpaid leave for military drills, training, or other temporary duty under military authority. Returning employee must be reinstated to former position with the same status, pay, and seniority, including any seniority that accrued during the leave of absence. Employer may not discriminate against an employee who is a member or an applicant for membership in the National Guard of Vermont or any other state. Members of the National Guard of Vermont or any other state ordered to state active duty by the governor have the right to take unpaid leave from civilian employment, and cannot be required to exhaust their vacation or other accrued leave.

State Laws on Military Leave (continued)

Virginia

Va. Code Ann. §§ 40.1-28.7:6, 44-93.2 to 44-93.4

Members of the Virginia National Guard, Virginia Defense Force, or the national guard of another state, called to active duty by the governor are entitled to take unpaid leave and may not be required to use vacation or any other accrued leave (unless employee wishes). Returning employee whose absence does not exceed five years must be reinstated to previous position or one with same seniority, status, and pay; if position no longer exists, then to a comparable position unless employer's circumstances would make reemployment unreasonable. Employee must apply for reinstatement, in writing, within (a) 14 days of release from service or related hospitalization if service length did not exceed 180 days, or (b) 90 days of release from service or related hospitalization if service length exceeded 180 days. Employer cannot discriminate against employees because of membership in state military service.

Members of the Virginia Civil Air Patrol are entitled to up to 30 workdays of leave while responding to an emergency mission and up to 10 workdays of leave for training for emergency missions, without loss of seniority or other benefits.

Washington

Wash. Rev. Code Ann. §§ 73.16.032 to 73.16.035

Employees in Washington who are members of the armed forces or the national guard of any state are entitled to take leave when called to active duty for training, inactive duty training, full-time national guard duty, or state active duty. Employees are entitled to be reinstated, following their military duty, to the position they previously held or one with like seniority, status, and pay. The time limit for requesting reinstatement depends on the length of the employee's military leave.

Employers may not discriminate against employees based on their membership in any branch of the uniformed services.

West Virginia

W. Va. Code §§ 15-1F-8, 15-1K-1 to 15-1K-9

Employees who are members of the organized militia in active service of the state of West Virginia or any other state have the same leave and reinstatement rights and benefits guaranteed under USERRA.

Employers with 15 or more employees must provide up to 10 days of leave to members of the Civil Air Patrol for training for emergency missions and up to 30 days for responding to an emergency mission. Employers may not discriminate against employees who have been employed for at least 90 days due to their membership in the Civil Air Patrol.

Wisconsin

Wis. Stat. Ann. §§ 111.321, 321.64, 321.65, 321.66

Employees who enlist, are inducted, or are ordered to serve in the U.S. armed forces for 90 days or more, or civilian employees who are asked to perform national defense work during an officially

State Laws on Military Leave (continued)

proclaimed emergency, may take leave for military service and/or training. Employees who are called to state active duty in the Wisconsin National Guard or the national guard of any state or U.S. territory, or called to active service with the state laboratory of hygiene during a public health emergency, are also entitled to take military leave. Upon completion of military leave, employees are entitled to reinstatement to their prior position or to one with equivalent seniority, status, and pay. A reinstated employee may not be discharged without cause for up to one year. Employers may not discriminate against employees based on their military service.

Employers with 11 or more employees must provide up to 15 days of unpaid leave (but not more than five consecutive days at a time) to members of the Civil Air Patrol for an emergency service operation, if it wouldn't unduly disrupt the employer's operations.

Wyoming

Wyo. Stat. §§ 19-11-103, 19-11-104, 19-11-107, 19-11-111

Employees of the armed forces or national guard of any state who report for active duty, training, or a qualifying physical exam may take up to 5 years' leave of absence. Employee must give advance notice of service. Employee may use vacation or any other accrued leave but is not required to do so. Returning employee is entitled to reemployment with the same seniority, rights, and benefits, plus any additional seniority and benefits that employee would have earned if there had been no absence, unless employer's circumstances have changed so that reemployment is impossible or unreasonable or would impose an undue hardship. Time limits set forth governing written application for reinstatement based on length of uniformed service. Employee is entitled to complete any training program that would have been available to employee's former position during period of absence. Employee may not be terminated without cause for one year after returning to work. Employer cannot discriminate against applicant or member of the uniformed services.

Worker Adjustment and Retraining Notification Act (WARN)

Statute: 29 U.S.C. §§ 2101 and following
To view the statutes, visit http://uscodehouse.gov and select "Title 29" and "Chapter 23."

Regulations: 20 C.F.R. §§ 639.1–639.10
To view the regulations, visit www.govinfo.gov and search "20 CFR 639."

Overview of WARN

The Worker Adjustment and Retraining Notification Act (WARN) requires certain larger employers to give some advance notice of an impending plant closing or mass layoff that will result in employment loss for a specified number or percentage of employees. The law was passed to help ease the transition for workers who lose their jobs in these circumstances. WARN requires employers to give notice not only to employees and unions that will be affected by the job cuts, but also to state government agencies that provide assistance to dislocated workers.

Definitions

Terms that appear in italics throughout this chapter are defined below.

Affected employees: Employees who may reasonably be expected to suffer an *employment loss* as a result of a proposed *plant closing* or *mass layoff* by their employer.

Employment loss: An employment loss is:

- an employment termination for reasons other than cause, voluntary departure, or retirement
- a layoff of longer than six months, or
- a reduction of more than 50% in an employee's work hours for six consecutive months.

An employee has not suffered an employment loss if the employer conducted a *plant closing* or *mass layoff* as part of a relocation or consolidation of its business and either:

- prior to the closing or layoff, offered to transfer the employee to a different employment site within a reasonable commuting distance with no more than a six-month break in employment, or
- offered to transfer the employee to any other employment site (regardless of commuting distance) with no more than a six-month break in employment, and the employee accepted this offer within 30 days of the offer or 30 days of the closing or layoff, whichever is later.

Facility: A building or buildings in which an employer operates.

Definitions (continued)

Mass layoff: A reduction in force that is not the result of a *plant closing* and results in an *employment loss* at a *single site of employment* during any 30-day period for:
- 500 or more employees (excluding *part-time employees*), or
- 50 to 499 employees (excluding *part-time employees*), if the number of employees laid off makes up at least 33% of the employer's active workforce.

Operating unit: An organizationally or operationally distinct product, operation, or specific work function within or across *facilities* at a *single site of employment* (for example, a sales force or production line).

Part-time employee: An employee who:
- works, on average, fewer than 20 hours per week, or
- has been employed for fewer than six of the 12 months preceding the date on which notice would be required under WARN.

Plant closing: The permanent or temporary shutdown of a *single site of employment*, or one or more *facilities* or *operating units* within a *single site of employment*, which results in an employment loss for 50 or more employees (excluding *part-time employees*), during any 30-day period.

Single site of employment: One geographical location of an employer's operations. A single site may consist of one building, an office or a suite of offices in a building, or a group of buildings that form a campus or an industrial park, for example. Separate buildings or areas that are not in immediate proximity may nonetheless constitute a single site of employment if they:
- are reasonably close together
- are used for the same purpose, and
- share the same staff and equipment (for example, two warehouses might be a single site if the employer rotates employees from one to the other).

Covered Employers

Only large private employers must comply with WARN, and then only if they carry out a plant closing or mass layoff as defined above.

Federal, state, and local governments are not covered by WARN and need not comply with its requirements.

Private employers are covered if:

- they have 100 or more employees, not counting part-time employees, or
- they have 100 or more employees (including part-time employees) who work a combined 4,000 or more hours per week.

In deciding whether they meet these eligibility requirements, employers do not have to count independent contractors. However, they must count workers who are on temporary layoff or on leave, if those workers have a reasonable expectation of being recalled or otherwise returning to work. For example, an employee who is taking family medical leave should be counted, because he or she is entitled to be reinstated under the Family and Medical Leave Act (FMLA). (See Chapter 8 for detailed information on the FMLA.)

Layoffs Covered by WARN

Not every reduction in force by a covered employer triggers WARN's notice requirements. An employer must comply with WARN only if it plans to conduct a:

- *plant closing*
- *mass layoff*, or
- plant closing or mass layoff that occurs in stages over any 90-day period.

For example, an employer with 150 employees would not have to comply with WARN if it laid off 20 workers in a 30-day period, because this would not constitute a mass layoff as defined by WARN. However, if the same employer laid off 20 more workers in each of the two following months, these combined layoffs would total more than 33% of its workforce in a 90-day period—and thus constitute a mass layoff as defined by WARN. This rule is intended to prevent employers from getting around WARN's requirements by conducting a series of smaller layoffs.

Covered Workers

All *affected employees* are entitled to notice under WARN. *Part-time employees* are entitled to notice, even though they are not counted in determining employer size under WARN.

Independent contractors are not covered by WARN: They do not count toward the plant closing or mass layoff minimum thresholds, nor are they entitled to notice.

Did You Know ...

- Before budget cuts were mandated in 2013, the Bureau of Labor Statistics (BLS) collected data on mass layoffs in the United States each year. In 2012, the last year in which BLS issued a report, there were 6,500 extended mass layoff events, resulting in the separation of more than 1.25 million workers.
- A study by the General Accountability Office (GAO) found that the issues most likely to be litigated in a WARN case are: (1) whether the job loss in question qualifies as a "mass layoff," and (2) whether the unforeseeable business circumstances exception applies. (This exception allows employers to give less than 60 days' notice; see "Exceptions," below.)

What's Prohibited

WARN prohibits an employer from carrying out a plant closing or mass layoff until 60 days after the employer gives written notice of its plans (see "What's Required," below).

What's Required

If a layoff is covered by WARN, the employer must give written notice of the layoff, 60 days in advance.

Who Is Entitled to Notice

An employer must provide written notice to:
- each affected employee, except those who are union members
- the bargaining representative(s) of all affected employees who are union members
- the state's dislocated worker unit (sometimes called the rapid response coordinator), and
- the local government in the area where the layoff will occur.

Key Facts

- WARN applies only to companies that have at least 100 full-time workers, or that have at least 100 workers (including part-time employees) who work a combined total of at least 4,000 hours a week.
- WARN applies only to large job losses: plant closings, in which an entire single site of employment, facility, or operating unit is shut down and at least 50 employees lose their jobs; or mass layoffs, in which either 500 full-time employees lose their jobs or 50 to 499 full-time employees lose their jobs and they make up one-third of the company's workforce.
- An employer can give less than 60 days' notice, or no notice at all, in limited circumstances.
- Employers that violate WARN can be required to pay up to 60 days' wages and benefits to employees who lost their jobs, but this amount can be reduced by any wages the employer paid the employees during that time and any other amounts the employer paid voluntarily and unconditionally.

Notice Contents

The employer's notice must be based on the best information available at the time the notice must be given. If that information proves to be wrong because of subsequent changes in events or inadvertent errors, the employer will not be liable.

The legally required contents of the written notice vary depending on the recipient:

- **Affected employees who are not union members** must be given a notice that states whether the planned action is expected to be permanent or temporary; whether an entire plant is to be closed; the expected date when the layoff or plant closing will begin; the expected date when the employee will be terminated; whether the employee will have bumping rights (that is, whether the employee can take the job of an employee with less seniority who isn't targeted for layoff); and the name and telephone number of a company official the employee can contact for more information. This notice must be written in language understandable to the employees.
- **Bargaining representatives of affected employees who are union members** must receive written notice stating the name and address of the employment

site where the layoff or plant closing will occur; the name and address of a company official to contact for more information; whether the planned action is expected to be permanent or temporary; whether an entire plant is to be closed; the expected date of the first termination; the expected schedule for the remaining terminations; the job titles of positions affected; and the names of the workers holding those positions.

- **State dislocated worker units and local governments** must receive a written notice that states the name and address of the employment site where the layoff or plant closing will occur; the name and address of a company official to contact for more information; the expected date of the first termination; and the number of affected employees. In addition, the employer must include the following information in the notice or maintain this information on site and make it available to the dislocated worker unit and local government agency on request: whether the planned action is expected to be permanent or temporary; whether an entire plant is to be closed; the anticipated schedule for making terminations; whether bumping rights exist; the job titles of positions affected; the names of the workers holding those positions; the name of each union representing affected employees; and the name and address of the chief elected officer of each union. (See "Agency Resources," below, for contact information for state dislocated worker units.)

Exceptions

In certain circumstances, an employer is not required to give notice, or can give less than 60 days' notice before a mass layoff or plant closing.

No Notice Required

WARN does not apply—and therefore, an employer need not give advance notice of a mass layoff or plant closing—in these circumstances:

- **Temporary facilities or projects.** If an employer closes a *facility* that was intended to be open only temporarily or lays off workers who were hired only for a specific project that is complete, no notice is required. However, this exception applies only if the laid-off workers understood when they were hired that their employment was limited to the duration of the facility or project.
- **Strikes and lockouts.** If a plant closing or mass layoff results from a union strike or an employer lockout, no notice is required.

Notice of Less Than 60 Days Allowed

In some cases, an employer may comply with WARN by giving as much notice as possible under the circumstances—even if the employer can't give 60 days' notice. If an employer relies on one of these exceptions, it must give as much notice as it can and state (as part of the written notice requirement) why it didn't give the full 60 days' notice that would otherwise be required:

- **Natural disasters.** If a natural disaster forces a mass layoff or plant closing, an employer may give less than 60 days' notice.
- **Unforeseeable business circumstances.** If the plant closing or mass layoff is caused by business circumstances that were not reasonably foreseeable at the time the employer should have given 60 days' notice, a shorter notice period is allowed.
- **Faltering company.** If a company is struggling financially at the time it should have given 60 days' notice of a plant closing, it can give a shorter period of notice. However, the company must show that it was actively seeking business or financial capital that would have allowed it to avoid or postpone the closing, and that it reasonably believed, in good faith, that giving 60 days' notice would have precluded it from obtaining the necessary business or money. This exception does not apply to mass layoffs.

How WARN Is Enforced

Individual Complaints

The only way affected employees, union representatives, or local government units can assert their right to notice under WARN is by filing lawsuits in federal district court.

Agency Enforcement

Although the Department of Labor published the regulations that interpret and explain WARN, Congress gave that agency no power to administer or enforce the law. Therefore, there is no administrative agency available to accept or investigate complaints of WARN violations.

Complying With WARN

Deadlines

Employers must provide the required written notice 60 days before a mass layoff or plant closing covered by WARN, unless an exception applies.

Reporting Requirements

WARN requires reporting to state dislocated worker units and local governments, as explained in "What's Required," above.

Posting Requirements

WARN does not impose any posting requirements.

Record-Keeping Requirements

WARN does not impose any special record-keeping requirements on employers other than those records that must be kept on-site and available for state dislocated worker units and local governments to inspect (see "What's Required," above, for more information).

Remedies

Employers that violate WARN (by conducting a plant closing or mass layoff without giving appropriate notice) may be ordered to:

- pay affected workers for all wages and benefits lost for the period of violation, up to 60 days. Some courts calculate the damages period as 60 calendar days, which works out to roughly 42 days of pay; others use 60 workdays as the measure, which results in larger damages awards. This amount may be reduced by any wages the employees were paid by the employer during that period and by any payments the employer made to the employees voluntarily and unconditionally. Payments the employer is already obligated to make—such as paying out accrued vacation time in states that require employers to do so—cannot be used to offset the damages amount, nor can wages earned from another employer (for example, if the employee immediately gets another job).

- pay a fine of up to $500 for each day of violation, if the employer fails to give notice as required to the state's dislocated worker unit, and

- pay the attorneys' fees and court costs of affected workers who sue the employer successfully for violating WARN.

Agency Resources

- A list of the name, address, telephone number, and email address of the coordinator of each state's dislocated worker unit

  State Rapid Response Coordinators
  www.doleta.gov/layoff/rapid_coord.cfm

- A detailed explanation of the rights and obligations created by WARN

  Employer's Guide to Advance Notice of Closings and Layoffs
  www.doleta.gov/layoff/pdf/EmployerWARN09_2003.pdf

- An explanation of the benefits available through state dislocated worker programs

  Rapid Response Services for Employers
  www.doleta.gov/layoff/employers.cfm

State Laws Relating to Plant Closings

Many states have also passed laws relating to plant closings and layoffs. The chart below provides basic information on these laws. If you need more information, contact your state labor department (see Appendix A for contact details).

State Laws on Mass Layoffs and Plant Closings

California

Cal. Lab. Code §§ 1400 to 1408

Covered employers: Industrial or commercial facility that employs at least 75 employees.

When law applies: Mass layoff (of at least 50 employees); relocation 100 or more miles away; or closing of industrial or commercial facility with at least 75 employees.

Notification requirements: Employer must give at least 60 days' advance notice, in writing, before mass layoff, relocation, or closing of facility. Notice must include the elements required by the federal WARN Act and must be provided to affected employees, Employment Development Department, local workforce investment board, and chief elected official of each city or county where job losses occur. Employer that fails to give notice to employees is liable for back pay and benefits for the period of the violation, up to 60 days or one-half the length of the employee's tenure with the company, whichever is shorter.

Exceptions: Notice not required if job loss due to physical calamity or act of war; or if employer was actively seeking capital that would have avoided or postponed job losses when notice should have been given.

Connecticut

Conn. Gen. Stat. Ann. §§ 31-51n, 31-51o

Covered employers: Industrial, commercial, or business facility with 100 or more employees at any time during the last 12 months.

When law applies: Permanent shutdown of facility or relocation of facility out of state.

Severance requirements: Employer must pay for existing group health insurance coverage for terminated employee and dependents for 120 days or until employee is eligible for other group coverage, whichever comes first.

Exceptions: Notice not required if facility closure is due to bankruptcy or natural disaster.

Delaware

Delaware Code Ann., tit. 19 §§ 1901 to 1911

Covered employers: Employers with 100 or more full-time employees, or 100 or more employees that work a combined total of at least 2,000 hours per week.

When law applies:

Plant closing: permanent or temporary shutdown of a single site of employment, or one or more facilities or operating units within a single site of employment, if it results in 50 or more employees (excluding part-time employees) losing their jobs during a 30-day period.

Mass layoff: reduction in force at a single site of employment that results in job loss for at least 500 employees, or at least 50 employees representing at least 33% of the total workforce, in a 30-day period.

Relocation: removal of all or substantially all of the employer's industrial or commercial operations to a location at least 50 miles away.

Notification requirements: Employers must give at least 60 days' notice of a mass layoff, plant closing, or relocation to affected employees, their representatives, the state department of labor, and the local workforce development board where the job losses will occur. Employers that fail to

State Layoff and Plant Closing Laws (continued)

provide notice are liable for back pay and lost benefits for up to 60 days.

Exceptions: Notice is not required if job loss is due to physical calamity, war, or act of terrorism; closure of a temporary facility; natural disaster; or strike or lockout. Notice is also not required if job losses were caused by unforeseeable business circumstances or if employer was actively seeking capital or business that would avoid or postpone job losses and employer reasonably believed that giving notice would have precluded acquiring such capital or business.

District of Columbia

D.C. Code Ann. §§ 21-101 to 32-103

Covered employers: Contractors and subcontractors who employ 25 or more nonprofessionals as food service, health service, security, janitorial, or building maintenance workers.

When law applies: When a new contractor takes over a service contract.

Severance requirements: Within 10 days after new contract is awarded, previous contractor must give new contractor names of all employees. New contractor must retain all employees who have worked for the past 8 months for a 90-day transition period. If fewer employees are needed, the new contractor must retain by seniority within job classifications; otherwise, employees may not be fired without cause during the transition period. After transition period ends, new contractor must give written performance evaluations and retain all employees with satisfactory performance.

Contractor whose contract is not renewed and is awarded a similar contract within 30 days must hire at least half of the employees from the former site(s).

Hawaii

Haw. Rev. Stat. §§ 394B-1 to 394B-13

Covered employers: Industrial, commercial, or other business entity with at least 50 employees at any time during the last 12 months.

When law applies: Permanent or partial closing of business; relocation of all or substantial portion of business operations out of state.

Severance requirements: Employer must pay dislocated worker allowance for 4 weeks to supplement unemployment compensation; amount is the difference between the employee's former weekly wage and the employee's weekly unemployment benefit. Employer who does not pay severance is liable to each employee for 3 months of compensation.

Notification requirements: Employer must give notice to employees 60 days in advance of closing or relocation. Employer who fails to provide notice is liable to each employee for back pay and benefits for the period of the violation, up to 60 days.

Illinois

820 Ill. Comp. Stat 65/1 to 65/55

Covered employers: Any business enterprise that employs at least 75 full-time employees or at least 75 employees who work an aggregate of 4,000 hours a week (not including overtime).

State Layoff and Plant Closing Laws (continued)

When law applies: Mass layoff (of at least 250 employees or at least 25 employees who make up 33% or more of the workforce); relocation; or plant closing (shutdown of a site or operating unit resulting in job loss for at least 50 full-time employees).

Notification requirements: Employer must give at least 60 days' written notice to affected employees, their representatives, the Department of Commerce & Economic Opportunity, and the chief elected official of each municipal and county government where job losses occur. Employer that doesn't give notice is liable for back pay and benefits for the period of the violation, up to 60 days or one-half the length of the employee's tenure with the company, whichever is shorter.

Exceptions: Notice not required if job loss due to completion of temporary project or closure of temporary facility; unforeseen circumstances; strike or lockout; physical calamity; or war; or if employer was seeking capital in good faith that would have avoided or postponed job losses when notice should have been given.

Iowa

Iowa Code §§ 84C.1 to 84C.5

Covered employers: Employers with at least 25 full-time employees.

When law applies: Business closing (permanent or temporary shutdown) or mass layoff that will affect 25 or more full-time employees.

Notification requirements: Employer must give 30 days' notice or amount of notice required by collective bargaining agreement. Employer may pay wages in lieu of notice.

Exceptions: Notice not required if job loss due to strike or lockout; unforeseeable business circumstances; or natural disaster; or if employer was seeking capital in good faith that would have avoided or postponed job loss when notice should have been given.

Maine

Me. Rev. Stat. Ann. tit. 26, § 625-B

Covered employers: Employers with at least 100 employees at any time during the last 12 months.

When law applies: Closing, discontinuation, or relocation of business operations at least 100 miles distant; mass layoff (job loss for at least 500 employees or at least 50 employees, if they represent at least 33% of the workforce).

Severance requirements: Employer must give one week of severance pay for each year of employment and partial pay for any partial year of employment to all employees who have worked for at least 3 years.

Notification requirements: Employer must give employees at least 60 days' notice, in writing, before relocating or closing. Employer must also notify the director of the Bureau of Labor Standards and municipal officials where plant is located. Employers initiating mass layoffs must report to the director, within 7 days, the expected duration of the layoff, and whether the layoff is definite or indefinite.

Exceptions: No fine for failure to give notice if closing is due to physical calamity or final order by the government, or if unforeseen circumstances prevent giving notice.

State Layoff and Plant Closing Laws (continued)

Maryland

Md. Code Ann. [Lab. & Empl.] §§ 11-301 to 11-304; Md. Code Regs. tit. 9 § 09.33.02.04

Covered employers: Employers with at least 50 employees that have been in business for at least one year.

When law applies: Shutdown of workplace or portion of operations resulting in layoffs of at least 25% of the workforce or 15 employees, whichever is greater, over any 3-month period.

Severance requirements: Employers are encouraged to follow Department of Labor voluntary guidelines for severance pay, continuation of benefits, and notification.

Notification requirements: Employers should provide 90 days' notice whenever possible.

Exceptions: Notice not required if job loss is due to bankruptcy; seasonal factors common to industry; labor disputes; or the closure of a construction site or temporary workplace.

New Hampshire

N.H. Rev. Stat. Ann. §§ 275-F:1 to 275-F: 12

Covered employers: Employers with at least 100 full-time employees or at least 100 employees who work a total of at least 3,000 hours per week.

When law applies: Plant closing (shutdown of a single employment site, facility, or operating unit resulting in job loss for at least 50 full-time employees); mass layoff (job loss for at least 250 full-time employees or at least 25 employees, if they represent at least 33% of the workforce).

Notification requirements: Employer must give 60 days' notice of plant closing or mass layoff to affected employees, their representatives, the state labor commissioner and attorney general, and the chief elected official of each municipality where job losses occur.

Exceptions: Notice is not required if job loss due to shutdown of a temporary facility; physical calamity; natural disaster; act of war; or strike or lockout. Notice is also not required if need for notice was not reasonably foreseeable or if the company was actively seeking capital, in good faith, that would have postponed or avoided job loss when notice should have been given.

New Jersey

N.J. Stat. Ann. §§ 34:21-1 to 34:21-7

Covered employers: Employers that have operated a business establishment for at least 3 years.

When law applies: Mass layoff (at least 500 full-time employees or at least 50 full-time employees that represent at least one-third of the full-time employees at that establishment); termination or relocation of operations resulting in job loss for at least 50 full-time employees.

Severance requirements: Employer that does not provide at least 60 days' notice must pay laid-off full-time employees one week of severance for each year of employment.

Notification requirements: Employers with 100 or more employees must provide 60 days' notice or such notice as is required by the federal WARN Act. Notice must be

State Layoff and Plant Closing Laws (continued)

given to affected employees, their collective bargaining units, the commissioner of Labor and Workforce Development, and the chief elected official of each municipality where job losses occur.

New York

N.Y. Lab. Law §§ 860 to 860-i

Covered employers: Employers with at least 50 employees.

When law applies:

- Plant closing: permanent or temporary shutdown of single site, facility, or operating unit that results in job loss for at least 25 full-time employees in a 30-day period.
- Mass layoff: reduction in force at a single site that results in job loss for at least 25 full-time employees representing at least 33% of the employer's workforce or at least 250 full-time employees in a 30-day period.
- Relocation: moving employer's entire operation at least 50 miles away.

Notification requirements: Employer must give notice at least 90 days before a mass layoff, plant closing, or relocation to affected employees, their representatives, the department of labor, and local workforce investment boards where job losses occur. Employer that fails to give required notice to employees is liable for back pay and lost benefits for up to 60 days.

Exceptions: Notice not required if job loss due to physical calamity or act of terrorism or war; closure of a temporary facility; natural disaster; or strike or lockout. Notice is also not required if job losses were not reasonably foreseeable or if employer was

actively seeking capital that would avoid or postpone job losses when notice should have been given.

Tennessee

Tenn. Code Ann. §§ 50-1-601 to 50-1-604

Covered employers: Employers with 50 to 99 full-time employees within the state.

When law applies: Closing, modernization, relocation, or new management policy of a workplace or portion of operations that permanently or indefinitely lays off 50 or more employees during any 3-month period.

Notification requirements: Employer must notify employees who will lose their jobs, then the commissioner of Labor and Workforce Development.

Exceptions: Notice not required if job loss due to closure of construction site; labor disputes; or seasonal factors common to industry.

Vermont

Vt. Stat. Ann tit. 21 §§ 411 to 418

Covered employers: Employers with 50 or more full-time employees; employers with 50 or more part-time employees each working at least 1,040 hours per year; or employers with a combination of 50 or more full-time employees and part-time employees each working at least 1,040 hours per year.

When law applies: Mass layoff (permanent layoff of 50 or more employees at one or more worksites in a 90-day period); business closing (permanent shutdown of a facility, permanent cessation of operations at one or more worksites that results in

State Layoff and Plant Closing Laws (continued)

layoff of 50 or more employees in a 90-day period, or the cessation of operations not scheduled to resume within 90 days that affects 50 or more employees).

Severance requirements: If employer fails to give notice, it must pay each employee up to ten days' severance pay and up to one month of continuing medical and dental coverage.

Notification requirements: Employer must give at least 30 days' notice to affected employees, municipal government, and employees' collective bargaining representatives. Employer must provide 45 days' notice to the Agency of Commerce and Community Development and the Vermont Department of Labor.

Exceptions: Compliance not required: when closing or mass layoff is caused by strike or lockout, by business circumstances that were not reasonably foreseeable, by disaster beyond the control of the employer, or due to the conclusion of seasonal employment or a particular project; when affected employees were hired with the understanding that their employment was limited to the duration of the season or project; or when the employer is actively trying to secure funds to avoid a closing or mass layoff and it reasonably believes that giving notice would have precluded securing such funds.

Wisconsin

Wis. Stat. Ann. §§ 106.15; 109.07

Covered employers: Employers with at least 50 employees in the state.

When law applies:
- Business closing: permanent or temporary shutdown of an employment site, facility, or operating unit(s) at one site or within one town that affects 25 or more full-time employees.
- Mass layoff: reduction in force that affects at least 25% or at least 25 full-time employees, whichever is greater, or at least 500 employees.

Employees include only those who have worked at least 6 of the last 12 months and work at least 20 hours a week.

Notification requirements: Employer must give at least 60 days' written notice to affected employees, their collective bargaining representatives, the Dislocated Worker Committee in the Department of Workforce Development, and the highest official in the municipality where job losses occur. Employer who fails to give required notice to employees is liable for up to 60 days of back pay and lost benefits.

Exceptions: Notice not required if job loss due to sale of company, if buyer agrees to hire affected employees with no more than 6-month break in employment; end of seasonal or temporary work; unforeseeable business circumstances; or disaster.

Federal and State Agencies

Federal Agencies

This section includes contact information for the federal agencies that enforce the laws covered in this book. You can find more information on each agency's authority, enforcement powers, and resources for employers in the chapter that covers the law the agency administers.

Department of Health and Human Services

Administration for Children & Families (ACF)
Office of Child Support Enforcement
330 C St., SW
Washington, DC 20201
https://oscetest.service-now.com/wf/webform.do

The ACF enforces PRWORA.

Department of Justice

Civil Rights Division
Office of the Special Counsel for Immigration-Related Unfair
  Employment Practices (OSC)
950 Pennsylvania Avenue, NW
IER, NYA 9000
Washington, DC 20530
Employer Hotline: 800-255-8155
TDD: 800-237-2515
www.justice.gov/crt/immigrant-and-employee-rights-section

The OSC enforces the antidiscrimination provisions of IRCA.

Department of Labor

Employee Benefits Security Administration (EBSA)

Frances Perkins Building
200 Constitution Avenue, NW
Washington, DC 20210
Phone: 866-444-EBSA
www.dol.gov/agencies/ebsa

The EBSA shares enforcement responsibility for COBRA with the IRS.

Employment and Training Administration (DOLETA)

Office of National Response
200 Constitution Avenue, NW
Washington, DC 20210
Phone: 866-4-USA-DOL
www.doleta.gov

DOLETA issued the regulations interpreting WARN, and has some explanatory resources available.

Occupational Safety & Health Administration (OSHA)

200 Constitution Avenue, NW
Washington, DC 20210
Phone: 800-321-OSHA
www.osha.gov

OSHA enforces the OSH Act and the whistle-blower provisions of Sarbanes-Oxley (SOX).

Veterans Employment and Training Service (VETS)

200 Constitution Avenue, Room S-1325
Washington, DC 20210
Phone: 866-4-USA-DOL
www.dol.gov/vets

The VETS enforces USERRA.

Wage and Hour Division (WHD)

Employment Standards Administration
200 Constitution Avenue, NW
Washington, DC 20210
Phone: 866-487-9243
TTY: 877-889-5627
www.dol.gov/whd

The WHD enforces the EPPA, FLSA, and FMLA.

Equal Employment Opportunity Commission (EEOC)

131 M Street, NE
Washington, DC 20507
Phone: 800-669-4000
TTY: 800-669-6820

www.eeoc.gov

The EEOC enforces the ADA, ADEA, EPA, OWBPA, PDA, and Title VII.

Federal Trade Commission (FTC)

600 Pennsylvania Avenue, NW
Washington, DC 20580
Phone: 202-326-2222
www.ftc.gov

The FTC enforces the FCRA.

Internal Revenue Service (IRS)

U.S. Treasury Department
1500 Pennsylvania Avenue, NW
Washington, DC 20220
Phone: 800-829-4933 (for businesses)
TDD: 800-829-4059
www.irs.gov

The IRS shares enforcement responsibility for COBRA with the EBSA.

National Labor Relations Board (NLRB)

1015 Half Street, SE
Washington, DC 20570
Phone: 844-762-NLRB
www.nlrb.gov

The NLRB enforces the NLRA.

Securities and Exchange Commission (SEC)

100 F Street, NE
Washington, DC 20549
Phone: 888-SEC-6585
www.sec.gov

The SEC enforces the complaint procedures provision of Sarbanes-Oxley (SOX).

U.S. Citizenship and Immigration Services (USCIS)

111 Massachusetts Avenue, NW
Washington, DC 20539
Phone: 800-375-5283
TDD: 800-767-1833
www.uscis.gov

The USCIS enforces the employment verification provisions of IRCA.

State Agencies

State Labor Departments

Note: Phone numbers listed are for each department's headquarters. Check the website for regional office locations and numbers.

Departments of Labor	
Alabama Department of Labor Montgomery, AL 334-242-8055 www.labor.alabama.gov	**Colorado** Department of Labor and Employment Denver, CO 303-318-8000 www.colorado.gov/CDLE
Alaska Department of Labor and Workforce Development Juneau, AK 907-465-2700 www.labor.state.ak.us	**Connecticut** Department of Labor Wethersfield, CT 860-263-6000 www.ctdol.state.ct.us
Arizona Industrial Commission Phoenix, AZ 602-542-4661 www.azica.gov	**Delaware** Department of Labor Wilmington, DE 302-761-8000 http://dol.delaware.gov
Arkansas Department of Labor Little Rock, AR 501-682-4500 www.labor.arkansas.gov	**District of Columbia** Department of Employment Services Washington, D.C. 202-724-7000 https://does.dc.gov
California Labor Commissioner's Office Department of Industrial Relations Oakland, CA 510-285-2118 www.dir.ca.gov/DLSE/dlse.html	**Florida** Department of Economic Opportunity Tallahassee, FL 850-245-7105 www.floridajobs.org

Departments of Labor (continued)

Georgia
Department of Labor
Atlanta, GA
404-232-7300
https://dol.georgia.gov

Hawaii
Department of Labor and Industrial
 Relations
Honolulu, HI
808-586-8844
https://labor.hawaii.gov

Idaho
Department of Labor
Boise, ID
208-332-3570
https://labor.idaho.gov

Illinois
Department of Labor
Chicago, IL
312-793-2800
https://illinois.gov/idol

Indiana
Department of Labor
Indianapolis, IN
317-232-2655
www.in.gov/dol

Iowa
Division of Labor
Des Moines, IA
515-242-5870
www.iowadivisionoflabor.gov

Kansas
Department of Labor
Topeka, KS
785-296-5000
www.dol.ks.gov

Kentucky
Labor Cabinet
Frankfort, KY
502-564-3534
www.labor.ky.gov

Louisiana
Louisiana Workforce Commission
Baton Rouge, LA
225-342-3111
www.ldol.state.la.us

Maine
Department of Labor
Augusta, ME
207-623-7900
www.maine.gov/labor

Maryland
Department of Labor, Licensing,
 and Regulation
Baltimore, MD
410-767-2241
www.dllr.state.md.us/labor

Massachusetts
Executive Office of Labor and Workforce
 Development
Boston, MA
617-626-7122
www.mass.gov/orgs/executive-office-of-
 labor-and-workforce-development

Michigan
Department of Licensing and Regulatory
 Affairs
Lansing, MI
517-373-1820
www.michigan.gov/lara

Departments of Labor (continued)

Minnesota
Department of Labor and Industry
St. Paul, MN
651-284-5005
www.dli.mn.gov

Mississippi
Department of Employment Security
Jackson, MS
601-321-6000
www.mdes.ms.gov

Missouri
Department of Labor and Industrial
  Relations
Jefferson City, MO
573-751-3215
https://labor.mo.gov

Montana
Department of Labor and Industry
Helena, MT
406-444-2840
www.dli.mt.gov

Nebraska
Department of Labor
Lincoln, NE
402-471-9000
www.dol.nebraska.gov

Nevada
Office of the Labor Commissioner
Las Vegas, NV
702-486-2650
https://labor.nv.gov

New Hampshire
Department of Labor
Concord, NH
603-271-3176
800-272-4353
www.nh.gov/labor

New Jersey
Department of Labor and Workforce
  Development
Trenton, NJ
609-659-9045
http://.nj.gov/labor

New Mexico
Department of Workforce Solutions
Albuquerque, NM
505-841-8405
www.dws.state.nm.us

New York
Department of Labor
Albany, NY
518-457-9000
888-469-7365
www.labor.ny.gov/home

North Carolina
Department of Labor
Raleigh, NC
800-625-2267
www. labor.nc.gov

North Dakota
Department of Labor and Human Rights
Bismarck, ND
701-328-2660
800-582-8032
www.nd.gov/labor

Ohio
Division of Industrial Compliance
Reynoldsburg, OH
614-644-2223
www.com.ohio.gov/dico

Oklahoma
Department of Labor
Oklahoma City, OK
405-521-6100
www.ok.gov/odol

Departments of Labor (continued)

Oregon
Bureau of Labor and Industries
Portland, OR
971-637-0761
www.oregon.gov/boli

Pennsylvania
Department of Labor and Industry
Harrisburg, PA
800-932-0665
www.dli.pa.gov

Rhode Island
Department of Labor and Training
Cranston, RI
401-462-8000
www.dlt.state.ri.us

South Carolina
Department of Labor, Licensing,
  and Regulation
Columbia, SC
803-896-4300
www.llr.sc.state.gov/labor

South Dakota
Department of Labor and Regulation
Pierre, SD
605-773-3101
www.dlr.sd.gov

Tennessee
Department of Labor and Workforce
  Development
Nashville, TN
844-224-5818
www.tn.gov/workforce

Texas
Texas Workforce Commission
Austin, TX
512-463-2222
https://twc.texas.gov

Utah
Labor Commission
Salt Lake City, UT
801-530-6800
800-530-5090
https://laborcommission.utah.gov

Vermont
Department of Labor
Montpelier, VT
808-828-4000
www.labor.vermont.gov

Virginia
Department of Labor and Industry
Richmond, VA
804-371-2327
www.doli.virginia.gov

Washington
Department of Labor and Industries
Tumwater, WA
360-902-5800
www.lni.wa.gov

West Virginia
Division of Labor
Charleston, WV
304-558-7890
https://labor.wv.gov

Wisconsin
Department of Workforce Development
Madison, WI
608-266-3131
https://dwd.wisconsin.gov

Wyoming
Department of Workforce Services
Cheyenne, WY
307-777-7261
www.wyomingworkforce.org

State Agencies That Enforce Laws Prohibiting Discrimination in Employment

Note: Phone numbers listed are for each department's headquarters. Check the website for regional office locations and numbers.

State Agencies That Enforce Laws Prohibiting Discrimination in Employment

United States
Equal Employment
Opportunity Commission
Washington, D.C.
800-669-4000
TTY: 800-669-6820
www.eeoc.gov

Alabama
Birmingham District Office
Equal Employment Opportunity
  Commission
Birmingham, AL
800-669-4000
www.eeoc.gov/field/birmingham

Alaska
Commission for Human Rights
Anchorage, AK
907-274-4692
800-478-4692
http://humanrights.alaska.gov

Arizona
Civil Rights Division
Arizona Attorney General
Phoenix, AZ
602-542-5025
877-491-5742
www.azag.gov/civil-rights

Arkansas
Little Rock Area Office
Equal Employment Opportunity
  Commission
Little Rock, AR
800-669-4000
www.eeoc.gov/field/littlerock/index.cfm

California
Department of Fair Employment and
  Housing
Elk Grove, CA
800-884-1684
www.dfeh.ca.gov

Colorado
Colorado Civil Rights Division
Department of Regulatory Agencies
Denver, CO
303-894-2997
www.colorado.gov/dora/civil-rights

Connecticut
Commission on Human Rights and
  Opportunities
Hartford, CT
860-541-3400
www.ct.gov/chro/site

State Agencies That Enforce Laws Prohibiting Discrimination in Employment (continued)

Delaware
Division of Industrial Affairs
Department of Labor
Wilmington, DE
302-761-8200
http://dia.delawareworks.com/
  discrimination

District of Columbia
Office of Human Rights
Washington, D.C.
202-727-4559
http://ohr.dc.gov

Florida
Commission on Human Relations
Tallahassee, FL
850-488-7082
800-342-8170
https://fchr.myflorida.com

Georgia
Atlanta District Office
Equal Employment Opportunity
  Commission
Atlanta, GA
800-669-4000
www.eeoc.gov/field/atlanta

Hawaii
Hawaii Civil Rights Commission
Honolulu, HI
808-586-8636
http://labor.hawaii.gov/hcrc

Idaho
Idaho Human Rights Commission
Boise, ID
208-334-2873
888-249-7025
http://humanrights.idaho.gov

Illinois
Department of Human Rights
Chicago, IL
312-814-6200
www2.illinois.gov/dhr

Indiana
Civil Rights Commission
Indianapolis, IN
317-232-2600
800-628-2909
www.in.gov/icrc

Iowa
Civil Rights Commission
Des Moines, IA
515-281-4121
800-457-4416 (in-state only)
https://icrc.iowa.gov

Kansas
Human Rights Commission
Topeka, KS
785-296-3206
www.khrc.net

Kentucky
Commission on Human Rights
Louisville, KY
502-595-4024
800-292-5566
www.kchr.ky.gov

Louisiana
Commission on Human Rights
Baton Rouge, LA
225-342-6969
http://gov.louisiana.gov/page/lchr

State Agencies That Enforce Laws Prohibiting Discrimination in Employment (continued)

Maine
Human Rights Commission
Augusta, ME
207-624-6290
www.maine.gov/mhrc

Maryland
Commission on Civil Rights
Baltimore, MD
410-767-8600
800-637-6247 (in-state only)
http://mccr.maryland.gov

Massachusetts
Commission Against Discrimination
Boston, MA
617-994-6000
www.mass.gov/orgs/massachusetts-
 commission-against-discrimination

Michigan
Department of Civil Rights
Detroit, MI
313-456-3700
800-482-3604
www.michigan.gov/mdcr

Minnesota
Department of Human Rights
St. Paul, MN
651-539-1100
800-657-3704
http://mn.gov/mdhr

Mississippi
Jackson Area Office
Equal Employment Opportunity
 Commission
Jackson, MS
800-699-4000
www.eeoc.gov/field/jackson

Missouri
Commission on Human Rights
Jefferson City, MO
573-751-3325
877-781-4236
www.labor.mo.gov/mohumanrights

Montana
Human Rights Bureau
Employment Relations Division
Department of Labor and Industry
Helena, MT
800-542-0807
http://erd.dli.mt.gov/human-rights/
 human-rights

Nebraska
Nebraska Equal Opportunity Commission
Lincoln, NE
402-471-2024
800-642-6112
www.neoc.ne.gov

Nevada
Equal Rights Commission
Las Vegas, NV
702-486-7161
www.detr.state.nv.us/nerc.htm

New Hampshire
Commission for Human Rights
Concord, NH
603-271-2767
www.nh.gov/hrc

New Jersey
Division on Civil Rights
Office of the Attorney General
Trenton, NJ
609-292-4605
www.nj.gov/oag/dcr/index.html

State Agencies That Enforce Laws Prohibiting Discrimination in Employment (continued)

New Mexico
Human Rights Bureau
Santa Fe, NM
505-827-6838
800-566-9471
www.dws.state.nm.us/Human-Rights-
  Information

New York
Division of Human Rights
Bronx, NY
888-392-3644
800-625-2267
www.dhr.ny.gov

North Carolina
Employment Discrimination Bureau
Department of Labor
Raleigh, NC
800-NC-LABOR
www.labor.nc/workplace-rights

North Dakota
Human Rights Division
Department of Labor and Human Rights
Bismarck, ND
701-328-2660
800-582-8032 (in-state only)
www.nd.gov/labor/human-rights

Ohio
Civil Rights Commission
Columbus, OH
614-466-2785
888-278-7101
www.crc.ohio.gov

Oklahoma
Office of Civil Rights Enforcement
Office of the Attorney General
Oklahoma City, OK
405-521-3921
www.oag.ok.gov/labor/civil-rights-
  enforcement-unit

Oregon
Civil Rights Division
Bureau of Labor and Industries
Portland, OR
971-673-0764
www.oregon.gov/BOLI/CRD

Pennsylvania
Human Relations Commission
Harrisburg, PA
717-787-4410
www.phrc.state.pa.us

Rhode Island
Commission for Human Rights
Providence, RI
401-222-2661
www.richr.ri.gov

South Carolina
Human Affairs Commission
Columbia, SC
803-737-7800
www.schac.sc.gov

South Dakota
Division of Human Rights
Department of Labor and Regulation
Pierre, SD
605-773-3681
http://dlr.sd.gov/human_rights/default.aspx

State Agencies that Enforce Laws Prohibiting Discrimination in Employment (continued)

Tennessee
Human Rights Commission
Nashville, TN
800-251-3589
www.tennessee.gov/humanrights

Texas
Civil Rights Division
Texas Workforce Commission
Austin, TX
512-463-2642
888-452-4778 (in-state only)
www.twc.state.tx.us/jobseekers/
  employee-rights-laws

Utah
Anti-Discrimination and Labor Division
Labor Commission
Salt Lake City, UT
801-530-6801
800-222-1238 (in-state only)
https://laborcommission.utah.gov/
  divisions/AntidiscriminationAndLabor/
  index.html

Vermont
Attorney General's Office
Civil Rights Unit
Montpelier, VT
802-828-3657
888-745-9195 (in-state only)
http://ago.vermont.gov/about-the-
  attorney-generals-offce/divisions/
  civil-rights

Virginia
Office of the Attorney General
Division of Human Rights
Richmond, VA
804-225-2292
www.oag.state.va.us/index.php/
  programs-initiatives/human-rights

Washington
Human Rights Commission
Olympia, WA
800-233-3247
www.hum.wa.gov

West Virginia
Human Rights Commission
Charleston, WV
304-558-2616
888-676-5546
www.hrc.wv.gov

Wisconsin
Equal Rights Division
Department of Workforce Development
Madison, WI
608-266-6860
dwd.wisconsin.gov/er

Wyoming
Labor Standards Office
Department of Workforce Services
Cheyenne, WY
307-777-7261
www.wyomingworkforce.org/workers/
  labor

Nolo Resources

Nolo offers a variety of resources on HR compliance and employment law.

Books

Nolo publishes many titles for employers, managers, and human resources professionals, including:

- *Dealing With Problem Employees*, a comprehensive resource for handling tough discipline and performance issues, including detailed information on minimizing legal exposure if you have to fire an employee.
- *Create Your Own Employee Handbook*, which provides all of the information and policies you need to draft or update your company's handbook, including access to policies you can cut and paste to create your own handbook.
- *The Essential Guide to Workplace Investigations*, a step-by-step guide to investigating complaints and misconduct, including detailed information on investigating harassment, discrimination, workplace violence, and theft.
- *The Job Description Handbook*, which explains how to create, use, and update job descriptions effectively, and includes access to a PowerPoint training presentation.
- *The Manager's Legal Handbook*, an introduction to many of the legal issues managers face every day, including discrimination, wage and hour issues, firing and layoffs, employee privacy concerns, protecting trade secrets, and much more.
- *The Employer's Legal Handbook*, a comprehensive guide to employment law, written with the small business owner in mind.
- *Consultant & Independent Contractor Agreements*, which provides all of the information and sample contracts you need to work well with independent contractors—and avoid having them reclassified as employees.

Nolo's Website

You can find free articles on a wide variety of employment and HR topics on Nolo's website, www.nolo.com, which includes articles on:

- hiring employees
- hiring independent contractors
- wage and hour laws
- personnel policies and procedures
- family, medical, and other types of leave
- discrimination and harassment
- workplace privacy
- firing workers, and
- obligations to workers who are leaving the company.

Index

NOLO *More from Nolo*

Nolo.com offers a large library of legal solutions and forms, created by Nolo's in-house legal editors. These reliable documents can be prepared in minutes.

Create a Document Online

Incorporation. Incorporate your business in any state.

LLC Formation. Gain asset protection and pass-through tax status in any state.

Will. Nolo has helped people make over 2 million wills. Is it time to make or revise yours?

Living Trust (avoid probate). Plan now to save your family the cost, delays, and hassle of probate.

Provisional Patent. Preserve your right to obtain a patent by claiming "patent pending" status.

Download Useful Legal Forms

Nolo.com has hundreds of top quality legal forms available for download:

- bill of sale
- promissory note
- nondisclosure agreement
- LLC operating agreement
- corporate minutes
- commercial lease and sublease
- motor vehicle bill of sale
- consignment agreement
- and many more.

www.nolo.com

△△ NOLO — Save 15% *off your next order*

Register your Nolo purchase, and we'll send you a **coupon for 15% off** your next Nolo.com order!

Nolo.com/customer-support/productregistration

On Nolo.com you'll also find:

Books & Software

Nolo publishes hundreds of great books and software programs for consumers and business owners. Order a copy, or download an ebook version instantly, at Nolo.com.

Online Forms

You can quickly and easily make a will or living trust, form an LLC or corporation, apply for a provisional patent, or make hundreds of other forms—online.

Free Legal Information

Thousands of articles answer common questions about everyday legal issues, including wills, bankruptcy, small business formation, divorce, patents, employment, and much more.

Plain-English Legal Dictionary

Stumped by jargon? Look it up in America's most up-to-date source for definitions of legal terms, free at nolo.com.

Lawyer Directory

Nolo's consumer-friendly lawyer directory provides in-depth profiles of lawyers all over America. You'll find information you need to choose the right lawyer.

FEMP6

CPSIA information can be obtained
at www.ICGtesting.com
Printed in the USA
JSHW031140261221
21540JS00004B/52